HOLD YOUR TONGUE

Also by James Crawford

Bilingual Education: History, Politics,
Theory, and Practice (1989)

Language Loyalties: A Source Book
on the Official English Controversy (1992)

HOLD

||||||||||||||||||||||||||||||||||||||||

i11758594

LCHECKIN: Mon May 13 2013 12:38PM

AUTHOR: Crawford, James, 1949-

306.44973 C73 1992

Sylvania Checkout Desk

||||||||||||||||||||||||||||||||||||||||

p1838562x

Please
Check Out

Mon
May
20

9990

HOLD YOUR TONGUE

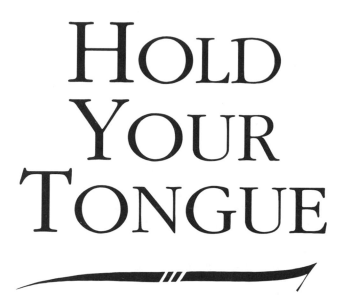

Bilingualism and the Politics of "English Only"

James Crawford

Addison-Wesley Publishing Company

Reading, Massachusetts • Menlo Park, California • New York
Don Mills, Ontario • Wokingham, England • Amsterdam
Sydney • Singapore • Tokyo • Madrid • San Juan
Paris • Seoul • Milan • Mexico City • Taipei

Library of Congress Cataloging-in-publication Data
Crawford, James, 1949–
    Hold your tongue : bilingualism and the politics of English Only /
James Crawford.
    p.   cm.
Includes bibliographical references and index.
ISBN 0-201-55044-X
1. Language policy—United States.   2. English language—Political aspects—United States.   I. Title.
P119.32U6C73   1992
306.4'4973—dc20   91-46614
                                                         CIP

Jacket design by Julie Metz
Text design by Diane Levy
Set in 11-point Sabon by Maple-Vail Composition, Binghamton, New York

1 2 3 4 5 6 7 8 9-MW-95949392
First printing, July 1992

To my mother and the memory of my father

Contents

Preface

There is nothing new about ethnic intolerance. But in the United States of the 1980s, it assumed a guise we had not seen before: the politics of English Only.

Traditionally taken for granted, our national tongue emerged as a cause célèbre, a civic passion touching nearly every state house, the U.S. Congress, and numerous municipalities. The fervor was not so much *for* English as *against* the growing prominence of other languages. "Bilingualism" had arrived, to the dismay of many monolingual Americans. Some claimed it was now easier to function in English when traveling abroad than in the immigrant ghettos of U.S. cities. Apparently today's newcomers, unlike their predecessors, felt no obligation to learn our language. Did they expect us to learn Spanish? shocked Anglo-Americans wanted to know. Whose country was this, after all? Most amazing, government was pursuing policies that seemed to discourage English acquisition: bilingual schooling, bilingual driver's tests, bilingual welfare forms, even bilingual assistance in the voting booth. Could we afford to accommodate millions of new Americans—literally scores of different language groups—each in their own tongue? Would Congress soon be translating its proceedings, United Nations–style, with every member listening through a headset? Where would it end?

Such anxieties and resentments have given rise to a movement to declare English the nation's official language. While the objective may seem innocuous, the proposed means are not. A constitutional English Language Amendment seeks to prohibit most uses of other tongues by government (federal, state, and local) and, in some circumstances, by individuals. Whether it would achieve these aims no one can say with certainty. But, if adopted, the measure would jeopardize a wide range of rights and services now available to non-English speakers, from bilingual clerks at city hall to the freedom of speech itself. At a symbolic level, Official English would be a way of telling newcomers, "Conform or get out." Indeed, that message has already been conveyed by the current agitation, polarizing several communities where Hispanics or Asians have settled.

Americans are not accustomed to quarreling over language. Earlier generations of nativists were usually too preoccupied with immigrants' race or religion to worry whether their English skills were up to snuff. Contrary to melting-pot mythology, newcomers often maintained their native tongues for generations on U.S. soil. Many fought for and, depending on their political clout, won concessions like bilingual public education, which was commonplace in nineteenth-century "German America." Moreover, this country has a kind of libertarian tradition where language is concerned—a democracy is not supposed to tell its citizens how to talk—which may explain the Founders' "oversight" when it came to mandating an official tongue.

This is not to say the tradition has been consistent. At various points in our history, linguistic minorities have faced policies of exclusion or coercive assimilation or both. Yet, unlike today's campaigns, these were normally aimed at particular groups for particular purposes—for example, in the 1880s, when federal authorities decided that "the first step . . . toward teaching the Indians the mischief and folly of continuing in their barbarous practices" was to force their children to attend English-only boarding schools; or in 1897, when Pennsylvania enacted an English-proficiency requirement for miners, seeking to bar Italians and Slavs from the coal fields; or in 1921, when Republicans in New York pushed through an English literacy test for voting, hoping to disfranchise one million Yiddish speakers who had an annoying habit of electing Democrats.*

What distinguishes today's English Only phenomenon is the apocalyptic nature of its fears: that the American language is "threatened" and, with it, the basis of American nationhood. We are warned that unless action is taken to halt our "mindless drift toward a bilingual society," the United States will soon be balkanized, divided, at war with itself. Ostensibly to defend "the primacy of English," a new cadre of zealots is working to restrict speech in other tongues. And there is a real chance that such proposals could become law; in several states, they already have.

*Source notes begin on page 297. Explanatory notes begin on page 261.

Worries about the slipping status of English in the United States come, ironically, at a time when English continues to spread as a world language, the undisputed medium of international business, science, and statecraft. To be sure, this country is more diverse, linguistically and otherwise, than it was a generation ago. Immigration is the major reason. Exotic cultural enclaves have appeared not only in coastal cities, but throughout the heartland. In 1960, how many citizens of Fort Smith, Arkansas, or Garden City, Kansas, would have foreseen a Vietnamese community in their midst? (How many had even heard of Vietnam?) Just as in the past, the newcomers find it natural to preserve remnants of their homelands—food, customs, religion, and language—that some Americans find jarring. The number of U.S. residents who speak a minority tongue at home increased by 41 percent during the 1980s. Yet at the same time, all available evidence shows that today's immigrants are learning English *faster* than ever before. By objective measures, bilingualism is no more prevalent now than in several earlier periods of U.S. history.

So what accounts for the new English Only mentality? Some say bigotry. It is no coincidence that the targets of antibilingual campaigns are frequently racial as well as linguistic minorities. Leaders of U.S. English, the major lobby promoting an English Language Amendment, have expressed an animus toward Hispanics in particular. This organization is an outgrowth of the immigration restriction movement. One of its founders has warned that Spanish speakers may use their "greater reproductive powers" to seize political control in the United States. ("Perhaps this is the first instance in which those with their pants up are going to get caught by those with their pants down!") A similar group, English First, complains: "Tragically, many immigrants these days refuse to learn English! They never become productive members of American society. They remain stuck in a linguistic and economic ghetto, many living off welfare and costing working Americans millions of tax dollars each year." It goes on to claim that "radical activists have been caught sneaking illegal aliens to the polls on election day and using bilingual ballots to cast fraudulent votes." The fact that U.S. English and English First have raised millions of dollars with such appeals suggests a sizable nativist constituency.

Nevertheless, it is a mistake to assume that enthusiasm for Official English is driven solely, or even primarily, by such prejudices.

According to opinion polls and election results, about three Americans in four are inclined to endorse the idea. Many ask: Shouldn't newcomers be expected to learn English, for their own good and the country's? What's racist about that? Nothing whatsoever. Bilingual accommodations are the issue. Should government be able to provide them, as needed, to ease immigrants' transition into this society? Should there be an affirmative *right* to certain services in minority tongues? Or should public-sector bilingualism be banned by law? When Congress passed the Bilingual Education Act of 1968 and the bilingual voting rights amendments of 1975, it galloped headlong into this arena with little foresight and almost no public discussion. Such an abrupt turn in policy was bound to provoke debate sooner or later. At last, language issues are beginning to receive some needed attention. It is only unfortunate that vital programs, for example, the schooling of limited-English-proficient children, are now held hostage to symbolic politics.

English Only flows from feelings of insecurity. Now that demographic changes of all kinds—greater mobility, nontraditional families, mass culture—are disrupting Americans' sense of community, there is a renewed search for unifying institutions. With ethnic warfare spreading in eastern Europe, many are wondering when it will reach our shores. Already there is talk of "tribalism" and "the disuniting of America" from those who fear that common ties are being frayed by group claims of all descriptions. Many fair-minded people, who otherwise cherish individual rights and cultural pluralism, are beginning to wonder whether the national tongue may be an exceptional case. Perhaps "unilingualism" is our best hope of managing diversity, the one bond that might keep us together. If so, it becomes too precious to risk and legislating conformity becomes justifiable.

It is the aim of this book to show how mistaken, how shortsighted, and how disastrous that view can be.

One

Guardians of English

For Mayor Barry Hatch, it was the ultimate act of cultural aggression. In barely a decade his hometown of Monterey Park, just east of Los Angeles, had become the Chinese Beverly Hills, home to thousands of affluent immigrants from Taiwan and Hong Kong. The newcomers bought out American businesses and re-stocked the shelves with Asian goods. Soon they were opening banks as well as ginseng shops, developing high-density malls and condo-miniums, and crowding the streets with new Mercedes. As longtime residents sold out, or were pushed out by rising rents, Anglo-Americans found themselves outnumbered by Asians, many of whom seemed to have little use for the English language. Not only was the din of Mandarin and Cantonese heard in shops and restaurants, but signs with Chinese characters began to sprout everywhere, emblems of the changing social order.

Now, in the fall of 1988, Taiwan had the nerve to send foreign aid. The Lions Club International of Taipei announced a donation of ten thousand volumes—in Chinese, naturally—to the Monterey Park public library. It was a very Asian gesture. A Chinese Ameri-can member of the city council, Judy Chu, had happened to meet the club's president, and he asked her what the Lions could do to express and reinforce the closeness they felt with their sister city, which many have begun to call "Little Taipei." Chu suggested a gift to the library, then struggling to meet the needs of Chinese readers. "But little did we dream it would be ten thousand books!" she recalls. "All kinds: a lot of children's books, cultural works, back issues of magazines. At least two thousand of the volumes were bilingual. Which I thought was terrific because any English-speaking person could read them and understand a little more about

Chinese culture. And there were things like a Chinese translation of 'Peanuts,' books that would help Chinese people enjoy themselves and acculturate themselves to this country." If accepted, the gift would more than double the library's well-thumbed holdings in Chinese, one-half of which were normally checked out at a given time.

While local Chinese were ecstatic, Mayor Hatch was livid. In the Taiwanese largess he saw yet another intrusion by arrogant guests who insisted on rearranging the furniture, imposing their own tastes, remaking Monterey Park to suit themselves. Hatch is a large white-haired man who teaches civics at a junior high school in nearby Bell Gardens. Punctuating his convictions with a made fist, he likes to stress what he calls "pro-America" values. But with his students increasingly Latino and Asian, and his school increasingly bilingual, Hatch feels besieged by alien cultures. "You know, I'm in the trenches with these people," he says. "We're allowing them to come in not only by hundreds and thousands, but by millions. And not only are we accepting their separate identity, their history, their loyalties, but *their language*—which is the first and most emotional issue a man has."

Though Barry Hatch once served as a Mormon missionary in Hong Kong and still claims fluency in Cantonese, in Monterey Park he has brooked no concessions to linguistic minorities. On his motion in mid-1988, the council voted to abolish the city's independent library board, then headed by a Chinese American. Meanwhile he pressed to limit expenditures for non-English-language materials. At one budget hearing he lectured the city librarian: "This is the United States of America, and nobody likes to walk into a public building and feel like they are in a foreign land."[1] Suddenly, with the Taiwanese Lions' donation, Hatch felt outmaneuvered.

If the Chinese wanted to keep the books, he announced, they should construct their own building rather than "encroach on space" for English-language volumes. "We built this little library with our own tax money," he explained. "We spend over a million dollars a year on it. It is an American library, paid for by American taxpayers, for the American public, and I don't see any need to turn it into a cultural center for any foreign group of people." Offended by the mayor's remarks, the Lions considered withdrawing their gift but thought better of it after hearing from library supporters and leaders of the Chinese community. Ultimately, Hatch was powerless to block delivery of the books. All he could do was boycott a dedication ceremony and refuse to sign certificates of appreciation to the donors. The expanded Chinese section has since become one of the most popular in the library.

Looking back, Hatch still contends that the Taiwanese had more in mind than a token of goodwill. "You've got to realize the attitude of these people," he says. "They're not coming to join; they're coming to conquer. They have to raise their little flag, and it's not always on a pole. They want Southern California to be an Asian part of the country. These people work in devious manners. And language is one of the most important tools they can use. *Language is the key that opens the door to taking this country and breaking it apart.*" Indeed, language became the fault line along which ethnic divisions grew in Monterey Park, a rift fostered in no small measure by Barry Hatch. The rhetoric of Chinese exclusion, long couched in racial terms, now assumed a more respectable form: the "legal protection of English."

"English is under attack," warns a new movement of civic activists. Two decades ago this idea would have struck most Americans as bizarre: the histrionics of literati, or perhaps a Dadaist charade. But in the uneasy eighties it attracted mass support. "Defend our common language!" became the rallying cry. No one had to ask, "From whom?"

Immigration to the United States has increased noticeably in recent years and, more important, its source countries have changed. In 1965, Congress abolished the national-origins quota system, a racially restrictive policy that long favored northwestern Europeans and virtually excluded Asians. As late as the 1950s Europe was still supplying more than half of all immigrants to the United States. By the 1980s the Third World was providing 85 percent of them, not counting the undocumented.[2] These newcomers were far less familiar, racially and culturally, and so was their speech. After half a century of decline, minority tongues were suddenly more audible and, to many Americans, more dissonant as well.

In 1981, for the first time, Congress entertained a proposal to designate English as the official language of the United States. The sponsor was Senator S. I. Hayakawa of California, a Canadian immigrant of Japanese ancestry who believed that concessions to linguistic minorities had gone too far. "English has long been the main unifying force of the American people," he asserted. "But now prolonged bilingual education in public schools and multilingual ballots threaten to divide us along language lines." A semanticist by profession, Hayakawa was best known for his college text, *Language in Thought and Action,* which explores a wide range of obstacles to effective communication. Oddly, the book never mentions bilingualism, a problem that seems to have escaped the author's notice until he entered politics.

On retiring from the Senate, in 1983 Hayakawa helped to found U.S. English, a Washington lobby to promote his constitutional English Language Amendment and similar measures at the state level. He served as the group's "honorary chairman" until his death in 1992. Started on a shoestring, U.S. English claimed 400,000 dues-paying members by decade's end. Over that time it raised and spent approximately $28 million on campaigns to "preserve the status" of English—or, more precisely, to limit public uses of other languages. Whether such restrictions are intended to encompass all or selected government programs, schools, broadcast media, workplaces, business advertising, and other domains have remained matters of dispute. Proponents have issued contradictory statements. Some have pressed merely to give English legal recognition, while others have sought to outlaw all public services in other tongues, up to and including emergency 911 operators,[3] and to crack down on private sector bilingualism as well.

The new guardians of English achieved few tangible changes in language policy during the 1980s. They did succeed, however, in placing a polarizing issue on the national agenda, a debate—conducted almost entirely in English—that produced misunderstanding and mistrust on all sides. Throughout the country language differences became a lightning rod for ethnic tensions:

- In Elizabeth, New Jersey, a city whose residents are 30 percent Hispanic, the mayor instituted a "Speak-English-Only" rule for city workers while performing their duties, except when other languages were needed to communicate with members of the public. He insisted it was "discourteous for City employees to converse in other than English in front of other City employees."

- A San Diego grand jury denounced schooling in languages other than English as "un-American." It asserted that "bilingual education promotes a type of cultural apartheid in that it encourages a dual society."

- Koreans in Philadelphia secured the city's permission to purchase and erect street signs in their native language. Posted in a racially mixed neighborhood, the signs soon became targets for vandalism and angry protests and had to be removed. Local German Americans, betraying an ignorance of their own history, objected that their ancestors had never enjoyed such advantages.

- A cooperative apartment building in Broward County, Florida, voted to restrict residency to persons able to speak and read the English language. "We screen everyone for the protection of our tenants," explained the co-op's president. "We don't want undesirables living here. And if we can't communicate with people, it creates a real burden."

- At a concert near Boston, when Linda Ronstadt and a mariachi band performed music from her recent album, *Canciones de mi Padre,* some members of the audience began to chant: "Sing in English." As Ronstadt continued to sing in Spanish, two hundred fans walked out.

- Responding to complaints from African-American constituents about Korean, Arab, and Hispanic merchants, an alderman in Chicago proposed that anyone seeking a retail grocer's license should have to pass an English-proficiency test. "If you don't know English, you can't understand the laws," he said. "You have to know more than Mexican."

The English Only movement came to Monterey Park in 1985, the same year it was named an "All-America City" by the National Municipal League and *USA Today*. Predominantly white until the 1960s, thanks to racial covenants and hostility toward the Hispanics, Asians, and blacks who dared move in, Monterey Park had by now overcome such overt manifestations of prejudice. While this was a praiseworthy achievement, it owed much to changing demographics. In the early 1970s a Chinese developer, Fred Hsieh, recognized the fortune to be made in Monterey Park's undervalued real estate, then selling at $5 a square foot, just a few minutes from downtown Los Angeles. Hsieh began promoting the city in Asian newspapers as an attractive site for investment and immigration. In Taiwan and Hong Kong, where capital was accumulating faster than productive ways to spend it and where educational and professional choices were limited by overcrowding, the lure of Southern California proved irresistible. By the mid-1980s Asians accounted for 51 percent of Monterey Park's 61,000 residents, as compared with only 3 percent in 1960. (Hispanics represented 31 percent, up from 12 percent, and non-Hispanic whites 16 percent, down from 85 percent; less than 2 percent were blacks.) Two Latinos, a Filipino, a Chinese immigrant, and an Italian American comprised the five-member city council. Meanwhile the price of commercial land had risen to $45 a square foot.

USA Today touted "the acceptance of ethnic diversity" and pronounced it "great for business." But these were by no means consensus views in Monterey Park. Had it bothered to look, the newspaper would have found that uncontrolled growth, rapid immigration, rising taxes, spiraling real-estate prices, traffic congestion, crime, pollution, and general culture shock had created a swarm of resentments now looking for a place to land. The ever-visible Chinese language provided a handy target.

For many oldtimers in town, the incomprehensible characters up and down Atlantic and Garvey, the main avenues of the business district, had come to symbolize an Asian takeover and, even more galling, the spectacle of immigrant success without dues-paying. Somehow the sight and sound of the Chinese language seemed disrespectful to the memory of earlier arrivals who had struggled to learn English—not to mention an insult to current residents, many of whom felt ignored by stores advertising primarily or exclusively in Chinese. It was disconcerting to head for Safeway and find instead the Hoa Binh Market, where the familiar had given way to the strange and there was no hope of deciphering product labels. Not only Anglos, but Latinos and Japanese Americans said they felt *alienated,* literally, in their own city.

The touchiness created by the Chinese signs was obvious to Lily Lee Chen, herself something of a symbol. The previous year she had made national headlines by becoming the city's, and the nation's first female Chinese American mayor. (City council members share the job on a rotating basis; Hatch served as mayor in 1988–89). It was Chen who courted *USA Today* and won its breathless accolades for Monterey Park. Unofficially but firmly, she began to pressure Asian merchants to post signs that were at least bilingual—if not to attract business from English speakers, then to make a gesture of goodwill. Most complied. In late 1985, a civic group's survey turned up only thirteen signs, out of hundreds identifying Chinese enterprises, that featured no English at all. Still, English translations did nothing to erase Chinese characters from the landscape or to pacify opponents who resented the newcomers and the development they had brought.

Frank Arcuri, a Monterey Park resident who relished combat on numerous local issues, proposed a solution. "By putting up Chinese-only signs, [business owners] are effectively discriminating against Americans, against non-Chinese people," he argued. What was needed was an ordinance mandating the use of English on all commercial signs "so everybody would feel welcome in our community." A part-time photographer and full-time gadfly, Arcuri wrote and published the *Monterey Park Voice,* a single-sheet "Newspaper for Investigative Journalism," which he used to lambaste political and personal enemies (including "Dragon Lady" Lily Chen), while reporting on the progress of his lawsuits against various politicians and arresting officers. For Arcuri the signs became a favorite hobbyhorse. "Monterey Park has turned into a segregated city, a Chinese-only city," he charged.

As usual Arcuri got nowhere with the council, and as usual he determined not to let the matter rest. He consulted S. I. Hayakawa. The former senator encouraged him to organize a citizen initiative but suggested a demand with broader impact: an ordinance declaring English the "official language" of Monterey Park.

This was a new idea to Arcuri, and to the community. Initially it seemed innocuous—for citizens, a simple reaffirmation of English as our common tongue; for immigrants, a way to exhibit new loyalties. In this society everyone needs to know English, seemed to be the message. Who could quarrel with that? Members of the city council probably would, Arcuri believed, and he hoped to use the issue to defeat them at the polls. Barry Hatch, himself considering a run for the council, also saw the measure's potential to grab voters' attention. In early fall the two joined forces and began circulat-

ing petitions to place Official English on the ballot. The response
was enthusiastic and broad-based. Of the 3,452 signatures gathered, according to the organizers, roughly one-third were Asian
(Chinese, Japanese, or Vietnamese), one-third Latino, and one-third
Anglo.[4]

But linguistic minorities soon perceived a more sinister tone in
statements by Arcuri and Hatch. Language seemed to be a subterfuge for an antiforeigner agenda. Making English official was a way
to say, "Let's put America first," Arcuri declared at a public meeting.

> English as a foreign language. America as a foreign country. It
> happened to Monterey Park, didn't it? It will happen to Amer-
> ica, if we don't do something about it. . . . Our city has bent
> over backwards long enough in an effort to accommodate our
> new immigrants. While it is easier for them to use their own
> language and culture, they must realize that they are making a
> negative impact on our city. They must adapt to our ways.
> They must use our language and respect our culture. . . . We
> now say, "Enough is enough." This is America; don't divide
> us. Don't isolate us by building a separate nation with your
> language and customs.

Attempting to strike a more diplomatic note, Hatch praised the "rich,
five-thousand-year history" of the Chinese immigrants and cited their
potential contributions to this country—if they would only assimilate. "We need to educate them," he said, "in the great spirit we
refer to as Americanism," which he defined as loyalty to the United
States, its traditions, and its language. "If the Chinese are learning
English, there is no need for the Chinese signs."

Give up your culture and adopt American ways, or go back from
whence you came. Speak English or you will be unwelcome here.
Change or face the consequences. Newcomers once oblivious to such
ultimatums heard them clearly now. As the punitive, *English Only*
tenor of the campaign began to emerge, they felt the animosity not
only toward their language, but toward their presence. Did all white
people feel this way? A great many, it seemed, were ready to hold
Asians to blame for the city's growing pains.

Hatch won the endorsement of the Residents' Association of
Monterey Park (RAMP), an influential organization that included
veterans of the Proposition 13 tax revolt. The group had long bat-

tled Asian developers, attempting to halt construction of what it called "tenement condos" and "buildings that block the sky." It also complained about declining sales-tax revenues, as financial and service industries displaced retail merchants and car dealerships. Over a photo collage of Chinese-owned banks, one of RAMP's brochures blared, "Developer Greed Can Destroy Our Community." It went on to denounce a compliant city council for allowing tax-generating (read: white-owned) businesses to be "pushed out." RAMP hoped to defeat the three council incumbents, all linguistic minorities, who would face reelection the following April. While the group's leaders took no position on the official language initiative, they were more than willing to ride the wave of antigrowth and anti-Chinese sentiment that it embodied.

"A lot of us became concerned because we were hearing what we called 'racism'—not imagined racism, but the real stuff," recalled Ruth Willner. A longtime resident and community activist, Willner helped to found the Coalition for Harmony in Monterey Park (CHaMP) to oppose the Official English drive. "We were distressed to hear the way people were talking about the immigrants," she said, "the whole tone of what was going on here. We decided there had to be a better way to handle this." CHaMP sought to reduce the polarization by placing a countermeasure on the ballot that would appeal to the full spectrum of ethnic groups. Its resolution opposed the English Only approach of Arcuri and Hatch, while simultaneously recognizing English as "our common language in Monterey Park" along with "our multiethnic and multicultural heritage."

The issue came to a head at a city council meeting on November 12, 1985. It was an acrimonious three-hour session in which English Only supporters and opponents alternately traded epithets and pleas for mutual understanding. Each side brought to bear its own reading of American myths and founding documents, while stressing the high stakes of the conflict.

Michael Eng, a Chinese American lawyer and CHaMP cochairman, opened the discussion with a warning: "If we want a civil war the likes of which we have never seen, in which neighbor is pitted against neighbor, immigrant against citizen, race against race, then vote for English Only." Beyond the measure's divisiveness, Eng said, it jeopardized essential services and "fundamental constitutional freedoms." Ruth Willner added that speaking English "should not be a loyalty oath. Being an American means respect for diverse traditions, cultures, and languages." Another CHaMP leader, Pete Hollingsworth, urged: "Don't accept oversimplified 'symbolic gestures' which serve to inflame rather than to inform. Let's teach English rather than mandate it." "How can denying the basic freedom of speech create unity?" asked Lucila Ríos, an instructor of English as a second language.

Hatch and Arcuri fumed, their appearances delayed by a hostile council, as speaker after speaker attacked Official English. When his turn finally came, Arcuri challenged the audience: "Has anybody here read the Constitution? The Constitution doesn't give you the right to exclude Americans from Monterey Park." Brandishing a copy, he presented it to Councilwoman Lily Chen, as the crowd began to chant: "Bigot, bigot, bigot." Arcuri, who later appeared in the *Los Angeles Times* wearing boxing gloves inscribed *Official* and *English*, and was flattered to be dubbed the "Rocky of Monterey Park," raised his arms over his head, champ-like.

Apart from the clowning, Arcuri articulated a viewpoint not far from the mainstream of the Official English movement. Though Hayakawa would later disown him as an extremist, in a message read during the meeting he praised Arcuri's "courage and vision." The former senator went on to criticize the high visibility of Chinese in Monterey Park, which he said raised the question "Where am I? Is this America?"

Arcuri's appeal was equally visceral. Doesn't the majority have rights, too? he asked. English speakers feel ostracized when minorities erect barriers of language and culture. When a shopkeeper advertises in Chinese only, that's bigotry on a par with segregated lunch counters in the Old South. Minorities talk about their freedom of speech, but what about freedom of communication in a language that can be understood by all? English has always been that language, the great unifier of the American people, and so it must remain. Waxing defiant amid the jeers, Arcuri vowed that English would become the official language not only of Monterey Park, but of California as well. Both predictions would prove correct, though not tonight.

After Hatch spoke along the same lines, provoking further pandemonium, the council accepted a huge stack of initiative petitions to place Official English on the spring ballot. But a week later they were disqualified by the city attorney as incorrectly drawn.[5]

(Arcuri later blamed the mistake on a "half-assed" lawyer to whom RAMP had referred him.) Legally justified or not, the move appeared heavy-handed and undemocratic. It further weakened the three incumbents, whose candidacies were already faltering because of perceived links to developers. On February 24, 1986, the council passed an ordinance requiring every business in Monterey Park to post a prominent sign in English identifying its purpose. But the action came too late to quench English Only fervor. Barry Hatch, along with two other "slow-growth" candidates backed by RAMP, won easily in the April 8 municipal election. By now, however, voters were wary enough of Frank Arcuri to nix his nascent career in public service. Shortly after the election, in attempting to revive the Official English issue before the city council, he was arrested for disrupting a public meeting and assaulting a police officer.

The anticlimax came in the wee hours of June 3, when the new city council, without further debate and virtually without witnesses, adopted a proposal by Hatch establishing English as the official language of Monterey Park. The measure, Resolution 9004, also denounced the Sanctuary movement and instructed local police to cooperate with federal authorities in apprehending undocumented immigrants. Mayor Monty Manibog, a Filipino, was the lone dissenter; another member abstained.

Predictably, passions flared for yet another round of dissension. CHaMP circulated its own petition calling for repeal of Resolution 9004, gathering an impressive four thousand signatures. The Taiwanese American Citizens League linked English Only to the veto of a housing project for the elderly and led hundreds of marchers to protest the council's anti-Chinese stands. Attempting to exploit this sentiment, a group of developers staged a campaign to recall Hatch and his council ally Pat Reichenberger. But the effort foundered, in part because of the organizers' transparent progrowth agenda and in part because of their crude tactics (for example, warning longtime Latino residents that the council was out to deport them to Mexico). Further muddying the waters, Councilman Cam Briglio, an Italian American, agreed to change his vote on Resolution 9004, which meant that English was unofficial once again. But not for long. Monterey Park's language battles would continue, thanks to the media attention they generated, as part of a wider war.

Sixty miles to the northwest, a similar conflict was unfolding in Fillmore, a dusty citrus community of ten thousand. Culturally, this is about as far as one can travel from the Los Angeles suburbs and remain in California. Set in a narrow valley hemmed in by mountains, the town has an out-of-the-past feel, with its seedy drive-ins and a business district divided by railroad tracks. Overdevelopment is no threat in Fillmore. Mexican Americans make up a slight majority of the population; many work in the orange groves and packinghouses that literally surround the town. César Chávez came here in the 1970s to lead a union drive, but it was crushed after a conglomerate bought out local growers, fired the workers, and evicted them from the land. The victims received little sympathy from Fillmore's city fathers, Anglo property owners who saw no need for unions. Still, race relations have improved since the 1940s, when restaurants and movie theaters were strictly segregated.

Ernest Morales, one of two Hispanics ever to serve on the city council, grew up here and attended the "Mexican school"—integration came only after World War II—and he remembers that "kids were punished for speaking Spanish" even on the playground. Fillmore has since adopted bilingual education, albeit grudgingly. Hispanics accounted for nearly two-thirds of the school district's enrollment by the mid-1980s, but officials were not overly solicitous about their needs. Facing a budgetary crisis one year, they began charging students from migrant camps 25 cents a day to ride the school bus into town. Not surprisingly, attendance suffered. The fee, which appeared to violate the state constitution's guarantee of "free public education," was later dropped in response to litigation.

At that time California law required schools to provide native-language instruction, in most instances, for children judged to be "limited-English-proficient" (LEP).[6] While some Hispanics in Fillmore no longer spoke much Spanish, immigration continued to bring substantial numbers of non-English speakers. LEP students accounted for more than 25 percent of the school population, but there were not enough bilingual classrooms to accommodate them all. Fillmore was thus failing to comply with state law. Feeling the heat from Sacramento, the school district announced in late 1984 that it planned to turn the San Cayetano School into a totally bilingual facility the following year. This meant that English-speaking students in grades K–3 would no longer be assigned to all-English classrooms.

On hearing the news, many Anglo parents were concerned. A few were apoplectic. Why should their children's education be slighted in order to coddle the Hispanics, who should be learning English anyway? Educators tried to explain that English-speaking students could learn just as effectively in bilingual classrooms and would have the added opportunity of learning Spanish. Unappeased, a group of seventy-five parents threatened to pull their children out of school. This got the school board's attention. A number of more flexible plans were explored so that parents could exercise their right (guaranteed by state law) to insist on all-English instruction for their children.

By this point, however, Senator Hayakawa's Washington-based group had gotten wind of the controversy. Soon U.S. English was advising the disgruntled parents about the evils of bilingual education for all students. No longer just a community issue, the debate took on ideological proportions. California's bilingual education law, with its insistence on native-language instruction, came under attack as an obstacle to English acquisition. Resolving to send a message to the state legislature, one of the parent organizers approached the city council with the idea of declaring English the official language of Fillmore. The proposal was mulled over in the local newspaper but aroused limited interest. At a meeting on April 23, 1985, about thirty residents showed up to debate the measure. Although several called it racially motivated and "a slap in the face" to Hispanics, the council could see no prejudicial intent. As Mayor Hub Cloyd said later, the nonbinding resolution "simply endorses a goal for all the people of the United States to be united under one official flag, one national anthem, one official seal, one citizenship, and one language." So, on a three-to-one vote, Fillmore became the first California municipality to pass an Official English declaration.

As word of the action spread, Mexican Americans were awakened from their habitual apathy about town politics. Ethnic relations had been tranquil of late, at least on the surface, but the English resolution ended the truce. Most Hispanics took it as a gratuitous insult—or worse, a symbolic reassertion of Anglo dominance that brought back memories of the "No Dogs or Mexicans" days of open discrimination. On May 5, *Cinco de Mayo*,[7] three hundred demonstrators marched through Fillmore carrying American and Mexican flags, along with signs reading, "Respect the Difference" and "English Yes, Force of Law No."

Ernest Morales now regretted his decision not to stand for reelection the previous fall. A civilian worker at the Point Mugu Naval Air Station, he had been a member of the council for sixteen years, including three terms as mayor, and had enjoyed close relationships with prominent Anglos. "I was a 'good Hispanic,' " he says in retrospect. "You know, I just served my time, didn't rock the boat. There was no polarization then." Though hesitant to enter the fray, he was disturbed by the English Only measure and the insensitivity behind it. As the town's most visible Hispanic leader, he felt obliged to articulate Hispanic grievances.

City officials were stunned by the community's reaction. At first they sought to blame it on outside agitators who were willfully distorting the council's intent. (One leader of the demonstration was a migrant organizer from nearby Oxnard.) The mayor's office distributed hundreds of handbills in English and Spanish calling the furor "a serious misunderstanding. . . . We are *not saying* the Hispanics in this community cannot speak their native language." But when Morales and other activists organized a Concerned Citizens Committee and demanded that the resolution be rescinded, the council refused. "They didn't want to back down to us," Morales believes. "They just dug in their heels."

More than seven hundred people turned out at the next city council meeting. For nearly five hours, speakers decried the divisiveness the resolution had brought. Gary Collins, the Anglo parent who had originally proposed it, received one of the night's loudest ovations when he joined those calling for repeal. Only a handful spoke out for Official English, but among them was S. I. Hayakawa, who had traveled down from the Bay Area for the occasion. Recognizable in his trademark tam-o'-shanter, the aging ex-senator was greeted with chants and catcalls on entering the auditorium. He proceeded to deliver a lecture on the international dimensions of language diversity, describing its consequences in countries like Belgium and India. Soon members of the audience began to interrupt with cries of "What about Fillmore?" Losing his composure, Hayakawa admonished the crowd: "I am trying to make a rational argument here. I am a linguistic scholar—I know these things." Official English was getting a bum rap, he insisted. "The problem is from the ambitious politicians here who are manipulating the Spanish people [sic]. Your leaders are creating dissension when I want to bring people together."

If that was in fact his goal, Hayakawa failed in Fillmore. The council declined to take further action, leaving a residue of resentment on both sides. Over the next few months, Hispanic activists led a campaign to recall Mayor Cloyd and two other council members, but it lost by a wide margin. In the next election, all three Hispanic candidates were defeated, including Ernest Morales. The language issue has since died down—and nothing has changed in the way the town conducts its business—but the estrangement lingers, says Morales. "After all this, a lot of people in the Hispanic community don't feel part of Fillmore anymore. We don't stop and chat [with Anglos] like we used to. We say hello. But I think the trust just isn't there, the feeling of mutual respect isn't there. Or the pride in community, as far as I'm concerned. I just don't feel at ease with these people anymore."

What Hayakawa did get was exposure. The dispute put U.S. English on the map, bringing the kind of national publicity that money cannot buy. Fillmore would soon be forgotten, but not the emotions stirred there. Threatened Anglo-Americans who previously had never heard of Official English now opened their checkbooks. Journalists and legislators began to take notice. Celebrity endorsers appeared on the U.S. English letterhead, including such unlikely xenophobes as Norman Cousins, Walter Cronkite, and Gore Vidal (all would later resign in embarrassment).

As if this were not enough, U.S. English had one last score to settle in Fillmore. It tried to get Ernest Morales fired from his job—or at least silenced by the threat. Stanley Diamond, chief of the lobby's California operations and a longtime aide to Hayakawa, wrote to the base commander at Point Mugu to complain that Morales was violating the Hatch Act, which bans partisan politicking by career federal employees. This was a serious allegation; Hatch Act violations are punishable by suspension or dismissal from the civil service. Yet, as the base commander explained in his response to Diamond, Morales had done nothing wrong. The law in no way prohibits civic activism, holding office in a nonpartisan system like Fillmore's, or speaking out on issues like English Only. First Amendment rights still apply.

During the first half of 1986, more than a million Californians signed petitions to qualify Proposition 63, an Official English amendment to the state constitution, for placement on the November ballot. This would be the first major test of Hayakawa's proposal. Fittingly, it was held in the residence of choice for newcomers to the United States. Twenty-eight percent of immigrants settled in California that year, including nearly half of the Taiwanese, Filipinos, Vietnamese, Mexicans, and Salvadorans, and there were growing enclaves of non-English speakers all around the state. Not just inner cities, but increasingly suburbs and small towns awoke to find immigrants and refugees on their doorsteps, usually in need of help. Few communities were prepared to cope with the cultural fallout, the racial tensions, and the practical demands on schools, courts, and social service agencies. Fillmore and Monterey Park gave a name to this nexus of problems—*bilingualism*—and suggested a way to strike back. Local English Only activists, however outrageous or insensitive, were of enormous benefit to Hayakawa's statewide campaign, not so much in elaborating an agenda as in defining a focus for voter frustrations. Indeed, leaving the details murky proved to be a winning strategy at the polls. Despite much unclarity about its implications, Proposition 63 passed with 73 percent of the vote.

In turn, a victory in trend-setting California thrust the movement into national prominence. Six months later, Official English bills were pending in thirty-seven state houses (not counting the eight in which such measures had already passed). By 1990, a total of seventeen states had adopted laws or constitutional amendments designating English as their official language. Sensitivity to the impact of immigration has been acute not only in California, but in Florida, Colorado, and Arizona, where voters also adopted English Only amendments in contests that pitted Anglos against growing Hispanic minorities. Yet the pattern is inconsistent. Among the eleven other states that elevated English to official status during the 1980s—Alabama, Arkansas, Georgia, Indiana, Kentucky, Mississippi, North Carolina, North Dakota, South Carolina, Tennessee, and Virginia—only the last has experienced a substantial influx of newcomers (mainly in the suburbs of Washington, D.C.).[8] Something larger is afoot than knee-jerk nativism.

It is safe to say that few voters or legislators had previously encountered the issue, or given it much thought. Even amid the hoopla created by Proposition 63, a national survey found that 64 percent of Americans believed the U.S. Constitution *already* specified English as the country's official tongue. On hearing otherwise, reactions generally ranged from Why not? to Why bother? When an

Official English bill passed almost unanimously in Arkansas in 1987, it was taken as a sign that silly season had arrived. Deadlocked over the state budget, legislators took time out to consider an official vegetable, an official rock, an official fish, and an official language. Before approving Official English in Mississippi, members of the General Assembly amused themselves by "debating" various amendments. One would have made the law contingent on all legislators' passing an English literacy test. Another declared: "The following words and terms will be no longer recognized in this state since said words and terms are either incomprehensible or are not of pure English extraction: *Y'all; hominy; canoe; up-air; down-nair;* and *yonder.*"

By contrast, linguistic minorities were usually quick to see the campaign as an affront to their heritage and a threat to their rights. Where they were present to raise such concerns—Puerto Ricans in New York, Chicanos in Texas, Crow Indians in Montana, Cajuns in Louisiana—they usually succeeded in derailing language legislation. Loath to alienate defined blocs of voters, most politicians scrambled to avoid the issue in these states, and Official English bills tended to expire in committee.

Where such measures reached the ballot, however, they proved unstoppable and, with the exception of a close contest in Arizona, scored easy wins. Voting "against English" was simply counterintuitive. If not English, then what? was the question that naturally asserted itself. The very fact that some people, mostly minorities, were opposing English as the official language seemed to confirm that English was threatened. No matter that 98 percent of U.S. residents above the age of four spoke English "well" or "very well," according to the 1980 Census. Or that immigrants were lining up for scarce seats in English-as-a-second-language classes. (On the day that Proposition 63 passed, more than forty thousand adults were on waiting lists for E.S.L. instruction in Los Angeles alone.) Nor was there much sympathy for claims that Official English would create an atmosphere of intolerance and invite acts of discrimination against linguistic minorities—that it would replay the rancor of Fillmore and Monterey Park on a larger stage.

Proponents of Official English were skillful in linking language to God and Country sentiments: national unity, loyalty, strength of purpose. To reaffirm English seemed to celebrate not only what Americans had in common, but also what they depended on to resolve their disputes. *E pluribus unum* came down to a matter of communication, in the same language. To convince voters otherwise, given the complexity of opposing arguments—hard to convey in thirty-second sound bites without name-calling or demagoguery, even if ad hoc "Vote No" coalitions had been able to afford television time in populous states like California and Florida—to defeat Official English under such constraints was virtually impossible.

Yet it would be misleading to suggest that opponents had no way of getting their views before the public. To the contrary, English Only campaigns received unrelenting and largely unfavorable coverage in newspapers like the *Los Angeles Times,* the *Miami Herald,* and the *Arizona Republic.* Establishment opinion, as articulated by editorialists and political leaders, was overwhelmingly negative: Official English was unnecessary, divisive, bigoted, dictatorial, mean-spirited, and unworthy of Americans who had long respected ethnic diversity. While this message was heard, it was singularly unpersuasive to the English-speaking majority. Abstract appeals to pluralism seemed to impress mostly minority groups and civil libertarians, who hardly needed convincing. Calls for tolerance failed to address the problems, real or imagined, created by a rapid influx of non-English-speaking immigrants. This was a populist revolt that elite voices were powerless to quell.

As the debate spread, Official English provided grist for the likes of Phil Donahue, Geraldo Rivera, and Morton Downey, Jr. It inspired activism by civil rights attorneys, educators, church and veterans' groups, and of course, a wide array of ethnic organizations. It seemed to cause friction wherever English speakers and minority language groups came in contact, not only in the Sunbelt, but in places like Holyoke, Massachusetts, and Suffolk County, Long Island. English Only was becoming a national phenomenon.

All the exposure did little, however, to resolve the central questions: What was the purpose of declaring English the official language? What were the intended effects, practical or symbolic? If the idea was merely to abolish bilingual education or bilingual ballots, why not seek such changes through legislation? If it was to enable more adult immigrants to acquire English, why not appropriate more funds for existing E.S.L. programs? Why was it necessary to amend the Constitution? *What was the point?*

There was no shortage of answers; indeed, that was the problem. Sponsors of Official English initiatives became a moving target for anyone seeking to pin them down about their goals. One day they appeared as jackbooted language police, the next as high-minded seekers of ethnic harmony. During a 1984 initiative against bilingual voting rights, they coined the term "English Only" but later disavowed the label and cried slander whenever it was applied. Shortly before launching the California English Campaign, Stanley Diamond gave an interview in which he accused corporations such as Philip Morris of promoting "dangerous divisiveness" by advertising in Spanish. He hinted that boycotts might be in the offing unless these businesses mended their ways. Diamond also organized a write-in campaign to Pacific Bell, protesting its *Páginas Amarillas en Español,* the Spanish-language Yellow Pages. "We will do everything we can to put this advertising in English only," he vowed. But Diamond dropped such threats when he began organizing for Proposition 63. The intent of the initiative, he now insisted, was solely to "protect English" as the language of state government. It would ensure that the legislature passed "no law that diminishes or ignores the role of English. . . . Languages in the home, church, private affairs, and private businesses are not affected."

Opponents, including Attorney General John Van de Kamp and Assembly Speaker Willie Brown, warned that approval of Proposition 63 might outlaw a wide range of bilingual accommodations, such as emergency operators, court interpreters, "pamphlets informing non-English-speaking parents how to enroll their children in public schools," and even foreign language teaching in tax-supported institutions. Hayakawa, Diamond, and other leaders of the campaign scoffed at these claims as desperation tactics. All essential rights and services would remain intact, they promised, portraying the initiative as largely symbolic: "This amendment recognizes in law what has long been a political and social reality. . . . [It] sends a clear message: English is the official language of California. To function, to participate in our society we must know English. English is the language of opportunity, of government, of unity. English, in a fundamental sense, is *US.*" (Presumably, other languages are *THEM.*) But what form would this message take? A simple resolution to "recognize reality" or a mechanism to shape it? Would English be "protected" with a ceremonial statement or through tangible steps to restrict the use and diminish the status of other tongues?

The proponents were more candid on November 5, the day after Proposition 63 passed. Assemblyman Frank Hill of Whittier unveiled his hit list: multilingual driver's tests, welfare applications, student-aid forms at state universities, and bilingual instruction in the public schools. J. William Orozco, the campaign's Southern California spokesman, called for the elimination of school notices to parents in other languages, arguing that "if you put crutches under these people, they're never going to learn English." And Stanley Diamond followed up on the one specific demand he had voiced during the campaign: an end to bilingual ballots in California, except where mandated by federal law.

As it happened, Proposition 63 had no *direct* consequences whatsoever. Attorney General Van de Kamp, who previously had fretted about the amendment's far-reaching impact, now concluded it was purely advisory, without binding effect on voting, schooling, or any other public function—although, as a political matter, bilingual education would soon feel the chill wind from Proposition 63 in the legislature. Like authorities in other states where Official English measures have passed, Van de Kamp could find nothing to enforce.

The voters' actual intent remained obscure. In various national surveys, respondents had overwhelmingly favored Official English, with support normally in the 60-to-80-percent range, sometimes higher. But when the proposal was defined to mean terminating bilingual services for those who needed them, opinion was evenly divided (47 percent for and 47 percent against in a 1987 CBS News/New York Times poll). A survey commissioned by U.S. English in Florida found likely voters more than eight to one in favor. Asked why, 45 percent responded that an English Language Amendment would ensure "that people who need to communicate for health and safety reasons always can"; 38 percent believed the measure would "make it easier for people who come to this country and don't speak English to eventually get ahead"; and only 8 percent hoped "to stop people from speaking any language but English." All unlikely outcomes, as experience would show.

No longer talking symbolism, an infuriated Stanley Diamond denounced Van de Kamp, Willie Brown, and their fellow Democrats in the California legislature for attempting to "cripple, gut, and emasculate the Amendment that was the Will of *THE PEOPLE.* . . . They are out to make Proposition 63 meaningless even though the Amendment won by large majorities in all their districts. Do they care about you the voter? *Hell,* no." Sounding like the ghost of Howard Jarvis, he pledged retribution at the polls: *"THE PEO-*

PLE are stirring, blood pressures are moving up. There is a whisper out there on the way to [becoming] a relentless, irreversible roar. Can you get away with this one? It's *HELL, HELL,* no." Diamond vowed to file lawsuits on behalf of the abused, English-speaking majority—an eventuality anticipated in the wording of Proposition 63—if state and local governments failed to heed its message and continued to offer bilingual services.

But once again, Official English advocates backed away from confrontation and from any hint of draconian designs rather than spoil their chances of passing more initiatives. By May 1987, Senator Hayakawa had renewed his claim that officializing English would "produce little or no change in people's lives." Then why bother with it? He advanced a creative new justification. It would serve as "an insurance policy" to prevent the declaration of any other official language in the United States. Did such a threat exist today? "Not yet," Hayakawa conceded, but he warned: "The non-English-speaking population is increasing vastly. If you get enough Hispanics, let's say in San Diego, California, to say the deliberations of city hall have got to be conducted in both Spanish and English, then you're going to have trouble on your hands." Trouble from whom? one might ask. From Hispanics or from those who fear and resent their empowerment? With an English Language Amendment, monolingual Americans could sleep more soundly, knowing that ethnic agitators would be forever thwarted in their plots to impose official bilingualism.

The looniness of Hayakawa's insurance policy should have been immediately evident. There is no challenger to English on the American horizon. Research by demographers such as Calvin Veltman shows that, in terms of language use, newcomers to the United States are assimilating more rapidly than ever before, a trend that includes the largest and allegedly most resistant group, Spanish speakers. By the time they have been in this country for fifteen years, 75 percent of Hispanic immigrants are speaking English on a daily basis, and 70 percent of their children become dominant or monolingual in English. (In contrast, the *grand*children of earlier immigrants were typically the first to become fully "anglicized.") Minority tongues are, of course, more commonly heard today than in the pre–1965 era of tight immigration restrictions. Linguistic diversity is likely to increase through the year 2000, as newcomers continue to arrive in large numbers. Yet, in the longer term, there are strong countervailing forces. Current projections show that, without the replenishing effects of immigration and without heroic efforts to revive indigenous tongues, all minority languages would gradually die out in this country, with the possible exception of Navajo.

In their language choices, immigrants—no less than longtime citizens—emulate those they admire, empathize with, or aspire to become. On the one hand, speech habits among the upwardly mobile gravitate toward the prestige variety, the language or dialect most associated with worldly success. On the other hand, those who prize their ethnicity may cling to native tongues in spite of—sometimes because of—their lower social standing. Simply put, language is inseparable from identity. The same principle applies whether one is considering speech training to shed a Brooklyn accent or wrestling with contradictory impulses about using Portuguese in the home.

For those who have appropriated the dominant language by birth, such choices rarely appear problematic. It is easy to take a pragmatic view. Conformity to majority preferences would seem to benefit everyone, providing equality of access and opportunity while removing a potential source of misunderstanding and mistrust. Why can't all Americans just use standard English? many ask, alternately questioning the intelligence and the motives of those who resist. Why would reasonable people handicap themselves by speaking a less useful, less accepted, less valued tongue? Today Anglo-Americans are increasingly posing such questions, oblivious to the dilemmas of language loyalty and language shift.

Even if acquiring a second tongue were as effortless as monolinguals are inclined to believe, speakers of African-American, working class, rural, and other stigmatized dialects, as well as languages other than English, are faced with a wrenching option: either advance by forsaking the customs and acceptance of their tribe, or preserve these linguistic links and be shunned by the larger society. Their choice is one of *status or solidarity* (to borrow the apt phrase of James and Lesley Milroy). Many will look back with regret, whatever their decision. Others, caught in a limbo of ambivalence, will never become articulate in either language. A fortunate minority becomes truly bilingual, at home in both worlds. But even they are likely to pay a social price, since their skill is more discouraged than rewarded by fellow Americans. Learning a "foreign language" in school (usually not too well) has higher prestige than acquiring the same language naturally (and thoroughly) in a minority community. As the Norwegian American linguist Einar Haugen complains: "Bilingualism has been treated as a necessary evil, a rash on the body politic, which time might be expected to cure without the need of calling in the doctors." No wonder that, for many, it is the first step toward monolingualism in the more powerful tongue.

In this country English tends to win out sooner or later, notwithstanding variations among immigrant groups. Joshua Fishman, a pioneer researcher in the dynamics of language shift, explains: "Generally speaking . . . the fewer the immigrants, the greater their dispersion, the greater their urbanization and education in the host language, and the greater their occupational interaction with the host society, the less likely it is that immigrants will be able to maintain intimate language and behavior networks." Social mobility is the crucial factor. It promotes contact with English speakers and thus increases incentives to speak the dominant language. More important, it breaks down relationships within the immigrant family. By the time this "last undisputed and indispensable domain" is penetrated by English, the ethnic language is doomed, Fishman argues. It "may linger on for metaphorical purposes (humor, insult, secretive identification), but its major vernacular role is gone." In the past, European immigrants normally completed the shift to English by the third generation.

Conversely, groups who were excluded from the mainstream (American Indians, Mexican Americans, Puerto Ricans, Chinese Americans) or who excluded themselves (Amish, Hutterites, Old Order Mennonites) got a late start on the road to anglicization. "Their language remained part of their ethnicity," Fishman says, not only because they had less to gain by learning English, but because, "unburdened" by economic opportunities, their family structures remained more stable. Naturally, this picture has changed as a result of civil rights reforms. Lowering color barriers in the 1960s had the effect of lowering language barriers as well—no doubt explaining the acceleration in English acquisition among nonwhite minorities. Anglicization is proceeding quite well, thank you, without the encouragement of an English Language Amendment.

Not that legislation could mandate patterns of language loyalty and language shift. Quite the reverse. Ukrainians who had stubbornly resisted the czars' attempts to eradicate their tongue, risking harsh penalties for printing a book or delivering a sermon or teaching a child in Ukrainian, abandoned their language voluntarily in the laissez-faire climate of the New World. On the other hand, language legislation does have the potential to exacerbate preexisting hostilities. Witness the civil war that has bloodied Sri Lanka for more than thirty years—a conflict often cited to illustrate the perils of bilingualism, but in fact an example of what can happen when language becomes an instrument of ethnic dominance. Active hostilities date from a 1956 decision to declare Sinhalese the sole official tongue, to the detriment of the Tamil-speaking minority.

That such factual considerations do not leap to mind, even as questions, for those who support Official English reflects a remarkable naïveté about the politics of language—perhaps predictable in a country where it has played a modest historical role, but nonetheless dangerous. Demagoguery thrives on unexamined assumptions. In the English Only mindset there are several:

- English has been Americans' strongest common bond, the "social glue" that holds the nation together.
- Linguistic diversity inevitably leads to political disunity.
- State-sponsored bilingual services remove incentives to learning English and keep immigrants out of the mainstream.
- The hegemony of English in the United States is threatened by swelling populations of minority-language speakers.
- Ethnic conflicts will ensue unless strong measures are taken to reinforce "unilingualism."

To accept these propositions, it is not necessary to dislike immigrants (though that cannot hurt), to speak English as a first language, or to belong to the John Birch Society. Some prominent advocates of Official English have foreign accents and liberal politics; surprisingly few have Anglo-Saxon surnames. One's linguistic repertoire is mutable, after all, unlike skin color. Newcomers can and often do trade in their native tongue for a more serviceable model, hoping to gain social acceptance, economic mobility, political clout, and myriad other advantages. Some of these assimilated first- and second-generation Americans are among the most militant exponents of English Only. Which makes it problematic to pin charges of nativism, ethnocentrism, or racism on those who hold such views. Still, the questions remain: Why the willing suspension of critical faculties about the status of English today? The yearning for cultural conformity? The ability to rationalize intolerance? Whence the *Anglo-paranoia?*

Even in Monterey Park, where Chinese seems ubiquitous, immigrants not long off the jumbo jet are working on their English. In fact, English is becoming the lingua franca among speakers of Cantonese, Mandarin, Taiwanese, and Chiou-Chou[9]—dialects of Chinese that are mutually incomprehensible to varying degrees. Asian parents, whose academic expectations range from high to astronomical, push their children to excel in English. Most years, the local Alhambra High School ranks among the top ten in Westinghouse science scholarships awarded nationwide. Students do not reach Berkeley, Stanford, and U.C.L.A. by studying in Chinese alone. Barry Hatch grudgingly concedes: "They're learning English sufficiently, the businessmen and so forth, the students naturally. They speak English. But they *prefer* Chinese, Vietnamese, and all these other languages."

Clearly, it's not just their tongues, but their hearts and minds he is after. It's not enough that immigrants acquire English; they must forswear allegiance to other languages. For Hatch and a growing number of Americans, bilingualism connotes divided loyalties.[10] A failure to identify with—respect—the heritage of this country. A desire to enjoy the benefits of citizenship without shouldering its obligations. A refusal to honor the prerogatives of those who came before. "This is a sovereign country," Hatch says. "This isn't an open land that nobody has laid claim to."

But today that claim's meaning is increasingly in doubt. At a time when it's tricky to say exactly what unites Americans and, for that matter, exactly who "Americans" are, bilingualism is a definable threat. Elevating English as an icon, a revered yet embattled symbol, has appeal for the insecure and the resentful. It provides a clear answer to the question "Who belongs?" And it gives comfort to those whose embrace of democracy is contingent on certain assumptions about race, ethnicity, and culture.

"One nation, indivisible" is the slogan Senator Hayakawa chose for the English Only movement. During his final years, he never tired of quoting Hector St. John de Crèvecoeur, a French immigrant to this country, writing in 1782:

> What then is the American, this new man? . . . *He* is an American, who leaving behind him all his ancient prejudices and manners, receives new ones from the new mode of life he has embraced, the new government he obeys, and the new rank he holds. . . . Here individuals of all nations are melted into a new race of men, whose labours and posterity will one day cause great changes in the world.

This passage may be read in different ways. Is political equality the miracle that produces the melting, that renders differences of origin irrelevant? Or is the new alloy—a unitary culture molded by a common language—the sine qua non of nationhood? Are unalienable rights universally shared? Or do they depend on conformity to Anglo-American values, traditions, and speech? An ambivalence on these points has always haunted our democracy. Which begins to explain why the matter of our national tongue, its legal status as well as its role in American identity, has been left unsettled.

Two

Polyglot Boarding-House

No one said English was threatened in 1787. As far as can be determined from Madison's sketchy notes, the matter of a national language never came up at the Federal Convention in Philadelphia. The word *English* appears nowhere in any draft of the U.S. Constitution, nor in any subsequent amendment. One hundred ninety-four years would pass before an English Language Amendment was first introduced in Congress.

Are we to assume that the Founders dispensed with the formality of an official tongue because, in their day, the hegemony of Anglo-Saxon culture was unchallenged? That the issue remained dormant over the years because few Americans, including immigrants, needed to be sold on the advantages of a common language? That large-scale bilingualism, especially in the operation of public institutions, was unthinkable in the United States before the present generation? These are plausible explanations, convenient for those who promote English Only legislation as a return to first principles: a way to reclaim America's lost purity, greatness, and—need it be said?—innocence. Convenient, but untrue. Such notions obscure a multilingual tradition that is unsurpassed in its variety and richness, while inventing for English a unifying role that it rarely enjoyed.

Certainly, language can serve as a shibboleth, a means to determine who belongs and who does not. At times it has marked immigrants and conquered peoples with a negative identifier, *un-American,* and has furnished a practical basis for discrimination, blocking equal access to justice, education, and voting. Language is always a potential source of political conflict because no "church–state" separation is possible. Government must decide on some medium for its operations (though not necessarily just one), and such decisions have repercussions. Even in private life, language choices are political choices, contingent on questions of power, status, and loyalty. Occasionally they take on a larger public meaning. Early in this century, during an extraordinary period of xenophobia, Anglo-conformity became a touchstone of "100 Percent Americanism."

Yet, for the most part, English has remained a dim star in the firmament of American nationalism. As a prideful symbol, it cannot compare to the place of, say, the French language in French national identity. To the extent that English has flared into patriotic significance—as when Noah Webster asserted that "a *national language* is a band of *national union*"—it has been inspired less by foreign competition than by a desire to declare independence from the mother country. Webster's particular plea was for spelling reforms that would differentiate American and British English (though he would later abandon this youthful enthusiasm). By some apocryphal accounts, American revolutionists even considered deposing the language of the oppressor in favor of German, French, Greek, or Hebrew. There is little evidence, however, that any of these alternatives was seriously discussed. No doubt Roger Sherman, a delegate to the Continental Congress, summed up the prevailing view when he quipped, "It would be more convenient for us to keep the language as it was and *make the English speak Greek.*"[1]

All kidding aside, the question of a national language was subordinated to a novel conception of nationhood. Early Americans saw themselves as exceptional: a people embarked on a noble adventure in self-government, united by a commitment to democratic ideals rather than by involuntary ties of ancestry. Here was a nation that anyone could join, simply by embracing the principles on which it was founded. Moreover, in the words of Tom Paine, it offered an "asylum for the persecuted lovers of civil and religious liberty from *every part* of Europe" (his emphasis). The traditional markers of nationality—language, customs, religion, and blood—were seen as outmoded, inconsistent with the universalism of the American experiment. Ethnic exclusiveness would have deflated Jefferson's grandiose conception of a government in harmony "with the rights of mankind." And there was a tendency to view language issues accordingly, through an ideological prism that focused attention on the clash between democratic and autocratic values.

Before 1981, the question of designating an official language had come up, albeit rarely, in state legislatures. But prior to Senator

Hayakawa's bill, the only such proposal ever considered in the U.S. Congress was to repudiate English and adopt "American" as the national tongue. The sponsor of this 1923 measure, Representative Washington Jay McCormick of Montana, explained his objectives as follows:

> I might say I would supplement the political emancipation of '76 by the mental emancipation of '23. America has lost much in literature by not thinking its own thoughts and speaking them boldly in a language unadorned with gold braid. It was only when Cooper, Irving, Mark Twain, Whitman, and O. Henry dropped the Order of the Garter and began to write American that their wings of immortality sprouted. Had Noah Webster, instead of styling his monumental work the "American Dictionary of the English Language," written a "Dictionary of the American Language," he would have become a founder instead of a compiler. Let our writers drop their top-coats, spats, and swagger-sticks, and assume occasionally their buckskin, moccasins, and tomahawks.

Other than sneers from Eastern literati (McCormick's real targets), the scheme received little notice and no Congressional action. It fared better in the Illinois legislature, where Chicago Irish politicians commanded sufficient clout to enact American as the state's official language, along with a few choice *whereas*es condemning the British Empire. The law remained on the books until 1969, when English was quietly rehabilitated.

Even if language had figured larger in the calculus of Americanism, during the Federalist Era there was another factor that weighed against language legislation. Early Americans recoiled at the notion of a state-sponsored culture, which they associated with Old World monarchs and aristocrats. It is no accident that the United States has no counterpart to the *Académie française,* despite periodic discussions about the need for a linguistic standard. "To this day," John Adams complained in 1780, "there is no grammar nor dictionary extant of the English language which has the least public authority." He argued that British inaction had handed the new nation an opportunity to seize leadership, to define and promote an American English throughout the world, thereby advancing American interests. Yet Adams was rebuffed by the Continental Congress when he sought its backing for an "American Academy for refining, improving, and ascertaining the English language." Subsequent schemes along these lines were also rejected as elitist and intrusive.

There was no elaborate ideology at work here, but rather an instinctive libertarianism. What business did government have in telling the people what to say or how to say it? And if an official standard for English were endorsed, which English would it be—the argot of the marketplace, the homespun idiom of the frontier, or (as critics suspected) the patter of Anglophile drawing rooms?

Elected leaders wisely avoided any role in such decisions, or they paid a political price. As one Senate supporter of an official language academy conceded in 1807, the idea was "considered so generally hostile to the interests & independence of the respective States, that there is hardly any thing more unpopular & less likely to be adopted." A century later President Theodore Roosevelt courted rebellion when he attempted to use the Government Printing Office to promote a system of simplified spelling. "I am not willing to vote to padlock the language," announced one Missouri congressman. Soundly repudiated, Roosevelt was forced to confine such innovations as *tho, altho, thru, thruout, thoro,* and *thoroly* to White House communications. As a matter of practical politics, Americans' linguistic decisionmaking has remained decentralized—left, if not entirely to schoolmasters, publishers, and unofficial grammarians like Webster, then at least to the states.

This laissez-faire spirit often extended to non-English-speaking immigrants as well. When the framers took no steps to give English constitutional status, it was not for lack of challengers, but in spite of them. At that time the dominion of English was at least as "threatened" by the presence of linguistic minorities as it is today. To cite the prime example: German Americans accounted for 8.7 percent of the U.S. population in the first census, a proportion comparable to that of Hispanic Americans (9.0 percent) exactly two centuries later. Although statistical data are fragmentary, it is likely that a higher proportion of Hispanics speak English now than Germans did then. It is almost certain that there are proportionally fewer non-English speakers in the 1990s than there were in the 1850s or the 1910s. Yet we now hear an unprecedented clamor for "the legal protection of English." All of which goes to prove that objective measures of language diversity do not determine the politics of language.

Myths, not facts, are generating strong feelings about bilingual-ism today, and these myths do not involve language so much as tradition. Do the new services for linguistic minorities violate an unwritten agreement that all citizens must know English, the chosen medium of our democracy? Conversely, do restrictions on other languages betray American values of respect for free speech and equal rights regardless of ethnicity?

It is possible to pick and choose, in *ahistorical* fashion, ample evidence to support either of these interpretations. But seeking to isolate a consistent American policy on language is a futile exercise. The most one can say is that ad hoc responses to diversity have varied along a scale from accommodation to tolerance to exclusion to repression, usually depending on forces that have nothing to do with language. As Daniel Boorstin has observed, Americans tend naïvely to assume that the Founders elaborated "a perfect and com-plete political theory, adequate to all our future needs." Faith in an "orthodox American creed" is especially misplaced when it comes to language policy. Here there are no first principles, no original sources of wisdom to draw upon. Moreover, this is a subject largely neglected by U.S. historians, who have tended to regard linguistic pluralism as a moot issue following the immigration restrictions of the 1920s. The acknowledged authority in the field, Heinz Kloss, is a German whose major work, *The American Bilingual Tradition,* was unavailable in English until 1977. Despite recent contributions by linguists such as Dennis Baron, Joshua Fishman, Kenji Hakuta, Shirley Brice Heath, Reynaldo Macías, and Geoffrey Nunberg, im-migrant historiography remains fixated on what John Higham has called "the sunny side of American life, the success of American institutions, the common bonds of an American national character."

Nevertheless, history remains essential to an understanding of the Official English controversy. Beyond clarifying the factual record—for example, the misconception that the American "common school" operated solely in English—it can supply a needed depth perception in evaluating current arguments. In exploring the past, we can rec-ognize familiar lines of language conflict: majority prerogatives ver-sus minority rights, "Americanization" versus ethnic pride, *unum* versus *pluribus.* We can appreciate how language attitudes change, chameleon-like, to reflect their political surroundings. We can rec-ognize and assess today's unique concerns, notably the claim that "the primacy of English" needs defending against the encroachment of other tongues. Finally, we can highlight the stakes of this debate, the extent to which, after two centuries of national experience, Americans are still struggling over basic questions of democracy.

An Anglocentric reading of U.S. history has always had its uses. Fear of faction, a recurrent theme in our political life and a special concern at its outset, has inspired a myth of denial: significant diversity either never existed, or it quickly "melted" away owing to New World conditions. Homogeneity is exalted as the nation's natural state and the key to its political success. Consider, for example, John Jay's rationale for Federalism, frequently cited by modern proponents of Official English:

> Providence has been pleased to give this one connected country to one united people—a people descended from the same ancestors, speaking the same language, professing the same religion, attached to the same principles of government, very similar in their manners and customs, and who, by their joint counsels, arms, and efforts, fighting side by side throughout a long and bloody war, have nobly established their general liberty and independence.
>
> This country and this people seem to have been made for each other, and it appears as if it was the design of Providence that an inheritance so proper and convenient for a band of brethren, united to each other by the strongest ties, should never be split into a number of unsocial, jealous, and alien sovereignties.

Jay's demographic portrait omits not only Indians and Africans—blind spots not unusual for the time—but even his own Huguenot and Knickerbocker ancestors. Then there were the Germans, for whose benefit the Continental Congress had translated numerous official documents, including the *Artikel des Bundes und der immerwährenden Eintracht zwischen den Staaten von New Hampshire, Massachusetts Bay* . . . (Articles of Confederation), and the French, in whose language it had printed revolutionary appeals hoping to rally Québécois support. These and other non–Anglo-Saxon groups were, of course, well known to Jay, an experienced politician, who would later coin the verb *to Americanize*. But for now, in pressing the case for centralized government, he found it convenient to ignore the potential for ethnic schisms.

Madison took a more forthright approach. He began by acknowledging that "all civilized societies are divided into different sects, factions, and interests." The problem was how to manage these contending forces within a democratic framework, not only to guard against a state of anarchy in which the people's liberty is sacrificed to factional interests, but simultaneously to prevent a *tyranny of the majority* in which the liberty of factions is crushed by the popular will. As Madison warned, "In all cases where a majority are united by a common interest or passion, the rights of the minority are in danger." Hence the need for a constitutional system of checks and balances to play factions against each other. "Whilst all authority in it will be derived from and dependent on the society," he explained, "the society itself will be broken up into so many parts, interests, and classes of citizens, that the rights of individuals, or of the minority, will be in little danger from interested combinations of the majority."

Its technical brilliance notwithstanding, Madisonian pluralism has worked imperfectly for the simple reason that it failed to address the unequal distribution of power in civil society. All factions were not created equal; some were not even free. Nor was the system insulated from demagogic appeals to prejudice, especially those involving race. Ethnocentrism has repeatedly fouled the mechanism, for example, when states used English literacy requirements to disfranchise unwanted minorities. The Bill of Rights has shielded certain freedoms, at least in theory, against the whims of majority rule. But redressing inequities among groups has proved elusive within a legal framework that apportions rights to the state on the one hand and to the individual on the other. The Fourteenth Amendment was nearly a century old before it did much to aid the victims of racial discrimination. Affirmative action–style remedies such as bilingual voting are controversial not only because of lingering ethnocentrism. An eighteenth-century political tradition lives on as well, in which rights and privileges based on group membership are anathema. This legacy, egalitarian in its time, now complicates efforts to appease the democratic demands of cultural minorities. The question of *language rights*—of an entitlement to non-English-language assistance from government, for example—remains especially murky.

It is also worth remembering that in 1787 cultural pluralism was a concept yet to be invented. Language, ethnicity, national origin—these categories appeared nowhere on Madison's list of factional troublemakers. Nor had they provided frequent cause for political strife; which may in part excuse Jay's omissions. His voice in *The Federalist* is that of an assimilated ethnic who saw no profit in advertising his roots, and of a patrician who conceived the body politic a bit narrowly. John Jay is also remembered for his comment, "Those who own the country ought to govern it."

Those who governed in those days were indeed a homogeneous lot, but hardly a cross-section of the American people, even if one ignores their propertied status. Their primarily English origins were shared by a mere 60 percent of the white population. Besides the Germans and French, there were Scots, Scotch-Irish, Irish, Dutch, Swedes, and Welsh, all substantial minorities, not to mention the Spaniards, several of whose vast holdings would soon be annexed.

Some of these groups anglicized readily—such as the Huguenots, fleeing Catholic persecution, who were only too eager to discard all that was French—while others clung fiercely to their native tongues. The Germans were especially stubborn. Rather than disperse evenly, they coalesced in *Sprachinseln,* or "language islands," the largest of which encompassed fifteen thousand square miles in eastern Pennsylvania. Crèvecoeur (in a passage never cited by Senator Hayakawa) describes "whole counties where not a word of English is spoken; and in the names and language of the people, they retrace Germany." Meanwhile Gaelic dialects thrived among Scottish Highlanders and the Irish, particularly in the backwoods. Up until the Revolutionary War, Swedish-speaking congregations in Delaware and New Jersey were served by ministers from the old country. The Dutch language continued to dominate much of the Hudson Valley, where it was virtually impossible to empanel an English-speaking jury more than a century after Peter Stuyvesant surrendered New Netherland to the British. In that year, 1664, Manhattan Island was already home to a cacophony of nationalities—including Portuguese Jews, Spaniards, Germans, Scandinavians, Finns, Bohemians, Poles, Italians, and Africans (both free citizens and slaves)—who jostled, courted, and swindled each other in eighteen different languages, not counting those of nearby Indians.

Between 500 and 1,000 indigenous tongues were spoken in North

America when white settlers arrived. Puritans like John Eliot learned to preach in local dialects of the Algonquian language, a skill they found indispensable in converting the Indians. Eliot spent fourteen years translating the Bible into Algonquian and published it in 1663 (a remarkable achievement, considering that fifty-four scholars had worked for seven years to produce the King James version). Using his knowledge of the language, he founded a string of "praying towns" throughout Massachusetts. These settlements also served the purpose of teaching the Indians English and acculturating them to European ways.

Southern colonies like Virginia and South Carolina resisted pressures to Christianize and anglicize their African slaves, arguing that linguistic unity would foster rebellion. Such fears later inspired "compulsory ignorance laws" that made it a crime to teach slaves, and sometimes free blacks, to read or write. William Smith, a slave ship's captain, explained the strategy of exploiting diversity:

> As for the languages of *Gambia,* they are so many and so different, that the Natives, on either Side of the River, cannot understand each other; which, if rightly consider'd, is no small Happiness to the *Europeans* who go thither to trade for slaves. . . . I have known some melancholy Instances of whole Ship Crews being surpriz'd, and cut off by them. But the safest Way is to trade with the different Nations, on either Side of the River, and having some of every Sort on board, there will be no more Likelihood of their succeeding in a Plot than of finishing the Tower of Babel.

African tongues gradually died out in North America as a result of dispersion, calculated or otherwise. Slaves were obviously unable to settle in familiar communities of language and kinship, as voluntary immigrants have done. Yet Captain Smith put too much faith in Babel. A lingua franca, originating as an English-based pidgin on the West Coast of Africa, spread quickly among African-Americans. Dubbed Plantation Creole (though it was spoken throughout the thirteen colonies), this language likely resembled Gullah, a dialect still spoken along the Georgia–South Carolina coast. Some of its "Africanisms" still survive in varieties of Black English.[2]

Fluency in more than one language was commonplace in eighteenth-century America, especially in the cosmopolitan "middle colonies." At least thirty-eight German-language newspapers were

published between 1732 and 1800. By the 1750s private schools in
Philadelphia offered instruction in German, French, Spanish, Italian, Portuguese, Latin, Greek, Hebrew, and Arabic. And a flair for
languages was by no means restricted to educated elites. To judge
from advertisements in contemporary newspapers, bilingualism and
often trilingualism were the rule rather than the exception among
indentured servants, both black and white:

> Run away . . . from *John Orr*, near *Skuylkill, Philadelphia*, a
> Servant Man named *James Mitchel*. . . . He has been a Trav-
> eller, and can talk *Dutch* [German], *Spanish* and *Irish*. [*Penn-
> sylvania Gazette*, November 5–12, 1749]

> Run away from *Joseph Forman*, of New-York . . . a Negro
> Man named JOE. . . . [This] country born, speaks good En-
> glish and Dutch. [*New-York Gazette*, February 14, 1763]

Inability to speak a language other than English was apparently unusual enough to be noteworthy:

> Run away from his Master, *Theodorus Van Wyck*, of *Dutchess*
> County, in the Province of *New York*, a Negro Man named
> JAMES, aged about 22 Years . . . can talk nothing but En-
> glish, and has a low Voice. [*New-York Gazette*, May 12, 1760]

No one thought to celebrate linguistic diversity during the colonial era, but few fretted about it, either. Pragmatic Americans could
always find their way around language barriers; there was so much
else to quarrel about. On the era's key test of loyalties, minority
language groups were neither more nor less likely to support Independence, or to defend the Crown, than the English-speaking majority. Distinctions other than ethnicity—backwoods versus metrop-
olis, Piedmont versus Tidewater, merchant versus farmer—were the
significant ones. In any case, English was rapidly gaining in status
and spread. As Peter Kalm, a visiting Swedish botanist, observed in
1750:

> Since English is the principal language of the land all people
> get to speak that and they become ashamed to talk in their
> tongue because they fear they may not in such case be real
> English. Consequently many Swedish women are married to
> English men, and although they can speak Swedish very well,
> it is impossible to make them do so, and when they are spoken

to in Swedish they always answer in English. The same condition obtains among the men; so that it is easy to see that the Swedish language is doomed to extinction in America.

Kalm saw linguistic assimilation operating in its most efficient mode, through consensus rather than coercion.

On rare occasions in colonial America, language did get mixed up in larger conflicts, as ethnic hostility overwhelmed more democratic impulses. Benjamin Franklin penned several tracts to express his alarm about the cultural transformation of Pennsylvania by German settlers. Arriving in increasing numbers each year, by 1755 the Germans represented more than 100,000 of the colony's 225,000 inhabitants. In a Malthusian rant published that same year, Franklin outlined his view of the demographic threat:

> Why should the *Palatine Boors* be suffered to swarm into our Settlements, and by herding together, establish their Language and Manners to the Exclusion of ours? Why should *Pennsylvania*, founded by the *English*, become a Colony of *Aliens*, who will shortly be so numerous as to Germanize us instead of our Anglifying them, and will never adopt our Language or Customs, any more than they can acquire our Complexion.[3]

Voicing an intolerance that sounds familiar today, Franklin complained about the proliferation of German schools, German newspapers, and German street signs. He was especially indignant about government operations in a foreign tongue:

> They begin of late to make all their Bonds and other legal Writings in their own Language, which (though I think it ought not to be) are allowed good in our Courts, where the German Business so encreases that there is continual need of Interpreters; and I suppose in a few years they will be also necessary in the Assembly, to tell one half of our Legislators what the other half say; In short unless the stream of their importation could be turned from this to other Colonies . . . they will soon so out number us, that all the advantages we have will not in My Opinion be able to preserve our language, and even our Government will become precarious.

Ahead of his time as usual, here Franklin anticipated several themes of modern English Only advocates—paranoia about a growing minority, warnings about bilingualism as a source of political instability, a call for immigration restrictions—although the idea of language legislation apparently never appealed to him. Ironically, as a young printer he had been eager to cater to the Germans' needs, publishing prayer books and a Bible in their language. In 1732, he founded the *Philadelphische Zeitung,* the first German-language newspaper in the Americas. But the Huguenot immigrant he hired as editor employed a quirky, nonidiomatic German that failed to impress the locals, and these ventures failed as more qualified German printers settled in Philadelphia. Bitter over his losses, Franklin later charged that "the Dutch underlive and are therefor enable [sic] to underwork and undersell the English who are thereby extremely incommoded."

Meanwhile Franklin the politician clashed with German pietists who resisted his calls to take up arms against the French and Indians. Whether pacifist or not, the Germans were renowned for their thrift and aversion to high taxes; naturally they tended to side with the Quakers in opposing military expenditures by the colonial government. Franklin's political frustrations no doubt magnified his annoyance about the language barrier, which insulated the Germans from his powers of persuasion. He went so far as to suggest that non-English-speaking enclaves posed a security threat on the Western frontier (a ludicrous idea, considering the Germans' historic enmity with the French).

In reality, the Germans were never a cohesive faction. Hailing from Württemburg, Hannover, Saxony, or the Rhineland, they arrived in Pennsylvania without a developed sense of nationality and often without fond memories of the fatherland, where many had suffered persecution. They tended to identify not as Germans, but as Mennonites or Dunkards, who wanted mainly to be left alone, or as worldly Lutherans or Calvinists, who began early to anglicize their names and intermarry with English speakers. While a common linguistic origin did little to bind the Germans together, ethnic slurs and accusations of disloyalty were not easily forgiven. In 1764, they turned out en masse to retire Franklin from the Pennsylvania Assembly.

To his credit, Franklin showed a willingness to modify his views about the Germans and their language. Late in life he supported a campaign to establish the country's first German-language institution of higher learning. Accommodation would prove not only a more humane, but a more effective policy in promoting acculturation, argued his friend Benjamin Rush. A German college would "open the eyes of the Germans to a sense of the importance and utility of the English language and become perhaps the *only possible means,* consistent with their liberty, of spreading a knowledge of the English language among them" (his emphasis). Dedicated in 1787 at Lancaster, the hub of Pennsylvania Dutch country, the school was named in honor of the old German-baiter himself. It is known today as Franklin and Marshall College.

Yet Franklin's high-mindedness about German education was hardly innocent of *Realpolitik.* Now that language was receding as a symbolic issue, ethnic alliances had shifted, and so had the public agenda. Pennsylvania was becoming a center of opposition to centralized government. Facing new adversaries, Franklin and Rush were eager to solicit the Germans' support for the Federalist cause. The German college was a cunning door-opener.

It would be misleading to suggest that the Founders welcomed large-scale immigration by non-English speakers. Even Jefferson, who bitterly opposed the Alien and Sedition Acts, dreaded an influx of Europeans who had lived under absolutist regimes:

> They will bring with them the principles of the governments they leave, imbibed in their early youth; or, if able to throw them off, it will be in exchange for an unbounded licentiousness, passing, as is usual, from one extreme to another. It would be a miracle were they to stop precisely at the point of temperate liberty. These principles, *with their language,* they will transmit to their children. In proportion to their numbers, they will share with us the legislation. They will infuse into it their spirit, warp and bias its directions, and render it a heterogenous, incoherent, distracted mass. [Emphasis added.]

Such concerns remained largely theoretical, however, owing to the limited number of immigrants. European wars and restrictions on emigration made the Atlantic passage dangerous until 1815, and the flow of newcomers did not resume in force until the 1830s. By now most of the nonanglophones who had settled during the colonial period were either shifting to English or isolating themselves from civil society.

So it was a group of involuntary Americans who first tested the new nation's commitment to equality for linguistic minorities. The Louisiana Purchase of 1803 doubled not only the territory of the United States, but its French-speaking population as well. And more significant than their numbers was the fact that Louisiana's French Creoles, Acadians, and francophone blacks were concentrated, along with a smattering of Spaniards and Germans, in settlements where English was rarely heard. How would such a community, culturally and physically remote from the capital, fit into the American system? Could these non-English speakers be trusted to govern themselves? On the other hand, could the United States in good conscience deny them this right?

President Jefferson was ambivalent. These were ticklish questions, coming at a time when the priorities of representative democracy and national expansion did not always coincide. Napoleon had agreed to sell Louisiana with the understanding that its inhabitants would be admitted "as soon as possible, according to the principles of the federal constitution, to the enjoyment of all rights, advantages, and immunities of citizens of the United States." Unfortunately, the Constitution offered no guidance whatsoever regarding the rights and status of annexed peoples, and the treaty lacked any enforcement mechanism. Louisianans therefore had to rely on the honorable intentions of American officials. Even as he signed the treaty, Jefferson expressed a private view that "our new fellow citizens are as yet as incapable of self-government as children."

The President revealed his rather imperial attitude by appointing a territorial governor who spoke no French. William C. C. Claiborne, a frontier lawyer and former congressman from Tennessee, proved ill-equipped for the job: inexperienced, thin-skinned, undiplomatic. But his most salient disability was his tongue. On arrival in New Orleans, Claiborne decreed that henceforth English would be the language of local government, reasoning that, as final arbiter of all civil proceedings, he had to be able to comprehend them. This arrangement proved none too popular in a territory where Anglo-Americans were outnumbered roughly seven to one. By the governor's own estimate, "not one in fifty of the old inhabitants appear to me to understand the English Language."[4] He reported back to

Washington: "Until . . . the progress of information shall in some degree remove that mental darkness which at present so unhappily prevails, and a general knowledge of the American Language, laws and customs be understood, I do fear that a representative Government in Louisiana would be a dangerous experiment." Acting on Claiborne's advice, in 1804 Jefferson drafted an Organic Act for the Orleans Territory that vested all authority in his own appointees. Nothing was said about statehood or about suffrage. The House approved an amendment promising local elections at some (unspecified) future date but later removed it on grounds that "representatives of no two parishes would perhaps speak the same language."

These developments came as a shock to Louisianans, who had generally welcomed the prospect of annexation. Despite the culture clash between the tradition-minded *ancienne population* and the aggressive newcomers, many Creoles had been intrigued by Jeffersonian ideas about natural law and unalienable rights. Now they felt betrayed. Mass meetings were called to draft a formal "remonstrance" to Congress, signed by two thousand heads of families. In stinging terms it condemned the hypocrisy of "absolute government" imposed by a nation (and a president) that had so recently declared independence from autocracy: "Are truths, then, so well founded, so universally acknowledged, inapplicable only to us?" A special sore point was Claiborne's "sudden change of language in all the public offices and the administration of justice," which had created chaos and hardships. Above all, the *vox populi* was stifled. "That free communication so necessary to give the magistrate a knowledge of the people, and to inspire them with confidence in his administration, is by this means totally cut off."

Delivered to Washington in December 1804, the Louisiana Remonstrance was an embarrassment for Jefferson and his party. Congress promptly rewrote the Organic Act, providing for an elected legislature and promising statehood when Louisiana's free population reached sixty thousand. The President also admonished Claiborne to revise his English-only policy. "I think it visible," Jefferson wrote, "that most of whatever discontent exists among the French inhabitants arises from the introduction of our language too suddenly." Besides appointing bilingual judges, Jefferson instructed the governor to maintain records and publish laws in both languages.

By 1806, the Louisiana legislature was translating relevant federal statutes into French.

Yet skirmishes continued over Jefferson's plans to Americanize the territory, in particular his futile effort to replace the French civil code with English common law. (To this day, Louisiana's legal system remains an uneasy marriage between the two.) Chafing at Creole legislators' resistance, the President proposed to enlist thirty thousand English speakers and settle them in Louisiana at government expense, ostensibly to serve as a frontier militia, thereby tipping the ethnic balance of the new state. But Congress declined to finance the scheme.

When Louisiana joined the Union in 1812, it retained a strong francophone majority—the first (and so far the last) state to be admitted in which native English speakers were clearly outnumbered. Uneasy about the precedent, Congress insisted on a state constitutional requirement that all laws and official records be published in the language "in which the Constitution of the United States is written." Yet there was no question of restricting official publications to English *only*. For much of the nineteenth century, Louisiana's statutes, legal notices, and other public documents were printed in French as a matter of course. The courts operated bilingually and so did the state legislature, where every speech was translated. (While the procedure was cumbersome, it had the advantage of giving tempers time to cool in an assembly known for its dueling.) Jacques Villeré, elected as the state's second governor in 1816, always addressed legislators in French because he spoke no English.

By the 1840s it was clear that the French language, while hardly threatened with extinction, had entered a period of decline. Migrants from elsewhere in the United States and abroad now accounted for half of Louisiana's white population, and ambitious young francophones increasingly used English in their business and professional lives. At a convention to rewrite the state constitution in 1845, Creoles made up fewer than one-third of the delegates, but a few old *habitants* waged an emotional campaign to shore up the status of French. They won provisions requiring certain legislative officers to "possess the French and English languages" and guaranteeing the right to address the legislature in either tongue. To a delegate named Pierre Soulé, the issue was nothing less than whether French speakers would continue to have a *voice* in the affairs of Louisiana:

That population that once had the property and every thing, that were the possessors of this vast territory . . . have yielded to the iron rule of time, and all that they ask of this new and unconquered population that have covered the land, is to be heard. They do not ask it as an act of generosity, but as an act of justice. Will you listen to their demands? That is the question.

Though the voice became enfeebled over the years, Louisianans chose not to silence it. A range of guarantees for francophone rights—bilingual public schooling, courtroom interpreters, translation of legal documents—survived in Louisiana law until 1921, except for a brief hiatus following the Civil War. A Reconstruction-era constitution struck most references to French as a way of punishing the Creoles for their support of the Confederacy. But when Democrats returned to power in 1877, French language rights were restored.

Nineteenth-century Americans had no horror of linguistic diversity in general, only of linguistic minorities in particular—though rarely were they conceived as such. Few would have thought to link the Creole planter, the Norwegian homesteader, the Chinese laborer, the Apache brave, and the Mexican *vaquero* on the basis of their limited English skills. No global ideology guided the politics of language, only specific attitudes toward specific tongues. These varied depending on speakers' race, nationality, religion, numbers, economic position, cultural distinctiveness, local history, and other factors governing a group's acceptance or rejection.

Frustrations about the pace of anglicization sometimes inspired heavy-handed projects to accelerate it, though generally in the context of larger policy objectives. The Indian Peace Commission of 1868, empaneled to investigate why Native Americans were resisting Manifest Destiny, concluded that "in the difference of language to-day lies two-thirds of our trouble." Conversely, in the spread of English, the commission saw a way of "civilizing" the enemy:

Through sameness of language is produced sameness of sentiment, and thought; customs and habits are moulded and assimilated in the same way, and thus in process of time the differences producing trouble would have been gradually obliterated.
. . . Schools should be established, which children should be

required to attend; their barbarous dialects should be blotted out and the English language substituted.

Thus began a federal initiative in cultural genocide, an explicit policy of remaking the Indian in the white man's image. Children were removed from their tribes, often forcibly, and sent to faraway boarding schools where they were punished when caught speaking any language but English. As one Commissioner of Indian Affairs articulated the goal in 1889: "They should be educated, not as Indians, but as Americans. In short, public schools should do for them what they are so successfully doing for all the other races in this country—assimilate them."

That Indians were managing their own affairs, training their own youth, practicing their own forms of government, learning to read in their own tongues—these were ideas that the U.S. government refused to entertain. A generation earlier, using the writing system developed by Sequoyah, Oklahoma Cherokees had established a bilingual school system and achieved a literacy rate exceeding 90 percent in their language. (By the 1850s tribal members were also more literate *in English* than their white neighbors in Texas and Arkansas.) Nevertheless, the federal boarding-school policy banned all forms of native-language instruction. Its architect, a cavalry officer named Richard Henry Pratt, once said: "I believe in immersing the Indians in our civilization and, when we get them under, holding them there until they are thoroughly soaked." The problem was that many students drowned in the process. In 1969, after a century of assimilationist education, a Congressional investigation found that 40 percent of Oklahoma Cherokees were literate in no language, 75 percent of their children were dropping out of school, and in one county, 90 percent were on welfare. But no one could say they didn't speak English.

Such coercive logic was rarely applied to European immigrants in the nineteenth century. To the contrary, policies toward these groups often went beyond laissez-faire into the realm of active accommodation. During the 1850s Louisville, Kentucky, was one of several municipalities that translated city-council minutes into German. Minnesota's 1857 state constitution appeared in five languages: English, German, Swedish, Norwegian, and French. Missouri published French and German editions of its governor's message, while Ohio and Pennsylvania did so in Welsh. Even Texas, never renowned for its spirit of ethnic tolerance, printed certain official documents in Spanish, German, and Czech.

Still, there was no national consensus on such *access rights* for linguistic minorities. New England, the most homogeneous region of the country, was far less accommodating than the cosmopolitan Mid-Atlantic region or the Mississippi Valley, where 1.5 million Germans had settled between 1830 and 1860. Immigrant votes were an important consideration in some areas, but not in others. Libertarian instincts sometimes prevailed and sometimes yielded to fears of disunion.

On the handful of occasions when formal requests were made, Congress declined to print its proceedings in languages other than English, although the votes were sometimes close. Besides objecting to the cost and the precedent (which it was feared might inspire such demands from numerous groups), opponents insisted that immigrants had a duty to learn English. But this was by no means a consensus view. In 1862, during routine approval of a federal agriculture report, the House of Representatives ordered twenty-five thousand copies to be printed in German. Justin S. Morrill of Vermont rose to denounce the move as "utterly subversive of the true doctrine of this country." It was essential, he declared, that "the foreign population which comes here [be] assimilated with and become Americans." To which Elihu B. Washburne of Illinois responded heatedly that German speakers were "honest, patriotic, and liberty-loving citizens of our country," who should not be "deprived of that information to which they are entitled." The House reversed itself the following day on a motion by E. P. Walton, another Vermonter, who argued that catering to the Germans raised "the question whether we are to have a national language or not."

It is no coincidence that this episode occurred at a time of secession and Civil War, when there was great anxiety about what, if anything, would keep the nation intact. As is often the case with symbolic politics, the language debate diverted energy from a real crisis to an imaginary one. Not only was there no question about the Germans' loyalty to the Union cause—one of their few common traits was opposition to slavery—but German was the language of command in numerous Union regiments from Pennsylvania, New York, Wisconsin, Missouri, Illinois, and other states.

By far the most important recognition of minority tongues was in the schools. Beginning with Ohio in 1839, a dozen states and territories passed laws explicitly authorizing bilingual public education. Several others gave it their unofficial blessing. German was pervasive, not just as a subject but as a medium of instruction, in the rural Midwest and in cities like Cincinnati, Indianapolis, Baltimore, Milwaukee, and St. Louis. Rather than support Irish-dominated parochial schools, German Catholics in New York City sent their children to public schools that offered German-language classrooms. Such education was usually bilingual, but not always. In 1888, Missouri's superintendent of public instruction complained, that "in a large number of districts of the State . . . the schools are mainly taught in the German language and sometimes entirely so. . . . Some of the teachers are scarcely able to speak the English language." German parents also sent their children to Catholic or Lutheran schools that strived to maintain *Deutschtum,* a cultural sense of "German-ness." By the year 1900, there were at least 600,000 children, about 4 percent of American elementary school enrollment, public and parochial, receiving part or all of their education in the German language. Smaller ethnic communities—Dutch, Scandinavians, Czechs, Poles, and Italians—were often successful in pressuring public schools to add their native tongues as subjects in the curriculum.

Language was always a potential trigger of conflict, but less so than several other ethnic traits. On the frontier, where non-English speakers were most likely to be found, there were countless concerns more vital than Anglo-conformity. Resourceful settlers learned not only to cope with language differences, but to exploit them to advantage (for example, in the legal theft of Mexican land grants in the Southwest). But as a political instrument, language usually lacked the symbolic power to mobilize members of the majority. Pre–Civil War nativists attacked immigrants for their Catholicism, intemperate lifestyles, or revolutionary politics, but seldom for their foreign speech.

Only in California did the Know-Nothings seek to restrict other languages—Spanish speakers were the prime target—in a campaign motivated more by race-hatred than any desire to defend the national tongue. Even there, language was seldom the weapon of choice when there were more blunt instruments available. Chinese immigrants were singled out for mob attacks, legally barred from employment in industry, disqualified from owning land, restricted to squalid Chinatowns, and forbidden to testify against whites in court. Naturally, they were also affected by language restrictions such as literacy requirements that kept American-born Chinese from voting, but English-only laws were usually the least of their worries.

Nineteenth-century language strife, when it did break out, tended to function as a surrogate, a way to act out other animosities, rivalries, or prejudices that for one reason or another could not be candidly expressed. Of the latter, religious bigotry was perhaps the most common. In the late 1880s it inspired a campaign to repress German-language schooling throughout the Midwest. The American Protective Association, an anti-Catholic secret society, was implicated in efforts to mandate English as the basic language of instruction in parochial as well as public schools. When Wisconsin and Illinois passed such legislation in 1889, prominent Germans denounced it as a nativist plot. Striking back, the *Chicago Tribune* described the protesters as "bigoted ultramontane sectaries . . . who are inspired by an inextinguishable hate of the American free-school system." It further characterized the debate as "a contest . . . between the right of Americans to make their own laws and the claim of an Italian priest living in Rome that he has the power to nullify them." In reality, German Lutherans were just as outraged as Catholics by state meddling with their schools, and their support proved decisive in winning the laws' speedy repeal.

Yet the conflict was also a harbinger of changing views toward language. Proponents of English education denied any hidden agenda. The only issue, according to Governor William D. Hoard of Wisconsin, was "the *duty* of the State to require, and the *right* of the children of the State to receive, instruction in the language of the country." The controversy focused sustained public attention on an unresolved question: how much cultural conformity was expected of Americans?

The Germans themselves were of several minds. Outside of *Pennsylvaniadeutsch* country, most colonial Germans had long since assimilated. Later immigrants, by contrast, often retained hopes of recreating a German nation on free soil, or of building isolated communities of God. Resisting English was a means to these ends. Such tendencies prompted assimilationists like Carl Schurz to lecture their brethren: "Let us never forget that we as Germans are not called upon here to form a separate nationality. . . . It is by unity of speech and harmony of thought that the ultimate American is to be the light of civilization." But this message was largely unavailing. Pride in *Deutschtum,* the tradition of Goethe, Schiller, and Mozart, was all that had sustained many immigrants in their difficult passage. Few were inclined to sacrifice it for some narrow vision of patriotism. Schurz himself insisted on an "iron rule" of German use at home and brooded over his younger children's preference for English.

In 1890, most German immigrants still drew a distinction between anglicization and Americanization. "There is no reason why we should hate English, nor is there any reason why a true American should not look upon German with tender regard," argued Conrad Krez, an opponent of the so-called Bennett Law, which mandated English-only instruction in Wisconsin. He continued:

> The English and German [have] lived together for 200 years as good neighbors in peace and amity without one attempt on either side to force his language on the other. They became one people without compulsory education laws, and the Germans were always good citizens and patriots. Why all at once this war on the Germans here in Wisconsin as well as in Illinois? For the Bennett law indeed means war. . . . [It is] a foolish law, a tyrannical law and an unconstitutional law. . . . As long as German is spoken in Wisconsin, equal justice, law, and constitutional freedom will never lack a defender.

Some of Krez's allies went so far as to propose that German be recognized as the *zweite Sprache,* or second language, of the state. One pamphleteer argued: "It is no more a *foreign* language than the English language, which like the German was not spoken by the natives of this Country, but was imported from foreign lands."

For the Bennett Law's defenders, this reaction confirmed that a language problem existed. Their leader was Governor Hoard, an earnest if bumbling Republican, who adopted as his 1890 campaign slogan: "The Little Schoolhouse: Stand By It!" Hardly a xenophobe, Hoard was by most accounts a naïve apostle of assimilationist education. He found it intolerable that some American-born children in Lutheran and Catholic schools were failing to learn English (a phenomenon eagerly sensationalized by the *Milwaukee Sentinel*). By election day the governor was warning that German-language instruction "will be a menace to the progress of civilization and the perpetuity of our institutions."

This assessment lacked credibility for the bulk of Wisconsin voters, a majority of whom were either immigrants or the children of immigrants. Everyone knew that most Germans learned English out of economic necessity. If some preferred to keep to themselves, send their children to parochial schools, and preserve their native tongue, where was the harm? Democrats recognized the political opening and exploited it. At every campaign stop, one candidate repeated the question: "What is the difference if you say, 'two and two make four' or *'zwei und zwei machen vier'?"* The Republicans had no effective answer. Soiled by the suggestion of nativism, they were buried in a landslide, losing the governorship, a majority in the legislature, and virtually every Congressional seat. (A similar fate befell Illinois Republicans two years later.) Never enforced, the Bennett Law was stricken from the books in 1891, although it appears to have had an indirect impact. Wisconsin's public schools redoubled their efforts to teach English, and while parochial-school attendance increased, the proportion of German instruction declined.

With imperialism came a new attitude toward the American language, among other assets. Politicians like Senator Albert J. Beveridge of Indiana began to speak of an "Anglo-Saxon impulse," a biological and cultural endowment that qualified the United States to administer the affairs of less gifted peoples. Beveridge preached a new gospel of Americanism: "The rule of liberty, that all just governments derive their authority from the consent of the governed, applies only to those who are capable of self-government." God had "been preparing the English-speaking and Teutonic peoples for a thousand years . . . to establish system where chaos reigns." The old rhetoric of freedom and equality gave way to race, language, empire—once-subliminal connections now articulated as part of the national discourse.

From its outset, U.S. colonial policy made the spread of English synonymous with what Whitelaw Reid, publisher of the *New York Tribune,* liked to call "the extension of ordered liberty in the dark places of the earth." There was no strategic plan, but an overpowering sense of Anglo-Saxon purpose that dictated the introduction of English as the language of government and education in the Philippines, Hawaii, and Puerto Rico. Especially in the last case—a thickly populated island of nearly one million people, virtually monolingual in Spanish, with a Castilian-Indio-African culture developed over four centuries—the attempt to impose English was quixotic, to say the least. Yet the difficulties were minimized by officials dispatched from Washington to investigate conditions. "The mass of Puerto Ricans are as yet passive and plastic. . . . Their ideals are in our hands to create and mold," reported Victor S. Clark, director of schools under the American military occupation. For the social engineer drawing up his blueprints, it was an exciting prospect:

> Another important fact that must not be overlooked, is that a majority of people of this Island does not speak pure Spanish. Their language is a patois almost unintelligible to the natives of Barcelona and Madrid. It possesses no literature and little value an an intellectual medium. There is a bare possibility that it will be nearly as easy to educate these people out of their patois into English as it will be to educate them into the elegant tongue of Castile.

Puerto Rico now became "Porto Rico." The anglicized spelling was officially maintained until 1932, appeasing the Yankee's vanity as much as his hard-edged tongue, a daily reminder of his resolve to northamericanize the island. "English is the chief source, practically the only source, of democratic ideas in Porto Rico," Clark asserted. Democracy, however, was not on the agenda. Samuel McCune Lindsay, appointed as Puerto Rico's commissioner of education in 1902, spoke more to the point: "Colonization carried forward by the armies of war is vastly more costly than that carried forward by the armies of peace, whose outposts and garrisons are the public schools of the advancing nation." He resolved, "as soon as pupils and teachers can be trained sufficiently in the use of the English language, to make it the official language of the school room."

By 1909, 607 out of Puerto Rico's 678 grade schools had been anglicized—an amazing feat at a time when English was spoken by only 3.6 percent of Puerto Ricans. While Spanish was retained as a subject, English became the basic medium of instruction. In practice, this meant that children spent much of their time parroting a language they had no occasion to use outside of class, while other subjects were generally neglected. Predictably, most students left school before completing the third grade.

Puerto Ricans naturally resented the subordination of their vernacular, which had the effect of denying an education to all but a few native elites. By 1913, the island's legislature was demanding the reinstatement of Spanish, but U.S. officials blocked the change. Thereafter, the issue became inseparable from the larger question of Puerto Rico's political status: a test of wills between colonizer and colonized, in which North Americans asserted their good intentions against Puerto Ricans' stated desires. Amid mass protests by teachers and students, Education Commissioner Paul G. Miller maintained in 1919: "As citizens of the United States, the children of Porto Rico possess an inalienable right to learn the English language."

The mandatory English policy would affect three generations of schoolchildren before it was finally scrapped, an acknowledged failure, in 1949. Spanish instruction was restored (over the objections of President Truman) only after the island had won a measure of political autonomy.

English was now an unabashed tool of empire. In the past the United States had wavered on the principle of self-government for linguistic minorities, especially where they commanded local majorities. Would it be prudent to extend the franchise to strangers whose languages and cultures made them unknowable and perhaps uncontrollable? On the other hand, would it be possible to deny these groups an equal voice in the American system without undermining the system itself? With the advent of colonialism, this kind of soul-searching went out of fashion. Jingoists now raised ethnocentrism to the level of principle: Anglo-conformity would be a condition of full democratic rights.

The new ethic was evident in policies toward New Mexico, an internal colony of sorts, where Spanish speakers still predominated half a century after the Mexican-American War. The territory had yet to become a state, unlike the more anglicized precincts of California, Texas, and Colorado. Accustomed to provincial isolation since 1598, New Mexico had changed little in the first decades of American rule. In the 1870s the territorial legislature still operated mainly in Spanish, with laws later translated into English. Jury trials were held in English in only two of fourteen counties. A mere 5 percent of New Mexico's schools used English as the language of instruction, while 69 percent taught in Spanish and 26 percent were bilingual. Then, quite suddenly, New Mexicans encountered the wider world of railroads, land speculators, and Anglo-American settlers.

In 1902, Senator Beveridge led a congressional delegation to the Southwest to investigate the question of statehood. Privately, the prophet of Anglo-Saxon destiny viewed Spanish speakers as a benighted group of half-castes, unqualified to govern themselves. So rather than conduct an impartial inquiry, he orchestrated it to reach a negative result. After a perfunctory tour and a closed-door hearing, the committee returned to Washington with a report that stressed New Mexicans' shortcomings. It noted, for example, that 33 percent could read neither English nor Spanish, while ignoring the remarkable progress made since 1870, when illiteracy stood at 75 percent. The Beveridge Report concluded:

> On the whole, the Committee feel that in the course of time, when education, now only practically beginning, shall have accomplished its work; when the mass of the people, or even a majority of them shall, in the usages and employment of their daily life, have become *identical in language and customs* with the great body of the American people; when the immigration of English speaking people who have been citizens of other states does its modifying work with the Mexican element; when all these things have come to pass, the Committee hopes and believes that this mass of people, unlike us in race, language, and social customs, will finally come to form a creditable portion of American citizenship. [Emphasis added.]

After further maneuvering, the statehood bill was defeated.[5]

By the time New Mexico finally joined the Union in 1912, migration had given Anglo-Americans a popular plurality over Hispanos and Indians, albeit a narrow one.[6] While consenting to statehood, Congress nevertheless sought to counteract what Beveridge termed "the curious continuance of the solidarity of the Spanish-speaking people." Enabling legislation instructed New Mexico and Arizona (admitted simultaneously) to adopt state constitutions establishing "a system of public schools, which . . . shall always be conducted in English" and making "ability to read, write, speak, and understand the English language sufficiently well to conduct the duties of the office without the need of an interpreter . . . a necessary qualification for all State officers and members of the State legislature."

But New Mexicans resisted these conditions. Delegates to the 1910 constitutional convention ratified several provisions that effectively undercut the language requirements: antidiscrimination protections for Spanish speakers in voting and education, a mandate for the training of teachers in Spanish, and the bilingual publication of state documents for twenty years. Congress subsequently backed away from the English requirement for office holding, fearing it might prove unconstitutional. And despite the mandate for English-language schooling, the legislature passed numerous laws creating loopholes for bilingual instruction. Linguistic libertarianism flowered in New Mexico, even as it began to wither elsewhere.

In 1906, Congress approved a major change in U.S. naturalization policy: citizenship would henceforth be denied to immigrants unable to speak English. This was the first language restriction of any kind to be enacted in federal law, and it signaled a significant shift in policy toward immigrants as well.

Americans had long recognized the human right to pull up stakes and move to a better place. Thus far the United States had been willing to take in virtually anyone with a white skin and a "yearning to breathe free." A certain self-righteousness was entailed in offering asylum to huddled masses, not to mention an appetite for their labor. Yet there was also an enormous faith in the nation's assimilative capacity, with its wide open spaces and pioneer traditions. Apart from the Chinese Exclusion Act of 1882, Congress had never distinguished between desirable and undesirable newcomers on the basis of ethnicity. (Nor had most nativists, for that matter, who despised foreigners in general.) But after 1890, the changing sources of the immigrant stream became a matter of public notice and concern. The arrival of new non-English-speaking groups—Jews, Italians, Greeks, Magyars, Poles—coincided with the "closing" of the frontier. Unlike the Germans and Scandinavians who came before, these immigrants settled mostly in urban centers, where their poverty, appearance, and manners attracted the horrified stares of Anglo-Americans. In a poem for the *Atlantic Monthly,* Thomas Bailey Aldrich captured the reaction of proper Bostonians:

Wide open and unguarded stand our gates,
And through them presses a wild motley throng—
Men from the Volga and the Tartar steppes,
Featureless figures from the Hoang-Ho,
Malayan, Scythian, Teuton, Kelt, and Slav,
Flying the Old World's poverty and scorn;
These bringing with them unknown gods and rites,
Those, tiger passions, here to stretch their claws.
In street and alley what strange tongues are these,
Accents of menace alien to our air,
Voices that once the Tower of Babel knew!

Unfavorable comparisons were now drawn between "new" and "old" immigrants. Francis A. Walker, president of the Massachusetts Institute of Technology, pronounced the new arrivals "beaten men from beaten races; representing the worst failures in the struggle for existence. . . . They have none of the ideas and aptitudes which . . . belong to those who are descended from the tribes that met under the oak trees of old Germany to make laws and choose chieftains." Walker laid the groundwork for a theory of "race suicide," a curious reversal of Social Darwinism, which warned that genetic inferiors might outbreed Americans of Anglo-Saxon stock, thereby threatening the social basis of democracy. This alarming prospect inspired a group of Brahmin intellectuals and politicians under the leadership of Senator Henry Cabot Lodge to found the Immigration Restriction League, an organization dedicated to the exclusion of eastern and southern Europeans. The device it chose was the literacy test—an ability to read forty words in any language—as a legal requirement for entry into the United States.[7]

Disagreements raged over the new immigrants' fitness to assimilate, but by 1906 there was a consensus that many were failing to do so. They were stereotyped as clannish and ignorant, easily manipulated by ward heelers and labor agitators, prone to criminality and licentious behavior. The language barrier made these problems seem all the more intractable, providing a convenient target for do-gooders and victim-blamers alike. Speaking English came to be viewed as an index of immigrants' social progress and of their willingness to embrace American ways and American loyalties. The House Committee on Immigration and Naturalization insisted that any newcomer who had met the five-year residency requirement for citizenship yet had failed to acquire English must "be so deficient in mental capacity . . . or so careless of the opportunities afforded to him . . . that he would not make a desirable citizen." Such immigrants tended to "remain not only aliens in law but aliens in sentiment," added the committee's chairman, Robert Bonynge of Colorado. Providing them an inducement to speak the language would have the effect of "safeguarding and elevating our citizenship" and of keeping Americans "a homogenous people." [8]

The naturalization bill passed with the English requirement intact, but not without numerous voices raised against this departure from the asylum principle. In a House debate that spanned several days, legislators came forward to tell of "honest, industrious, and God-fearing" constituents, living in rural enclaves or working long hours in factories, who simply lacked the time and opportunity to learn English. Several congressmen took pains to identify "old" immigrants in this category—Germans in Iowa, French Canadians in Minnesota, Dutch in Michigan. In an impassioned speech, George Burgess of Texas argued that "whatever troubles have come to us by immigration, none of them have rested on ignorance of English." Except majoritarian fears, he might have added.

Besides unprecedented levels of immigration, the years 1890–1914 marked a period of widening class divisions, as American labor took a revolutionary turn. Though disproportionately represented in basic industry, the foreign-born were largely unorganized—*shunned* would be more accurate—by the nativist craft guilds of the American Federation of Labor. The Industrial Workers of the World, founded in 1904, soon filled the vacuum of leadership with frank calls to class struggle. Though internationalist in principle, the I.W.W. recognized that overcoming splits within labor's ranks sometimes meant organizing along nationality lines and catering to workers in their native tongues. In 1912, during the Bread and Roses Strike in Lawrence, Massachusetts, Wobblies conducted mass meetings in more than twenty languages. Ethnic solidarity proved crucial to the strikers' victory by thwarting the textile mills' strategy of divide-and-conquer.

Worried capitalists were watching. Many drew the conclusion that industrial peace was threatened not by workers' conditions, but by a lack of English skills that insulated them from free-enterprise values. Frances Kellor, a crusader for immigrant education, recruited employers to her cause by stressing this concern: "Strikes and plots that have been fostered and developed by un-American agitators and foreign propaganda are not easily carried on among men who have acquired, with the English language and citizenship, an understanding of American industrial standards and an American point of view."

This appeal proved effective. Before long, the boards of Kellor's enterprises read like a Who's Who of American business. These philanthropists sponsored conferences for politicians and educators, developed curricula and didactic pamphlets for immigrants, pressured cities to expand night-school classes, and even financed "Americanization" programs by the federal Bureau of Education. In 1915, Kellor joined forces with the Board of Commerce of Detroit, a city where 75 percent of residents were foreign-born, to stage an "English First" campaign. The goal was to enlist employers' help in persuading workers to learn the language—as a patriotic gesture, an avenue to promotion, and often a condition of continued employment. Many firms followed the lead of Henry Ford, who set up English classes after work and notified his foreign-born employees: "This School was established for your benefit and you should be glad of this opportunity. . . . There is no excuse for your remaining away from school."

It was not enough that newcomers acquired English. As Samuel Rea, president of the Pennsylvania Railroad, insisted in one of Kellor's leaflets, "They must be induced to *give up* the languages, customs, and methods of life which they have brought with them" (emphasis added). Only in this way could subversive thoughts be rooted out.

Had it not been for World War I, worries about English might well have remained restricted to factory owners and settlement-house workers. But conflict in Europe had the effect of highlighting the persistence of Old World ties, language among them, and it raised a new specter: "hyphenated Americanism." This was an age of discontent, as captive nations chafed under the Kaiser, the Czar, and the Austro-Hungarian Monarchy. Refugees who had been prevented from developing a literate culture in their homelands now did so in America, and many hatched liberation movements as well. Lithuanians described the United States as "the second birthplace of the nationality." For others, the act of immigrating itself—the loneliness, the indifferent or hostile reception, the yearning for the familiar—fostered an ethnic consciousness. Even those who planned never to return home tended to remain preoccupied with developments there. As the United States was drawn into war, immigrants were drawn into politics *as ethnic minorities.*

Most noticeable were the German Americans. More than 8 million strong in 1910 (including 2.5 million immigrants), they remained the largest nonanglophone group and, thus far, the most tolerated, a "racially" and culturally preferred minority. German was the language of more than 550 publications, along with countless singing societies, gymnastics associations, private academies, and other institutions dedicated to preserving *deutsche Kultur in Amerika.* On the eve of war, the German American writer Julius Goebel ridiculed the melting pot notion as "a sort of forced uniformity [which] would mean the destruction of all that we regard as holiest in our people and its culture . . . our speech, our customs, and our views of life." In 1914, such views were within the mainstream of ethnic opinion. But when German organizations and newspapers began agitating for U.S. neutrality, *Deutschtum* was suddenly discovered to be a "pan-German" plot to prevent assimilation and thereby aid the Kaiser.

"A hyphenated American is not an American at all," proclaimed Theodore Roosevelt. This slogan aptly summarizes the xenophobia that followed. Beginning as a popular rage against German-ness, it flowered into paranoia toward foreign influences of all kinds. "100 Percent Americanism" demanded absolute loyalty, which was understood to mean absolute conformity, especially in matters of language.

The United States's entry into the war brought sweeping restrictions on German speech. While some were innocuous—sauerkraut was renamed "Liberty cabbage"; hamburger became "Salisbury steak"—many involved wholesale violations of the First Amendment. Under the guise of preventing espionage, numerous communities and some states banned the use of German in public places: schools, churches, lecture halls, trains, even on the telephone. One could be fined $25 for speaking German on the streets of Findlay, Ohio. Public libraries in Chicago and Cincinnati removed German volumes from the shelves. School officials in Columbus collected

German textbooks and sold them to a wastepaper company for 50 cents a hundredweight (a sensible alternative to the book burnings in other Ohio towns). Authorities in St. Louis and Milwaukee closed down German theaters. German conductors and opera singers faced harassment in several cities. In an editorial entitled "Westerners Do Things Thoroughly," the *New York Times* praised South Dakota's quasi-official vigilantes, the State Council of Defense, for outlawing religious services, public speeches, and all forms of instruction in German. It supported "even more far-reaching prohibitions" by the governor of Iowa but questioned why neither state had yet restricted the German-language press. (Foreign-language periodicals already had to file a translation of their contents for approval by the postmaster.[9]) In midwestern states alone, nearly eighteen thousand persons were charged with violating anti-German statutes and emergency decrees.[10] Meanwhile school boards throughout the country were abolishing the study of German as a foreign language.

Proselytizing for linguistic unity became a mainstay of the civil defense effort. Secretary of the Interior Franklin K. Lane sponsored a conference on "Americanization as a War Measure" primarily to address the internal security risks posed by non-English speakers. And German was not the only casualty. In the space of a single year, fifteen states designated English as the sole language of instruction in both public and private schools; several went so far as to prohibit foreign language teaching in the elementary grades (a ban later struck down by the U.S. Supreme Court).

As the war ended and the Red Scare began, Americanization was sold as revolution insurance. Homefront warriors like the National Security League and the American Defense Society turned their attention to the menace of "aliens . . . neither speaking nor thinking American." Their activities included a campaign against foreign-language advertising in New York subways. (The A.D.S. went on to promote anti-Semitism as well, financing a 1920 edition of *The Protocols of the Elders of Zion*.) Teddy Roosevelt was a prominent adviser and spokesmen for both organizations. On their behalf, he argued it was time to strike an explicit bargain with immigrants: full rights in exchange for full assimilation. Government would provide opportunities for newcomers to learn English, but those who failed to do so within five years would be deported. The immigrant should "be treated on an exact equality with every one else," T.R. said in a message to the American Defense Society, for it is an outrage to discriminate against any such man because of creed or birthplace or origin. But this is predicated upon the man's becoming in very fact an American and nothing but an American. If he tries to keep segregated with men of his own origin and separated from the rest of America, then he isn't doing his part as an American. . . . We have room for but one language here, and that is the English language, for we intend to see that the crucible turns our people out as Americans, of American nationality, and not as dwellers in a polyglot boarding-house.

Rooseveltian absolutes notwithstanding, this statement captures the basic logic of Anglo-conformity. Indeed, it has been dusted off and returned to service by modern advocates of Official English.

In 1920, however, Congress declined to approve a compulsory Americanization bill. The measure under consideration would have given states a financial incentive to require attendance at night-school classes for non-English speakers under the age of forty-five (and all illiterates under twenty-one). Though the Senate was willing, the House refused to go along. Opponents focused on the measure's unprecedented expansion of federal power, as well as its $12.5 million price tag. Subsequently, a few states adopted such laws on their own but generally neglected to appropriate enough money to run the classes.

By now the country's enthusiasm for assimilating immigrants was nearly spent. Exclusion seemed a simpler route to homogeneity. Throughout this period there had been those who argued that biological destiny made Americanization a hopeless cause for certain "racial" types. In 1913, the psychologist H. H. Goddard administered I.Q. tests at Ellis Island and determined that 79 percent of Italians, 80 percent of Hungarians, 83 percent of Jews, and 87 percent of Russians were "feeble-minded" (that is, below a mental age of twelve). Massive testing of army recruits during the war, including a multiple-choice quiz about American culture, turned up shocking confirmation of the new immigrants' inferiority. It seemed that "Nordics," who had arrived earlier, consistently outscored "Alpines" and "Mediterraneans," a finding that greatly impressed the old Anglo-Saxonists. Now came a new crop of pseudoscientists positing a hereditarian basis for virtually every human trait. Eugenicists like Harry H. Laughlin, consultant to the House Immigration Committee, warned that the recent arrivals "present a higher percentage of inborn socially inadequate qualities than do the older stocks. . . . We in this country have been so imbued with the idea of democracy, or the equality of all men, that we have left out of consideration the matter of blood or natural inborn hereditary mental and moral differences. No man who breeds pedigreed plants and animals can afford to neglect this thing."

Duly armed with this kind of academic wisdom, Congress was prepared to enact a series of restrictive laws to protect the nation's genetic legacy. Beginning in 1921, a new quota system based on national origins effectively curtailed immigration by eastern and southern Europeans. Signing the decisive 1924 law, President Calvin Coolidge said, with characteristic matter-of-factness: "America must be kept American."

And so it was. With fewer newcomers each year, the problem of minority languages began to fade in the public mind. A tyranny of majority attitudes obviated further repression. There was no need to legislate Anglo-conformity now that it was well established as the acid test of Americanism. Some immigrants continued to resist assimilationist pressures, but increasing numbers embraced the new monolingualism. Minority tongues declined rapidly in ethnic churches and schools. Foreign-language newspapers survived the Red Scare only to starve for lack of subscribers. Detached from their sources, Old World cultures soon lost their vitality and appeal for the young. Grandparents and grandchildren grew apart, often incommunicado, as the second generation began to rear its offspring in English only. Along with the American dream, these immigrants bought the Americanization ethic. Half a century would elapse before it faced a serious challenge—not from Euro-ethnics, but from groups who had been here all along yet had never been invited to assimilate.

Three

Strangers in Their Own Land

In the fall of 1986, as Californians prepared to vote on Proposition 63, no less an authority than the state's attorney general, John Van de Kamp, announced that the Official English initiative would violate the Spanish language rights guaranteed under the Treaty of Guadalupe Hidalgo. He asserted that this 1848 accord, which ended the Mexican-American War, gave Spanish coequal status with English as a language of government in California and other territories ceded to the United States. While acknowledging that the provision "never has been implemented," Van de Kamp warned that it still might be invoked to void an English Only amendment.

Legalities aside, the issue was significant. The case for Official English relies on the fabled immigrant bargain: conformity to "American" ways in exchange for American freedoms and opportunities. These foreigners knew that English was spoken here, the reasoning goes, and if they didn't like it, they should have stayed home. What gives them the right to demand special programs like bilingual education in the public schools? According to its sponsors, Proposition 63 was needed to set the record straight: "This amendment reaffirms California's oneness as a state, and as one of fifty states united by a common tongue."

On the other hand, if speakers of other languages have a prior claim—if they were here first, before Anglo-Californians came on the scene, and were systematically denied access to adequate schooling in English—this argument loses its moral authority. The myth of "oneness" is shattered. Suddenly the English Language Amendment must be weighed against a historical assertion of minority rights. No longer is it purely an "immigrant issue," a set of policy choices affecting the generic non-English speaker, or an abstract discussion of cultural cohesiveness versus cultural diversity. Now the debate raises specific questions of justice, of language rights, for groups whose history in this country predates anglicization.

Native Americans are the most obvious example. Indian peoples consented to the dominance of English in the same way they consented to resettle on reservations. Their "bargain" was made at the point of a gun. Federal Indian schools were conceived as an extension of military policy, a kind of cultural counterinsurgency aimed at replacing Indian values with those of "civilization." But coercive assimilation became, in effect, another broken treaty. Learning English did little for Indians' social or economic advancement, despite the sacrifices it entailed, notably their own means of self-expression. To deny the legitimacy of indigenous languages today is to advocate finishing the job of cultural genocide, an argument that not even U.S. English is prepared to make. So the organization concedes the right of Indians to preserve their ancestral tongues on the reservation. At the same time, it insists that those who leave to enter the dominant society should be "governed by the same principles" as immigrants. Of course, this begs the question of the Indians' original land base, but, as Senator Hayakawa once said of the Panama Canal, "We stole it fair and square."

Owing to most voters' limited attention span when it comes to Indians, U.S. English has seldom had to defend this precarious position. By contrast, the claims of Mexican Americans, a large, organized, and vocal minority, cannot be so easily dismissed. Although Latinos in this country are typically regarded as immigrants, which many are, others can trace their ancestry back four centuries in the Southwest. Historically speaking, English speakers are the recent arrivals there. Few Anglo-Americans felt obliged to learn the language of the conquered, but Spanish continued to thrive, and not merely because of reinforcements from Mexico. More important, the language cemented a way of life, an autonomous culture maintained not merely by tradition and geography, but frequently by enforced segregation.

Thus the Treaty of Guadalupe Hidalgo—specifically the question of what rights, if any, it reserved for Spanish speakers—has become a sensitive point in the Official English debate. Supporters of Proposition 63 were quick to attack the attorney general's expansive interpretation. They presented him with a copy of the treaty, which, as it happens, contains no explicit mention of language. Ergo, no legal basis for Spanish language rights, according to U.S. English. An embarrassed Van de Kamp backed down. Apparently it never occurred to him to research the treaty's history. Had he done so, he might have stood his ground.[1]

A proud young republic in 1848, Mexico had been humiliated by the defeat of its armies and the plunder of its lands. It resented North American pretensions to racial and cultural superiority, in particular the missionary arrogance of Manifest Destiny. But the most painful blow to Mexico's national honor, even more severe than surrendering half its sovereign territory, was abandoning some seventy-five thousand of its citizens to become, as one minister expressed it, *"extranjeros en su propia patria,"* strangers in their own land. Nicholas Trist, chief of the U.S. peace delegation in Mexico, reported back to Washington that "the condition of the inhabitants of the ceded or transferred territory is the topic upon which most time has been expended." In a letter to Secretary of State Buchanan, Trist italicized what he perceived to be an "overpowering" concern of the Mexican negotiators: *a perfect devotion to their distinct nationality, and a most vehement aversion to its becoming merged in or blended with ours.* Hence their insistence on "the right of Mexicans residing there to continue there, retaining the character of Mexican citizens."

Echoing the words of the Louisiana Purchase, the Treaty of Guadalupe Hidalgo provided that the new Spanish-speaking citizens of the United States "shall be maintained and protected in the free enjoyment of their liberty and property, and secured in the free exercise of their religion without restriction."[2] For the Mexicans and, as events would show, for sympathetic *norteamericanos,* these promises implied some recognition of the Spanish language: its special role in the Southwest and its speakers' need for reasonable accommodations from their new government. This did not mean official bilingualism—a strict equality of the two languages—but rather the equal protection of Spanish speakers under U.S. law, that is, unrestricted access to legislatures, courthouses, and schools regardless of their English-speaking ability. These were concessions comparable to what Louisianans had won.

In practice, however, Mexican Americans would rarely enjoy the language rights or political status accorded to the Creoles, or even to nineteenth-century immigrants from Europe. As a racially mixed, culturally distinctive, and above all, *conquered* people, Spanish speakers bore a weight of history that speakers of French, German, or Norwegian did not.

The first of those burdens was Hispanophobia. Since the sixteenth century, Spain's imperial competitors had popularized what came to be known as the Black Legend. Relying on exaggerated accounts—for example, Bartolomé de Las Casas's claim that conquistadors had slaughtered twenty million Indians—English propagandists stereotyped the Spaniard as uncommonly violent, ignorant, bigoted, fanatical, gold-seeking, and deceitful. "From the point of view of tolerance, of culture, and of political progress," writes Julián Juderías, a debunker of the myth, Spain was portrayed as "a lamentable exception among European nations." More than a popular prejudice, the Black Legend has long influenced intellectuals in the English-speaking world. It can be found in the work of historians like Walter Prescott Webb, who wrote in 1935: "Without disparagement it may be said that there is a cruel streak in the Mexican nature, or so the history of Texas would lead one to believe. This cruelty may be a heritage from the Spanish of the Inquisition; it may, and doubtless should, be attributed partly to the Indian blood."

There is no question that Spaniards often treated indigenous peoples with brutality and contributed, directly and indirectly, to genocide—crimes that provoked considerable debate and soul-searching among Spanish Catholics. During the heyday of the mission system in California from 1769 to 1834, more than 53,000 Indians were rounded up and "converted" by forcible means such as imprisonment, then held in servitude. Only after learning the Spanish language and customs were they allowed to live in towns alongside the *gente de razón* (literally, "people of reason," or whites of Hispanic origin), where they remained prey to exploitation and mistreatment. The hypocrisy of the Black Legend, however, is to ascribe such evils to a single European empire. As if the slavedriver's lash and the cavalry's massacre were somehow more humane in the United States. If anything, the condition of California Indians worsened with the coming of U.S. rule. Threatened with enslavement and homicide by lawless forty-niners, they enjoyed limited protection from the authorities. California's native population declined steadily in proportion to settlement by whites—from an estimated 300,000 in 1769 to 100,000 in 1834, 58,000 in 1870, and 17,000 in 1913—owing to the combined effects of vigilantism, peonage, disease, and alcohol. While Spaniards were by no means innocent in this calamity, neither have they concocted a legend to shift the blame.

On becoming U.S. citizens in 1848, Spanish speakers also had to contend with Anglo-Americans' stark views on race, unlike the chiaroscuro caste distinctions of the Hispanic world. At that time an uncompromising system of white supremacy, ideological as well as practical, was essential to the South's survival as a slave economy. Political rights for mixed races represented a dangerous precedent. Senator John C. Calhoun sought to block statehood for the mestizo-populated lands seized from Mexico, arguing that "the greatest misfortunes of Spanish America are to be traced to the fatal error" of miscegenation. During debate on the Texas state constitution in 1845, one delegate sought to prohibit Mexicans from voting. "I fear not the Castilian race," he explained, "but . . . those who, though they speak the Spanish language, are but the descendants of that degraded and despicable race which Cortez conquered." While this proposal did not prevail, such notions rationalized a system of bullying and inequality for *Tejanos* not unlike Jim Crow in the post-Reconstruction South.

Finally, Mexican Americans inhabited the quintessential Darwinian environment: the frontier, newly opened to exploitation. Outside of New Mexico, numbers were against them. As a defeated and unpopular minority, they were routinely denied equality under the law, such as it existed, and were sorely disadvantaged in competing with Anglo-Americans or European immigrants. When gold was discovered at Sutter's Mill on January 24, 1848 (nine days before the Treaty of Guadalupe Hidalgo was signed), native Spanish speakers represented a slight majority of California's nonindigenous population. A year after the Gold Rush began, they were outnumbered approximately seven to one, and their relative strength continued to dwindle.[3]

English speakers, particularly the "Mexicanized Yankees" who had arrived years earlier and intermarried with the locals, were initially disposed to be magnanimous. There was no question that the

1849 constitutional convention would be conducted in both English and Spanish, and that its proceedings would be printed in both languages. Delegates unanimously approved a provision guaranteeing the bilingual publication of California laws. But the spirit of tolerance soon evaporated in the heat of gold-seeking and land-grabbing. *Gringos* jealous of veteran miners from the Mexican state of Sonora (who had pioneered early gold-panning and milling techniques) prevailed on the state legislature to enact a punitive Foreign Miners Tax. Meanwhile the U.S. Congress favored Anglo squatters and speculators over Mexican grantholders in the California Land Act of 1851. Forced to prove title to their lands in a language and legal system that was foreign to them, native *Californios* gradually lost most of the 14 million acres they had held on the eve of statehood; 40 percent of the holdings were sold to pay the fees of English-speaking lawyers.

In 1855 came a rash of legislation designed to harass Spanish speakers: a mandate for English-only instruction in all schools, public and private; the notorious "Greaser Law," an antivagrancy statute that targeted "persons who are commonly known as 'Greasers' or the issue of Spanish and Indian blood"; and prohibitions on the *Californios'* popular pastimes: "bull, bear, cock or prize fights, horserace, circus, theatre, bowling alley, gambling house, room or saloon, or any place of barbarous or noisy amusements on the Sabbath." Legislators also flouted the constitutional requirement for Spanish publication of state laws. Francisco P. Ramírez, editor of *El Clamor Público,* a Spanish-language newspaper in Los Angeles, questioned how citizens could be expected to obey laws they could not understand. Yet he later conceded in a moment of despair: "What language they may be published in does not matter much—in Kanaka or in Chinese it is the same if we are always to be governed by Lynch Law. Everyone understands perfectly the words 'Hang! Hang!' "

The tyranny of the majority was consummated at California's 1878–79 constitutional convention. Not a single native Spanish speaker was represented among the 153 delegates. Dominated by the antiforeigner Workingmen's Party, the convention is best remembered for its unabashed racism and vindictiveness against Chinese immigrants. "This State should be a State for white men," said one delegate, articulating the predominant mood. "We want no other race here." The convention then proceeded to the matter of language. Not content to eliminate the printing of laws in Spanish, it inserted a new requirement: "All laws of the State of California, and all official writings, and the executive, legislative, and judicial proceedings shall be conducted, preserved, and published in *no other than the English language*" (emphasis added). California thus became the nation's first English-only state.

Considering the nativism of the time, the provision itself is less surprising than the controversy it aroused. James J. Ayers of Los Angeles reminded fellow delegates that

> in the treaty of Guadalupe Hidalgo there was an assurance that the natives should continue to enjoy the rights and privileges they did under their former Government, and there was an implied contract that they should be governed as they were before. . . . It would be wrong, it seems to me, for this Convention to prevent these people from transacting their local business in their own language.

Charles Beerstecher of San Francisco also found implicit in the treaty "the right of having laws of this State printed in Spanish, and having the judicial proceedings of this State, at least in certain districts . . . conducted in the Spanish language." Such practices, he added, were common in parts of the East and in "the Western States generally, with their cosmopolitan population." Judge Horace Rolfe of San Bernardino County predicted that the English-only mandate would throw local courts into chaos, producing gratuitous errors and injustices. Considering that the "English-speaking people of the State are the new comers," he argued, they had certain obligations toward Spanish speakers. "I say when we take their country and the people, too, and make American citizens of them, we must take them as they are and give them an equal show with us whether it was so contracted in the treaty or not."

Backers of the amendment, however, had no patience with either legal or ethical objections. They were intent on consolidating the power of white Anglo-Americans, not on unifying a multiethnic state. Unlike latter-day apostles of Official English, none even bothered to suggest that Spanish speakers' interests might be served by learning English. Delegate W. J. Tinnin was typical:

Thirty years have elapsed since this portion of the country became a portion of the Government of the United States, and
the different residents who were here at that time have had
ample time to be conversant with the English language if they
desired to do so. This is an English-speaking Government, and
persons who are incapable of speaking the English language
certainly are not competent to discharge public duties. We have
here in the Capitol now tons and tons of documents published
in Spanish for the benefit of foreigners.

"Do you call the native population of this State foreigners?" Judge
Rolfe interjected. "They had ample time to learn the language,"
Tinnin replied. The English-only clause passed on a vote of 46 to
39 and remained part of California's constitution until 1966.

In actuality, however, there is no evidence that this provision ever
prevented the translation of public proceedings into Spanish. As the
tides of nativism receded, so did symbolic concerns about the language of government. California retained an official state translator
until 1897 and a statute providing for certain bilingual publications
until 1933. There is no record of any serious complaints. Courts
required that state business he transacted in English, but not solely
in English.[4] The constitution had little perceptible effect on anyone's language choices. At times, to suit political or administrative
purposes, the state operated bilingually; otherwise it did not.

For most Anglo-Americans, the Treaty of Guadalupe Hidalgo is
long forgotten. But it has remained fresh in the historical memory
of Mexican Americans, a reminder of promises unfulfilled, yet also
a recognition of their special status. This is the treaty's larger, mythic
significance: though its homeland was conquered, a *nation* lived on,
conscious of certain guarantees by the conqueror. Even if Spanish
language rights have remained ambiguous, never fully defined or
exercised, there is an official claim on file. The U.S. government has
acknowledged that Spanish speakers are not just another immigrant
group, but a people with deep roots in the Southwest. In effect, the
treaty says that Mexican Americans cannot be forced into a Euro-
ethnic mold. While they swore political allegiance to the United States,
renouncing their heritage was never part of the deal.

Naturally there is more to the question of Spanish language rights
than how to interpret an ancient agreement. Treaty or no treaty, as
Judge Rolfe suggested, a democratic country cannot annex a group

of people, deny them effective access to government, and remain true to its principles. (That way lies colonialism, of which Puerto Rico remains a glaring example.) Nor may it suppress or denigrate minority cultures in the name of *e pluribus unum*. Precisely to avoid ethnic divisiveness, a democracy must guard against discrimination on the basis of language. It also would be wise to take affirmative steps to promote equality, either by facilitating assimilation or by safeguarding minority rights—in particular, the freedom of expression. Ideally, it should do all of these things, so as to make unity consensual rather than coerced.

Cultural self-determination is not a legal or moral imperative so much as a political one: a question of popular will. If the experience of Mexican Americans had paralleled that of German Americans—a gradual loss of the mother tongue as they moved from the backwaters into the broader currents of U.S. society—all special claims for Spanish would be moot. No one is demanding reparations for the anti-German excesses of World War I, however regrettable, because Germans have largely dissolved into the English-speaking mainstream. But social inequality has persisted for many Spanish-speaking Americans and, with it, the vestiges of second-class citizenship. It is well to remember that assimilation entails majority acceptance as well as minority acculturation. As long as Latinos remained the objects of racial discrimination in the Southwest, there was little to be gained by becoming *agringado*—northamericanized—and much to lose in solidarity with their own people. Many continued to identify with Mexico, a sovereign nation that, though seldom able to protect their interests, still granted them a measure of respect. Even today, a century and a half after the fall of the Alamo, native Texans still refer to themselves as either "Americans" or "Mexicans."

All of which begins to explain why Spanish has shown such a remarkable tenacity in the United States. When it overtook German in numbers of mother-tongue speakers sometime in the 1950s, immigration was undoubtedly a factor (less from Europe, more from Latin America). Yet nearly 40 percent of Spanish speakers were native-born of native parentage, according to estimates by Joshua Fishman. That is, they were at least third-generation Americans, a pattern that defied the tendency toward rapid erosion of European immigrant languages. Clearly, something different was happening in the Southwest. A failure to address it—a determination to ignore or subordinate Spanish and its speakers—was a choice that brought long-lasting consequences, not least of which is the continuing dissension over bilingualism.

It is commonly alleged that Spanish-speaking Americans have resisted English out of cultural pride, peasant backwardness, lack of ambition, and more recently, ethnic militancy. That Hispanic leaders have fostered "linguistic ghettos" so as to control patronage and preserve their own influence. Indeed, that these motives, rather than any sound pedagogical theory, underlie today's programs in bilingual education. The prevalence of such assumptions not only among ethnocentrists, but among otherwise enlightened Americans, testifies to a profound ignorance about the Hispanic experience. In the Southwest its predominant feature has been exclusion, not separatism.

Certainly, in 1848, few Spanish speakers were inclined to abandon their native tongue because of a remote change in government. Yet they had no principled aversion to the new language of power. While crusading against English-only policies in the 1850s, Francisco Ramírez added a bilingual page to *El Clamor Público* as a way of nudging his readers to acquire English. If French and German immigrants could learn the language, he asked, "why not Mexicans and those of Castilian descent?" By remaining non-English speakers, they would leave themselves vulnerable to "cunning 'sharpers.' " This attitude was typical among the urban middle class. In 1887, *Tejano* parents in El Paso founded a private school to teach their children English, so as to prepare them for public schools that were neglecting this task.

Throughout most of the Southwest, however, life continued to creep its leisurely Latin pace. For inhabitants of isolated villages and ranchos, the impetus to speak a second language was minimal to nonexistent. English acquisition was rarely a practical option in any case before the twentieth century. "We have not had the means or facilities to learn [English]," editorialized *El Independiente* of Las Vegas, New Mexico, in 1904. "Even knowing this, there has been no lack of those who want Spanish to be a prohibited language, and that those who speak it be despoiled of their franchises and rights of citizenship." The newspaper predicted that the "darts of contempt and proscription" directed at Spanish speakers

will not be an impediment for those sons and descendants who
may learn the English language when they have sufficient opportunities to learn it. But until that time comes, it is necessary
that they do not allow [Spanish] to be trampled under foot or
cut down by those who, with an axe of a different language,
would like to relegate Spanish-speaking people to a state of
isolation and political slavery.

Such was the predicament of Mexican Americans: limited in their
chances to acquire English, yet penalized and disparaged for speaking Spanish. And bear in mind that New Mexico was a haven of
tolerance compared to other Southwestern states. Even there, contrary to the expectations of *El Independiente,* the problem of linguistic inequality did not vanish with the advent of public schooling
in English. Strict policies of English-only instruction seemed, para-
doxically, to make matters worse.

The Americanization campaign took a different path in the
Southwest, where assimilationist rhetoric clashed with the reality of
school segregation. Educational policy toward Mexican Americans
was, in the words of Guadalupe San Miguel, Jr., a study in "cross-
purposes." It was a grand hypocrisy that exhorted Spanish speakers
to learn English while leaving in place the obstacles that kept them
from doing so. Annie Webb Blanton, the Texas superintendent of
public instruction, outlined the case for coercive anglicization in a
1923 pamphlet:

A state may, with safety, admit as residents only those capable
of being assimilated—those who can adopt its standards of living, its language, and its ideals of citizenship and of government. . . . But what of those who, while availing themselves
of the advantages of the land which our forefathers wrested
from Mexico, do not desire to become one with its citizens?
Who prefer to keep up, here, the language of the mother country, and who cling to the customs and the institutions which
had a part in bringing about conditions which drove them to
seek refuge in a more fortunate land? . . . This is the land
of liberty, but has not the war taught us that too great a degree of certain kinds of liberty is unsafe even in a democratic
country?

So strong was its insistence on English that in 1918 Texas enacted criminal penalties for teachers speaking anything else in the
classroom, except to teach foreign languages in the upper grades.
(As a concession to reality, certain countries along the Mexican border were later exempted.) Yet state authorities did little to ensure
that Spanish-speaking students got an adequate education—or any
education, for that matter. Local authorities tended to be lax
in enforcing compulsory school laws. One reason was that Texas
long based its state aid to education on a district's school-age population, rather than on the number of students enrolled. This enabled local officials to keep school taxes among the lowest in the
country by discouraging the attendance of Mexican Americans. A
statewide survey in the late 1920s found that only half of Hispanic
children were in school; of these, three-quarters were in the first
three grades. Fewer than one in twenty made it to high school.

Cost was not the only factor guiding Anglos' attitudes. Paul S.
Taylor, a sociologist who studied race relations in South Texas during the Depression years, recorded their candid reservations about
the schooling of "Mexicans." A large grower worried about the
potential loss of his workers: "If the Mexicans get educated, they
will go to the cities where they can get more [income]." A ranch
foreman opined that cultured Hispanics "think it is a disgrace to
work. The illiterates make the best farm labor." One school superintendent said his local school board "told me they wanted to keep
the Mexicans ignorant. They cited a landowner who had trouble
with a Mexican over cotton seed." (On learning he had been cheated,
a tenant farmer had sued for back wages.) Another school official
said he enforced truancy laws only during the slack season, when
"there's nothing for the Mexican children to do out of school, so
[ranchers] want them in school to keep them out of trouble."

Texas law did not mandate separate facilities for Mexican American students (as it did for black students), and in some instances
they attended classes with white Anglo children. But schools often
justified the segregation of Spanish speakers on instructional grounds,
citing a need for special help in overcoming their "language defi-
ciency." In practice, such assignments were normally based on ethnicity rather than on children's command of English. As one rural
superintendent told Taylor: "When I first came to this school the
Mexicans had lice and odor. We did not want them in the same
school." Patterns of segregation varied. In some South Texas dis-

tricts, children who completed the early grades in "Mexican" schools were allowed to attend "American" middle or high schools; in others they were advised to "go to San Antonio," more than a hundred miles away, for further education.

Meanwhile the Texas Department of Education pressed teachers to enforce, "throughout the school day, [a policy] requiring English only be spoken on the playground as well as the classroom." This was commonly misconstrued to mean that students were committing a crime by using Spanish on school property; violators were treated accordingly, like little outlaws. Hardly an inducement to academic success. At this stage, however, the language question was overshadowed by more rudimentary demands for equality.

A quarter century before *Brown v. Board of Education,* a civil rights movement began to stir among Mexican Americans in Texas. In 1928, parents organized a school boycott in Dimmit County to protest the insensitive treatment of their children. In 1930, they sued to halt construction of a "Mexican" school in Del Rio, a border town where fewer than five Hispanics had received high school diplomas during the previous fifteen years. Nevertheless, federal courts found no discriminatory intent and accepted local authorities' "educational" excuses for separate facilities. Finally, in 1948, Mexican American parents prevailed in a lawsuit against the segregated school system of Bastrop County. Grouping children for English instruction did not justify separate "Mexican" schools, a U.S. district judge concluded. Nor was it permissible to dump Hispanics automatically into remedial classes; such placements had to be based on a scientific assessment of each student's language abilities. While African-American children were not directly affected, the arguments raised in these and related cases in California laid the groundwork for *Brown.*

The organization driving this movement and steering its litigation was the League of United Latin American Citizens. Founded at Corpus Christi in 1929, LULAC differed from earlier mutual aid associations by stressing acculturation to Anglo ways and absolute loyalty to the United States as essential to Latino advancement. Drawn from the professional and entrepreneurial classes, LULAC's founders emphasized self-help through education, along with legal and political action to dismantle discriminatory barriers. A major aim was to encourage and assist Mexican Americans in learning English. In view of LULAC's active opposition to the English Only movement of the 1980s, the following section of its constitution seems more than a little ironic:

> The acquisition of the English language, which is the official language of our country [sic], being necessary for the enjoyment of our rights and privileges, we declare it to be the official language of this organization, and we pledge ourselves to learn and speak and teach same to our children.

Fluency in the majority tongue was deemed necessary, if not wholly sufficient, to reduce the odds against Hispanic success. Equality was unthinkable without English. Still, out of practical necessity, LULAC was often forced to hold meetings in Spanish, despite its strict rule limiting membership to U.S. citizens.[5] And the organization counseled no rejection of its members' heritage. True bilingualism was LULAC's ideal. It advised: "Learn to handle with purity the two most essential languages, English and Spanish."

In Depression-era Texas, this was a high ideal indeed. Outside of a few private schools, opportunities for children to perfect their Spanish skills were practically nil. The legislature finally relented, in keeping with the Good Neighbor Policy toward Latin America, and in the 1940s it allowed the introduction of Spanish into elementary schools. Yet the focus was entirely on foreign language training for Anglo children. A paternalistic philosophy held that Mexican Americans would have no incentive to learn English if allowed to rely on the "crutch" of their native tongue. As a teacher from Harlingen explained the policy, "We use no interpretation in our school work. . . . If they can't talk English, they don't talk."

The futility of the "sink or swim" approach was not lost on Mexican American educators, who in this period began to advocate experimentation with bilingual methods. Roqué Wellborne, an Austin teacher, wrote in 1941: "The time has come when we should decide that our Hispano-Texans shall not be a people without a language, speaking neither English nor Spanish well, but that they shall be a bilingual people having a good, useful knowledge of both languages." The most influential voice in this period was that of George I. Sánchez, a LULAC leader and an educational psychologist at the University of Texas. He believed the single-minded stress on English was at the root of Hispanic students' failure—or, more to the point, of the schools' failure in teaching them:

Imagine the Spanish-speaking child's introduction to American education! He comes to school, not only without a word of English but without the environmental experience upon which school life is based. He cannot speak to the teacher and is unable to understand what goes on about him in the classroom. He finally submits to rote learning, parroting words and processes in self-defense. To him, school life is artificial. He submits to it during class hours, only partially digesting the information which the teacher has tried to impart. Of course he learns English and the school subjects imperfectly!

Sánchez argued for adapting the curriculum to the child, rather than vice versa. The home language and culture should be seen as a foundation, not an obstacle to be dismantled. Students could start learning basic subjects in Spanish from the first day of school, instead of falling behind until they acquired English. This was commonsense pedagogical advice: build on what children already know. Before it was heeded, however, another generation of Mexican Americans would endure an avoidable form of *mis*education. The obstacles to change in Texas and elsewhere had nothing to do with pedagogy. The problem was political, and so was the remedy.

The Bilingual Education Act of 1968 was the inspiration of Senator Ralph Yarborough, a Texas populist who hoped to break what he saw as a cycle of injustice in the Southwest. War and annexation had reduced Spanish speakers to a powerless minority, which in turn encouraged their economic exploitation, perpetuated by the educational neglect of their children in English-only classrooms. Viewed in this light, sink-or-swim schooling was not merely ineffectual; it was a linchpin of social inequality. Yarborough conceived bilingual education as a special entitlement for Mexican Americans, rather than a program to serve all linguistic minorities. For immigrants, he argued, the "decision to come here carried with it a willingness to give up their language, everything. That wasn't true in the Southwest. We went in and took the people over, took over the land and culture. They had our culture superimposed on them. They did not consent to abandon their homeland and to come here and learn anew." Yarborough's bill was enacted virtually without controversy, except on this point. Before final passage, the senator accepted the political and pedagogical wisdom of expanding coverage to all students of limited English-speaking ability.

By 1973, the federal government was spending $45 million to support bilingual education in twenty-six different languages. Not only were these school programs teaching English and other basic subjects, but many strived to develop skills in mother tongues as varied as French, Russian, Portuguese, Cantonese, Cree, Yup'ik, and Chamorro. Linguistic minorities saw in the Bilingual Education Act an opportunity to maintain, and in some cases to revive, their cultural identities. Grants awarded under the new law helped to develop orthographies for American Indian languages that had never been written. Others enabled immigrant children to learn about the civilization of Spain or China, about their ancestors' role as explorers or railroad-builders, and other matters that Anglocentric textbooks had previously slighted.

There is no question that the reemergence of bilingual education lent legitimacy (not to mention needed subsidies) to minority self-expression. Now there was talk of a "bilingual movement," particularly among Hispanics who remembered the indignities of entering school with a "language handicap." Bilingual instruction was hardly a panacea, but it removed the stigma from—more than that, it attached value to—proficiency in languages that had previously commanded little respect. It is no wonder that the Bilingual Education Act stirred an outpouring of ethnic pride.

At the same time, this phenomenon has enabled critics to characterize the law as little more than a political sop to Spanish-speaking militants. "To a large extent, the educational arguments were window-dressing," writes the political scientist Abigail Thernstrom.

> The chairmen of the House and Senate committees did not call witnesses—in the sense of experts on the educational and political questions raised by the legislation—but (with few exceptions) lobbyists. Ethnic activists—mostly Hispanics—came to testify on the bill's necessity. . . . [By authorizing federal funding] the Bilingual Education Act made painless the capitulation of local educational authorities to demands from ethnic groups for an ethnically-oriented program.

Another neoconservative academic, Diane Ravitch, alleges that "advocates [for bilingual instruction] press its adoption regardless of its educational effectiveness. . . . The aim is to use the public schools to promote the maintenance of distinct ethnic communities, each with its own cultural heritage and language." Ravitch frets that such "politicization" has undermined the teaching of English: "The child who spends most of his instructional time learning in Croatian or Greek or Spanish is likely to learn Croatian, Greek, or Spanish." Extending this logic, U.S. English leader Stanley Diamond describes bilingual education as "part of a political movement for the official establishment of foreign languages in this country." Other opponents have linked bilingual education to affirmative action (a "jobs program" for Hispanic teachers) and to separatist schemes by Chicano radicals (an internal security threat).

Undeniably, the Bilingual Education Act had a political motivation, but the critics have not found it, any more than they have grasped the law's pedagogical rationale. For those seeking to understand the evolution and goals of bilingual education, the legislative history provides a useful starting point. Yet Thernstrom's account illustrates the blinders that many American intellectuals bring to the subject. Apparently unable to see beyond the surnames on the witness list, she misses the linguistic arguments altogether and reduces the equity arguments to an assault on "the melting-pot ideal."

To describe the witnesses as "ethnic activists—mostly Hispanics" (as opposed to "experts") is a distortion, to put it charitably. Thernstrom somehow overlooks the linguists, psychologists, curriculum specialists, economists, school superintendents, principals, teachers, social workers, labor and business leaders, state legislators, and other public officials—of varied ethnic backgrounds—who testified from academic or practical experience. A tiny proportion of the witnesses represented what could be called advocacy groups (though that in itself denotes no lack of expertise), such as the Puerto Rican Educators' Association, the National Congress of American Indians, and the National Education Association. Because Yarborough convened hearings in San Antonio, Corpus Christi, and Edinburgh, Texas, as well as in Los Angeles, New York, and Washington, a number of community leaders were also able to appear. Slightly less than half the witnesses were of Hispanic origin[6]—perhaps tainting the proceedings for those who share Thernstrom's theory of an ethnic conspiracy, but excusable for anyone willing to consider other scenarios.

Contrary to the critics' assumptions, at that time bilingual education was still a revolutionary concept, even among Mexican

Americans. Though it had been common in the nineteenth century among German immigrants, the continuity was broken by World War I. Native-language instruction remained illegal in a majority of states. Moreover, in the 1960s, psycholinguists had just begun to challenge the notion that bilingualism was a cognitive disability, a source of mental confusion that justified replacing children's first language with English. Educational researchers were recognizing that, far from unique to the Southwest, underachievement was predictable wherever children were denied access to education in their vernacular. "Submersing" students in a new language on the first day of school not only interrupted their intellectual development but threatened to retard it permanently. This treatment was also quite demoralizing. A. Bruce Gaarder, head of modern-language programs for the U.S. Office of Education, explained to Yarborough's subcommittee:

> Language is the most important exteriorization or manifestation of the self, of the human personality. If the school, the all-powerful school, rejects the mother tongue of an entire group of children, it can be expected to affect seriously and adversely those children's concept of their parents, their homes, and . . . themselves.

In this context, bilingual education seemed a promising if somewhat speculative alternative. When Dade County, Florida, launched a bilingual program for Cuban refugees in 1963, it was the first in an American public school in nearly half a century. Similar experiments followed in Laredo, Texas; Calexico, California; Rough Rock, Arizona; and a handful of other locales. Nevertheless, few educators, much less "ethnic activists," were aware of these efforts. LULAC remained wedded to the idea of intensive English instruction. Its Little Schools of the 400, a preschool program financed by Gulf Oil and the state of Texas, was a well-meaning but misguided attempt to remedy Hispanic academic problems by drilling children in four hundred basic English words.

The National Education Association, through its Tucson Survey on the Teaching of Spanish to the Spanish Speaking, organized the first broad discussion of bilingual education. Conducted in 1965–66, the survey made clear that the prevalent sink-or-swim approach resulted in "confusion, failure, and frustration." Despite some improvements in teaching English as a second language, only 5 percent of Mexican American children were enrolled in special E.S.L. programs. It was routine to hold students back for a year or more while they learned English, leaving them overage for their grade and thus more likely to quit school before graduating. In Texas, Hispanic dropout rates approached 80 percent. Veteran educators like José Cárdenas of San Antonio had come to the conclusion that "just about anything was better than the existing situation." Meanwhile there were a number of academic researchers and Romance language teachers who believed that a dual-language approach was theoretically viable.

The N.E.A. brought these forces together, along with Senator Yarborough, Texas State Senator Joe Bernal, Congressman Mo Udall of Arizona, and other legislators, at a pivotal conference in Tucson on October 30–31, 1966. Politically speaking, this marked the birth of the bilingual movement. The two senators would become influential converts, returning home to sponsor the first bilingual education legislation. Initially, however, both were skeptical.

Educational orthodoxy had long held that, to succeed in school, Hispanic children needed to "practice" their English as much as possible and to refrain from speaking Spanish during school hours. "It was a rejection of one to accomplish the other," recalls Bernal, now a school administrator in San Antonio. "And it made a lot of sense at the time" to teachers, parents, and students "wanting to come into the system." Whereas the idea of learning English through the medium of Spanish seemed, on first encounter, "ridiculous."

Growing up on the West Side of San Antonio in the 1940s, Bernal had attended a high school where 99 percent of the enrollment was Mexican American. As a student council leader, he helped to enforce an English-only policy on school grounds. Each student was given a ribbon with the legend, "I Am an American—I Speak English," and urged to turn in classmates overheard using Spanish. Violators faced corporal punishment, after-school detention, and other forms of discipline. Later, as a teacher in the 1950s, Bernal fined his pupils a penny for each lapse into Spanish (saving the proceeds to spend on Halloween or Christmas parties). "And I used to collect a lot of money from these kids," he laughs ruefully. "The parents knew about it and they were very supportive," believing that their children must learn good English, whatever the cost.

Such victim-blaming attitudes and practices were pervasive in Texas schools before the advent of bilingual education. Hispanic under-achievement was ascribed to "speaking the wrong language," and Hispanics generally accepted the blame. "It's the crowning touch," says José Cárdenas, "when society gets the victimized population to agree to their guilt for having been victimized."

On visiting his old high school in the late 1960s, Bernal found that otherwise successful students, perfectly fluent in English, still had their grades docked or their bottoms paddled for speaking Spanish outside of Spanish class. By now he sensed that something was wrong. Mexican American children were being told, in effect, "You can't be yourself." Spanish was all they heard in the barrio—perhaps it was all their parents could speak—but it wasn't good enough to use at school, even informally. Clearly, this implied something about the students themselves. "When you take a kid's language away from him," Bernal says, "you take away his self-esteem. You take away the culture, his ties to his family, his grand-parents, and you leave him out there—this hurts—at a very, very early age, being a nonsuccess by being unable to cope with the lan-guage."

To be punished for speaking Spanish only deepened the stigma. It was a humiliation that set children apart, alienated them from English-speaking teachers and classmates. And it tended to remain vivid in the mind, as Hispanic adults of a certain age can attest. Those who wonder at the evangelical fervor of some bilingual edu-cators might consider the recollection of one from South Texas:

> I come from a small town close to Corpus Christi, where, ever since I can remember, it was a sin to speak Spanish at school. Our family always spoke Spanish at home because it was easier and it was my first language. Somehow, eating potatoes and meat doesn't sound quite as appetizing as *papas con carne*. Those words mean more to me in Spanish, as they bring to mind the smell of hot flour *tortillas* cooking over a *comal* with *salsa pi-cante* and *frijoles refritos*. So not speaking Spanish at school was almost a conscious effort on my part.
>
> I was on the girls' basketball team. I was so proud of that and I loved playing the sport. . . . [But] there was an ugly part that I remember very well, as if it was yesterday. We had

an Anglo principal (the only Mexicans on staff were the cafeteria workers and the custodians) who . . . had given instructions to the basketball coach for us not to speak Spanish off campus on any of our trips.

All the Mexican girls would get on the bus and sit in the back. We spoke English, but when you're in an informal setting, there are certain things that just don't translate—like the meat and potatoes. So we sprinkled our girl talk with Spanish. It was so neat to get on the bus and go to Sinton and Taft and some of the other towns. But on every one of our trips, the coach would assign an Anglo girl to monitor us in case we spoke Spanish. She would write our names down and turn us in to the coach. The next day we would get paddled for being on the list.

What a crime! Never mind that we won the game. . . . Win or lose, we the Mexican girls on the basketball team always lost.

With English-only rules, as with school segregation, the purported aim of teaching English was a subterfuge. Prohibiting Spanish was a political act.

More than anything, says Joe Bernal, this realization opened his eyes to the virtues of bilingual education. In 1969, he led a successful campaign in the Texas legislature to decriminalize teaching in languages other than English (formerly punishable by a fine of $100 a day and the loss of a teacher's license). The law did not mandate bilingual programs but at least gave them official sanction, he explains. "No longer were we going to be told we were not legitimate just because we were Spanish-speaking. The bilingual approach said, 'You don't have to apologize for your parents. You don't have to apologize for your culture being a little different.' "

If that sounds like a "political" agenda, no doubt it was. Mexican Americans took up the cause of bilingual education as they had taken up school desegregation a generation earlier—as a step toward social equality. For their children it promised both opportunity and a measure of dignity that they themselves had been denied. Instilling ethnic pride was not merely a worthy end in itself, but also a pedagogical means. Until the mark of inferiority was erased from their culture, as a group Latino children would remain forever behind:

discouraged, rebellious, prone to drop out. At minimum, schools needed to remove the taboo attached to Spanish; better yet, they could use it constructively in the classroom. The devaluation of Spanish was a social phenomenon, after all, not an educational necessity. It certainly made no practical sense in a region where the language remained a vital medium of commerce (along the border, sometimes the only medium). Why not turn students' "disability" into an asset to be developed, perhaps even shared with Anglo students? An eminently reasonable question—but a naïve one. Bilingual education was more than an issue of language; it was an issue of power.

In the late 1960s a new wave of school boycotts spread throughout South Texas, combining demands for bilingual education with attacks on discriminatory practices. The latter ranged from the use of English I.Q. tests on Spanish-speaking children to the exclusion of Hispanic candidates for homecoming queen. For the Chicano militants who led these struggles, it was only natural to regard language as a matter of self-determination. "You've got a handful of *gringos* controlling the lives of *muchos mexicanos*," charged José Angel Gutiérrez, founder of La Raza Unida Party. Suppressing Spanish was one strategy for maintaining this "colonial" relationship. After leading a successful boycott in Crystal City, Texas, La Raza Unida won an electoral majority on the school board and proceeded to institute bilingual programs from kindergarten through the third grade. Obviously, there were political motives behind these educational reforms. Introducing Spanish into the schools encouraged students to identify *as Chicanos*, to discover a latent self-respect that is crucial to any group asserting its rights. Pride in the language was integral to Aztlán, the nationalist vision of an autonomous Southwest reunited culturally, and perhaps politically, with Mexico.

For a brief time such ideas flowered. Yet they never took root among Mexican American masses, politicians, or educators. José Cárdenas, who was superintendent of San Antonio's Edgewood school district during that period, describes them as "extremist [views] that no one took seriously except the critics of bilingual education."

Even La Raza Unida's innovations never approached the separatist "politicization" that English Only proponents decry. Crystal City owed its reputation as "Spinach Capital of the World" to an abundance of impoverished, illiterate farm labor. In the surrounding Zavala County, the median Hispanic educational level was 3.1 years in 1970. Gutiérrez and his allies, who had ousted a conservative school board untroubled by such statistics, were not about to trifle with their constituents' hopes for better schools. La Raza's introduction of bilingual methods was pedagogically grounded and administered. By contrast, the reaction of Crystal City Anglos was entirely extracurricular. Local authorities indicted a high school teacher for using Spanish during a history lesson (charges were later dropped). In nearby Uvalde, when parents and students demanded bilingual instruction, Texas Rangers were called in to crush their peaceful boycott.

Summing up Mexican American attitudes in the late 1960s, Cárdenas emphasizes that "the paramount concern was improving the performance of our kids." As long as their language needs were neglected, Hispanics would be denied an equal opportunity to learn. The value of desegregation was limited if it meant "equal treatment" of non-English-speaking children in English-only classrooms. As the Supreme Court later agreed in *Lau v. Nichols,* that approach made a "mockery" of equal opportunity. Mexican Americans embraced bilingual education, Cárdenas explains, mainly because it promised "a better way of teaching English, without academic retardation." It would ease the *transition* between the two languages at no cost to a child's overall development. Secondarily it offered a chance for the *maintenance* of mother-tongue skills, enabling a student to become equally adept in the two languages.

For the experts who urged Congress to authorize experiments in bilingual education, there was no contradiction between proficiency in English and proficiency in the native tongue. Quite the contrary. There was evidence that two goals were mutually reinforcing, that linguistic skills—literacy, for example—were "transferable" between languages. During hearings on the Bilingual Education Act, witnesses advanced a number of arguments for maintaining minority tongues. There would be *societal benefits* (conserving rather than wasting language resources), *individual benefits* (making bilingualism a job skill by adding biliteracy), *psychological benefits* (improving attitudes toward school and self, with favorable effects on achievement), and perhaps *cognitive benefits* (enhancing mental flexibility—though the evidence here was inconclusive). While bilingual programs were normally labeled as either transitional or maintenance, the distinction was misleading, because there was no pedagogical reason why children had to abandon their native tongue in the process of learning English. It was in the realm of politics where the two approaches would prove worlds apart.

For a nation committed to Anglo-conformity, "a better way of teaching English" was one thing. A means of preserving minority languages was quite another. Did the Bilingual Education Act aim to make the melting pot more efficient or to render it obsolete? On this point the legislative history is ambiguous. "We must take advantage of the language pluralism that exists in our Southwest," urged Senator Joseph Montoya of New Mexico during deliberations on the bill. "Comprehensive bilingual education programs . . . can give to all [students] the best of both worlds in terms of language, culture, and cooperation in daily life." But Senator Frank Lausche of Ohio, a native speaker of Slovenian, objected that when he attended school "they did not teach me Slovenian in order to [teach me] English." Why was it necessary for children to study native languages they already knew? he wondered. "What are we to do if there is a Hungarian neighborhood in Toledo that finds it wants Hungarian taught in its schools?"

Sensitive to the minefield he was traversing, Senator Yarborough stepped gingerly. As sponsor of the legislation, he explained: "It is not the purpose of this bill to create pockets of different languages throughout the country . . . not to stamp out the mother tongue and not to make their mother tongue the dominant language, but just to try to make these children fully literate in English, so that the children can move into the mainstream of American life." Yarborough assured his colleagues that funding would be available only where academic problems could be traced to a non-English-speaking environment. Satisfied with this answer, Lausche backpedaled, asking "whether all of us should not be expert in at least two languages—perhaps three," and recommending "a knowledge of Latin" for everyone. This was the extent of the Senate's "debate" over objectives. In the House, where thirty-six bilingual education bills were pending (including one sponsored by freshman Representative George Bush), there was even less controversy.

It seemed that Congress wanted to be on record favoring multiple language skills and assimilation, too. The potential contradiction was suppressed. Also known as Title VII of the Elementary and Secondary Education Act, the new law was perceived as an antipoverty effort, designed to aid a deserving group thus far overlooked by the Great Society.[7] Its major emphasis was remedial, to help underachieving children make the transition to English.

Nevertheless, the law's stated purpose remained vague: "to develop and carry out new and imaginative elementary and secondary school programs . . . [for] children of limited English-speaking ability." No attempt was made to dictate teaching methods or even to define the concept of bilingual education. The door was left ajar for language maintenance and enthusiasts exploited the opening. By 1971, the U.S. Office of Education was advising grant applicants: "It must be remembered that the ultimate goal of bilingual education is a student who functions well in two languages on any occasion." Hardly a radical notion, considering that ever since *Sputnik* the federal government had been spending lavishly to improve foreign language teaching. Yet this reading of the Bilingual Education Act was not widely shared. As far as Congress was concerned, "we were in there to overcome [students'] 'bilingual problem,' " recalls Albar Peña, the first director of Title VII programs. "There was an obsession that if they were not English-speaking at the end of the first grade that the world would come to an end."

Yarborough's legislative strategy had succeeded brilliantly in the short term. But the absence of substantive debate created long-term confusion about the law's aims. Worse, it invited a backlash. The Bilingual Education Act marked a major policy shift—never before had the U.S. government recognized the special needs of non-English-speaking students, much less supported efforts to perpetuate their languages—and yet its rationale remained obscure to the public. A vote in Congress did nothing to alter attitudes about Americanization or the social biases that supported them.

There was little resistance as long as bilingual education merely meant no-strings funding for school districts that chose to apply. But soon it was clear that this was not just another poverty program. By the mid-1970s bilingual education was being applied as a civil rights remedy, imposed where local authorities had neglected non-English-speaking students, and an instrument of ethnic pluralism, used to bring diversity into the curriculum. It was an expanding commitment that entailed the recruitment of teachers in numerous tongues, as well as in E.S.L., not to mention the training of a new corps of bilingual administrators. In sum, the federal government had thrown its weight behind a costly and far-reaching change in the way American schools were run—all with minimal discussion or scrutiny. It was at this point that the premises of bilingual education came under serious criticism.

Much of the attack focused on the goal of language maintenance, which at first glance appeared to contradict the goal of English acquisition. Some members of Congress expressed shock in 1977 when the first national study of Title VII–sponsored programs reported that 86 percent of teachers endorsed maintenance as one of their aims. Surreptitiously, it seemed, federal bureaucrats and ethnic activists had twisted bilingual education's thrust by 180 degrees. But another conclusion largely escaped notice: when teachers were actually tested, 50 percent lacked proficiency in their students' native tongue. These findings reflected on the one hand the program's expectations—teachers knew they were supposed to endorse maintenance (then in vogue)—and on the other hand its realities. "Bilingual" education was often bilingual in name only, with classes taught almost exclusively in English, a phenomenon that helps to explain its disappointing results in early evaluations.

A simultaneous blow came from Noel Epstein, education editor of the *Washington Post,* in an influential monograph blasting bilingual education as a policy of "affirmative ethnicity." Epstein's parallel with antidiscrimination law was apt, in the sense that bilingual education promised more than equal access to an English-speaking society; it legitimized once-denigrated cultures and implied an interest in preserving them. But at the same time, his terminology conjured up images of minority set-asides, "forced busing," and other federal ventures in social change that a growing number of white Americans found threatening. It was this pejorative connotation that Epstein stressed. Again, with bilingual education, government seemed to be going too far in righting historic wrongs.

What was curious about Epstein's case against language maintenance was that he had no quarrel with the end result. Bilingualism was fine, even laudable, for the individual student. It was the motivation of "bilingual backers" and the thought of appeasing them that he found hard to stomach. If all they sought was "a way of sustaining and building valuable national language resources, opening new worlds to all . . . [language maintenance] would raise no serious social or political issues." But Epstein perceived a broader agenda among Hispanics, a plan to enhance "ethnic identities through more extensive use of the native language and culture." This offended his conception of public education:

> The issue—and this cannot be emphasized too strongly—is *not* the unquestioned importance of ethnicity in individuals' lives, any more than it is the unquestioned importance of religion in individuals' lives. The issue is *not* the right or the desirability of groups to maintain their languages and cultures. The issue is the government role. The overriding question is whether the federal government is responsible for financing and promoting student attachments to their ethnic languages and cultures, jobs long left to families, religious groups, ethnic organizations, private schools, ethnic publications and others.

According to this view, it was legitimate to spend public funds to promote *nonethnic* language instruction, for example, to teach Spanish to English speakers, or English to Spanish speakers. Yet if maintaining Spanish as a native tongue would encourage "ethnic attachments," that was another matter—the social costs outweighed the educational benefits. Hispanics had every right to pass on their heritage to the next generation, of course, but not at taxpayers' expense. The symbolism of public schools elevating "ethnic languages and cultures alongside English" was unacceptable. It might result in the "ghettoization" of linguistic minorities, encouraging "greater separation" rather than "greater integration." Teaching Spanish to Spanish speakers would also divert resources from "those who are most in need": non-English-speaking children. Therefore, bilingual education should be kept strictly transitional, with students reassigned to regular classrooms as soon as they could cope.

Epstein was not unaware of the contradictions of this position. He acknowledged the folly of discarding children's mother tongue in elementary school "and then requir[ing] them to study language as a subject in the later grades." Still, as a matter of public policy, he insisted on a Chinese Wall between bilingual and foreign language instruction.

Congress endorsed this schizophrenic approach in 1978. It voted to restrict Bilingual Education Act grants to programs that would *replace* minority tongues with English. In other words, it resolved to spend tens of millions to encourage children to forget the same languages that it had been spending tens of millions to promote under the National Defense Education Act of 1958. Apparently, legislators could afford a departure from fiscal sanity, but not the scandal of "affirmative ethnicity."

During Congressional hearings in June 1977, shortly after a version of Epstein's monograph appeared in the *Washington Post*, Representative Albert Quie of Minnesota grilled the federal director of bilingual education: "Do you think that we ought to become a bilingual nation like Canada, where we would print everything in two different languages?" The official, John Molina, responded:

> The idea is so far-fetched that I don't really give it too much thought. . . . I think the English language is here to stay, and it is pretty solid, and I think the American culture is pretty solid, and I don't share the fear of those who feel that this program is going to split ethnic groups into war camps.

But such worries were not easily assuaged. Reinforced by newcomers from south of the border, Spanish speakers were an expanding, and increasingly demanding, minority. To the north, separatists had recently come to power in the province of Quebec and were preparing to enact French Only legislation. Still smarting from the traumas of Vietnam, black nationalism, Watergate, and OPEC, white Anglo-Americans were hypersensitive to any further challenge to their hegemony. However unlikely, the idea of "official bilingualism" was now on the table, apparently an option for the first time in U.S. history.

In this new context, bilingual education became less a question of pedagogy than a question of prestige. By placing its imprimatur on language-maintenance programs, government would be approving new terms for Americanization. No longer would immigrants have to surrender a central feature of their identity as part of the bargain; bilingualism would be allowed, even encouraged. English—and "Americanism"—would no longer be an either/or proposition. For many, this renegotiation seemed to devalue the ordeal of earlier newcomers and their hard-earned *nonethnic* identity. "Fairness" demanded that today's non-English-speaking groups be treated just like yesterday's: no special help, no exemption from sink-or-swim. Of course, none of these resentments was made fully explicit. What was said was that government had "no responsibility" for perpetuating "ethnic languages." That, however attractive on educational grounds, such a policy might become "divisive."

This argument, first elaborated by Noel Epstein, foreshadowed the basic logic of English Only. While minority tongues were tolerable in private—freedom of speech and all that—they were problematic in the public realm. Or, as a leader of U.S. English later expressed it through her thick German accent, "Being bilingual, bicultural is the greatest ability for a person; it is a curse for a nation." Although Americanization was too chauvinistic a concept to revive for the 1980s, the new mindset was familiar: one flag, one language. *Englisch über Alles.* Behind the public-spirited rhetoric lurked the anxieties of Anglo-Americans. Raising the status of minority languages would inevitably diminish that of English and its speakers. Perhaps the change would be slight at first. But once bilingualism got a foothold, who knew where it might lead—pressures for Anglos to learn Spanish? Hispanic cultural enclaves in the United States? Who would be the strangers then?

Four

Tribal Politics

Miami is where Anglo-Americans' worst fears converge: a U.S. city overrun and finally hijacked by foreigners. A place where Americanization has given way to Latinization and where the natives, more than the newcomers, feel pressure to adapt. A community where the Cuban influence is so pervasive that one must learn Spanish or cease being a full participant. *¡Bienvenido a Miami!* To resist the bilingual imperative here is to invite daily indignities—trouble finding a sales clerk who speaks good English; Hispanics joking in the elevator about God-knows-what (the grim Anglo, perhaps?); a growing section of the newspaper that is inaccessible. And worse than the language barrier, there is an attitude that rankles: an obvious disdain for English. Though most Cubans can function in both worlds, they clearly prefer their own, as if, given a choice, they find the Anglo's lacking. So they have recreated Havana without Castro on American soil, using Spanish to consolidate their new regime. For many Old Miamians there is a sense of losing one's country, of being dispossessed by language.

This vision is not altogether paranoid. Many Hispanics see what is essentially a mirror image of the same reality. Osvaldo Soto, a Cuban American attorney, contends that Miami has supplanted Madrid and Buenos Aires and Mexico City as "the capital of the Spanish language." An extravagant idea, befitting an extravagant new center of Latin American finance, trade, media, and tourism. A boomtown that Cubans feel could never have happened without them. Soto's presumption is itself indicative of Miami's uniqueness. Who would dare make such a claim for Los Angeles or New York, cities that are home to considerably larger Spanish-speaking populations?

The difference is that Spanish has attained a status in Miami that it enjoys nowhere else in the continental United States. Though hardly a threat to replace English, it is a bold competitor for market share that, at least for now, holds an enviable edge in demographics. From less than 5 percent in 1959, Hispanics have expanded to 49 percent of Greater Miami's residents (and 62 percent of the city's). Not only Cubans, but Puerto Ricans, Colombians, Nicaraguans, Venezuelans, Peruvians, Dominicans, and other Latinos are flocking to Miami. More important, their Spanish is far from the marginalized vernacular of Los Angeleños or Nuyorricans. Spoken in boardrooms as well as barrios, it feels like a world-class language, for which no apologies need be made. (Even resentful Anglos will concede that bilingualism has been good for business.) Maurice Ferré, a Spanish-speaking former mayor of Miami, once observed:

> You can be born here in a Cuban hospital, be baptized by a Cuban priest, buy all your food from a Cuban grocer, take your insurance from a Cuban broker, and pay for it all with a check from a Cuban bank. You can get all the news in Spanish—read the Spanish daily paper, watch Spanish T.V., listen to Spanish radio. You can go through life without having to speak English at all.

He was not exaggerating.

What is most remarkable, however, is that Spanish has thrived in Miami while banned as a language of government. County officials here are forbidden by law to post a sign, translate a meeting, print a form, or distribute a pamphlet in Spanish, to subsidize a Hispanic arts festival, or to allow Spanish-language programming on the community-access cable T.V. channel. (The principle applies equally to Haitian Creole, Vietnamese, Yiddish, Russian, and other minority tongues of local importance.) Public expenditures "for the purpose of utilizing any language other than English, or promoting any culture other than that of the United States, [are] prohibited." In short, Dade County, Florida, is home to the nation's strictest English Only ordinance. Enacted by citizen initiative in 1980, the law has survived several attempts at repeal. In 1988, Floridians adopted English as their state language by a vote of 84 to 16 percent. Though not exactly outlawed—and certainly not in retreat—Spanish is officially unwelcome here.

How this came about is a story of Cuban chutzpah and Anglo

estrangement, bilingualism in public manners and the job market, nativist hysteria and hate-mongering talk shows. Most of all, it is a tale of tribal politics. The so-called antibilingualism campaign not only marks the birth of the movement for Official English but reveals the raw impulses that spawned it. Before all the prettifying rhetoric about "our common language" and its "unifying role," there was Dade County: revenge of the Anglos.

The Antibilingual Ordinance was mean-spirited on its face. Though amended in 1984 to create loopholes for health, emergency, and tourist services, the original law allowed for no exceptions. If county funds were involved—including expenditures in Miami, Hialeah, Sweetwater, and other majority-Latino jurisdictions—any use of a language other than English, whether to warn about an approaching hurricane or to communicate with patients at the county hospital, was verboten. Supporters made little attempt to conceal their motives. In a *Miami Herald* exit poll, more than half of the non-Hispanic whites who voted for the initiative said they hoped it "would make Miami a less attractive place to live for Cubans and other Spanish-speaking people." Nearly an equal number said that, while they doubted the wisdom of English Only government, they endorsed it "to express my protest" about bilingualism. Whatever the practical impact on non-English speakers—no one expected them to give up their native tongues overnight—the law would declare them personae non gratae until they did so.

It was no accident that the antibilingual vote came shortly after Fidel Castro's decision to open the port of Mariel, releasing a new and often troublesome wave of Cuban refugees. About 125,000 landed in South Florida between April and September of 1980. Largely unskilled, non-English-speaking, racially mixed, and including a small but salient minority of violent criminals, mental patients, and other misfits, the Marielitos put strains on the community's resources and goodwill. As street crime and welfare costs soared, Miamians' sympathy plummeted. In the *Herald*'s November exit poll, 74 percent of all voters agreed that "the recent refugee influx has made Dade a less desirable place to live."

Earlier-arriving Cubans, during the first wave of 1959–1962 and the "freedom flights" of 1965–1973, had enjoyed a very different reception. Indeed, it would be hard to find a more favored group of newcomers. Before it ended in 1974, the federal Cuban Refugee Program provided nearly $1 billion in resettlement assistance, covering everything from food, clothing, and child care to English instruction and college loans. A substantial portion went to the Dade County Public Schools, both directly and through a program to retrain and recertify Cuban teachers. These funds, along with a Ford Foundation grant, enabled the district to launch its first experiment in bilingual education at the Coral Way School. This was an unabashed Spanish-maintenance program for Cuban children and at the same time a Spanish "immersion" program for Anglo children. The goal was fluency in both languages for both groups—just the kind of bilingual education that would become anathema fifteen years hence. In 1963, however, no one perceived any affront to the melting pot.

Perhaps this was because the Cubans were regarded not as traditional immigrants, but as "guests" of the United States who were temporarily down on their luck. Most were expected to return home when Castro fell. Under the circumstances it was natural for the Cubans to preserve their language; it would have been unfair to insist on Anglo-conformity. Bilingualism in this context was politically innocuous. Thousands of English-speaking Miamians began to study Spanish—the Dade County schools offered a sixteen-week course for just $5—in hopes of making the refugees feel welcome, courting their business, and later, attracting their votes. As the Cubans began to compete, building their own successful enterprises, *Se habla español* became a popular advertising pitch among Anglo shopkeepers.

Local boosters also saw the potential to turn Spanish to the city's economic advantage. Whereas New York and New Orleans had long dominated Latin American finance and trade, respectively, Miami was now in a position to exploit its favorable geography. So when Bernardo Benes, a Cuban banker, approached the Metro-Dade Commission about improving Hispanic access to public services, it gave him literally more than he had bargained for. On April 16, 1973, the all-Anglo commission voted to declare Dade County bilingual and bicultural and to designate Spanish as "the second official language." Not a single dissenting voice was heard; when one commissioner recorded his vote as "*¡Sí!*" the audience gave him a standing ovation.

Though spelling out no explicit obligations, the resolution was more than ceremonial. It led to the translation of street signs, public meetings, and election ballots, along with tax bills, parking tickets, trade-licensing exams, and some 4,500 pages of county documents. It committed the county to hiring more bilingual employees and established a Division of Latin Affairs to handle community relations, disseminate information through Spanish-language media, and otherwise cope with the need for bilingual services, which was considerable. Hispanics now made up one-quarter of Dade County's 1.3 million residents. A language census conducted around this time turned up 155,000 adults who spoke Spanish most of the time, 44 percent of whom were illiterate in English. On the other hand, 75 percent of younger Latinos were proficient in both languages.

By now the realization was dawning that a Cuban counterrevolution was not imminent and that, regardless of Fidel's fate, there would be a permanent Hispanic presence in South Florida. Cuban exiles were beginning to think of themselves as Cuban immigrants and to seek U.S. citizenship. By 1973, a majority of new arrivals were expressing their intention to remain in the United States. Meanwhile there was a surge in immigration from elsewhere in the Caribbean. From 1970 to 1975, Spanish speakers outnumbered other newcomers to Dade County by twenty-six to one. Economic opportunity and political democracy, plus a vibrant Latin culture, added up to a powerful attraction, and not just for huddled masses. Miami was also becoming a base of operations, as well as an upscale shopping mall, for South American oligarchs and millionaires.

The Cuban diaspora continued apace. While its class status has been exaggerated—managers and professionals were overrepresented, but always in the minority—its prosperity has been accurately portrayed. By the mid-1970s Cubans headed five local banks and owned 8,500 businesses, more than a third of Dade County's total.

With Hispanics' increasing investment came an increasing interest and aggressiveness in civic life. The bilingual-bicultural declaration was a foot in the door. In 1974, barely a year after its passage, a Cuban-led coalition accused the county manager of "ignoring" the mandate for Spanish-language services and demanded a larger share of county jobs. This was a familiar ethnic scenario, but for the Cubans it signaled a departure from the obsessive politics of exile. Another indication was the emergence of the Spanish-American League Against Discrimination. Though its name suggested a civil rights organization, SALAD was the vehicle of a new *Cuban American* elite, young professionals seeking traditional positions of power: local judgeships, college vice-presidencies, school-board seats, and offices in county government. Yet, with its acronym, SALAD threw down a gauntlet before old notions of Americanization. "We were looking for an appealing way to say that America is not the melting pot that the myth would have us believe," explains its founder, Javier Bray. "It is a salad bowl. It is a combination of all the ingredients . . . [contrary to] the nation-building myth that says we must become all the same. Americanism is that process of orchestrating all this diversity into something unique, but without asking anyone to give up what they are."

Not that there was much danger of Cubans being seduced or cajoled into abandoning Spanish. A group of economists led by Alejandro Portes followed the experience of newcomers arriving in 1973 and determined that, after six years in Dade County, a full 45 percent still had no knowledge of English and another 32 percent had limited proficiency, while only 9 percent could be considered fluent. (In self-reports rather than objective tests, they rated themselves a good deal higher.) Nevertheless, most of the Cubans were well informed about U.S. society through Miami's Spanish-language newspapers and television. And their economic progress was substantial, considering their limited job skills on arrival, relative to those of earlier Cuban exiles. After six years, one-fifth owned their own businesses and two-fifths owned their own homes. Here the ethnic enclave was performing its familiar role, facilitating the immigrant's gradual adjustment to the host society. Only its scale and efficiency were unusual. Living and working in Spanish, many Cubans felt little urgency about learning English—much like the Germans, Norwegians, Greeks, and other groups before them, who for a time had succeeded in building insular communities.

Still, there was something different about the Cuban attitude. Arriving with plenty of human capital, if little of the other kind, better educated than the immigrant norm, older and thus more *formed* as cultural beings, they were less vulnerable to assimilationist appeals. Most Cubans struggled at first, but without losing their distinctive self-confidence. As they rose, some propagated the legend that pre–1959 Miami had been little more than a breeding ground for alligators (a suggestion that still enrages local Anglos). There is no question that the Cubans' timing was propitious. "We came here to a city that was in gestation," explains Max Castro, a sociologist whose family arrived in the first wave of refugees.

> It's not true that the Cubans built Miami. But we came into a young metropolis that had not yet been consolidated in the way that New York City, for example, had been consolidated when it welcomed, or didn't welcome, the Puerto Ricans. Cubans have become a constituent element here, as opposed to arriving in a city that was already defined and trying to break into very long-established, crystallized structures. So we had that advantage. And, though I'm not too comfortable with the idea of national character, Cubans are known for being very assertive and aggressive, and there's some truth to that.

The Cubans also brought a different experience of language. Unlike Mexican Americans, they had never been humiliated at school for speaking their native tongue or persuaded that their children must speak only English to get ahead. Unassailable in their anticommunism, they felt no need to forsake Spanish as a token of loyalty to the United States. Most Cubans were slow to recognize the stigma that Anglo-Americans have attached to minority languages. (In the Portes study, it was the anglicized Cubans who perceived more bias against themselves and others.) While intolerance is no stranger to Spanish-speaking countries, linguistic purity has seldom been its object. Caribbean culture is a melding of sight and sound, taste and movement, a swirl of dialects, creeds, and races. Fusion, not refinement, is its operative principle. So nothing in the Cubans' background had prepared them for the Anglos' aversion to Spanish, which made little sense except as an expression of ethnic animosity. As any American must know, their war was with Castro, not with *Cubanismo*. Why should they renounce it now?

Bilingualism is the immigrant's natural accommodation to new realities, albeit a temporary one in most cases. Diglossia, or the stable coexistence of two languages, each commanding its own sphere of social functions, has been virtually unknown in the United States. English is so overpowering in close contact that minority tongues quickly give way, retreating to the domains of home and hearth, church or synagogue, fraternal lodge, ethnic press, and private school. To the extent that these institutions thrive in isolation, so does the mother tongue, although adult immigrants must still learn survival and, usually, job-related skills in English. Immigrant children are more likely to achieve an equal fluency in both languages. As they desert the constricted world of their elders, however, they find less and less reason to speak anything but English. Monolingual to bilingual to monolingual. Such is the pattern for urban immigrants in twentieth-century America.

But not for the Cubans—at least, not so far. Their pattern is contradictory. On the one hand, it would be premature to assert that diglossia has arrived, that bilingualism is institutionally secure in Miami, despite its Spanish language enclave, ever expanding to accommodate new waves of immigrants. Mayor Ferré was right about the possibility of "going through life" without speaking English. But this observation is "very misleading," argues Max Castro. "Cuban Americans aspire for their children to go to law school, medical school, and you can't do that in Spanish." Responding to a 1985 survey, 98 percent of Hispanic parents in Dade County said that it was essential for their children to "speak and write English perfectly" (compared with only 94 percent of Anglo parents). On the other hand, Castro adds, while Cubans identify increasingly with the United States, "this is not an either/or proposition, either American or Cuban. There's a search for an integration of those identities." Why choose one or the other when one can have the Miami Sound Machine? For the younger generation, there is no dilemma of status or solidarity, no temptation to escape the ghetto and its language, because there is nothing claustrophobic about Latin Miami. Quite the reverse: it is English-speaking Miami that often seems a bit limited.

Here bilingualism is much more than a temporary adjustment. For Miami's Hispanics—not just Cubans—it has become a preferred way of life, a philosophy of have-your-cake-and-the-Anglos'-too, an insistence that Spanish be an essential ingredient in the city's future. Bilingualism signifies a resolve to make assimilation work both ways. A "unique orchestration of diversity" indeed.

SALAD's revisionist ethnicity, though sometimes hard to distinguish from the rhetoric of cultural pluralism, differs in this crucial respect. It expects reciprocity—which makes the language connection essential. Linguistic pluralism offers more than lip service to diversity; it becomes a mechanism for ethnic leveling. SALAD expresses this idea as "English Plus." Another coinage of Javier Bray's, the slogan has become a catchy alternative to English Only. It is a doctrine that concedes the primacy of English in the United States but opposes an exclusive franchise, stressing the economic, social, and educational benefits of multiple language skills. As Bray explains:

> English Plus should be a rational way to say, "Hey, don't feel threatened; let's put this [English Only] nonsense aside and move on to greater things." . . . This narrowing of who is an American on the criteria of language reduces the humanity of all of us. Hispanics are going to be as skillful in the use of English as anyone. But don't shut the door to other languages. Don't shut the door to that *plus* that makes us even more universal, more open to the rest of the world.

And, he might have added, more open to the Latin world in particular—not only to its córdobas and bolívars and pesos, but to its peoples.

The 1980 census, taken just prior to the Mariel influx, reported that two out of five Dade Countians were now of Hispanic origin. This was the demographic basis of bilingualism and also its outcome. No slogan, however reasonable, could mask the political threat. A power shift was in progress, and language was its most obvious feature. As immigration swelled, Anglo-Miamians' scattered gripes gathered into a full-scale backlash.

The English Only movement originated not in any elaborated ideology, but in everyday frictions at the shopping mall and the workplace, as strangers, acquaintances, and even friends found themselves cast in a cross-cultural melodrama. Suddenly the mundane act of going through a checkout line or taking a coffee break could become a political encounter. A scene might ensue because someone spoke the wrong language to the wrong person in the wrong setting—or because someone perceived this to be the case and responded with hostility. There were no accepted rules of etiquette where bilingualism was concerned, only clashing opinions about what was appropriate:

- Was it impolite to speak a language that some people within earshot might not understand? Or was it permissible, when conversing in a public place, to exclude casual bystanders in this way? What about customers or coworkers, who might wonder whether they were objects of discussion?

- In a social gathering, should bilinguals stop speaking in Spanish whenever a monolingual English speaker approached? Or should they feel free to engage in "code-switching" between languages, a popular conversational style among Latinos that made most Anglos feel left out?

- Did the same principles apply regardless of language? Was it equally discourteous to speak English in the presence of non-English speakers as to speak Spanish in the presence of non-Spanish speakers? Or was English always appropriate, but Spanish only sometimes?

- How should one address a stranger of indeterminate ethnicity? In the majority language of the city (Spanish) or of the nation (English)? And how should the stranger respond when an incorrect assumption was made?

There was—and is—no forum to settle such questions, or even to discuss them rationally. So Miamians caught in tense situations either bit their tongues or acted out their prejudices.

This type of politics has little to do with liberalism or conservatism. It is incidental to one's considered views on foreign policy or civil liberties or even language education. Reactions to bilingualism come straight from the gut. In Miami it is usually an Anglo lodging the complaint and a Latino resenting it. Enos Schera, a leader of the antibilingualism campaign, lists a few of the grievances that spurred him to get involved:

Overuse of Spanish was driving people up the wall. You'd go down to your county agency and you could barely understand the people working behind the counter. They'd mainly address you in Spanish first, and when you'd tell them you didn't speak Spanish, only then did they convert back over to English. In other words, we were treated like we were foreigners and they were the legitimate person that was born here. I've even gone into a store where one woman—she was a teenager, I guess, working behind the counter—addressed me in Spanish. I said, "What?" She repeated it and I said, "Well, I'm sorry, I don't speak Spanish." And she said, "Why not?" and threw the change down, utterly perturbed because I don't speak Spanish. See, I look like I'm Cuban, really. But even so, even if I look it, in Miami the courtesy should be shown to the people of the town. You should address them in English first, and if you find out that they don't speak English, then it would probably be correct to convert to Spanish.

Schera's solution is simple. As newcomers, Hispanics must bear the full burden of adjustment, accepting the linguistic status quo that prevailed before 1959. The suggestion that Anglos have the option of learning Spanish, or at least learning to tolerate it, is too far-fetched to consider: "When you live under the American system of laws, the American system of culture, the American language that goes along with the culture, and a group of refugees comes in, it's upon their incumbency to learn your language, your culture, adopt your system, and assimilate. This is what's been happening since 1900 by the millions upon millions. Why should this trend be reversed just because all of a sudden we have an overabundance of foreigners?" Schera has a point. Linguistic etiquette was no problem when immigrants were subordinate minorities who deferred to English speakers, embracing Anglo-conformity out of fear, pragmatism, or conviction—or at least keeping their native tongues discreetly out of earshot.

But the traditional pecking order no longer holds in Miami. With numbers and economic status, Hispanics have the option of ignoring Anglo sensitivities—in fact, of ignoring Anglos altogether. They assert the right to express themselves without inhibition, whether that means sticking to Spanish or darting impulsively between languages. There is no intent to exclude, bilinguals insist. Code-switching is rarely calculated or even conscious. Certain thoughts and feelings are simply easier to broach in one language than the other. (Hence the cliché that one makes money in English and love in Spanish.) This phenomenon holds doubly true in a bicultural environment. For much of the community, Spanish is "the language of conversation and familiarity and emotion and greeting and religion," says Mark Gallegos, a Mexican American lawyer who spends much of his day speaking English at a downtown firm. Among younger Latin Miamians, bilingualism has become second nature. An adjustment that is both spontaneous and sensible, under the circumstances.

So Hispanics tend to judge Anglos' distaste for other tongues as irrational at best. If consenting adults choose to communicate among themselves in Spanish, "Spanglish," or Pig Latin, why should that offend? Do English speakers claim the right to eavesdrop on private conversations? If they want to sample the flavors of Latin Miami, why not learn Spanish? If not, why worry about something that does not concern them? Or is there something unstated behind all these objections—bigotry, for instance?

This is not to say that Hispanics are insensitive to the complications of bilingualism. Some, if not all, will acknowledge there are occasions when monolinguals have cause to feel put down or screened out by language. Osvaldo Soto, a tireless trumpet for English Plus, is nonetheless quick to concede: "When I have somebody speaking Yiddish next to me, or I hear the [Haitian] patois, I react—'They might be saying something about my person'—which is very normal." Small paranoias are only human.

Yet larger pathologies are also at work. In Dade County, the same ethnic scenario is replayed with striking regularity, a story one hears again and again: *My friend and I were walking down the street (or standing on line or taking a lunch break), speaking Spanish, absorbed in our discussion, when a strange Anglo accosted us and said, "This is America—speak English," then disappeared. And Americans had the nerve to say Cubans were rude! Such an incident was inconceivable in Havana or Madrid or, for that matter, in any cosmopolitan city. With typical arrogance, the Anglos claimed to cherish freedom of speech but failed to recognize this right for anyone but themselves. Where did the Constitution say anything about English?*

Certainly, no more than a few Anglo-Miamians take it upon themselves to correct their neighbors' language behavior. But numerous others seem to support the cause. There is a sense of righteousness about resisting Spanish, as if it stood for all the indignities and injustices of a foreign occupation. When one's birthright is at stake, a lapse in civility becomes a rather small sacrifice.

That's the message of Terry Robbins, Dade County's best known scourge of bilingualism, who speaks of preserving the "legacy" of English for her grandchildren. Beginning as an organizer for U.S. English, Robbins later left the national group to found Dade Americans United to Protect the English Language. "Hispanics are free to speak Spanish in public," she grants.

Only don't expect Americans to like it or keep quiet about it. . . . Freedom of speech also extends to the public, which is free to object to the possibility that a foreign language, Spanish, may become the primary language of Dade County. . . . I say it's precisely because of the large numbers of Hispanics who have come here, that we ought to remind them and better still educate them to the fact that the United States is not a mongrel nation. We have a common language, it's English, and we're damn proud of it.

Robbins's ire has also been directed at the U.S. Postal Service (for delivering junk mail in Spanish), Little League baseball (for flying the Cuban flag at games), and the City of Miami (for naming streets after Cuban heroes). "We've been José Martí'd to death," she complains.

How does one measure the impact of hateful rhetoric? In threats received? Hostile glances noted? Friendships never consummated? One certain effect has been bureaucratic action against Spanish, notably in the workplace. In the most celebrated case, local Burger King franchises bowed to demands by some customers for an English-only fast-food experience. A management decree warned workers that "communications . . . in the Spanish language will not be tolerated." The responsible executive (a Cuban, as it happened) explained cryptically that employees had been "speaking Spanish and not getting the orders right. We're talking about no pickles, heavy onions, whatever." Higher-ups quickly disowned the policy after Hispanics threatened to "have it their way" at other restaurants. It was not long before Burger King joined McDonald's in posting Spanish menus at selected locations, setting off a new protest campaign by Terry Robbins.

In a contradiction typical of Miami's language wars, employers were resorting to English-only mandates at the same time they were recognizing the value of bilingual skills. By the late 1970s monolingualism was becoming a noticeable handicap in the job market. Want ads began to specify fluency in Spanish as a requirement for lowly positions that involved dealing with the public. Suddenly Anglos found themselves less desirable candidates for jobs as sales clerks, receptionists, waitresses, and gas pump attendants (many stations were now Cuban-owned). Non-Hispanic youths had a harder time finding menial summer work.

By far the most acute effects, however, were felt in the black community, already in worse straits than in most American cities. In the early 1960s, just as the barriers of segregation began to fall, Miami's blacks had found themselves competing with white, overqualified Cuban exiles. Soon they were displaced from service jobs they had long taken for granted. As the local Urban League president explained, "Hotel managers on the Beach didn't want a brother from Liberty City as a doorman when they could get a former attorney from Havana who spoke Spanish, English, and French." When Cubans moved up, their places were usually taken by new refugees. As a group blacks remained near the bottom of the ladder, receiving little of the job training, educational assistance, or minority set-aside contracts lavished on the Cubans. During the 1970s the Small Business Administration loaned $7.86 to Hispanics for every $1 it loaned to blacks in Miami, although the population ratio was only two to one.

Now the one edge blacks had previously enjoyed—language—had turned into a liability. Immigrants were much more likely to have the bilingual skills that many bosses were demanding. Even Haitian refugees, the most wretched of the recent arrivals, tended to know Spanish and occasionally found positions with Cuban employers, whereas African-Americans rarely did. Cubans naturally preferred to hire fellow Spanish speakers with whom they felt comfortable, whether or not language skills were relevant to the job. This pattern prevailed both in small enterprises and in factories with hundreds of workers, which might employ Afro-Cubans, Haitians, and Dominicans, but few if any American-born blacks. "Internally, everything is done in Spanish," explains Ghislain Gouraige, a Haitian banker. "If you call on a Latin company as an English speaker, the reception you get is completely different. Even though the son of the owner has the capacity to speak English to the banker and the lawyer and the accountant, the decision-making process is completely in Spanish. And that reinforces the continued usage of the language."

Gouraige is bullish on bilingualism. "A lot of business that's done in this town is done because people here speak Spanish," he says. "It attracts entrepreneurs and capital that otherwise wouldn't come here." At the same time, he acknowledges the problems that Spanish poses for black Miamians:

In New York City, blacks and Puerto Ricans tend to live close to each other. With the rap music and the Latin disco, you'll see a lot of intermingling and interaction. So among black Americans, especially the so-called underclass, there's a greater receptivity to Spanish [than among whites]. They don't at all feel threatened by it. But here it's a completely different story. Blacks don't speak a lot of Spanish, don't make an effort to. They feel left out, and they tend to blame the Cubans for that. And the Cubans, frankly, have tended to say, "That's not our problem." Which has caused a lot of tension. Blacks who grow up here don't feel the city is theirs anymore. A lot of them leave Miami and don't come back.

Language was among the numerous frustrations that led to Miami's three-day race riot in May 1980, which claimed eighteen lives and an estimated $200 million in property damage. After investigating the riot's causes, the U.S. Commission on Civil Rights concluded that "bilingual requirements sometimes mask intentional racial discrimination." No doubt. But precisely how much discrimination remains an open question. In a city where many residents are basically monolingual in either English or Spanish, bilingualism is a valuable job skill, if not always an essential one—which makes it hard to draw the line between a bona fide requirement and an unreasonable barrier. Should a downtown bank insist that all tellers be proficient in Spanish, or is it sufficient to have only a few on hand? Should monolingual English speakers be hired as security guards, considering the chance of encountering monolingual Spanish or Creole speakers in a life-or-death situation? If managers can conduct meetings in English only, why not in Spanish only, if they believe that would enhance productivity? Where does business necessity end and employer prejudice begin? And how about workers' rights, including the right to extra compensation for bilingual skills?

Few cases are as clear as that of two African-American women whose applications for $3.40-an-hour cleaning jobs were denied in 1984 because they spoke no Spanish. Though language had no obvious relevance to pushing a vacuum cleaner through a deserted office building, the contractor had chosen to run its crews in Spanish for reasons unexplained (to promote efficiency? to keep immigrant workers isolated? to favor Hispanics?). After some resistance the company capitulated to civil rights advocates and agreed to hire the women and reimburse them for lost wages. Nevertheless, Beverly Barnes and Shirley Drayton became household names in Dade County and soon attracted national attention. "This is our home," Barnes told the *Miami Herald*. "They came over here. I don't see why I have to go through changes." As a single mother living with two teenagers in a one-bedroom apartment, she needed a second job to save up for her own home. When did she have the time to learn Spanish? And why should she?

Disgruntled Anglos were eager to portray the incident as representative, a tip-of-the-iceberg glimpse of discrimination against English speakers. In fact, the complaint was the first of its kind ever received by Dade County's Fair Housing and Employment Board. Yet it confirmed a widespread perception of inequity. The plight of blacks, little noticed before the riot, served to strengthen white Anglos' faith in their own indignation. Ethnic finger-pointing acquired a liberal veneer. Let's take care of our own deserving poor, the argument ran, before opening the door to all of Latin America. Things had gone too far when native-born Miamians had to learn a foreign language to survive in their own community. With relish, many Anglos took up blacks' case against Hispanics, blaming Cuban success, Cuban numbers, and Cuban insensitivity for the breakdown in race relations. For their part, Cubans tended to disclaim any responsibility for the American phenomenon of white supremacy. And angry blacks had no intention of letting anyone off the hook. Nineteen eighty was the year that everyone's patience ran out.

As Liberty City smoldered, boatloads of Marielitos were arriving daily in Key West. Most of the refugees made their way to Miami, along with thousands of Haitians fleeing starvation and Tontons Macoutes. That year the local unemployment rate more than doubled, to 13 percent, as a housing shortage drove up living costs. Elderly residents became prey to non-English-speaking muggers in Miami Beach (while street crime in Cuba apparently declined). With drug-related shootouts spilling into quiet neighborhoods, Dade County dealers sold more than forty thousand handguns in a twelve-month period. Miamians who could afford to do so retreated behind iron gates and high-tech security systems. In one survey 75 percent of non-Hispanic whites said that "if it were practical," they would move elsewhere. "We are a community in trauma,"

announced County Manager Merrett Stierheim. With public officials seemingly impotent to cope, a populist revolt appeared imminent; only a focus was needed.

Communication across ethnic lines was limited. Sometimes it
seemed the only open channel was talk radio, medium of the opinionated, the embittered, and the wacko. Both English- and Spanish-
language stations exploited these markets with rosters of celebrity
talkmeisters, all competing for the title of most controversial. Naturally, few Anglos were able to sample exile-oriented stations like
WQBA, *La Cubanísima* ("the most Cuban"), but the English-
language talk shows drew a huge, mixed audience hungry for combat.

One of the top-rated hosts was WNWS's Neil Rogers, known for
his open-season-on-Cubans format. Five nights a week, throughout
the spring of 1980, Rogers had made raw meat of the Marielitos;
in July he turned to bilingualism. Emmy Shafer, a Russian-born immigrant who claimed to be fluent in six languages, phoned in to
complain about Spanish. Her diatribe, repeated often in the coming
months, went something like this: "I don't feel like I'm in America
anymore. I don't feel like I'm in Miami anymore. No matter where
you go, you hear Spanish. This is not Cuba, and we're not going to
put up with it anymore. I want to live in America again." The
switchboard went crazy. When excited listeners asked what they
could do, Rogers put them in touch with Shafer and a movement
was born.

Equally important, a target was found for Anglo frustrations. Shafer
called special attention to Dade County's budget for bilingual services, recently swelled by the Mariel influx. Besides translating public meetings and documents, the Division of Latin Affairs helped
Spanish speakers apply for property tax abatements and register to
vote, coordinated the celebration of Hispanic Heritage Week, supplied newspaper columns and programs for Spanish T.V., and even
produced a series of radio spots, entitled *Conservemos Nuestro
Idioma*, which aimed to "improve the quality and variety of the
Spanish language as used nowadays." When costs for tourist promotion and federally supported programs were added in, the bill
for Spanish-language government came to more than $1.3 million a
year.

For Shafer this was "Cuban-pandering" at its worst, a way of excusing Spanish speakers from their duty to learn English. Arriving here in the 1950s after surviving a Nazi concentration camp, she had enjoyed no such exemption, nor had she sought one. Why should Dade County give in to Cubans demanding special privileges? This appeal had a special resonance in Miami, with its large population of Euro-ethnics, notably Jews. While some still spoke Yiddish or other Old World tongues, this had always been a private matter. Never in memory had ethnic languages received state support. It seemed unfair to change the rules now.

A former waitress and model with little political experience, Shafer was an unlikely leader. No matter. A grass-roots movement had been poised, merely awaiting direction. With donated office space and a cadre of volunteers, she founded Citizens of Dade United. Over the next month the group gathered more than 44,000 signatures to put the Antibilingual Ordinance before county voters. Neil Rogers helped at the outset by broadcasting the group's telephone number, generating hundreds of calls a day. Soon petitioners were sweeping the haunts of middle-class Anglos—condominiums, swimming pools, beauty salons, and shopping centers. Shafer kept her message simple, with newspaper ads urging, "STOP wasting our TAX DOLLARS to Promote Bi-Lingualism: ONE LANGUAGE, ONE COMMUNITY."

For the record, Citizens of Dade United insisted it had nothing against Hispanics. Yet its leaders provided ample evidence to the contrary in press interviews and campaign rallies, singling out Cubans as loud, obnoxious, clannish, and violent. Midway through the campaign, Shafer announced she was sleeping with a .38 by her pillow after receiving numerous threats, including one from Omega 7, an anti-Castro terrorist cell based in Union City, New Jersey. "She had *santería* chickens in her bird-bath," adds Enos Schera, a confidant. (In recent years he has refused to reveal Shafer's whereabouts, hinting at security concerns.) While such incidents cannot be independently confirmed, there is no question about the verbal volleys exchanged throughout the fall. Hispanic leaders repeatedly hurled the epithets "bigot" and "racist," and Shafer's forces responded in kind: "If you want to speak Spanish, go back to Cuba."

While rational debate was not entirely lacking, its impact was dubious. Both the *Herald* and the *Miami News* dissected the proposed ordinance in their news columns and condemned it editorially at every opportunity: "divisive . . . carelessly worded . . . a threat to Dade stability." A coalition organized by the Greater Miami Chamber of Commerce spent $50,000—five times as much as proponents—to warn that the measure would exacerbate an already strained situation. Yet the initiative passed easily, with 59 percent of the vote. One reason was that many Latinos were not yet citizens. Though they represented 41 percent of Dade County's population, they accounted for only 17 percent of its registered voters. In exit polls, five out of six said they opposed the antibilingualism measure, which most perceived as a deliberate affront to Spanish speakers. But their votes were insufficient to offset the 71 percent support among non-Hispanic whites. Blacks, perhaps more sensitive to antidiscrimination arguments raised during the campaign, put aside their economic rivalry with Hispanics and rejected the initiative by 56 to 44 percent.

As opponents had predicted, passage of the ordinance had the effect of spreading rather than settling language conflicts. Battles flared throughout the 1980s over what the voters had intended, what the law really said, and whether it was a mistake. From the beginning the ordinance produced migraines for county officials. In drafting the initiative, Citizens of Dade United had taken a blunderbuss approach. Government would operate "in the English language only," bilingual meetings and publications would be forbidden, and no public funds would be spent to "utilize" other languages or to "promote" other cultures. Period. Shafer and her allies apparently had given no thought to the consequences for health care, elderly services, disaster relief, or even tourism. This meant that in many cases officials were now forced to choose between violating the new law and neglecting the general welfare. Predictably, they resorted to a bit of both.

Attempting to steer a middle course (thus pleasing no one), the county attorney's office issued a series of legal opinions interpreting the Antibilingual Ordinance. It concluded, for example, that Metro-Dade government was forbidden to

- distribute bilingual materials on fire prevention, even if printed with outside funding;
- provide Spanish-language recordings for the popular Tel-Consumer hotline;
- subsidize ethnic celebrations such as the Kwanza and Goombay festivals, Mariel Festival of the Arts, and Israeli Jubilee;

- publish Metrorail schedules and mark bus stops in languages other than English;

- sponsor Spanish classes for county judges (although state-funded classes were deemed permissible).

On the other hand, county libraries could continue to purchase Spanish-language books and the police department could employ bilingual 911 operators. (Both exceptions drew fire from English Only leaders.) Because the Dade County school system is a separate governmental entity, its bilingual education programs were not directly affected by the ordinance. Nor was there any effect on functions mandated by federal or state law, such as bilingual voting and court interpreters.

Yet applying the ordinance was neither simple nor expeditious. For county agencies there were countless situations in which public safety, convenience, courtesy, equity, or common sense dictated the use of languages other than English. Except that—who knew?—it might now be illegal. Subject to interpretation and reinterpretation, the law may have cost Dade County more in legal consultations and managerial time than it saved in reduced services for non-English speakers. In terms of community relations, the price was much higher. The ordinance led to such gratuitous insults as the suspension of civil marriage ceremonies in Spanish and Creole (until the county attorney determined they were unlikely to promote a foreign culture). Then there was the matter of *los animales* at the Dade Metro-zoo. In 1982, when an Anglo couple offered to donate $3,000 to post Spanish signs at the county-run facility, Emmy Shafer and her allies protested this attempt to circumvent the law. Zoo officials even received complaints about the display of Latin species names—wasn't that an illegal use of public funds? After three years of bickering, the Spanish signs finally went up, though objections continued.

On the matter of public health and emergency services—always a sensitive issue for English Only proponents—the original ordinance was uncompromising. Among the more celebrated effects, doctors at the county's Jackson Memorial Hospital were prevented from giving patients a prenatal care pamphlet in Creole, and "Danger—Third Rail" signs, warning transit riders about a 700-volt electrical hazard, had to be posted in English only.[1] At times antibilingual leaders denied they had intended such restrictions. Yet for years they resisted efforts by Jorge Valdés, the lone Hispanic on the county commission, to authorize humane exceptions to the law's coverage.

For Enos Schera it was a matter of principle: "How do you defend taking county tax dollars and dispersing them for Spanish speakers, not caring about the emergency services, the rights, of 160 other ethnic classes?" (Schera has calculated this figure based on his communications with ham radio operators in 160 countries.) He reasons that "the Constitution and the Civil Rights Act say all people must be treated equal. Now how equal is it going to be to provide Spanish for Spanish speakers and tell the rest, 'Go fend for yourself; we do not care for your emergencies in German; we do not care about services in Polish'? If you're going to give it to one, you've got to provide it to all. Of course, it wouldn't work. You cannot have the Tower of Babel in county, state, or federal government. So we're back to one language."

Emmy Shafer, a bit more adept in the political arts, came to recognize that risks to public health and safety made the ordinance vulnerable to repeal. By 1984, she saw it was time to strike a compromise with Valdés. The resulting amendments, as approved by the county commission, created loopholes for hospitals, elderly and handicapped programs, "emergency services relating to police, fire, ambulance, medical, rescue and hurricane preparedness," and tourist promotion. This took the pressure off, appeasing practical concerns without altering the law's political symbolism. Yet instead of dissipating, as most hysterias do, antibilingualism continued to gather steam.

Three years later, when Valdés again called for repeal of the ordinance and the commission tentatively agreed to let the voters decide, English Only supporters exploded. Neil Rogers orchestrated their outrage into a symphony of abuse. He predicted "a verbal bloodbath or even a real bloodbath" if the vote were allowed to proceed. After Rogers broadcast the commissioners' phone numbers over the airwaves, the county switchboard was jammed for three days. Among the 1,800 calls that got through were a bomb scare and death threats aimed at Jorge Valdés. Support for the referendum vanished, not only on the Metro-Dade commission, but even among SALAD and other Cuban organizations, who hoped that canceling the vote would prevent further divisiveness. With his allies deserting him, Valdés reluctantly ended the repeal campaign. But this did little to slow the English Only forces, already planning for their next battle.

The 1984 compromise inserted a new clause in the Antibilingual Ordinance: "English is hereby declared to be the official language of Dade County." This marked a significant change in emphasis. English Only was to assume a more respectable guise—Official English—and a more sophisticated appeal. The following year Senator Hayakawa's organization launched the Florida English Campaign, a statewide ballot initiative. Its approach was positive: "Traditionally, the U.S. has been able to forge unity from diversity primarily because the English language provided a common meeting ground. This amendment affords us an opportunity to reaffirm our national unity, and Florida's intrinsic adherence to it." Forget the genius of the Founders, the spirit of the pioneers, the principles of representative democracy. Above all, it was English that had made the American system possible. Our common language was "no longer *a* bond, but *the* bond between all of us." Safeguarding "the primacy of English" thus became a patriotic obligation, the moral equivalent of defending the flag.

These arguments could hardly have withstood the assault of a high-school civics class. How seriously Floridians took them is impossible to know. But clearly, there was a will to believe among those who needed to put a benign face on the politics of resentment. Raw antibilingualism gave way to a "pro-English" orientation—"I ♥ English" read the bumper stickers—which focused less on Cubans' misbehavior and more on Anglos' altruistic intentions. Bilingual services sent an erroneous message, the campaign argued: "It is misleading to imply to language minorities living in the United States that they can take full part in American life without learning English." An Official English amendment would correct this misunderstanding.

Yet the difference between Official English and English Only was essentially cosmetic. Inherent in the idea of legalizing a single language for public use was the restriction, to a greater or lesser extent, of other languages. This was how the message about English would be delivered. Non-English speakers would face "inconveniences" when dealing with government (in the parlance of Florida English), and these would create "incentives" to anglicize. However one tried to dress this up, it was a program of exclusion and coercion.

To lead the Florida campaign through its final phase, in 1988 U.S. English recruited Dr. Mark LaPorta, a young internist from Miami Beach. With his irrepressible good humor and civility in public debates, LaPorta personified the new look of Official English. "Mr. Moderate," opponents called him. He could hardly be called anti-Spanish, having learned the language to better serve his patients. Nor was he part of Dade County's antibilingual contingent (whom he came to regard as "the rednecks on the English Only side"). Rather than Cuban-baiting, LaPorta stressed good-government themes, notably the need for a "linguistic convention" for public business. He had learned about U.S. English through a mailing that warned of plans by the Federal Aviation Administration to license non-English-speaking pilots. This was typical fundraising hype—the regulation applied to recreational fliers who never communicate with air-traffic controllers. Yet for LaPorta, the prospect of Babel in South Florida's crowded skies seemed to epitomize government's bumbling response to bilingualism. As he explains,

> I just happened to grab onto the association that tied together airplanes, the F.A.A., conventions. It was almost like a hallucinogenic stream of thoughts, free associations. I thought of all the situations I'd seen—metric versus English, Macintosh versus I.B.M.—where things had gone crazy because no convention was ever established. We all agree to use dollars, don't we? Now all [the Florida English Campaign] said is: "You want to build your business in Spanish? That's your private enterprise, and government should stay away from those things. But when it comes time to report back to government, we choose a currency of communication, just as we choose a currency of dollars for paying taxes."

An honest argument constructed from false premises is perhaps the most difficult to refute. LaPorta's reasoning assumes that a common medium of communication is lacking in this country (not true), or at least threatened by bilingualism (improbable). That choosing an official tongue would obviate this problem in the future (speculative) by prompting newcomers to learn English (naïve), without affecting private uses of other languages (unlikely). And finally, that the human consequences of all this would be minimal (myopic).

In fairness, Mark LaPorta is perceptive enough to see that imposing Official English is not without its complications. He concedes the campaign itself has been traumatic but justifies it with a medical metaphor: "I made the analogy—and I never wanted to be disparaging about this—that an infection has been present for a while and it's causing you pain. And we're going to operate. Now, during surgery, you'll have some more pain. But afterwards, when it's done, things will be better. It will be just a bad episode in your overall growth and development." Diagnosis and treatment are, of course, the relevant questions here. Before slicing up the body politic, one should know the answers. Or, to torture the metaphor one last time, Dr. LaPorta must determine whether bilingualism is a cancer, an irritant, or a useful organ, and whether excising it will improve or destroy the patient's health. Surgery is no field for enthusiastic amateurs.

Nevertheless, this ingenuous approach—antibilingualism without ethnic name-calling—proved appealing to the vast majority of Anglo voters. Several factors accounted for the final outcome: an ineffectual response by opponents, a tide of anti-Hispanic sentiment in northern and central Florida, and an overwhelming, knee-jerk support for the amendment from the outset. LaPorta concedes that some of his allies were eager "to get back at the Cubans." Still, he maintains that few voters really "wanted to hurt anybody." He's probably right. Ethnic insensitivity is not the same as ethnic animus. Yet neither did Official English supporters fret about the potential fallout, which would rain down not on themselves, but on their neighbors.

English Plus advocates had no realistic hope of defeating the initiative. In a confidential statewide survey they commissioned three months before the election, respondents favored Official English by five to one (an uncannily accurate forecast of the final outcome). Among numerous voter classifications—age, sex, party, ethnicity— only Latinos deviated from the pattern of overwhelming support. Perhaps the most discouraging news was that 54 percent of Floridians who had an opinion agreed with the statement *We are losing control of our state to foreigners.* The pollster concluded: "This will be an extremely tough race to win. . . . The dynamics powering support for the amendment are deeply rooted and not necessarily subject to rational persuasive efforts."

Starting late, lacking the resources for a media blitz, and receiving tepid support from Miami's Cuban establishment, opponents also squandered what few opportunities they had. Their campaign organization, Speak Up Now (SUN) for Florida, played down arguments about civil rights and ethnic harmony, instead choosing to emphasize pocketbook issues:

> If foreigners do not feel comfortable in Florida, they will take their business elsewhere. The result would be a loss of jobs and millions in revenue. Florida cannot afford to say: "Come to Florida, but only if you speak English." In addition, the [amendment's] English-only emphasis in our schools will contribute to our lack of competitiveness in world markets.

Here was English Plus in its most sanitized, nonthreatening form. The problem was that few voters found it credible. Among all the conceivable dangers posed by Official English, a boycott by non-English-speaking tourists and trading partners was perhaps the most far-fetched.

While the business community was generally sympathetic to English Plus, especially in South Florida, it knew a lost cause when it saw one. Consequently, SUN for Florida raised only a fraction of the $1 million it had hoped to spend on television time. And yet, trying to maintain the fiction that Official English was "not a Hispanic issue," the group failed to mobilize its one identifiable bloc of grass-roots supporters. Jon Weber, the young attorney who directed SUN for Florida, went so far as to discourage high-profile involvement by Latinos, fearing that might offend Anglos. His so-called "Hispanic gag order" created resentment and exacerbated a culture clash inside the English Plus campaign.[2]

Florida's Conference of Catholic Bishops, its popular Republican governor, Bob Martínez, and all its major newspapers opposed the initiative as unnecessary, ignorant, divisive, threatening to minority rights, and likely to bring ridicule on the state. Even the conservative William Bradford Reynolds, U.S. assistant attorney general for civil rights, supported a lawsuit to keep Official English off the ballot, arguing (unsuccessfully) that the campaign's failure to circulate petitions in Spanish had violated the federal Voting Rights Act. But Florida voters paid little heed. On November 8, 1988, Amendment

11 passed with ease in all sixty-seven of the state's counties, including Dade, where it won 61 percent of the vote.

For opponents, the campaign's one high point came on election night, after the proportions of the landslide had become clear. Jon Weber appeared alongside Mark LaPorta at the Florida English victory party, and the two leaders issued a joint statement of conciliation, televised live on several Miami stations. Among other things, they agreed that the Antibilingual Ordinance was now superfluous. LaPorta announced that Florida English would support its repeal. "Over my dead body," shouted Enos Schera. The crowd, mostly Dade County regulars, rushed the podium, knocking aside microphones and T.V. lights. As LaPorta tells it, "I'd been duped. Whether it was a joke or whether [SUN for Florida] deliberately lit the fire under the bigots on our side, I don't know. But I fell for it. The scene was surreal—it was like a war zone. No one touched me, but they came close." And the viewing audience got an eyeful. "These guys are a bunch of neanderthals," Weber said later. For once the losers felt vindicated.

L aPorta's medical metaphor proved misplaced. Official English did nothing to alleviate tensions. If anything, the issue of bilingualism was more confused following the vote. Hispanics did not stop speaking Spanish in public, to the surprise and annoyance of some Anglos. Predicted cutbacks in bilingual services did not materialize, a reflection of Cuban Republicans' influence in the state legislature and the ineptitude of English Only proponents. Meanwhile Latin American tourists and entrepreneurs paid no more attention to the new amendment than they had to the Antibilingual Ordinance.

What did change was the ethnic climate. "I think the main effect that the amendment had was to create more alienation," observes Max Castro from his vantage point as director of Greater Miami United, a community relations organization. "The campaign itself whips up people's resentment about Spanish and Spanish speakers, creates a white heat; it exacerbates what [Anglos] have already been feeling. And for Hispanics, the vote creates a lot of pain, feelings of hurt. I've heard people say, 'I didn't realize how much our neighbors or coworkers disliked us and how much they resented us. Is that what they've been feeling all along?' " There was political fallout as well. "The fact that 84 percent of the voters agreed with

Official English puts [advocates for] migrant children, or foreign-born children, on the defensive. It makes it more difficult to get bilingual education programs discussed and analyzed in a rational way."

The most visible short-term impact was what Castro calls "language vigilantism," as some Anglos took it on themselves to enforce the amendment, telling Hispanics, in effect: "This law is on the books and you are going to speak English now." Two days after the vote, a supermarket cashier in Coral Gables was suspended when he turned to coworkers and asked after a friend, *"¿Dónde está Jorge?"* Later that week a high school administrator in West Palm Beach told students to stop using Spanish on campus. At a Miami department store, customers attempting to place telephone orders in Spanish were denied service. A Dade County mortgage company began refusing checks with amounts written in languages other than English. Yet, in these and countless similar incidents, there was no institutional edict for English Only. All were cases of individual initiative by Anglos who either misunderstood the Official English amendment or felt it gave them license to strike back against Spanish.

Hispanics braced for more trouble. The League of United Latin American Citizens and the American G.I. Forum, two predominantly Chicano organizations, announced plans to monitor the impact of Amendment 11. They took out ads in Spanish-language media to solicit allegations of language discrimination. Their lawyers were ready. But a year later, according to Robert Canino, the LULAC representative in Dade County, not a single complaint had been received. Among Florida employers there was no stampede to impose English Only rules. In fact, following publicity over the supermarket cashier's case, a few rescinded such policies that they had previously imposed. While unofficial rudeness persisted, it was not subject to litigation.

Many Cuban leaders have tried to ignore the issue. Why give English Only activists needless publicity? they reason. By now Hispanics have learned to live with the Antibilingual Ordinance. As a practical matter, its restrictions are minimal, explains Mark Gallegos, because so many Spanish speakers are employed in local government. On the other hand, he believes the law remains "a smoldering coal in the woodwork of this community, and it will certainly flare up again."

Animosity was reignited in the summer of 1989, during a special election to replace the late Congressman Claude Pepper. Emerging from the primary, the two major candidates seemed to offer voters a clear ideological choice. The Dukakis Democrat, Gerald Richman, and the Reagan Republican, Ileana Ros-Lehtinen, disagreed on virtually everything. Yet, as the campaign developed, all issues of substance were overshadowed by a single question: ethnicity. In the end, the choice came down to Jew versus Cuban, Anglo versus Hispanic.

Lee Atwater, chairman of the Republican National Committee, set the tone at the outset when he said it was time for the Eighteenth Congressional District—which encompassed Little Havana as well as Miami Beach, Liberty City, Coral Gables, and other non-Hispanic precincts—to send a Cuban American to Congress. Richman begged to differ: "This isn't an Anglo seat, it isn't a Jewish seat, it isn't a Cuban American seat. It's an American seat." Not an unreasonable response, except that Richman insisted on repeating it in every speech. "American seat" became his campaign slogan, mantra, and theme song, a transparent appeal to anti-Cuban sentiment. Ros-Lehtinen made it her issue as well, blasting "Richman's racist view of America" and refusing to appear with him at campaign forums because "bigotry is not debatable."

Meanwhile U.S. English injected itself into the race on Richman's behalf. Its English Language Political Action Committee sent out thousands of letters warning that "an election emergency is imminent. . . . A single, malicious state senator, Ileana Ros-Lehtinen [has already] blocked implementation" of Amendment 11 in Tallahassee. Think of the damage she could do in Washington![3] Richman, to no one's surprise, turned out to be an Official English supporter (though he professed to tolerate unofficial bilingualism). The previous spring Ros-Lehtinen had helped to kill legislation that would have required English Only documents in state and local government. In a partisan role reversal, Florida Republicans cited threats to civil liberties, while Democrats seemed determined to ignore them.

In the Eighteenth District race, for the first time the language issue worked to Anglos' disadvantage. Preelection polling found that, of those who had made up their minds, twenty-seven of twenty-eight Cubans planned to vote for Ros-Lehtinen and twenty-four of twenty-five Jews for Richman. But the split went further. Miami's Puerto Rican community, which rarely agreed with the Cubans on anything, went overwhelmingly for the Republican, while many white conservatives crossed over to join blacks and liberal Anglos on the Democratic side. A massive Hispanic turnout proved decisive. Ros-Lehtinen won easily, becoming the first Cuban American to serve in the U.S. Congress.[4] Her election suggests that Spanish speakers' political strength, which has always lagged behind their economic and cultural influence in South Florida, is beginning to catch up. One day soon, in place of token representation on the county commission and school board, they will command majorities. No doubt their first act will be to repeal the Antibilingual Ordinance.

Still, the anachronism lives on. English Only remains in force, the legal language of government offices staffed increasingly by Spanish speakers. Unofficial Miami attracts not only immigrants, refugees, tourists, and investors, but also Americans of promise and ambition who happen to be bilingual. Mark Gallegos came from New Mexico because he saw Miami as a multicultural boomtown, with all the "color and excitement and food and controversy and conflict and ideas and motivations that come from an infusion of immigrants, whether they be Hispanic or otherwise." Ghislain Gouraige, a Haitian immigrant whose family settled in upstate New York, says that after he finished Harvard Law School, "Miami was the logical place to set up shop. We have a Little Haiti here, a pretty well-focused Haitian community. And Miami is not just tolerant. It's an international city where Spanish is spoken. That gives you more leeway to feel you can speak your own language—Creole, Portuguese, French."

When Univision, the Spanish-language network, decided to relocate its production and news operations to Miami (from New York and Los Angeles, respectively), there were several considerations. Florida was a right-to-work state. Miami's airline connections to Latin America were unequaled. On the creative side, there was a seemingly bottomless pool of bilingual talent. And there was something else, according to Joaquín Blaya, the Chilean immigrant who heads Univision: "It's nice to live in a place where we're first-class citizens." This is a feeling that many Latinos say they can capture nowhere else in North America.

What all this portends for English remains uncertain. There are those who argue that the old assimilation patterns will hold for Spanish-speaking Miamians, the main differences being Hispanics' proximity to their points of origin and continuing migration by fellow countrymen. (And, as Max Castro notes, "The Polish and the Italians didn't have Univision.") These factors may postpone the shift to English, the argument goes, but are unlikely to prevent it. Already the older generation is expressing alarm about the erosion of Spanish, which is clearly under way. In a 1985 survey of Cuban American students at Miami-Dade Community College, an astounding 86 percent said they preferred to use English when speaking with friends. Javier Bray blames this trend at least in part on the public schools' neglect of Spanish. Contrary to the popular image, he says, Dade County's bilingual programs are "fiercely transitional."

Yet there are others who see something unprecedented happening in South Florida, where a third of Hispanics speak no English and 97 percent speak their native language in the home. There is little indication that Spanish is losing status in the way that other immigrant languages have done. While English seems secure enough, its monolingual monopoly seems unlikely to return. Bilingualism is becoming institutionalized, a new way of living and doing business. And perhaps a new way of identifying as Americans.

This is what Anglos find so upsetting. The threat they perceive is not so much to English as to the images and loyalties that English conveys. In that sense much has already been lost. Lifelong residents—not all, but many—mourn the passing of an idyllic, pre-Cuban Miami when no one worried about Spanish, the language of gardeners and band leaders, and white Anglos never felt excluded. In the words of one old-timer, it was "a city where front doors were left open so its people could enjoy the cool tropical breezes, a city rich in history and pride, a city of pioneers and people who cared." But today, she continued in a letter to the *Miami News,*

> Miami is a city where we destroy our history for parking garages and high-rises. . . . It is a city of cocaine use and drug battles on our streets. It is a city of rudeness, and of trash and tacky signs, of tall, bland buildings which hide our once resplendent view of Biscayne Bay. And yes, it is a city where an unwanted language is forced upon us. It is a city where American citizens cannot obtain jobs cleaning offices at night because they do not speak Spanish. It is a city wherein after twenty-five years many cannot communicate in the language of the

country they chose. It is a city which opened its doors to our Cuban neighbors and received no thank yous; a city which slams the same doors shut on the Haitians. It is a city of the absurd. . . . And it is my city . . . I am not leaving.

Blaming the Cubans for all that has gone wrong recalls a less glorious feature of Miami's past: anti-Semitism. The stereotypes are virtually identical—loud, pushy, arrogant, avaricious, hedonistic, cunning, clannish—except that language, not religion, is the Cubans' salient identifier. And the Jews now find themselves cast in the role of an established group resisting an upstart competitor. The irony is not lost on Osvaldo Soto, who has boyhood memories of visiting Miami Beach in the 1940s, when hotels still posted signs like *Rooms with Views and No Jews* and *Gentiles Only; No Dogs.* "To me it was a big surprise," he says, to learn that many of Dade County's English Only activists are Jews, "because I know how much they have been discriminated against."

Sadly, the experience of being scapegoated provides no immunization against scapegoating others. Tribal politics is by definition unprincipled: self-serving, visceral, intolerant—yet not entirely irrational. Cubans are mistaken to assume that antibilingual fervor reflects little more than racism. Anglos' dispossession is real. Whatever the *Herald* and other civic boosters may say about the progress that Spanish has brought, there is no hiding the complications or the attendant shifts in power and status. For Old Miamians, "that language" is always there to remind them of unwelcome changes. English Only laws can never restore the city they knew. Still, if Anglos can no longer feel undisputed ownership of their community, they can at least make Hispanics feel their rage.

Five

Old Ethnics and New

Both apologists and detractors have characterized English Only as a revolt against Babel, a reflexive response to diversity. Whether one calls it civic-mindedness or xenophobia, this movement is a reaction to the demographic changes of the 1980s. All at once, it seemed, the world was on the move and large portions were bound for the U.S.A. In numbers, this migration could not match that of Europeans at the turn of the century,[1] but it more than compensated in variety. The new immigrants and refugees brought with them more exotic dialects, more hues of complexion, more ways of thinking and acting than Americans had previously encountered. As the newcomers' visibility increased—and they were hard to miss—so did concerns about the costs, not so much financial as social and cultural. Could America absorb this flow of amazing heterogeneity while remaining, well, America?

The fear is hardly without precedent. Over the years this nation of immigrants has been, in equal measure, a nation of nativists: proud of our immigrant roots, yet dubious about the current crop. It is one thing to welcome individuals and families, hardworking, freedom-loving, eager to contribute and adopt "American" ways— Statue of Liberty immigrants, appreciated mainly in retrospect. It is quite another to admit masses of political or economic refugees who exert strains on our schools, welfare agencies, and criminal justice system, and who seem in no hurry to acculturate—Marielitos, boat people, illegals from south of the border. These latter images now predominate.

Many natives are wondering: will the strangers blend in or will they remain non-English-speaking, unskilled, hard to educate, and burdensome to the taxpayers? Most frightening is the prospect of a balkanized society in which the *pluribus* overwhelms the *unum*. Will the United States soon be torn by ethnic strife? Perhaps it is time to impose some limits. Hence the enthusiasm for legislation designed to convey the message *English spoken here*. It is significant that the two state official-language laws enacted before 1978 (by Nebraska in 1920 and Illinois in 1923) date from another era when the nation feared for its unity and the urge to "Americanize the alien" proved irresistible.

Still, this explanation is not entirely satisfying. If English Only is a generic reaction against foreign-ness, why is it so selective about its targets? Before the current waves of immigrants, there were Poles on Chicago's Northwest Side, Italians in Boston's North End, Portuguese in New Bedford, and French Canadians in Lewiston, Maine, keeping their vernaculars alive in churches, public and parochial schools, civic clubs, newspapers, and radio programs. During the so-called ethnic revival of the 1970s, congratulations were in order for anyone able to utter a few words of the mother tongue. Yet there was no antibilingual backlash, no undue concern about these groups' neglect of English. Nor is there today. In Odessa-by-the-Sea—also known as Brighton Beach, Brooklyn—Soviet Jewish immigrants can speak as much Russian as they like without being accosted by self-righteous Anglos. Bilingualism is a problem, it seems, a cause for political agitation, only when it involves Third World immigrants, notably Hispanics and Asians. Euro-ethnics have never come under attack from the modern English Only movement. Indeed, many have joined it.

Meet George Kouloheras, second-generation American and senior member of the Lowell, Massachusetts, school board. Now in his late seventies, he remains fluent in his native Greek and even ventures a bit of Spanish now and then. Yet, alarmed at the expansion of bilingual education, Kouloheras has successfully promoted an initiative to declare English the official language of Lowell. The measure, which won 72 percent voter approval, has no binding legal effect. But it makes a statement, he explains:

Don't come here and dictate to me, "Why should I learn English?" If you're in America, do as the Americans do. If you don't wish to learn English, then go back where you came from. That's an awful thing to say. Who am I to tell anybody, "Go back where you came from"? Because my parents would have to go back to Greece. But we should never be threatened about English. Language is what binds us together—nothing else, absolutely nothing else.

My parents could only speak one language, their ethnic language. So when I went to school, I couldn't speak English. And in months, a very short period of time, I learned. I spoke Greek, I spoke English, I went on to college. So we have been able to do it. I hate to say "we" and "they"—people take offense at that, you know—but there's got to be a way to separate the oranges from the bananas. If there are those who've been able to learn English, everybody should be able to do it.

We are the "old" immigrants, in this case primarily Greeks, Poles, French Canadians, Portuguese, and Irish. *They* are Lowell's recent arrivals: Cambodians, Laotians, Vietnamese, Puerto Ricans, and other Latinos. As a public official, Kouloheras presides over—many would say, inflames—a tense rivalry between the two. Almost from the beginning, ethnic competition has been fierce in Lowell, birthplace of the industrial revolution in the United States. Textile magnates soon learned to exploit divisions among immigrant workers, using each wave of newcomers to undercut prevailing wage levels. More and less established groups have fought constantly over jobs, housing, and political clout. While these struggles continue, the main battle has shifted to the schools. In particular: what accommodations will be made for students who are limited in English, how will equal education be achieved, and at what cost?

These controversies were perhaps inevitable. From a negligible presence in 1980—604 of Lowell's 92,418 residents—Asians expanded to an estimated one-quarter of the population by decade's end,[2] while the Hispanic community doubled, to about 10 percent. Language is an obvious marker of ethnic boundaries. In an immigrant neighborhood known as "the Acre," Spanish and Khmer seem ubiquitous. On the other hand, so does Greek. According to the 1980 Census, 2,930 of the city's residents reported speaking Greek in the home and, of these, two-thirds were American-born. Yet virtually none of Lowell's Greek Americans have come forward to challenge the English Only campaign.

Before exploring this paradox, let us consider the central premise of George Kouloheras and countless others who share his views. Is there something unique about the immigrants of the 1980s? Are they indeed failing—or, worse yet, refusing—to learn English?

In 1911, the federal Dillingham Commission completed a four-year, forty-two-volume study of the "new immigration" of that period. The findings were discouraging. It seemed that Jews, Italians, Greeks, and Slavs had "congregated together in sections apart from native Americans and the older immigrants to such an extent that assimilation has been slow as compared to that of earlier non-English-speaking races." The study noted in particular the new groups' "backwardness" in English acquisition, relative to the Germans and Scandinavians who preceded them, and took this to be a sign of resistance to Americanization. As the historian Oscar Handlin has demonstrated, however, the commission paid little if any attention to its own data in reaching this and similar conclusions. In making comparisons among groups, it ignored such factors as economic status and length of residency in the United States. The Dillingham Report mostly reiterated stereotypes purporting to prove, in its words, the "undesirability" of contemporary immigrants.

Similarly, today's English Only zealots have rarely attempted to muster evidence for their charge that newcomers are resisting English, apart from out-of-context statements by flamboyant Latinos or statistics on the growth of Spanish-language advertising or aspersions about bilingual education as a promoter of "linguistic ghettos." In short, they have offered no factual support for the claim that anglicization is slowing down.

At first glance, this seems like a question that could be easily settled. English-speaking ability is susceptible to objective measurement and comparison; it can be plotted on graphs. But what is at issue here is more complicated. It involves *language attitudes* as well as language behavior. Many Anglo-Americans perceive that immigrants no longer feel a compelling need or obligation to acquire English and that, as a result, many are no longer doing so. Such suspicions are confirmed every time a minority language is heard in public or a new demand is made for bilingual services. No doubt there are ethnic biases at work here, but there are also legitimate questions about trends too obvious to ignore. Over the long term, should we expect a growing percentage of the U.S. population to be non-English-speaking? Or will immigrants and indigenous minorities continue, gradually but inexorably, to adopt English as their usual tongue?

This problem is at the heart of today's dispute over officializing English, and it deserves more scrutiny than it has thus far received. Because of the glacial progress of language shift, immediate experience is an unreliable gauge. A generation from now, Anglo fears of a Hispanic takeover in Miami or a Chinese regime in Monterey Park may seem as misplaced as Henry James's "sense of dispossession" on returning to New York in 1904 to find a "Yiddish world" in which the "immensity of the alien presence" menaced "the consecrated English tradition." As yet, Spanish and Chinese show no signs of going the way of Yiddish. But immigrant cultures have never remained intact for long under the atomizing pressures of American life. Historically, language has been among the most vulnerable ethnic traits. So it would seem rash to premise a multilingual future on a decade's worth of impressions.

This is not to say that subjectivity is irrelevant. How do today's immigrants feel about acquiring English and about retaining their native tongue, for themselves and their children? Have they consciously forsaken the melting pot for the salad bowl? Do their sense of loyalty to the United States and eagerness to adopt its ways differ substantially from those of Euro-ethnics? Unambiguous answers are elusive. A pollster can elicit many different responses, depending on how such questions are posed, and often the responses are enigmatic. English Only forces have made much of surveys in which a majority of U.S. Latinos have identified themselves as "Hispanic first, American second." Surely Teddy Roosevelt, were he alive today, would call this treason. But what does it really denote besides a strong sense of ethnicity? The same surveys have found Spanish-speaking parents virtually unanimous in wanting their children to learn "perfect" English. Social attitudes are best evaluated in the context of real controversies and measurable data. So let us begin with the objective side.

What are the current patterns of minority language use, and do they differ from those of earlier periods? How soon are immigrants speaking English and how regularly? Are there variations by ethnicity, education, income, geography, and so forth? Above all, *what is their rate of anglicization*—that is, how rapidly are they abandoning their native tongues and adopting English as their usual language?

It is unfortunate that the demographic research on these issues remains so primitive. Sweeping historical comparisons are risky because census questions about language have been inconsistent and poorly formulated. In 1910, 1920, and 1940, all Americans were asked what language they had first learned in the home. But in 1960, this question was restricted to the foreign-born; no statistics were gathered for the children and grandchildren of immigrants, whose language choices can only be estimated. In 1970, the mother-tongue question reappeared for all groups, but in ambiguous form: "What language, other than English, was spoken in this person's home when he/she was a child?" Many respondents interpreted this to mean "Did anyone in the home speak another language during your childhood?" The result was an explosive "growth" in the linguistic minority population (45 to 50 percent higher than in surveys that inquired about the "usual language" of the home). In 1980 and 1990, the mother-tongue issue was dropped entirely in favor of a single question about *current* usage: "Does this person speak another language at home?" Again, the phrasing may have artificially inflated the estimate of linguistic minorities. (Think of all the high school students practicing their French.) Worse, without a question about respondents' *native* language, there was no reliable way to chart patterns of language shift. In the blunt appraisal of Calvin Veltman, author of the only comprehensive U.S. study in this field, these "extremely poor questions . . . render the data obtained useless" for analyzing rates of anglicization.

Veltman's own work draws mainly on the 1976 Survey of Income and Education conducted by the National Center for Education Statistics. By all accounts, this is the best designed study of its kind, based on a representative sample of 150,000 American households. Questions were precise and comprehensive, including place of birth, year of immigration, educational history, English proficiency, and language spoken in various contexts. Unlike the 1980 Census, it collected comparative data on respondents' mother tongue and usual language. (The verdict: 13 percent of U.S. residents had linguistic minority backgrounds; 7 percent remained regular speakers of languages other than English.) Too bad there are no plans to repeat this survey for the latest waves of immigrants. Veltman insists that "the data in this study show the world doesn't change rapidly over such a short time frame." Still, the 1976 snapshot was taken just after the upswing in Asian and Hispanic immigration and just before the refugee influx from Southeast Asia and Central America. It would be helpful to have current figures for these groups, who are now accused of failing to assimilate.

A further caution is that most evidence about language behavior comes from "self-reports." When the 1980 Census determined that only 2 percent of U.S. residents (excluding preschool children) spoke English "not well or not at all," this finding was based on judgments by the speakers themselves. Obviously, there is much room for bias in self-assessments. Values like ethnic solidarity or identification with the larger society tend to influence responses about how well or how often one speaks a given language.

All that said, there are still significant conclusions to be drawn from recent research. First, *there is no evidence that linguistic assimilation is slowing down.* To the contrary, the process appears to be speeding up. This phenomenon is best documented in the case of Hispanic immigrants, whose anglicization rate has increased by 4 to 5 percent per decade over the past half century.[3] Moreover, there are broad, generational patterns that corroborate this trend. Immigrants traditionally have learned enough English to get by, while remaining dominant in their native tongue; their children have become bilingual, using the ethnic language less as they grow older; and the grandchildren have been raised largely as monolingual English speakers. But by 1976, according to Veltman, virtually all ethnic groups were reaching or approaching "a two-generation model of anglicization." A substantial shift to English—often accompanied by a substantial loss of the native language—now begins with the children of immigrants.

Second, *there are differences in anglicization rates among immigrant groups.* Of those who arrived during the 1960s, by 1976 Chinese speakers were the least likely to have adopted English as their usual language (26.3 percent),[4] followed by Hispanics (29.1), Greeks (29.7), and Portuguese (29.9). Most likely to anglicize were Scandinavians (99.8), Germans (89.2), Japanese (78.8), Filipinos (71.5), Koreans (69.3), and Arabs (68.7). Falling at points in between were speakers of French (59.2), Italian (53.4), and Polish (47.4). These patterns conform to no simplistic typology of "old" versus "new," or European versus Third World, immigrants. Instead, the crucial variables appear to be social and economic—for example, continued ties to the ethnic homeland, level of educational attainment, and prospects for upward mobility.

Third, *there are significant age and regional variations in language shift*. The younger an immigrant on arrival in the United States, the more likely that he or she will become dominant or even monolingual in English. According to Veltman's analysis, 70 percent of Spanish speakers who settle here before the age of ten become anglicized by adulthood and 10 percent abandon Spanish altogether. Hardly a pattern of resistance to assimilation. Also contrary to stereotype, Hispanic anglicization rates in urban barrios surpass those in rural areas like South Texas. With more and more Spanish-speaking immigrants choosing to settle in cities, this is another factor speeding the acquisition of English.

Fourth, *there is limited institutional support for the maintenance of minority languages*. Adult language use in the home plays the most significant role in passing on mother-tongue skills to the next generation. Yet more and more immigrant parents are inclined to speak English with their children. While ethnic churches, private schools, organizations, and newspapers have traditionally helped to perpetuate immigrant languages, it is doubtful that these domains are growing in importance (most appear to be declining). Certainly, during the 1980s there was a proliferation of Spanish-language media in response to Hispanics' increasing numbers, status, and buying power. Whether and to what extent these trends will counteract the erosion of Spanish remain to be seen. Despite speculation that bilingual education delays linguistic assimilation, so far there is no evidence to support this claim.[5]

Finally, *immigration is the paramount reason for linguistic diversity in the United States*. Veltman reports that, without constant reinforcements from the old country, languages other that English tend to decline rapidly among immigrants after about fifteen years of residence here. This explains why most European tongues are dying out and why Spanish and Chinese are thriving. It also accounts for the anomalies of Miami, Monterey Park, and other cities where the number of non-English speakers is growing, even as English acquisition accelerates among Latinos and Asians. While multilingualism seems certain to persist, it is likely to ebb and flow, more like a tide than a climatic change. So far there is nothing in the forecast—whether or not immigration continues at a rapid pace—to suggest a long-term challenge to the dominance of English.

On this question, however, who pays attention to objective evidence? Not many Americans are even aware of it. This suits the aims of U.S. English, which has barely acknowledged the existence of Veltman's research, while continuing to bemoan "the erosion" of our national language. A sophisticated Washington lobby, it knows that stereotypes pack a more powerful wallop than statistics. Everyone has heard anecdotes about immigrants who have been here five, ten, fifteen years and still haven't learned English—not because they can't, but because they won't. There is no question that such individuals exist today, just as they existed during the Americanization era. Only the latter have been forgotten. Turn-of-the-century immigrants' eagerness to belong is romanticized, their insularity ignored. In 1910, owing to the unskilled nature of most industrial jobs, it was far easier to survive with little or no English than in today's high-tech economy.

Monolinguals also have a tendency to underestimate the difficulty and time involved in acquiring a second language. The conventional wisdom holds that newcomers simply need to be "immersed" in English, a job traditionally performed by the public schools—and quite well, according to melting-pot mythology. No one seems to remember that most of the old immigrants dropped out of school at an early age. One valuable feature of the Dillingham Report was its extensive survey of enrollment and performance data for the 1908–9 school year. According to an analysis by the education historian Joel Perlmann, in New York City only 13 percent of twelve-year-old students whose parents were foreign-born went on to high school (as compared with 32 percent of white children of native parentage). It is hard to count the remaining 87 percent as successfully "melted."

Moreover, European immigrants often sent their children to parochial schools or private after-school programs where the ethnic language was taught. In Lowell some Greeks still do, determined to keep their heritage alive—but not at public expense, stresses George Kouloheras. "It was done by the community; it wasn't done with taxpayers' dollars," he says proudly. For him, this is a crucial issue. "We have six languages in the Lowell public school system." Besides English, bilingual classes are taught in Khmer, Lao, Portuguese, Spanish, and Vietnamese. "I don't mind teaching those languages," he says, "but don't do it with my tax dollars. We have enough problems making them literate in English." There is no Greek bilingual program in the public schools, and parents have not requested one, Kouloheras adds. "I wouldn't allow it in Lowell. I'm not opposed if it's part of our curriculum, like German, like Latin, as a foreign language. But I don't want to spend a penny to perpetuate any *ethnic* language. That's where I draw the line. We have one American culture, and that's what [the schools] should perpetuate from here on. Our own personal culture, we carry that at home."

Such distinctions are lost on newly arrived Asians and Latinos, who simply want an education for their children. Many also want their own language and culture preserved. Not as an alternative to English—for they know their children's future is in this country—but why should social progress mean a loss of cultural identity? Why can't they become Americans without forgetting they are also Laotians or Colombians? These aspirations are essentially the same as those of European immigrants, past and present. What difference does it make whether they are pursued in public rather than private bilingual programs? As a practical matter, for ethnic communities unable to afford their own schools, government funding can mean the difference between equal education and "sink-or-swim" neglect. But as a matter of attitude, how does it imply any refusal to assimilate? After all, parochial schooling has traditionally meant a retreat from the social mainstream; today's newcomers are fighting for admittance. Why has bilingual public education become such a point of contention between new and old ethnics? The immigrant experience in Lowell suggests some answers.

About twenty thousand Greeks arrived here between 1895 and 1922, making Lowell the third largest Greek enclave in the United States. Most settled in the Acre, a downtown slum being vacated by upwardly mobile Irish. Founded in 1821 at the confluence of the Concord and Merrimack rivers, Lowell rose on the site of a "praying town" where John Eliot once ministered to the Pennacook Indians. The city was built by and for the textile industry, featuring an elaborate system of locks and canals to power the mills, and dormitories for the New England "farm girls" who formed the first workforce. But there was no housing for immigrant laborers, who were not part of the original plan. So the Irish erected a shantytown on vacant land near the mill district. By the time the Greeks came on the scene, as historian Peter Blewett describes it, "the Acre was infested with disease, misery, and death. . . . The wooden tenement houses, built close together, showed no design for life: sun and air reached only a few of the rooms. Generations of tubercular people spat on the floors and left a killing bequest to those who followed them."

As new arrivals, the Greeks were last in the pecking order. They took the lowliest mill jobs, earning as little as $3 to $4 a week (children made less) at a time when rents averaged $1.50. Male immigrants greatly outnumbered females, and they slept several to a room, often without sanitary facilities. Garbage was strewn in yards and alleyways. Tuberculosis, virtually unknown in Greece, infected one in four Greek residents of the Acre by 1910. Other groups shunned them as unclean; many of the remaining Irish quit the neighborhood in what today would be called "white flight." A riot ensued, the legendary Battle of the Knives, when Irish youths tried to prevent Greeks from drinking at a public fountain. Interethnic violence is another Lowell tradition.

Yet, at the same time, the Acre provided an indispensable safety net. Its inhabitants were typically rural and unsophisticated, young people without prospects in Greece following the collapse of the currant market in the 1890s. They had heard of Lowell from *patrioti,* fellow countrymen, who wrote glowing letters home. Arriving at Ellis Island without a word of English, many wore tags to mark their final destination. The fortunate ones had relatives or sponsors to meet their trains and to reassure them that, yes, this landscape of brick, snow, soot, and grime was Lowell, city of their dreams. Others would have been helpless without mutual aid societies and less formal (sometimes exploitive) networks for finding a room and a job. Equally important were the diversion and companionship they found in coffeehouses, a Greek institution that took root in the Acre. In their heyday Lowell had more than thirty of these establishments, where men could meet friends from their town or village, talk Greek politics, read Greek newspapers—twenty-two were published in Lowell at various times—and sip strong (though nonalcoholic) brew. On these and other storefronts, the Hellenic alphabet gradually replaced English.

For immigrants in a harsh environment, language offered a co-

coon of warmth and security. Nicholas Karas, in an oral history of Lowell's Greek Americans, records the experience of one teenager arriving around 1910:

> When I stepped into the Appleton [Mill], it seemed like a terrible place. I was from the village, from the mountains, the Grevena of Macedonia. There I had been a *joubano* [shepherd] tending sheep; I had taken care of farm animals like chickens and pigs. Still my fear didn't last very long because there were many boys and girls—well, mostly boys—from Greece in the factory. On the floor, out of one hundred people, eighty or more were Greek; the others were *xeni* [strangers]. There were a lot of *patrioti,* so you didn't feel alone. No matter what else happened to you, you spoke Greek, you heard Greek; you didn't feel as if you had come to a completely strange land. . . . We learned English here and there, but only in Greek could we express our deepest feelings.

He could just as well have been speaking for French Canadians, Poles, Portuguese, Lithuanians, Armenians, or any of the non-English-speaking groups who comprised a majority of Lowell's population. By 1912, only 20 percent of the city's residents were native-born of native parentage. Seldom mixing with other nationalities, either in the mills or outside, the new arrivals felt little pressure to perfect their English. Some planned to return to their homelands and developed no interest in American life. The old country and the ethnic neighborhood defined their frame of reference.

The Greeks were especially insular. Their rates of naturalization and political participation were the lowest of any ethnic minority. In 1910, out of 1,208 Greek males of voting age in Ward 2 (the Acre), only eight were on the register. They further isolated themselves by resisting trade unions and sometimes offering their services as scabs, although in 1912 their cooperation proved decisive in a general strike led by the I.W.W. Greek parents often discouraged their children from socializing with non-Greeks, hoping to shield them from American influences.

But what most set the Greeks apart was their zeal to retain their native tongue. For one thing, it was a link with their past, a treasured symbol of Hellenism. Modern Greeks liked to say their language "gave light to the world." Then there was its significance in the Orthodox ritual. As a Greek American bishop reminded his flock,

"The Greek language is the language of the Gospel, a privilege that only the Greek people have." Finally, it was a reminder of national pride and resistance. During the period of Ottoman rule in Greece (1453–1821), when their native tongue had been suppressed, clerics had taught it secretly to children in cellars and monasteries. So language held a special place in the Greeks' appreciation of their heritage—far more than for most ethnic minorities.

Despite their limited resources, Lowell's Greeks invested heavily in bilingual schools to teach the second and third generations. Churches continued to perform this role, financed by a "bread tax" of one cent for each loaf their members consumed. At the largest of these institutions, the Hellenic-American School, all subjects were taught bilingually, so that students would emerge fluent in both English and Greek. For those attending public schools, Greek "afternoon schools" and Sunday schools were established. Contemporary accounts indicate that, at least during the community's early years, parents were less anxious that children learn English than that they keep up their Greek.

It was the Commonwealth of Massachusetts that exhibited the most concern about English acquisition. Beginning in 1898, the state required cities and towns with over ten thousand residents to offer night-school English instruction at no cost. Lowell set aside two buildings for Greeks and hired Greek teachers to conduct what were essentially bilingual classes for adults. By 1907, more than nine hundred Greek students were enrolled in the city's evening schools. Attendance was voluntary, but gradually the emphasis on anglicization became more coercive. In 1913, the state made it illegal to employ workers below the age of twenty-one who were illiterate in English, unless they could prove attendance at evening schools.[6]

In Brahmin circles there was considerable hand-wringing about resistance to compulsory school laws, especially among the Greeks. "There is great difficulty in applying this rule," wrote Henry Pratt Fairchild, a Yale sociologist and author of *The Melting Pot Mistake,* "for the Greeks are inveterate liars when it comes to matters of age—or anything else that will interfere with their doing what they want to do." Clearly, these foreigners bore watching. The Dillingham Report contained a special section on "the Greek Padrone System" alleging the large-scale exploitation of Greek shoeshine boys by adults who "kept their help in ignorance of the English language." The Massachusetts Commission on Immigration added: "The arrival of from 70,000 to 100,000 newcomers each year, most of whom are unable to speak English and consequently—if neglected or ignored—are subject to the abuses, the misdirection, the prejudices of exploiters and irresponsible agitators—cannot but strain the social fabric to the breaking point." Here was a security risk that justified state action "to eliminate what we look upon as un-American tendencies in the foreign born."

Previously ignored, immigrants were suddenly the center of attention, bombarded by politicians, employers, newspapers, and civic organizations with the message that *to belong, one must learn English*. The Lowell Board of Trade organized an Americanization committee, with representatives drawn from each of the city's ethnic communities. The tenor of the times is evident in a 1919 advertisement by a local bank:

BECOME AN AMERICAN CITIZEN

Two things are essential—To speak, to read, to write the English Language and to have a Bank Account. Then with the American flag flying over your home, YOU ARE SAFE and your children are safe. Then you count. Without these two essentials, you don't count. In Rome do as the Romans do. In America do as Americans do. Save money. Get ahead.

Middlesex Trust Co.

Lowell's Greeks were responsive to these appeals. At the urging of community leaders, many attended English classes and applied for citizenship, having adjusted to the idea of remaining permanently in the United States. Still, a sizable number resisted any retreat from their Greek identity. Conflicts flared between partisans and critics of Americanization, among other things. (Squabbling over Old World politics, Lowell's Greek Orthodox community split into three separate parishes in the 1920s.)

Language was caught up in these currents of shifting loyalties. After centuries of resisting foreign occupation, some regarded any retreat from Greek ways as an act of betrayal. Yet America was not the Ottoman Empire. Here there was no language repression, notwithstanding the heavy-handed tactics of some Americanizers. Immigrants had choices. *The Loyalist,* an influential periodical, counseled them to choose acculturation: "We Greeks must recognize that Americanism is but the offspring of Hellenism." It condemned "the exclusive Greek school," arguing that it showed ingratitude to delay children's acquisition of English. More traditional Hellenists responded in 1923 by founding the Greek American Progressive Association, whose paramount aim was to preserve their language and culture.

While the dispute was not soon resolved, ultimately the odds favored Anglo-conformity. The 1924 immigration law reduced the entry quota from Greece to 307 per year, less than one percent of the prewar level. In 1948, Congress reopened the gates to refugees from the Greek civil war, but few *patrioti* arrived in the intervening years. The net effect was linguistic erosion. Adult immigrants became a dwindling and aging sector of the community. Their children associated increasingly with English speakers; many resented being forced to study a language that seemed at best unconnected with American realities, at worst a source of shame when their parents used it in public. By the 1940s the G.A.P.A. was beginning to hold functions in English. The largest Greek Orthodox church added an English-language section to its Sunday school in 1963.

Anglicization was further hastened by the breakup of the ethnic neighborhood. A large section of the Acre was leveled in 1939 to make way for public housing. As urban renewal continued over the next two decades, many Greek-owned bakeries, coffeehouses, and shoeshine parlors were displaced. Textile jobs had begun to migrate south after World War I; by the 1950s the last of the big mills were closing. Young families moved to other parts of Lowell or left the city altogether. It was mostly older Greeks who chose to stay in the Acre, although new immigrants continued to settle there. Only a handful of Greek businesses, mainly restaurants, remain. But the community is still anchored by Holy Trinity Church, a gold-domed Byzantine edifice, and the Hellenic-American School, where children continue to receive part of their day's instruction in Greek.

Meanwhile the "Massachusetts Miracle" in high-tech industry was transforming Lowell from a city of chronic blue-collar unemployment into a mecca for scientists and engineers. Wang Laboratories, the computer firm, relocated its headquarters to Lowell in 1978. That same year the National Park Service turned abandoned textile mills into a tourist attraction. As more than $500 million in redevelopment funds poured in, downtown buildings were rehabilitated and convention facilities were built. All of which was good news for the city as a whole, but not for the Acre, which suddenly found itself vulnerable to development—a classic case of urban decay on the edge of a boom. Blocks of slums were now coveted for condos. Rents soared, even as landlords allowed triple-decker flats to deteriorate. Longtime residents were forced to look elsewhere for affordable housing.

The Greek exodus also coincided with the arrival of Puerto Ricans and Colombians in the 1970s[7] and Southeast Asians in the 1980s. Nicholas Karas, the Acre's oral historian, describes the period as one of "physical destruction and social breakdown," when houses were boarded up and whites fled. The Greeks tended to associate their new neighbors with rising levels of crime, vandalism, arson, and garbage. Those who remained, for financial or sentimental reasons, were understandably disgruntled. As their neighborhood declined, taxes were rising, city services were strained, lifelong friends were departing, and non-English-speaking strangers were moving in. For "the survivors," as Karas calls them, "so many sights and sounds of the Acre had disappeared—of the Greek family community that they had created." It is not hard to imagine where they placed the blame.

S tarting from the opposite side of the world, decades later and for different reasons, Cambodians have followed a path to Lowell that is remarkably similar to the Greeks'. Forced to leave a chaotic homeland, they arrived largely without English or job skills and often without literacy, drawn by the promise of plentiful (if low-paying) jobs and by an enclave of familiar people, religion, and language. As it did for the Cubans, the U.S. government established a resettlement program with the idea of dispersing Southeast Asians throughout the country. But once again the policy proved futile. Feeling lonely or unwanted in scattered outposts, many refugees began a secondary migration to communities like Lowell. By the mid-1980s it was the second largest Cambodian community in the United States (after Long Beach, California) and was home to smaller concentrations of Laotians and Vietnamese.

There was no compelling reason for Cambodians to choose Lowell. It was true that An Wang, a Chinese American and the city's largest employer, had taken a special interest in their plight, and that a Buddhist temple had opened in nearby Chelmsford. The state of Massachusetts was also accommodating, setting aside state funds to hire interpreters in social service agencies. Yet, as with Greek immigrants in the past, the snowball factor seems to be most significant: Cambodians simply followed Cambodians who happened to settle in Lowell. Ravuth Yin, a young refugee who landed initially in New York City, explains: "I had a lot of friends here telling me about jobs, about the temple, about the strong community, about the stores and the restaurants." He smiles. "I missed my own food." So in 1985 he moved to Lowell. Now he helps others adjust, working as a housing counselor for the Cambodian Mutual Assistance Association, an organization that also provides job training, English classes, liaison with welfare agencies, youth programs, after-school tutoring, and child care. Laotians and Vietnamese operate their own M.A.A.'s.

At first the Asians received the "model minority" treatment, stereotyped as hard workers and fast learners, cooperative and respectful guests who would benefit the city. High-caliber newcomers, people said, unlike some we could mention. Whether implicit or explicit, the comparisons were always unflattering to Latinos, Lowell's *unmodel* minority in the eyes of many whites. Yet the cultural traits that smoothed the refugees' reception often proved a disadvantage. "The Puerto Ricans," sighs one Lao community leader. "It's so easy for them to get up and yell, 'We want this!' For us, we hide our faces and whisper to ourselves, 'We want this.' But give us a couple more years; we're still learning." One result of the model-minority syndrome was Lowell's laxity in addressing, or even acknowledging, the enormity of the Southeast Asians' plight: educational, economic, and psychological.

Few of the Cambodians had escaped the trauma of losing immediate family members during the Pol Pot regime and the turmoil that followed Vietnam's invasion of their country. Ravuth Yin is not atypical. Both his parents were shot by the Khmer Rouge, and a younger brother and sister died by starvation and disease. But unlike most of his contemporaries, he has managed to complete high school and a year of college classes toward a degree in social work. Many refugees missed out on education altogether while languishing for years in camps near the Thai border. When these areas were not being overrun by guerrilla skirmishes, authorities often discouraged schooling. Having no idea which country would accept them, the refugees had limited incentives to study English, or much else. "Anybody who was school-age between '75 and '83 was in big trouble," says Elma Vaidya, who coordinates English-as-a-second-language programs for the Cambodian M.A.A. Barely literate in their own tongue, these students have had an especially hard time with English. As rural people lacking factory experience, many have also had difficulty finding jobs in the computer industry, even before the late 1980s, when the Massachusetts Miracle turned into the Massachusetts Mirage.

Still, most remain determined to learn the language and build a future in the United States. "We Cambodians want to live in this country forever," says Ravuth Yin. "Except the elderly. They don't understand the system here, and they get stuck in the house all day long, just watch T.V., even though they don't understand it, just watch the picture. They don't speak English. How can they go communicate with other people? That's why they want to go back to the old country, because of the language barrier." But adjustment has been a trial for all age groups—dealing with landlords, employers, social workers, and police in a strange new environment. Perhaps most frustrating has been the Southeast Asians' relationship with the public schools.

As recently as 1975, only 4 percent of Lowell's students were racial minorities, according to Peter Kiang, a sociologist at the University of Massachusetts. By 1987, the proportion was 40 percent and growing. Nearly 2,000 of the city's 12,650 schoolchildren were enrolled in bilingual classes, and each week brought the arrival of twenty-five or thirty more students who were limited in English. The schools were understandably overwhelmed. Massachusetts law mandates bilingual education for limited-English-proficient children wherever there are enough students to make it practical. But recruiting teachers certified in Spanish was hard enough. Where was Lowell to find bilingual instructors who were competent in Khmer, Lao, or Vietnamese? On a more basic level, where was it to find the classroom space? With declining enrollments in the 1970s, little thought had been given to the replacement of decrepit school buildings, some more than a hundred years old.

Nevertheless, the major obstacles to change were political. Community sympathy for the refugees began to dissipate as their numbers and needs increased. The Lowell School Committee treated the newcomers as an uninvited burden, a drain on finances and existing programs. Consequently, the schools were slow to assess or respond to children's language difficulties. As if to justify their inaction, administrators often praised the refugees as highly motivated, quick to learn English, and appreciative of their new opportunities. One told the *Lowell Sun:* "The Southeast Asians know they have to make it here and that's it. Whereas [Puerto Ricans] think they have two homes." In fact, there was dissatisfaction among all of Lowell's linguistic minorities about the quality of education. Some refugee students excelled, especially the earlier-arriving Vietnamese, who tended to be the children of professionals or business people. But for every Asian valedictorian, there were scores of Asian underachievers, disoriented in a new culture yet receiving little or no special help. Nearly 70 percent of Laotian students quit Lowell High School in a single year, complaining about the lack of Lao-speaking teachers and guidance counselors and even books in their language. Dropout rates were high among Cambodians as well.

Most upsetting to parents, however, was the segregation of newly arrived Asian and Hispanic students. By the spring of 1987, Lowell was housing many of these children—to say *teaching* would be stretching it—in makeshift "classrooms": janitors' closets, hallways, storage rooms, staff lounges, even bathrooms, as well as recreation areas in the local Boys Club and Y.M.C.A. Pupils were expected to learn while crammed among pool tables and pinball machines. They had little contact with white English-speaking children. In one elementary school, sixty Southeast Asians were taught English in a gymlike room nicknamed "the echo chamber," where instructors blew whistles to control the noise and grew hoarse from shouting to be heard. The dilapidated state of the facilities was obvious to the students; many asked why they could not attend regular schools.

In several of these practices, Lowell was in blatant violation of state and federal civil rights laws. Facing a potential loss of subsidies, not to mention litigation by angry parents, the school superintendent decided it was time to act. He proposed a modest desegregation plan that involved "pairing" two schools and busing white and minority children between them. But the school committee rejected the idea. George Kouloheras led the opposition with an impassioned appeal to protect "the civil liberties of the majority," the white students who he said were "getting kicked around."

A lifelong resident of the Acre and an amateur wrestler in his youth, Kouloheras has cultivated a street-fighter image—the journalistic cliché "no stranger to controversy" is often applied—sometimes extending to physical assaults on his opponents (including two

mayors of Lowell). He is also among the city's most popular politicians. A rakish figure who sports a white handlebar moustache,
he has been returned to office every two years for nearly three decades, usually leading the field on the strength of Euro-ethnic votes.
So when that constituency sought his help in defense of "neighborhood schools," Kouloheras responded. State bureaucrats in Boston
could "take the minorities and do what they want with them," he
proclaimed, but Lowell was not going to bus majority students.
"They're the future of this city." Turning the tables on his critics,
Kouloheras charged that bilingual programs were responsible for
segregation. He called on the committee to endorse pending legislation to repeal the state's bilingual education law and to declare
English the official language of Massachusetts.

White parents cheered from the galleries. Hostility toward the
newcomers was now out in the open: *What gives Southeast Asians
and Hispanics a right to come here and disrupt our children's lives?*

Lowell's minority communities got the message. Their leaders denounced Kouloheras's politics of division. Educational neglect was
bad enough (if nothing new), but brazen discrimination was too
much to bear. The perception that their children were being victimized by bigots jarred parents into action. A statewide Hispanic organization, Parents United for the Education and Development of
Others (PUEDO), and the multiethnic Coalition for a Better Acre
began door-to-door organizing. Multicultural Education, Training,
and Advocacy (META), a public-interest law firm specializing in
bilingual education cases, offered its services. The stage was set for
a confrontation over language.

It came on the evening of May 6, 1987. More than a hundred
parents, primarily Southeast Asians and Latinos, turned out for a
school committee hearing to discuss alternatives for desegregation.
Limited English speakers for the most part, they filed into the Lowell High School auditorium with trepidation. This was not a politically experienced crowd. Except for the Puerto Ricans, few in attendance were U.S. citizens. For some, it was the first taste of how
public business is conducted here. Many brought from their home
countries a well-founded fear of officialdom, or like the Laotians
whispering their demands, they felt internal constraints when it came
to challenging authority. Yet these hesitations were offset by the
sense of crisis about their children's schooling. Determined to be

heard, and determined to hear what transpired, the parents had brought along their own unofficial translators.

The proceedings had just begun when George Kouloheras called them to a halt, objecting that languages other than English were being spoken. "I have been an advocate of education, a champion of education, since 1962," he said, "and all these years I've [conducted meetings] in English. I'm an American." For Kouloheras, this was a point of principle, as he explained later: "I will not compromise the integrity of the school committee meeting. . . . English has united a diverse nation and fostered harmony among its people. Let us not reject the 'melting pot' ideal." Ready to fight for ethnic harmony, he moved that the interpreters be silenced. When the motion failed to carry—committee members were evenly split—Kouloheras walked out of the meeting, forcing its adjournment for lack of a quorum. Angry parents followed him outside and epithets were exchanged. In the next day's newspapers, Kouloheras was quoted as saying, "Those bastards who speak Spanish . . . are the worst of all in this city." He later added that "the Southeast Asians are the true immigrants. But the Hispanics are transients; they're crossing the border back and forth."

Even by Lowell standards, the ethnic references were extreme. Several city officials and the *Lowell Sun* denounced Kouloheras's statements as racist. Offended Latinos, joined by the Cambodian and Laotian M.A.A.'s, picketed city hall. Massachusetts education officials announced that, in the absence of a desegregation plan, Lowell was on the verge of losing $2.4 million in state aid. For weeks the furor continued. Finally, the committee came up with a plan. It authorized the use of portable classrooms to ease overcrowding, coupled with a "controlled choice" arrangement that would involve some busing of students. While this seemed to pacify the state, minority parents continued to question the quality of instruction.

Kouloheras has asserted that Spanish speakers want "a bilingual-bicultural nation" so they can avoid learning English, whereas Asians "want their children mainstreamed. Like some have said to me: 'I don't want my children to learn Khmer in school. I'm not going to go back to Cambodia. This is my home now.' " But when one listens closely to Lowell's Asians and Latinos, there is no evidence of any split on issues of assimilation. At the Cambodian M.A.A., Ravuth Yin explains: "English is the language of this country. We're learning, you know. But we want to keep our own also, to keep our own things from our own country." Alex Huertas, a Puerto Rican parent who heads Lowell's chapter of PUEDO, expresses it this way: "Everybody who comes here knows they have to learn English. But that doesn't mean we have to forget our language and culture."

If anything, the events of May 6 brought the two groups together. Although Puerto Ricans, the more vocal critics, bore the direct assault, Cambodians and Laotians were also troubled by Kouloheras's actions. Why was it necessary to cancel a hearing because parents wanted it translated? What did that have to do with helping newcomers learn English or with ensuring fairness in the schools—or with being "an American"? How did busing and bilingualism connect? For the first time, many Asians began to understand what the Latinos had been talking about. That all the bickering over language was not *about* language, just as the desegregation struggle was not really about "neighborhood schools." That English Only was a coded way of saying Whites Only.

Prominent Cambodians and Laotians joined Puerto Ricans in suing the school committee. The parents sought not only to abolish separate and unequal classrooms, but to revamp Lowell's feeble bilingual programs as well. "There is no true desegregation," argued the plaintiffs' attorney, Camilo Pérez-Bustillo of META, "without comprehensive, affirmative efforts to provide equal educational opportunities." For linguistic minority students that meant "insuring access to effective and appropriate language programming." With this line of reasoning, META has won a number of mandates for bilingual instruction in federal court. Aware of its weak legal position, the school committee ultimately chose to settle the case before trial (with Kouloheras dissenting). The agreement featured reforms in bilingual curriculum, teaching materials, student assessment, and staff training, as well as an innovative "dropout recovery" program designed to entice back students the system had previously shortchanged.

As schools prepared to open in the fall of 1987, opponents of desegregation used a term that conjured up violent images: "forced busing." No one had forgotten Boston in the 1970s, and no parent wanted to see that conflict replayed in Lowell. The reality, however, was that the new desegregation plan affected mainly bilingual students; it required busing for only a handful of nonminority children who were recent arrivals to the system. Kouloheras grabbed headlines anyway by threatening to escort one white first-grader to his neighborhood school and to stage a sit-in, if necessary, until the child was admitted. Though he never went through with the stunt, the George-Wallace-in-reverse role was good publicity for his reelection bid. Staying in character, Kouloheras blamed "extraneous mercenaries" for the school controversy, "interlopers [who] have no genuine concern for our school children or the city of Lowell." In campaign advertisements, he warned that busing would be "a *fiasco,* creating *chaos* in our schools," and that *"BILINGUAL EDUCATION* is presently a self *perpetuating failure costing millions."* Some of his cronies were more blunt: Lowell was being overrun by minorities and whites were being victimized.

One day in mid-September, the bus failed to show up for two Cambodian brothers, Vanthy and Vandy Phorng, aged eight and thirteen, respectively. So they seized the opportunity to skip school and went fishing in the Pawtucket Canal, a murky waterway that bisects the Acre. The boys had a fine morning, catching several fish. But as they started for home, they encountered two white boys yelling slurs about Asians. The brothers tried to avoid a fight, Vanthy said later, but one of the white boys punched Vandy then dragged him down some steps and pushed him into the water. Though placid for much of its length, the canal is punctuated by locks and floodgates that discharge dangerous currents. Just below one of these gatehouses was where Vandy went under. Vanthy ran for help, but by the time his brother could be pulled out, it was too late. The white assailant, an eleven-year-old fifth grader, was charged with murder.

Race-baiting politicians were not directly responsible for the tragedy, yet neither were they innocent in this and numerous lesser incidents. As in Boston a decade earlier, school children in Lowell acted out the fear and loathing of their elders. *Us* versus *them.* Natives versus strangers. Youth violence proliferated along racial and linguistic borders defined by adults.

No one disputed that Lowell's resources were strained as a result of the refugee influx, or that it would cost plenty to honor the settlement with minority parents. Quality education never comes cheap. But the state was picking up more than 90 percent of the bilingual program costs, and the federal government provided additional mil-

lions in the form of refugee-impact aid, including a special appro-
priation to assist sites of secondary migration like Lowell. For its
part, the city raised some municipal fees and cut some services to
defray expenses. These budgetary skirmishes brought added turbu-
lence to local politics, already buffeted by conflicts over housing
and development, just as the high-tech economy began to decline.
Discontented whites found it easy to blame Southeast Asians for the
new austerity. Still, money was hardly the main issue.

What most bothered majority residents was the idea of entitlement: the *right* of newcomers to descend on Lowell, place burdens
on the community, and gain advantages unavailable to earlier immigrants. It seemed so unfair. Most of the refugees were not even
citizens, yet they could sue the school system and win preferential
treatment, forcing the diversion of resources not merely to teach
English, but to preserve their native tongues. Bilingual education
seemed to belittle the struggle of past immigrants who had pros-
pered by dint of individual effort, as well as the sacrifice of identity
that struggle had entailed. Greek and Polish and Franco-Americans
now retained only vestiges of their heritage: the ethnic food, the
church, the fraternal order. Except among older people and recent
immigrants, the language was largely gone, and with it the keys to
cultural memory. The third and fourth generations found themselves acting more and more like generic (that is to say, Anglo-)
Americans. Their ancestors had to earn membership in this club,
but now it seemed that anyone could be admitted free, even without
bothering to learn English. The more Euro-ethnics pondered these
ironies, the more outraged they felt. And the more determined to
put things right.

In the fall of 1989, George Kouloheras drafted an Official English
resolution, gathered the required twenty signatures, and won city
council approval to place it on the ballot. A longtime activist for
U.S. English, he won the national group's endorsement for the initiative, financing it as part of his reelection campaign. "Kouloheras
Strongly Supports English," ran a typical appeal. "The English language is one of the basic fibers which unites our community, our
society, and our nation. Over the past two weeks English has been
under attack and nearly beaten to death by its vociferous opponents
here in Lowell."

Local political figures were split, though a majority leaned in favor. Virtually none of the city's Southeast Asians were eligible to

vote in the school committee and council races, and only a few hundred Latinos were registered. Considering the unpopularity of bilingual education, backing English Only seemed like a cheap way to buy white votes. What harm could it do? some candidates asked, noting that the measure was nonbinding. For others, the vote appeared to be a pointless exercise. With no tangible issue at stake, why stir up needless animosity? The lines were sharply drawn. Again the civil rights–linguistic minority coalition came together, but this time with broad support from civic and religious leaders. The *Lowell Sun* denounced Official English in front-page editorials. More than fifty members of the clergy issued a rebuke to those who would divide "Anglo against Hispanic, English-speaking against non-English-speaking, native born against immigrant, Euro-American against Asian-American."

Opponents dubbed the English Only proposition "the bigot bill," casting it as a referendum on Lowell's feelings toward immigrants. For Charles Gargiulo, cochair of the Coalition for a Better Acre, the question was whether linguistic minorities would continue to be scapegoats for dislocations brought on by redevelopment and a slumping economy. "Whenever the ethnic landscape of a community is totally altered in a short time," he said, "there's a fertile terrain for English Only. Primitive fears get mobilized. People assume that the federal government is giving [refugees] too much, that their taxes are going to go up." Himself a descendant of Italian and French Canadian immigrants, Gargiulo was impatient with those who would revise the past to promote a sentimentalized brand of ethnicity. "Some of my own relatives left school in the fifth grade without learning to read English," he recalled. "If bilingual education works, why throw it out just because your ancestors didn't have it? Child labor also existed for immigrant families in the 1890s. Should we return to those days, or should we progress as a society?"

Mayor Richard Howe criticized the initiative as a diversion from real problems posed by the refugee influx. In an unconstructive way, he said, Official English simply "brought to the surface the latent anger, the resentment, the frustration" about change. Howe joined Congressman Chester Atkins, former U.S. Senator Paul Tsongas (a member of Lowell's Greek community), and Daniel Lam, head of the Massachusetts Office for Refugees and Immigrants, in warning that approval might imperil efforts to secure federal aid. As Lam explained: "Our job will become much more difficult if Lowell approves a referendum that is hostile to immigrants and refugees. Because communities that support English Only laws are telling newcomers loudly and clearly, 'We don't want you here.' "

That, however, was precisely how many whites felt. The measure passed, 14,575 to 5,679. Considering the paucity of linguistic minority voters in Lowell and the wide margins in Official English referendums elsewhere, organizers like Alex Huertas counted this outcome as something of a victory. But others in the community took it hard. Among Cambodians, says Ravuth Yin, "a lot of people feel that this time they eliminate our mother tongue, and in a couple of years maybe we have no more temple, no more culture." He believes English Only has sent a contradictory message about democracy, American-style: "For the Cambodians, the United States is a free country, peaceful, a lovely country. The Constitution of the United States gives more opportunities to the people than to the government. But right now it is not a hopeful country in terms of speaking. We have a lot of people who don't speak any English [who still need] to understand about the system in this country. That's why we want English Plus. It doesn't mean we want to take anything from American people."

Speaking personally, he adds: "I love to be part of this country. But even after I become an American citizen, I still think when people ask me, 'What is your nationality?' I will say right away, 'I am Cambodian.' " He laughs. "Very difficult to change." Meanwhile he worries about his daughter and her cousins, raised by relatives in an English-speaking household. "I try to speak Khmer to them, because I think in another five years they're going to forget their own language," he says. His child, soon to start the first grade, speaks too much English to be assigned to the bilingual program, and as yet, the temple offers no after-school Khmer classes (the idea is seen as too controversial). Ravuth Yin hopes this will change before Cambodian children lose their culture entirely. He explains, "I love to keep my own language because this is where I came from." Again he laughs. "There's no place like home."

This is a feeling that Euro-ethnics understood well, and none better than the Greeks. It explains why they can still tolerate—indeed, enjoy—hearing *patrioti* speak the ancestral tongue, and why some strive to keep the language alive for their children. Even now it is possible to study Greek from kindergarten through college without leaving Lowell. Yet, on an intuitive level, most Greeks sense a divide has been crossed; for them, unlike Latinos and Asians, there is no going home again. Should they attempt, literally, to do so, all but a few would need an interpreter. Their choice has been one of *either/or*—no hyphen allowed—while the new immigrants seem to have struck a better deal. Bilingualism at taxpayers' expense seems yet another case of "minorities" getting a free ride. For resentful white ethnics, English Only offers the hope of exacting a higher price, a way to reaffirm "one nation, indivisible" while sanctifying their own group's sacrifice on the altar of 100 Percent Americanism. The essential issues of language and culture remain the same. It is the country's racial alignment that has changed.

Six

Hispanophobia

Raúl Yzaguirre, president of the National Council of La Raza, minces no words: "U.S. English is to Hispanics as the Ku Klux Klan is to blacks." However harsh that analysis may seem, it is the consensus among Latino leaders, from rightist Cubans to liberal Chicanos to radical Puerto Ricans. English Only has united them like nothing else in recent memory. They perceive it to be a campaign of intolerance, aimed in particular at Spanish and its speakers. To their ears "the legal protection of English" sounds a lot like "equal rights for whites": a demand inspired by the paranoia of the dominant group, a backlash against Hispanic advances in civil rights, education, and political empowerment. In a word, racism.

After one listens to the anti-Hispanic (not to mention anti-Asian) ravings of some English Only proponents, the word seems apt. Yet it remains a blunt instrument—imprecise, confusing, and of course, crushing when it scores a direct hit. U.S. English was concerned enough about the allegation that by 1985 it was holding internal workshops on "Answering the Charge of Racism." On the other hand, the word can have a boomerang effect against those who hurl it too freely. To casual observers of the Official English debate— that is, to most monolingual Americans—the label often appears irresponsible. What does race have to do with language, after all? Is it racist to suggest that immigrants need to learn English to prosper in this country? What's wrong with encouraging them to enter the mainstream rather than remain apart? These are reasonable questions, and, to judge from results at the polls, critics of Official English have been unconvincing in their answers.

Taking further wind from their sails, in 1987 U.S. English hired

Linda Chávez, a former high-ranking official in the Reagan administration, as president of the organization. She was an ideal choice for the job. A seasoned Washington operative, well connected on Capitol Hill and among "movement" conservatives, Chávez was an experienced television performer, attractive and articulate, with a knack for arguing extreme positions without sounding shrill. And naturally, her ethnicity was no handicap in rebutting charges of racism. "Hispanics who learn English will be able to avail themselves of opportunities," she liked to say. "Those who do not will be relegated to second-class citizenship. I don't want to see that happen to my people." Official English implied no animus toward immigrants, she insisted. Measures like Proposition 63 were aimed at correcting misguided policies that hindered newcomers' assimilation into American life. Besides, Chávez told one group of skeptics, 73 percent of California voters can't be racist. Falling into the trap, some members of the audience shot back, "Oh, yes, they can!" (Who's paranoid now?)

Emotional attacks on Official English have done little to win over the undecided and often have had the opposite effect. Debating the issue on the *Donahue* show in 1986, Arnold Torres, a lobbyist for the League of United Latin American Citizens, berated an opponent: "You don't agree with what we are saying because you're a bigot." This type of name-calling aided leaders of U.S. English in portraying themselves as victims of unprincipled, ad hominem attacks. It also reinforced their claim that "professional Hispanics, as distinguished from Hispanic professionals," oppose the English Language Amendment not on its merits, but because it threatens their status as ethnic brokers.

S. I. Hayakawa, the organization's honorary chairman, turned the issue around, suggesting there was something racist about bilingual services: "All of us who are naturalized immigrants are deeply offended when government assumes we don't understand English." As a "minority" himself, the former senator could get away with ethnic generalizations that whites could not. "Why is it," he once asked,

> that no Filipinos, no Koreans object to making English the official language? No Japanese have done so. And certainly not the Vietnamese, who are so damn happy to be here. They're learning English as fast as they can and winning spelling bees

all across the country. But the Hispanics alone have maintained there is a problem. There [has been] considerable movement to make Spanish the second official language. The Hispanic lobby said we're going to teach the kids in Spanish and we'll call that bilingual education.

Anglo-Americans inclined to embrace such stereotypes, but conflicted about their fairness, could now take comfort in hearing them expressed by an Asian immigrant.

Yet few Asians would have designated the late senator as their spokesman. He long ago alienated fellow Japanese Americans by defending the U.S. government's decision to intern them during World War II (a period he spent teaching semantics at the Illinois Institute of Technology). Indeed, he seemed to enjoy himself most when courting controversy. Hayakawa's political career was launched by television images that showed him, as president of San Francisco State University, tearing the wires out of a sound truck operated by antiwar demonstrators. (They had refused to offer him the microphone, he said, thus abridging his freedom of speech.) Years later, when picketed for his English Only stance, the senator said he was "awfully glad" to see the protesters. "Every time they bring out a big enough demonstration against me, I've won out in the long run."

Though the racism charges persisted, U.S. English became increasingly effective in spreading its message. By 1988, all but two of the fifty states had at least considered legislation to declare English their official language, and thirteen had adopted such measures—most of them in response to lobbying by U.S. English. A remarkable feat for an interest group founded only five years earlier. Single-handedly, it had placed a new idea on the national agenda, grown into a $6-million-a-year operation, and recruited more members than Common Cause. It was on its way to adding three more states to the Official English column through initiatives in Florida, Colorado, and Arizona. Then came catastrophe.

A month before election day, the *Arizona Republic* published excerpts of a confidential memorandum by the chairman of U.S. English that seemed to confirm everything the critics had been saying about racism, and more. At last, the smoking gun. Here was a document that dropped the pretense of defending "our common language" and explained the "threat" in candid, demographic terms. Unless something was done, it warned, the United States would face a Hispanic takeover through immigration and high birthrates:

> *Gobernar es poblar* translates "to govern is to populate." In this society where the majority rules, does this hold? Will the present majority peaceably hand over its political power to a group that is simply more fertile? . . . Can *homo contraceptivus* compete with *homo progenitiva* [sic] if borders aren't controlled? Or is advice to limit one's family simply advice to move over and let someone else with greater reproductive powers occupy the space? . . . Perhaps this is the first instance in which those with their pants up are going to get caught by those with their pants down! . . .
>
> How will we make the transition from a dominant non-Hispanic society with a Spanish influence to a dominant Spanish society with a non-Hispanic influence? . . . As Whites see their power and control over their lives declining, will they simply go quietly into the night? Or will there be an explosion? . . . We're building in a deadly disunity.

The memo was a frank revival of the "race suicide" theory: American institutions were imperiled by a new wave of fast-breeding immigrants. Its author was Dr. John Tanton, an ophthalmologist from Petoskey, Michigan, and a "cofounder" of U.S. English, along with S. I. Hayakawa. In reality, it was Tanton who had approached the senator with the idea, the organizational acumen, and the big donor contacts. Hayakawa agreed to serve in a ceremonial capacity, signing direct-mail appeals and op-ed articles and making occasional public appearances. As chairman, Tanton held the reins of U.S. English from the beginning. He handpicked the staff, presided over the board, and set policy directions, while keeping a low profile that enabled him to continue his medical practice part-time and to focus on big-picture questions that preoccupied him. Of the latter, the most pressing was what he termed "the Latin onslaught." Not surprisingly, Tanton was also an advocate of tighter immigration restrictions. In 1979, believing that the volume of newcomers had overloaded the nation's assimilative mechanism, he founded the Federation for American Immigration Reform (FAIR), a lobbying group similar to U.S. English. He served as its chairman until 1987.

Yet Tanton was hardly the right-wing fanatic that many critics assumed him to be. His roots as a citizen-activist were in two movements long associated with liberalism: ecology and population control. Tanton has said that growing up on a Michigan farm made him "a congenital conservationist." Beginning in the 1960s, he became active in the Sierra Club, the National Audubon Society, and like-minded groups. Environmentalism led in turn to the problem of too many humans. After starting a Planned Parenthood chapter in northern Michigan, Tanton joined Zero Population Growth, rising to become its national president in the mid-1970s. By now, however, the "population bomb" scare had subsided. Americans were having, on average, fewer than 2.1 children per couple—what demographers call "replacement level fertility" for industrialized nations. In other words, the U.S. population would start gradually to decline were it not for an extraneous factor: immigration. It was to this threat that Tanton now turned. "More and more countries, most of them poor and less developed, are reaching the point of excessive population, resource depletion, and economic stagnation," he wrote in 1975. "Their 'huddled masses' cast longing eyes on the apparent riches of the industrial west. The developed countries lie directly in the path of a great storm from the Third World."

While sympathetic to these concerns, neither the Sierra Club nor Zero Population Growth wanted to make a crusade of immigration restriction. The issue simply had too many racial overtones. As one former Z.P.G. staffer explained, Tanton and his allies "talk in very legitimate terms, about protecting our borders and saving the nation's resources and so on. But the trouble is, after you've heard them, you want to go home and take a shower."

Breaking with his squeamish colleagues, Tanton went off to start FAIR, determined, as he later recalled, to defy "the taboo that in 1979 proscribed discussion of the immigration issue." In fact, this was a time of growing interest in the subject. President Jimmy Carter responded by appointing a commission to study U.S. immigration policy and recommend changes (which it did in 1981). What Tanton really meant was that a philosophical departure from the asylum principle—only recently revived by the 1965 immigration law—coupled with cries of alarm about Third World invaders and calls for strict quotas, was bound to be politically suspect. This created special problems for a lobby like FAIR, observed the historian Otis Graham, one of its original board members. During the Anglo-

Saxonist era, he noted, "certain intellectuals much concerned with racial purity" had given nativism a bad name. "Though the country has moved far beyond the racial attitudes of fifty, even twenty years ago, there seems still to linger the assumption that restrictionist ideas must somehow derive from the reactionary side of the national character." As a corrective, Graham argued that FAIR must reposition its agenda: "The restrictionist case can and must be articulated from centrist, and even liberal or radical, perspectives."

Accordingly, the organization settled on a strategy of emphasizing the economic and political impact of immigration on average Americans, while shying away from the more sensitive issues of assimilation and pluralism—a populist appeal that left ethnic resentments implicit. In its fundraising letters FAIR did not hesitate to target Hispanic newcomers, undocumented Mexicans in particular, as a menace to the general welfare. Yet it rarely mentioned the impact of the Spanish language or raised the specter of cultural separatism. When Tanton tried to steer the group in that direction, its board of directors resisted. So once again he was forced to create a new vehicle.

U.S. English took the opposite tack, focusing on language while avoiding immigration. Privately, Tanton believed the two issues were "inextricably intertwined," but as a tactical matter they had to be kept separate. To charge linguistic minorities with refusing to assimilate and simultaneously to propose limiting their numbers smacked of ethnic intolerance, a return to the old nativism. It would reveal an impolitic analysis—shared by several (though not all) leaders of FAIR and U.S. English—that the problem was not merely the *quantity* of new immigrants, but the *quality:* too many Hispanics.

The two organizations also shared a suite of offices, a multimillionaire benefactor, a general counsel, a political-action-committee treasurer, a direct-mail wizard, a writer-publicist, and of course, John Tanton as C.E.O. Gerda Bikales, executive director of U.S. English for its first four years, was previously an employee of FAIR. There was constant fraternization, even intermarriage, between the two staffs. And yet, both organizations went to great lengths to conceal these connections.[1] Opponents of Official English naturally did what they could to expose them, but to limited effect. While journalists profiled the many faces of Dr. Tanton (small-town visionary and beekeeper extraordinaire) and began to trace his expanding network of tax-exempt "public interest" groups, few people paid much attention. Not until his memo surfaced did the full extent of his agenda become visible.

Tanton had written the paper for a private study group drawn principally from U.S. English, FAIR, and allied organizations. He dubbed it WITAN, after the Old English *witenagemot,* or council of wise men to advise the king. Tanton later explained: "It was a whimsical name that we chose for a group of people who meet a couple of times a year to talk about the general problems of language and assimilation and population, to gather wool about what the future may hold. Sort of a think-tank." Sort of a repressed symbol of Anglo-Saxon pride, he might have added. A name that conveys images of blond-haired warriors meeting under the oak tree "to make laws and choose chieftains." (As a put-on, Dr. Mark LaPorta of the Florida English Campaign once informed his opponents that WITAN meant *"white man* in Druid," prompting an embarrassing press release. But LaPorta was not far off the mark. *WASP Power* would be a good loose translation.) This kind of nostalgia for a more homogeneous society was precisely what Graham, a regular at WITAN conclaves, had warned against. So attendance was strictly by invitation only and the proceedings were never publicized.

As the Proposition 63 campaign raged during the fall of 1986, WITAN gathered in its sanctum to ponder the implications of demographic diversity in California. Tanton's memo was a study guide to readings on the subject, taking what he later termed a "Socratic approach" of posing provocative questions. Most of these involved the impact of Hispanics on American life:

> Will Latin American migrants bring with them the tradition of the *mordida* (bribe), the lack of involvement in public affairs, etc.? . . . Is assimilation a function of the educational and economic level of immigrants? If so, what are the consequences of having so many ill-educated people coming in to low paying jobs? . . . What are the differences in educability between Hispanics (with their 50 percent dropout rate) and Asiatics (with their excellent school records and long tradition of scholarship)? . . .
>
> Will Catholicism brought in from Mexico be in the [Latin] American or the European model? . . . What are the implications . . . for the separation of church and state? The Catholic

church has never been reticent on this point. If they get a majority of voters, will they pitch out this concept? . . .

Is apartheid in Southern California's future? The demographic picture in South Africa now is startlingly similar to what we'll see in California in 2030. . . . A White majority owns the property, has the best jobs and education, has the political power, and speaks one language. A non-White majority has poor education, jobs, and income, owns little property, is on its way to political power, and speaks a different language. . . . Will there be strength in this diversity? Or will this prove a social and political San Andreas fault?

As usual Tanton was a bit hazy on the facts. Political involvement in Latin America varies by country, but as measured by electoral turnout, it is generally higher than in the United States. Mexico has a long history of anticlericalism that has minimized the church's influence in government. Two languages, not one, are spoken by South African whites (English and Afrikaans). These points are minor, but symptomatic of his biases. Although Tanton subsequently argued that the memo had been "mis- and mal-interpreted," he concluded it with the observation: "This is all obviously dangerous territory." Little did he know.

When the story broke on October 9, 1988, Linda Chávez was preparing to leave for her home state of Colorado to stump for Official English. The trip already promised to be difficult. Growing up poor in Denver, of Mexican American and Irish Catholic parentage, Chávez had traveled far and climbed high. She began as a liberal aide on Capitol Hill, then drifted rightward during her seven years in the employ of Albert Shanker, president of the American Federation of Teachers. In 1983, based largely on her writings for neoconservative journals, Ronald Reagan chose Chávez to direct his revamped Commission on Civil Rights. Later he brought her to the White House to direct the Office of Public Liaison. Thanks to appearances on shows like *MacNeil/Lehrer* and *Good Morning America* and a credible run for the U.S. Senate from Maryland, Linda Chávez was, at age forty-one, among the nation's most prominent Hispanics. Back in Denver, however, her success had aroused little of the hometown pride one might expect. Many viewed her as a traitor who had sold her surname to anti-Hispanic causes—first the assault on affirmative action and now the English Only movement. This woman who spoke no Spanish herself presumed to lecture others on the evils of bilingualism and, worse, to represent Official English as beneficial to "her people." The former was contemptible, the latter unforgivable.

Ironically, Chávez now insists that she has never approved of language legislation—including the English Language Amendment—and that she made clear this rather significant reservation before Tanton hired her in the summer of 1987. (At the time she told a journalist, "I would never, ever, agree to join a cause I didn't agree with.") Chávez explains that, despite her distaste for state-supported bilingualism, she saw Official English as a mistake: "It's the conservative, almost the libertarian, in me that says, 'Why are we doing this?' I couldn't stand up and say it was going to solve the problems people thought it was going to solve. Nor was I ever in favor of 'language police' to stop people from speaking another language." English Only initiatives seemed "meaningless" in states like California and Colorado, with growing numbers of assimilated Hispanics like herself, and even in the border state of Arizona, where "second-generation Hispanics are mostly English dominant." Rather than polarizing people with pointless resolutions, Chávez says she would have preferred to emphasize the narrower and more achievable goals of limiting bilingual education and abolishing bilingual ballots—pursuits that U.S. English regarded as less glamorous and therefore less appealing to contributors.

Yet neither side in the transaction had to be seduced. Out of work since her 1986 Senate campaign, Chávez plainly needed the job, which not only paid $75,000 a year but kept her face before the public. For his part, Tanton could not resist the public relations coup of recruiting a Hispanic to represent the organization. Not that Linda Chávez had any warm following among Latinos—quite the contrary—but Anglos who craved reassurance about the high-mindedness of U.S. English had no idea of the animosity that her name aroused.

Arriving in Boulder to debate Colorado's attorney general, Duane Woodard, Chávez was expecting a rough-and-tumble exchange over Official English. But she was stopped short by questions about the Tanton memo. Suddenly racism no longer seemed like such a wild charge. Reporters wanted to know: did she agree that Latinos threatened to corrupt U.S. institutions, merge church and state, and breed white Americans into oblivion? Though aware of WITAN and somewhat troubled by it, Chávez replied that she had neither seen the memo nor heard her boss express the sentiments it contained. And she was "very disturbed" to hear them now. Meanwhile word arrived that Walter Cronkite had resigned from the U.S. English advisory board, an association he termed "embarrassing," and asked that his name be removed from the group's letterhead. "I cannot favor legislation," Cronkite explained, "that could even remotely be interpreted to restrict the civil rights or the educational opportunities of our minority population."

Linda Chávez remembers "feeling I was in an absolutely impossible situation." She regarded the memo as "repugnant and not excusable," blatantly "anti-Catholic and anti-Hispanic." As for Tanton's defense that he was merely raising issues for discussion, she countered, "There are ways in which you can ask questions that beg certain answers that are not dispassionate and disinterested." Returning to Washington, where the U.S. English board was scheduled to meet that weekend, she issued a he-goes-or-I-go ultimatum. In the event, they both chose to resign amid a new series of disclosures.

It had always made Chávez nervous that Tanton closely guarded the details of U.S. English finances and kept many of the pertinent files in Michigan. Until mid-1988, the organization was part of a corporate entity known as U.S. Inc., essentially a pot of tax-deductible contributions that the doctor ladled out to his favorite causes. Unbeknownst to Linda Chávez—a free-market conservative who describes her own position as "aggressively pro–legal immigration"—the beneficiaries included anti-immigration groups like FAIR, Americans for Border Control, and Californians for Population Stabilization. After a year of insisting that U.S. English had no ax to grind on immigration, Chávez says she felt betrayed that Tanton had concealed these ties. She was even more dismayed to learn about some of his funding sources.

In the spring of 1988, when grass-roots efforts to qualify the Arizona initiative foundered and U.S. English needed an emergency infusion of cash to hire professional canvassers (at a cost of $1 per signature), Chávez says Tanton turned to an anonymous donor, Cordelia Scaife May. The name meant little to her at the time, other than its association with the Mellon fortune. A reclusive heiress whose personal wealth is estimated at more than $500 million, May turned out to be the largest contributor to U.S. English, FAIR, and Population-Environment Balance (yet another Tanton-linked group). During the 1980s she donated at least $5.8 million to this network of organizations via her Pittsburgh-based Laurel Foundation and personal trust funds.[2] May's support was kept in the strictest confidence. By 1986, according to federal tax documents, she had given U.S. English $650,000—a sum equivalent to more than 10 percent of its total expenditures—but in an interview that year, the group's executive director, Gerda Bikales, denied U.S. English had received any such grants, insisting that its funding came entirely from "membership."

Cordelia Scaife May is the sister of Richard Mellon Scaife, a preeminent funder of the New Right, but her own philanthropic interests run toward population control efforts irrespective of political ideology, a legacy from her childhood friend and mentor, Margaret Sanger. Married twice, though briefly, May is childless and believes the world would benefit if others followed her example. (Her car once displayed a bumper sticker reading *Stop the Stork.*) Like Tanton, she seems concerned with a particular source of population growth. Her funding decisions have increasingly favored groups working to reduce fertility in the Third World or to limit the flow of Third World immigrants.

In 1983, May's foundation spent $5,000 to help distribute an obscure French novel, *The Camp of the Saints,* by Jean Raspail. Taking the form of a futuristic allegory in which starving refugees from the Ganges invade Europe, the book is a white racist's call to arms. Nothing less than Western civilization is at stake, the author warns in his preface. "We need only glance at the awesome population figures predicted for the year 2000 . . . seven billion people, only nine hundred million of whom will be white." The alternatives are stark: race solidarity now or race suicide later. Raspail is contemptuous of muddleheaded humanitarians who refuse to address the alien threat—in the novel they resist shooting dark-skinned intruders on sight—until it is too late to save white society. Fashionable "antiracists" are portrayed as quislings who open the gates to foul-smelling hordes that proceed to slaughter Frenchmen and rape their women. All in all, a parable to inspire today's Jeremiahs on the immigration question.

As it happened, Linda Chávez had reviewed the book when it was first translated in 1975 and found it chilling. "Raspail preaches racial mistrust and hatred as a natural condition of man," she wrote. "One need go no farther than his characters' own words to argue that he preaches genocide as well." When a journalist informed Chávez about May's role in promoting *The Camp of the Saints*, other connections clicked. She recalled seeing a U.S. English staff member carrying around a copy of the book. The organization's attorney, Barnaby Zall, had recently praised it as "a prophetic work." And Garrett Hardin, one of Tanton's WITAN associates, had cited it approvingly: "Will America, like invaded France in Raspail's novel, continue to be immobilized by ambivalence in the face of a silent invasion? If we cannot muster the will to protect ourselves, we will find that we have shared not wealth, but poverty with our invaders." This was a cult book, Chávez realized, and she was a leader of the cult. Not what she had bargained for.

Had she needed further reason to flee the building, it was provided by the Pioneer Fund, another distressing link with the white supremacist fringe. Dedicated to "race betterment" through eugenics, this secretive foundation has been FAIR's third largest benefactor, contributing $680,000 to its operations between 1982 and 1989.[3] Again Otis Graham's advice was ignored. Rather than keep a discreet distance from racial nativists, Tanton accepted their checks.

The Pioneer Fund was founded in 1937 by Harry H. Laughlin, former "expert eugenics agent" to the House Immigration Committee, who had convinced Congress of the genetic "inadequacy" of eastern and southern Europeans. Immigration restrictions were essential, he insisted, because newcomers contributed to "the germ plasm of the future American population."[4] Writing to the Pioneer Fund's millionaire patron in 1936, Laughlin described its objectives as follows: "practical population control . . . by influencing those forces which govern immigration and the sterilization of degenerates, and which influence mate selection and number of children differentially in favor of American racial strains and sound family-stocks." His first project was to distribute films popularizing what he termed "Applied Genetics in Present-Day Germany," that is, the Nazi program of forced sterilization for persons judged to be of inferior heredity. Enamored of Heinrich Himmler's *Lebensborn*, or Aryan breeding farms for S.S. members, Laughlin sought "to encourage high fertility by junior flying officers of especially superior heredity." The foundation established a scholarship program for the third child of Army Air Corps pilots.

Responding to its critics in 1989, the Pioneer Fund vigorously denied any racist, fascist, or anti-Semitic leanings. It stressed its continuing support for genetic research at reputable institutions, for example, a University of Minnesota study of hereditary traits in identical twins reared apart. It insisted that Laughlin, who died in 1941, "was in the mainstream of U.S. thought during the early 1930s, as witnessed by our restrictive immigration laws and by the sterilization laws in over half our states."

Certainly, Laughlin reflected—not to mention reinforced—the prejudices of his time and class. Another founding member of the Pioneer Fund was John Marshall Harlan, future Supreme Court justice. Other intimates included Senator James Eastland of Mississippi and Representative Francis E. Walter, chairman of the House Un-American Activities Committee. Yet, long after Hitler's atrocities had clarified the implications of eugenics and other ventures in "scientific" racism, the Pioneer Fund continued quietly to support what it terms "the study of human variation," including efforts by Arthur Jensen and William Shockley to prove the intellectual inferiority of blacks. In the 1970s it financed antibusing seminars in Boston and Louisville by Ralph Scott, an activist in the National Association for Neighborhood Schools. In the 1980s it subsidized a "comparison of the nonverbal intelligence of Hong Kong and California schoolchildren" by the so-called Institute for the Study of Educational Differences. And the Pioneer Fund aided the Institute for Western Values—the same group Cordelia May paid to distribute *The Camp of the Saints*—in publishing the autobiography of Thomas Dixon, the novelist whose writings glorified and helped to revive the modern Ku Klux Klan.

Asked about these unsavory connections in September 1988, John Tanton professed to know nothing about the foundation beyond its support of the "Minnesota twins" study. During his years as chairman of FAIR, a period when the organization received half a million dollars from the Pioneer Fund, it seems his curiosity was never aroused. Why was this funder of genetic research so interested in immigration? "I guess they just see it as an important population question for the country," Tanton replied.[5]

Linda Chávez divined a more sinister meaning in all this. Putting together Tanton's memo and funding sources, she saw a clear pat-

tern and knew others would see it too: "This nexus of issues—
population control, immigration control, and language policy—certainly gives the impression that [U.S. English] is biased against Hispanics." That was not something she wanted on her résumé. Chávez
moved quickly to sever all ties with U.S. English, Tanton, and his
contributors. After a bit of persuading, the chairman himself called
it quits later the same day. The resignations were front-page news
in Florida, Colorado, and especially Arizona, where Official English
plummeted in the polls. (Though it subsequently passed in all three
states, the margin of victory in Arizona was barely one percent.)
Several press accounts played up the anti-immigrant and forced-
sterilization angles, which tended to merge in the public mind. Soon
came an incendiary T.V. spot, sponsored by opponents of the Arizona initiative, that pictured concentration camp victims staring out
from behind barbed wire.

John Tanton struck back, accusing his critics of "character assassination" and "the Big Lie." He admitted having "said some things
badly and awkwardly" in his WITAN memo but insisted it was
unfair "to silence any discussion of demographic change by labeling
anybody raising the issue as a racist." As for his funding sources, it
was "guilt by association" to suggest that he shared their views.
Tanton protested that he was only three years old when the Pioneer
Fund was founded. How was he to know about Harry Laughlin's
activities? And what did the Laurel Foundation's support for *The
Camp of the Saints* have to do with FAIR and U.S. English?[6] It was
foolish "to believe that a nonprofit organization is responsible for
every action ever taken by any contributor who gives it money." To
insinuate that big donors and recipients might have some ideological affinity—preposterous!

It is true that some conspiracy theorists have been hasty in alleging a "Nazi connection" where the evidence supports nothing more
than opportunism and greed. But it was not the first time Tanton
had exhibited a willful innocence in his choice of allies. In 1985,
U.S. English released a list of forty-two ethnic organizations that
had endorsed the English Language Amendment. Among these were
five émigré groups—the Bulgarian National Front, the Byelorussian-
American Veterans Association, the German American National
Congress (better known by its evocative German acronym, DANK),
the National Confederation of American Ethnic Groups, and the
Romanian American National Congress—that figured in a minor

scandal for the Bush presidential campaign of 1988. All were associated with members of the Republican Heritage Groups Council
who left the campaign following allegations about their ties to Nazis and Nazi collaborators. To take just one example, DANK leader
Austin App was author of *The Six Million Swindle,* a book that
claims the Holocaust never happened. Gerda Bikales denies that she
or "anyone else at U.S. English" knew about the background of
these organizations, whose endorsements were solicited by a U.S.
English volunteer. Certainly, it is hard to believe that Bikales, herself a Holocaust survivor, would have approved of such bedfellows.
On the other hand, fanaticism about one issue can induce blindness
about others. Bikales once argued in *Washington Jewish Week* that
"language disunity" was a significant cause of World War II.

Since his departure Dr. Tanton has produced a voluminous literature in his own defense, including a fifty-two-page exegesis of his
memo, which ran but seven pages in the original, and a letter of
explanation mailed to scores of supporters. His writings are seasoned with homilies from the Great Books ("There is nothing, says
Plato, so delightful as the hearing or the speaking of truth") that
convey a self-conscious rectitude in the face of adversity. Tanton
presents himself as a kind of civic physician attempting "early diagnosis" of society's ills. At the same time he complains about being
driven from U.S. English by unprincipled opponents: "It is a sad
day for America when someone who has devoted his life to public
involvement[7] has to step down because of McCarthyite tactics."
Being called a racist, he says,

> is a nearly fatal accusation, like being accused of being a com-
> munist in the 1950s. I shall have to live with the taint of this
> charge for the rest of my life. But let me make my necessary
> denial, no matter how inadequate: No, I am not a racist. I
> want to bring all members of the American family together to
> share in our Thanksgiving feast—but I also want us to be able
> to speak to each other when we're gathered around the table.
> Make no mistake, my desire for national unity is my real sin.

Who is John Tanton—misunderstood prophet or high priest of
ethnic purity? After working with Tanton for fourteen months,
Linda Chávez still isn't sure. "It's hard to describe him," she says.

"He's so foreign to my way of thinking. Clearly, he feels himself embattled. I have a sense of this man who lives on the edge of Lake Michigan in a very WASPy community, feeling himself surrounded by people coming into the country who may encroach upon his territory. He's obsessed with the population issue. There's a sense that his way of life is passing." A self-described conservative "ideologue," Chávez says she was always puzzled by Tanton's coterie, whose beliefs seemed to her to lack internal consistency. While their leader maintained a "dispassionate quality," some followers betrayed "a clear animus toward Mexican immigrants," while espousing an orthodox liberalism on other matters. At the one WITAN retreat she attended, Chávez recalls being baited mercilessly for her Reaganite views on the Strategic Defense Initiative. "I just don't know what to make of these people," she concludes.

Katherine Holmes, who served as U.S. English research director in 1988–89, is more blunt in her appraisal of Tanton. "My opinion is that the guy is a racist," she says. "Not in the K.K.K. definition, but as someone who sees the world in terms of groups of people of different colors." Fired by U.S. English after making known her disgust for the WITAN memo, Holmes is no disinterested observer. (Nor is Linda Chávez, who terms her involvement with the group a professional "disaster."[8]) But Tanton's preoccupation with race is well documented, for example, in a 1988 rumination about projections that the United States could become a "majority minority" society by the year 2020. Sometime soon, he writes, "the formation of a White political caucus, along with all the others, will be reasonable and justified."

U.S. English leaders have long been aware that their movement's appeal is based, at least in part, on white racism. Chávez says that soon after taking the U.S. English job, she received several abusive letters from members who resigned to protest the appointment of a Hispanic president. Subsequently she commissioned an internal attitude survey to gauge the prevalence of such views, which the organization's pollster called "the redneck factor." It turned out that among regular contributors to U.S. English, a sizable minority harbored anti-Latino biases. When asked what had prompted them to support the organization, 42 percent endorsed the statement: "I wanted America to stand strong and not cave in to Hispanics who shouldn't be here."[9] It would be hard to elicit a more candid admission of ethnic intolerance. But "redneck" seems a misnomer when one considers the overall "membership profile" of U.S. English. According to the survey, only 10 percent of contributors came from blue-collar backgrounds. In addition, they were disproportionately male (67 percent), elderly (75 percent were sixty or older), affluent (33 percent had incomes above $50,000), college-educated (60 percent), conservative (67 percent), Republican (71 percent), and northern European in origin (68 percent). Among the 385 respondents who identified their ethnic heritage, there were no Mexican Americans, no Cubans, two "other Hispanics," two Asians, and three blacks.

In 1985–86, the organization sponsored a write-in campaign to support Secretary of Education William Bennett in his attacks on the Bilingual Education Act. Numerous U.S. English members responded with complaints about communities being "overrun with all sorts of aliens," wetbacks on welfare, and out-of-control Hispanic birthrates. A typical correspondent reasoned: "At the rate the Latinos (and nonwhites) reproduce, [we] face a demographic imbalance if we do not change several of our dangerously outdated laws. Make English the official language everywhere in the U.S.A." Asked about these letters by a reporter, Bikales replied:

> I do not believe at all that we are responsible for any of this. This is a mass movement. Anybody can and does join U.S. English.[10] We do our very best to put out responsible ideas, responsible policies. We're not hate-mongers. [But] you've got this wide-open situation with hundreds of thousands of people in a state of utter frustration, just watching English erode under their very feet, with the government not giving a damn. There's no doubt that as long as our political leadership is going to continue to bury its head in the sand, we are going to have this kind of situation that's . . . somewhat out of control.

Had U.S. English taken any steps to repudiate this type of support? "Well, I'm talking to you," she replied. "I'm making it perfectly clear."

Tanton and his associates often seemed to believe that their credentials as Save the Whales–type activists would deflect the charge of exploiting racism. Rather than target conservatives as potential contributors, to the dismay of Linda Chávez U.S. English preferred to use the Greenpeace mailing list. Several of Tanton's lieutenants were veterans of the Michigan environmental movement. "The issues we're touching on here must be broached by liberals," he insisted in the WITAN memo. So it was a setback when Norman Lear's People For the American Way, one of the few liberal lobbies still thriving in Washington, became an active opponent. Tanton's memo, the group charged, had "laid bare the ugly core of the English Only movement . . . racism, plain and simple." It called on Saul Bellow, Alistair Cooke, Arnold Schwarzenegger, and other celebrity endorsers to join Walter Cronkite in quitting the U.S. English advisory board.[11] Kathryn Bricker, a Tanton aide who replaced Chávez at the helm of U.S. English, met with leaders of People For to ask them to reconsider. We're very well-meaning, she pleaded, *we're liberals like you,* and was surprised when no minds were changed.

Tom Olson, former P.R. director for U.S. English and another casualty of Bricker's housecleaning, believes the Tanton network does reflect "a bizarre kind of liberalism." He explains, "They feel they are an elite, an intelligentsia capable of providing leadership, using the powers of government to mold the future. But when you get into what motivates them, they are concerned about shaping demographic trends. They see people—cultural, racial, and immigrant groups—as a negative factor on the environment." For these would-be social engineers, it's a short step from the idea that people cause pollution to the idea that people constitute pollution (some more than others). If these are liberals, then they have misplaced their civil rights sensors somewhere along the way.

Of course, American nativism has never been a monopoly of the political right. Jefferson's warnings about immigration were later popularized by Know-Nothings who sought to exclude Catholics and others believed to exert "a blighting and withering effect upon republican institutions." This century's Americanization campaign, notwithstanding its worries about revolutionary syndicalism, was largely a Progressive affair. Promoting Anglo-conformity implied that immigrants could be remolded, an alternative to the Anglo-Saxonist view that certain types were unassimilable. Tanton & Co. seem ambivalent on this point where Hispanics are concerned. But what truly distinguishes their brand of nativism is the object of its paranoia: culture, not politics. While Latinos are regarded as a demographic menace, there is no hint of a Red Scare—only anxieties about decline in the status and lifestyle of white Americans.

WITAN is where the ideological threads get woven together. "This is a group that John Tanton has selected personally," Olson says, "to sit around talking about action plans to solve the world's problems." WITAN's 1989 roster included Bricker and Bikales; Otis Graham and his brother Hugh, board members of FAIR and U.S. English, respectively; Roger Conner, Dan Stein, David Simcox, and Cordia Strom, staff members of FAIR and its spin-offs; Matt Gallagher, direct-mail fundraiser for FAIR and U.S. English; Gregory Curtis, president of the Laurel Foundation; former governor Richard Lamm of Colorado, now head of the doomsaying 21st Century Fund (another Tanton venture); and the ecologist Garrett Hardin, professor emeritus at the University of California, Santa Barbara.

Of these, Hardin has been most influential, less for his expertise on environmental matters than for the conceptual framework he calls "lifeboat ethics." This is essentially a rationale for portraying narrow self-interest as farsighted altruism. Simply put, if rich nations try to rescue too many Third World refugees, the lifeboat will sink and everyone will drown. Better to preserve high living standards for some humans than risk losing them for all. In "The Tragedy of the Commons" and other essays, Hardin highlights the contradiction between individual and community interests in a world of finite resources, or "carrying capacity." Immigration benefits starving individuals, he argues, but not the host society that must be taxed to feed them, nor the human race as a whole.

To illustrate his Malthusian paradox, Hardin gives the example of a deer herd that has overpopulated its territory and is beginning to starve. Although animal lovers are tempted to intervene to keep the deer alive, it is kinder to the species to let nature take its course, culling the unfit and producing a smaller but healthier herd. "In game management," he explains, "the concept of 'sanctity of life' is intolerable." So far this is a familiar line of ecological reasoning. But the object of Hardin's parable is the problem of human population. "Man is a part of nature," after all. If he exceeds the carrying capacity of his environment, the species is threatened.[12] Artificial measures, such as famine relief to Ethiopia or Bangladesh, are thus "counterproductive" because they tolerate Third World inaction on birth control. Ditto for the "escape valve" of emigration to the United States. Americans should not let a sentimental attachment to the sanctity of life blind them to these realities, he says, citing Comte: "The Intellect should always be the servant of the Heart, and never its slave." In Hardin's case, one gets the feeling that this is not much of a dilemma. As a practical way to combat illegal immigration, he has proposed erecting a two-thousand-mile electronic fence along the Mexican border to zap *los mojados* into submission.

Reactions to Hardin's ideas have been appropriately intense. "Isn't it great that you can be moral and also defend your advantages as an affluent Westerner," observes Charles Keely, a population specialist at Georgetown University. "I find it repugnant that anybody could have such utter contempt for other human beings." For the nutritionist Jean Mayer and the anthropologist Margaret Mead, the same word came to mind in describing lifeboat ethics: "obscene."

More germane to the language question is the concept of *cultural* carrying capacity, which Hardin has expanded beyond the exigencies of biological survival to include intangibles like "values" and "quality of life." As such, it is a more versatile instrument for justifying ethnic homogeneity. "Cultural carrying capacity," he postulates, "is inversely related to the richness of the culture." In plain language, the more refined our standard of living, the less room we have for riffraff, unless we are prepared to lower our standards. Gerda Bikales takes the idea further in a polemic against bilingual education, arguing that growing numbers of non-English speakers "may well have stressed the cultural carrying capacity of our schools to the breaking point and perhaps beyond. We are caught in a vise by an inescapable arithmetic—even more new immigrant students are piling up every day on top of others still to be absorbed in the regular classroom. . . . If we do not wish to permanently turn our educational system into an engine for churning out members of a new multinational state *who share neither language nor values,* we must markedly slow down immigration" (emphasis added). Too many newcomers, too many strange tongues, too many undesirable cultures for the country to assimilate.

English Only advocates reserve their harshest judgments for one culture in particular: that amalgam of imperial and indigenous traditions, incorporating Castilian, Galician, Moorish, Aztec, Mayan, Taino, and West African elements, known loosely as "Hispanic." Not that nativists indulge in such fine distinctions. What concerns WITAN is a monolithic set of bad habits that it deems inimical to the American experiment, a "Latin" psychology that breeds underdevelopment, antisocial behavior, authoritarianism, educational failure, overpopulation, and of course, bilingualism. This is an updated version of the Black Legend. The villains are no longer ruthless conquistadors, but "ethnic bosses" who keep their people in bondage.

Former governor Lamm, whose views often parallel those of John Tanton, expresses alarm that 40 percent of U.S. immigration today comes from Latin America. "There's not a [single] successful nation south of our borders," he says. "We're bringing in immigrants who don't have the same culture, who don't have the same patterns of success." Spanish speakers insist on forming "ethnic enclaves so large that [they] can live in the U.S. and never learn to speak English or to assimilate into our culture." All this bodes grave consequences for the future, Lamm warns. "Demography is destiny. A nation succeeds only if a vast majority of its citizens succeed." Large numbers of Hispanics don't seem to be making it, he insinuates. Will they drag the rest of us down as well?

Similar views are expounded by other Official English activists. Lou Zaeske, head of the Texas-based American Ethnic Coalition, describes Chicano leaders as "political *patrones* [who] encourage people to think of themselves as Hispanics rather than as Americans." Their motive, he charges, is to transplant Mexico's way of life to the United States: "It's a conquistador mentality, back to Hernando Cortez, when he took the gold from the Aztecs. . . . He had the Indians do the work, but they were nothing more than glorified serfs. How do you keep somebody trapped like that? You encourage them to look inward into their group by way of ethnicity and language." Texans died at the Alamo, Zaeske says, to free themselves from "the tyranny, the discredited socioeconomic system that is Mexico even to this day." Why should they stand by now and allow a peaceful takeover through bilingualism?

"The new generation of Hispanic leaders is trying to benefit politically by [encouraging] linguistic separatism," charges Larry Pratt, president of English First, a group created in 1986 to mine the lucrative field opened by U.S. English.[13] Pratt warns of a Quebec-like future in which "Spanish-only requirements" would be imposed in places like Miami. "Fidel Castro would be welcomed by some because of his encouragement of the 'linguistic integrity' of the area." Either Pratt is abysmally uninformed about Cuban Americans or, more likely, he is playing to the crudest of anti-Hispanic prejudices.

The English First newsletter is replete with articles like "Hispanic Activists Get Rich from Non-English Speakers" and "Texas: Schools and Services Geared to Spanish-Speaking."

Amid the heated exchanges over racism—are English Only backers engaging in it? exploiting it? motivated by it?—one wonders how the question can ever be answered with finality. Tanton is correct on one thing. In the United States today, there is no greater stigma than to be judged a white racist. No public figure will cop to this charge, not even the former Klansman David Duke of Louisiana. (As it happens, he, too, has a penchant for English Only rhetoric.) Yet this is also an age of shameless Willie Hortonism, in which mainstream politicians like George Bush can exploit racism for partisan gain. They evade punishment by the voters because there is no consensus on the meaning of the term. To some, racism denotes a set of hereditarian judgments about "educability" or criminality. To others, it implies virtually any kind of animus or stereotype based on ethnic origin. This is a classic problem of semantics: words get in the way of settling differences. No matter that we're all speaking English.

Still, in the context of the language debate, a final verdict on the charge of racism is unnecessary for one to reject the restrictionist position. Undoubtedly, there is a spectrum of views among the leaders and followers of U.S. English. But is there any crucial distinction to be drawn between those who regard Latinos as genetically inferior and those who class them as culturally undesirable? Or between the eugenicists' "biology is destiny" and WITAN's "demography is destiny"? Does it really matter whether these zealots believe that Spanish speakers are incapable of acquiring English or that they refuse to do so out of laziness, backwardness, or disloyalty? The hidden agenda of English Only is to highlight the *cultural costs* of immigration so as to build support for restrictions against certain groups. Whatever the thought process, the end result is bigotry.

Though not fatal, John Tanton's self-inflicted wound drew plenty of blood at U.S. English. The organization was forced to retrench and concentrate on defending against bad press rather than waging new offensives. Over the next three years, only one additional state adopted an Official English measure (Alabama, in 1990), with minimal help from U.S. English. Formerly gung-ho supporters like Senator Steve Symms and Representative William Broomfield withdrew their sponsorship of the English Language Amendment. The Democratic and Republican hierarchies, never enthusiastic about Official English, now shunned the proposal and the proponents. During a national television appearance, First Lady Barbara Bush described the idea as "a racial slur."[14]

Internally, U.S. English staff and board members were polarized between Tanton loyalists and detractors. Stanley Diamond, a member of the latter camp, took over as chairman but remained in San Francisco while executive director Kathryn Bricker ran day-to-day operations. According to the cover story, Tanton had broken off all involvement with the group. But he continued to fax regular advice and directives to Bricker, who hired a $135-an-hour public relations consultant to rehabilitate the image of her former boss, along with that of the organization. Six months after his departure, Tanton had the nerve to schedule a WITAN meeting at the U.S. English office (though it was later moved in response to staff complaints). Meanwhile the new director found it easier to fire associates of Linda Chávez than to hire competent replacements or to keep them on the payroll after they learned about WITAN.

The only phase of U.S. English operations that did not suffer was finances. Direct-mail appeals, increasingly refined and targeted to reliable donors, continued to generate the $10, $20, and $50 contributions that had always accounted for the bulk of the group's income. Giving also proceeded apace from foundations willing to overlook the Tanton episode. Although the organization's income of $5.5 million in 1989 was down slightly (from $6.2 million in 1988), the decline was understandable in a nonelection year.

What is less easily fathomed is how U.S. English has managed since 1984 to finance costly ballot initiatives and lobbying efforts while retaining its status with the Internal Revenue Service as a tax-exempt, charitable organization. This classification, known as 501(c)(3), is an enviable one for groups that raise money from the public because it gives contributors an incentive to be generous: they may deduct the amount of donations from their federal income tax. To qualify for such treatment, an organization has to meet strict standards. It must engage in legal, nonprofit activity (educational, religious, scientific) and must not involve itself in political campaigns or "substantial" efforts to influence legislation. Minimal lobbying expenditures are allowed—5–20 percent of the organization's annual budget. While "providing information" to Congress is not considered lobbying, urging citizens to write their representatives in support of legislation, or to cast their own votes for state ballot measures, most definitely is. The I.R.S. also rules out 501(c)(3) status for groups, regardless of their spending habits, whose primary objectives can be achieved only through changes in law.

Where does U.S. English fit in? In fundraising appeals it has described itself as "a national public-interest organization dedicated to establishing English as the official language of the United States. We are fighting to restore the English-only ballot and limit bilingual education to a transitional role." Should such an organization be treated as a charity for tax purposes? That is a question of legal interpretation. But it is hard to see how the stated goals of U.S. English could be accomplished other than through legislation or how it could avoid spending a significant portion of its resources on lobbying. To be sure, there is nothing illegitimate about a nonprofit organization working actively to shape public policy. It simply qualifies for a less favored treatment: supporters cannot take a tax writeoff for their contributions, although the organization's noncommercial income remains exempt from taxation. Many Washington interest groups operate under two entities—an "educational" foundation and an "action organization" without restrictions on advocacy. Most take care to keep the finances segregated (for example, conducting separate fundraising drives) so as to keep 501(c)(3) activities above suspicion. The law's rationale is clear. While groups engaged primarily in charitable work deserve to be subsidized by the taxpayers, those dedicated primarily to lobbying do not.

U.S. English also uses an "action organization" to finance legislative activities, but it operates a bit differently. First its charitable arm raises money on a tax-exempt basis. Then it passes a generous portion of the proceeds to the U.S. English Legislative Task Force, the lobbying arm, which distributes the funds to state initiative campaigns or uses them for other forms of lobbying.[15] In 1988, for example, 99.2 percent of the $305,027 spent to promote Official English in Arizona was provided in this way. That is, less than one percent ($2,412) was covered by nondeductible contributions raised in Arizona. U.S. English also transferred large amounts of cash to the California, Florida, and Colorado campaigns via the same route, not counting its direct expenditures in court to keep Official English on the ballot. While these activities may conform to the letter of the law—5–20 percent of $6.2 million allows a big loophole for lob-bying—they appear to contradict its spirit. A sizable portion of the tab for U.S. English activism has been picked up by American tax-payers. It is worth noting that English First, for all its warts, iden-tifies itself as a lobby and raises no funds on a tax-exempt basis.

It also seems significant that the English Language Political Ac-tion Committee, which rewards congressional allies of U.S. English and punishes adversaries like Congresswoman Ileana Ros-Lehtinen of Florida, is operated by Barnaby Zall, the lawyer for U.S. En-glish.[16] Yet, in response to two inquiries by the Federal Election Commission, Zall has insisted that "ELPAC is an independent PAC and is not connected with any other organization. . . . Most work is done by volunteers." A most active "volunteer" in the commit-tee's 1989 attempt to defeat Ros-Lehtinen was Steve Workings, for-mer coordinator of state campaigns for U.S. English, who spent a week in Miami supervising ELPAC's six-figure effort. There is noth-ing improper in an association between U.S. English and ELPAC, as far as the F.E.C. is concerned (provided there is full disclosure). But for the I.R.S., it raises a bright red flag when a "charitable" organization works in tandem with a political action committee.

By the fall of 1990, allegations of lavish expenditures—political and otherwise—had become a splitting issue within U.S. English. After an internal audit concluded that Stanley Diamond had im-properly spent the organization's money on a personal vacation and other perks, the chairman responded to his critics by threatening to reveal much more to the I.R.S. In a bizarre handwritten letter, drafted but never mailed, he confessed to federal authorities:

> This is a report of the illegal activities of U.S. English; of myself as its Chairman and its Board of Directors since 1986. The Board of Directors of U.S. English authorized payments to me of $2,000 per month for "consulting" each month [sic]. In fact, there was no "consulting." The "consulting" fee was a front, a conduit for political activity, for political contributions in sup-port of or opposition to candidates for State or Federal offices and for support of or opposition to State & Federal legislation affecting the goals of U.S. English. The Board, in approving the "consulting" fee, knew such payments were for political activ-ity, were illegal & would not be reported as "lobbying" expen-ditures.

> Further, my field expenses and expenses of the San Francisco office of U.S. English were, at least, from 50% to 75% for political activity, all illegal under the 501c3 charter. . . . My estimate is that approximately $150,000.00 was expended illegally by me and the San Francisco office, none of which was reported as "lobbying."

Diamond sent the letter to Leo Sorensen, a Tanton ally who was agitating for his resignation but was instead forced off the board in an ensuing power struggle. Sorensen interpreted the document as blackmail: either allow Diamond to continue as chairman or he would wreck U.S. English and implicate its officers in wrongdoing. The confession remained a secret until factional infighting broke out shortly after the death of S. I. Hayakawa on February 27, 1992. When the letter surfaced in *Legal Times,* a weekly newspaper in Washington, Diamond denied its accuracy, describing it as "a reflection of some inner problems" at U.S. English.

U.S. English has financed one notable venture unrelated to legislation. Under what it calls Project Golden Door, it has supported private efforts to promote adult English literacy. At the Cambria English Institute in Los Angeles, for example, U.S. English grants have supported a "revolving loan program" for immigrant students. It has also produced workbooks and videotapes to teach "survival skills" in English (for example, how to call 911) and has encouraged employers to offer job-site English classes. The organization added this philanthropic focus after taking flak for its refusal to support expanded federal subsidies for adult E.S.L. instruction. When such legislation was introduced in 1986 by the Congressional Hispanic Caucus, Gerda Bikales said the job could be handled more effectively by the private sector, citing the "moral obligation" of Spanish-language television stations to teach English. The measure later passed, authorizing up to $32 million annually for an English Literacy Grants Program. But it received no backing from U.S. English.

This episode raised a few eyebrows among innocents who had assumed that U.S. English cared about helping immigrants to learn the national language. Hence Project Golden Door, announced with much fanfare in 1987, along with an alleged first-year commitment of $650,000. A year later Stanley Diamond was quoted as saying the project's budget would rise from $700,000 in 1988 to $2 million in 1989—generous figures by comparison with other private efforts in the field. But U.S. English financial reports tell a different story: grants for English-literacy programs totaled just $42,000 in 1987 and $50,000 in 1988, about one percent of the organization's overall expenditures. Its annual report is vague on whether any such grants were awarded in 1989; none is itemized on its federal tax return. Moreover, the bulk of this funding came from a single source, the Weingart Foundation of Los Angeles. Without unduly exerting itself or dipping into its direct-mail riches, U.S. English simply passed along these donations and reaped the public-relations benefits.

Yet it would take more than a few token English courses to exorcise the ghost of John Tanton. By the summer of 1990, it was clear that Kathryn Bricker had no plan to dissociate the organization from her longtime mentor. Nor was her own performance gratifying, what with continued turnover and dissension on the U.S. English staff. So Diamond moved to replace Bricker and (soon after) to oust Bikales, another Tanton retainer, from his board of directors. Ronald Saunders, the new executive director of U.S. English, was a prize catch. Formerly a bilingual teacher and administrator, fluent in Spanish and knowledgeable about education policy, Saunders had recently headed the National Clearinghouse for Bilingual Education. Like Linda Chávez, he was a disarming choice, able to put critics off balance (as well as a number of shocked friends and associates). Also like Chávez, he had been unemployed for several months before taking the job.

Saunders wisely declined to take responsibility for anything said or done by his predecessors. His only comment on the Tanton debacle was to note that "mistakes" were made and that Tanton was no longer connected with the organization. "One of the things I am about is to change the perception of U.S. English," Saunders explained shortly after coming on board, insisting that the group had been misunderstood by the many and maligned by a few. In reality, it was "an inclusionary organizaton and a unifying organization." Instead of restricting anyone's rights, Official English would be a "liberating" measure, a way to avoid "de facto linguistic apartheid." As for the charge that U.S. English was exacerbating ethnic hostility, he responded: "My feeling is that the divisiveness is not coming from this movement. My feeling is that the divisiveness is coming from people who make their living stirring things up."

While refusing to identify these agitators, Saunders seemed eager to burn bridges with his former colleagues. Asked whether he agreed with the assessment of his boss, Stanley Diamond, that bilingual educators are little more than *políticos* seeking "the official establishment of foreign languages in this country," he replied: "Are there people who use kids as a shield, just like Saddam Hussein? I would say yes, there are people in the schools who have absolutely no concern whether those kids learn anything."[17]

Rather than leap headlong into new initiatives, Saunders used the organization's formidable treasury to rehabilitate its image. One advertisement that appeared in the *Christian Science Monitor, Commentary,* and other publications featured a multicultural group of children smiling over the legend "In America, We Share Something Valuable That Makes Friendship Possible" (i.e., English). The promotional copy, which bore the U.S. English logo but made no mention of Official English, continued, "We, the undersigned, recognize the value of our common language and support efforts to enable all Americans to learn English—the language of equal opportunity." About fifty signatures followed: Walter Annenberg, Julia Child, Margaret Truman Daniel, Angier Biddle Duke, Howard Fast, Whoopi Goldberg, Barry Goldwater, Charleton Heston, C. Everett Koop, Eugene McCarthy, Dudley Moore, Richard M. Nixon, Norman Podhoretz, Dith Pran, Eric Sevareid, Abigail Van Buren, and other luminaries still willing to carry the baggage of U.S. English.

It would be hard to find fifty Americans of any description who would oppose this message. Virtually no one—certainly not the Hispanic leadership—denies the value of a common tongue or the need to make English instruction universally available. But like the rhetoric of "a color-blind society" now favored by the enemies of civil rights, "the language of equal opportunity" signifies something less benign than its surface meaning would imply. In an English Only America, only English speakers would enjoy equal rights, including the right to speech itself.

Seven

Language Rights and Wrongs

"Congress shall make no law . . . abridging the freedom of speech." Although the First Amendment is the best known and arguably the most cherished section of the Bill of Rights, as circumstances change its meaning is inevitably disputed. The language restrictionist campaigns of the 1980s raised a new series of questions. Does freedom of speech apply simply to the ideas expressed or does it extend to the *medium* of expression? May government require that only English be used in certain contexts and that other languages be silenced? Once again, the Founders saw fit not to address these matters directly. Perhaps they considered the answers to be self-evident or the questions trifling: the content of speech is normally its controversial, hence endangered, component—not the tongue chosen to convey it. Most likely, they failed to foresee the advent of an English Only movement.

Thus it fell to Judge Paul G. Rosenblatt to make the first ruling on the constitutionality of Official English. Arizona's Proposition 106, so far the most restrictive of these measures, provided the test case. Two days after it passed in November 1988, a state employee sued in federal court to block the initiative from taking effect. María-Kelly F. Yñiguez, an insurance claims adjuster in Arizona's Risk Management Division, argued that Proposition 106 violated her First Amendment rights by making her "afraid to speak Spanish at work." She was joined in the lawsuit by Jaime P. Gutiérrez, a state senator from Tucson, who believed that if Proposition 106 were allowed to stand, he would be breaking his oath to uphold the

Arizona Constitution every time he communicated with a constituent in Spanish.

The amendment seemed unambiguous. Unlike the vague Official English declarations adopted in several other states, Arizona's initiative was brazen about its English Only intent. In drafting the measure, Barnaby Zall, the attorney for U.S. English, had sought to avoid repeating mistakes in the wording of Proposition 63 two years earlier. The California amendment, a general statement about the need to "preserve, protect, and strengthen the English language," has thus far been interpreted as a symbolic gesture. To the chagrin of its sponsors, it has yet to outlaw any bilingual services in California. So Zall equipped Arizona's version with teeth that no one could ignore: "This State and all political subdivisions of this State shall act *in English and no other language*" (emphasis added). The restriction was defined to include

  (i) the legislative, executive, and judicial branches of government;

 (ii) all political subdivisions, departments, agencies, organizations, and instrumentalities of this State, including local governments and municipalities;

(iii) all statutes, ordinances, rules, orders, programs, and policies;

 (iv) all government officials and employees during the performance of government business.

It was the last paragraph that raised the most First Amendment worries. While on the job, it appeared, public servants would be forbidden to speak languages other than English, except under limited circumstances. To ward off criticisms that Official English would imperil essential rights and services, Zall exempted certain government functions from the amendment's coverage. The state would be allowed to "act in a language other than English"

 (a) to assist students who are not proficient in the English language, to the extent necessary to comply with federal law, by giving educational instruction in a language other than English to provide as rapid as possible a transition to English;

 (b) to comply with other federal laws;

    (c) to teach a student a foreign language as part of a required
        or voluntary educational curriculum;

    (d) to protect public health or safety;

    (e) to protect the rights of criminal defendants or victims of
        crime.

Otherwise Proposition 106 left no apparent leeway to use minority
tongues in the public sector. Could such broad restrictions pass constitutional muster?

    Yñiguez and Gutiérrez were not the only Arizonans concerned
about this question. Public school teachers and principals feared the
amendment would rule out communicating with parents in languages other than English. Employees of Arizona's Division of Developmental Disabilities wondered whether they could continue to
offer translation services in Braille and American Sign Language, as
well as Spanish, Navajo, and Hopi. Professors at state universities
worried that Indian-language programs, not covered by the exemption for *foreign* language teaching, would now be outlawed. Judges
predicted chaos in civil courts if interpreters were banned in di-
vorce, bankruptcy, and personal injury cases. Governor Rose Mofford announced that Arizona's trade office in Taiwan, if forbidden
to operate in Chinese, would have to close. A spokeswoman for the
Arizona Lottery said that Spanish-language advertising might have
to be canceled. The state Board of Pardons and Paroles suspended
parole hearings for prisoners unable to speak English until the le-
gality of translators could be clarified.

    As usual U.S. English dismissed such interpretations as "scare tac-
tics." The organization commissioned a legal analysis by Jim Henderson, a prominent Phoenix attorney, who concluded that "the initiative will not make substantial changes in existing laws or
government practices in Arizona." Those who predicted draconian
effects from Proposition 106 were "attempting to play on emotions" or "ignoring what it says." Barnaby Zall added that the
amendment was intended to affect only "official" business. To
"act in English" would apply, for example, to signing a contract,
but not to printing tourist pamphlets in French, German, or Japanese.

    Less partial observers had a different reading. Paul Bender, dean
of the Arizona State University Law School, believed the measure
was so poorly drafted as to contradict its sponsors' stated goals—

for example, by preventing a teacher from speaking another language to help adults learn English (not covered by the exemption for federally mandated programs). Proposition 106 also threatened to disrupt "the administration of justice," warned Judge Noel Fidel of the Arizona Court of Appeals. "It's always troubling when people try to use the constitution for . . . inflammatory, symbolic purposes and then say, 'We'll leave it up to the courts to sort it out.'"

If helping Arizonans to acquire English was the sponsors' real aim, State Representative Armando Ruíz of Phoenix had been willing to oblige. In early 1988, he proposed an alternative initiative that read, in part:

> It shall be the official policy of the State of Arizona to promote proficiency in English, the common language of the United States, while recognizing Arizona's unique history, languages, and diversity. . . . The State of Arizona shall provide the opportunity to learn and be proficient in the English language and guarantee the right and freedom to learn and use other languages.

The proposal went further than previous English Plus resolutions by officially recognizing a "common language" and asserting, in effect, a right to English classes as well as to protection against English Only restrictions. Ruíz won bipartisan support for his plan from U.S. Senators Dennis DeConcini and John McCain, Representatives Mo Udall and Jim Kolbe, and others. But U.S. English refused to endorse the measure, objecting that it "would create a new constitutional 'right' to 'use other languages' [that] could bring us closer to an officially bilingual society." Unable to pay professional canvassers more than $111,000, as U.S. English did, Ruíz and his volunteers gathered only two-thirds of the 130,000 petitions needed to qualify their ballot measure. So the voters were left with a simple yes or no choice on Proposition 106.

In the view of Arizona's business and political establishments, Official English was likely to benefit no one but trial lawyers, who could cash in on the ensuing litigation. J. Fife Symington, a Phoenix developer (and later governor), predicted it would jeopardize the state's ability to compete in international markets and to attract overseas investors. In Arizona, unlike Florida, this argument had credibility because the English Only measure was so explicit and because the warning was reiterated by leaders across the political spectrum. The state's entire congressional delegation and its recently impeached governor, Evan Mecham, not usually a zealot on behalf of civil rights, joined forces to attack the initiative. The sole public figures of stature who expressed support were retired U.S. Senator Barry Goldwater and Arizona Senate President Carl Kunasek (who lost some credibility when it came to light that he had printed his business cards in Chinese at taxpayers' expense).

The broad opposition coalition almost prevailed. Proposition 106 passed by a mere 11,659 votes out of 1,157,259 cast—the first and so far the only occasion an Official English initiative has faced a close challenge at the polls.

After the election Attorney General Bob Corbin followed the lead of his counterparts in other Official English states and pronounced the measure to be essentially ceremonial: "Proposition 106 requires official acts of government to be in English. It does not prohibit the use of languages other than English that are reasonably necessary to facilitate the day-to-day operation of government." Corbin's opinion was not legally binding, but it did clarify the state's policy of winking at English Only: the amendment would not be enforced. At all levels public business would continue to be conducted primarily in English and, when appropriate, in other languages as well. Municipalities like *Mesa* (Table), *Casa Grande* (Big House), and *Ajo* (Garlic) would be allowed to keep their names.[1] Common sense would prevail. Politically speaking, Corbin could not have chosen a safer course. Opponents of Proposition 106 were mollified, their worst fears assuaged, and proponents felt vindicated by the attorney general's statement.

At this point Judge Rosenblatt could have considered the issue moot. After all, the state of Arizona had denied any intention of imposing an English Only policy on its employees and officials. Was it now reasonable for Yñiguez and Gutiérrez to fear retribution for speaking Spanish on the job? While authorities remained free to revise Corbin's interpretation, and private parties still might sue to enforce a more restrictive interpretation, these were hypothetical threads on which to hang a lawsuit. Rosenblatt could have dismissed the case and left any future disputes to be resolved by Arizona judges. But he believed the First Amendment questions deserved an answer in federal court.

The issue was larger than the measurable impact of Official English legislation—for example, discipline against state workers who used other languages—because the potential for mischief did not end there. "As the Supreme Court has noted," Judge Rosenblatt wrote, "the danger associated with laws which limit First Amendment rights is to a large extent one of self-censorship, which is a harm that can be realized even without an actual enforcement action." A credible *threat* of state censorship is sufficient and that is what he found. The "plain language" of Proposition 106 was so "overbroad" that it created "a realistic danger of, and a substantial potential for, the unconstitutional application" of English Only restrictions. Yñiguez was correct to argue that Proposition 106 had a "chilling" effect on her exercise of free speech. It was Corbin who had performed a "remarkable job of plastic surgery upon the face of the ordinance."[2] Official English—at least in its Arizona version—was incompatible with the First Amendment.

On procedural grounds the judge removed the attorney general and another state official from the case. (Senator Gutiérrez also lacked standing, Rosenblatt ruled, because the executive branch had no jurisdiction to impose English Only restrictions on legislators.) This left Governor Mofford, an opponent of Proposition 106, as the only defendant in a position to appeal, and she declined to do so. But a federal appellate court later granted U.S. English standing to seek further review. "We are fighting that decision," explained then–executive director Kathryn Bricker, "because this judge in one fell swoop said we're going to have a multilingual government." She claimed that Rosenblatt had granted public employees the "right to use any language they chose while performing their official duties," and the public be damned. A rather shocking position for a conservative, Reagan-appointed judge to take.

Rosenblatt's distinction, of course, was one of several that English Only proponents refuse to acknowledge. Yñiguez's right to speak a language other than English when appropriate—for example, to communicate with Spanish-speaking insurance claimants—does not imply an unconditional right to speak Spanish at any time, if that would mean neglecting the needs of English-speaking claimants. On the other hand, providing reasonable accommodations for linguistic minorities is not the same as "multilingual government." In no way does it imply coequal status for languages other than English.[3] Finally, there is a world of difference between recognizing English as the *common* language of government in this country, a reality that no one disputes or seeks to change, and designating English as the *only* language of government (with a few narrow exceptions). Yet for many advocates of Official English, the two are synonymous—they believe that "linguistic unity" can and should be coerced—and this is what makes the proposition such a vexed legal question. Though the goal may appear innocent, the means would restrict the liberties and endanger the welfare of Americans whose English is limited, an already disadvantaged group.

The decision in *Yñiguez v. Mofford* was an unexpected victory for the opponents of Proposition 106, whose hopes had relied more on the Fourteenth Amendment than the First. That is, they had emphasized the discriminatory impact of Official English, only secondarily noting its threat to free speech. Some English Plus activists had even criticized Yñiguez and Gutiérrez for bringing a weak case. Yet, not surprisingly for a conservative, Judge Rosenblatt was content to dispose of Proposition 106 on First Amendment grounds and to stop before reaching the more contentious territory of "equal protection." It is here that most future battles over language rights are likely to be waged.

"No State shall . . . deprive any person of life, liberty, or property, without due process of law; nor deny to any person within its jurisdiction the equal protection of the laws." The Fourteenth Amendment was designed to check the power of government to abridge fundamental freedoms. It was, in effect, a fail-safe mechanism for those occasions when Madisonian pluralism broke down and "interested combinations" of whites, males, Protestants, native-born, English speakers, or other majorities conspired to strip minorities of their rights. In its historical context the amendment sought to address the ultimate challenge of ethnic pluralism: how to incorporate newly freed slaves into a democratic system. Sadly, federal judges often proved susceptible to the same racist biases as other Americans. For decades they were parsimonious in applying the amendment's Due Process and Equal Protection clauses to outlaw state-sanctioned discrimination against African-Americans and other unpopular groups. Then, in 1923, came the *Meyer v. Nebraska* case, a landmark in U.S. constitutional law that also set a precedent for minority language rights.

Robert Meyer, a teacher in rural Nebraska, was convicted of violating the state's English-only school law of 1919, which prohibited the teaching of foreign languages in the elementary grades. Meyer's crime, as described by the Nebraska Supreme Court, was "that between the hour of 1 and 1:30, on May 25, 1920, he taught the German language"—using a book of Bible stories—"to a ten-year-old boy, a pupil in the [Zion Evangelical Lutheran] school, who had not passed the eighth grade." For this the malefactor was fined $25. The pastor of Meyer's congregation testified at his trial, explaining that many church members were German immigrants and their English was poor. "In order to keep the parents and children in a religious way," he said, "and not diminish the influence of the parents in the home . . . for that reason we wanted to have the children learn so much German that they could be able to worship with their parents." But this argument did not satisfy Nebraska's highest court. The religious nature of a lesson "could not act as a shield" for the illegal teaching of German, it ruled.

> The law affects few citizens, except those of foreign lineage. Other citizens, in their selection of studies, except perhaps in rare instances, have never deemed it of importance to teach their children foreign languages before such children have reached the eighth grade. In the legislative mind, the salutary effects of the statute no doubt outweighed the restriction upon the citizens generally, which, it appears, was a restriction of no real consequence. . . .
>
> The Legislature had seen the baneful effects of permitting foreigners, who had taken residence in this country, to rear and educate their children in the language of their native land. The result of that condition was found to be inimical to our own safety. To allow the children of foreigners, who had emigrated here, to be taught from early childhood the language of the country of their parents was . . . to educate them so that they must always think in that language, and, as a consequence, naturally inculcate in them the ideas and sentiments foreign to the best interests of this country.

Here was the tyranny of the majority that Madison had warned about. "A restriction of no real consequence" for "the citizens generally" singled out German Americans, Nebraska's principal ethnic minority at the time, for a special burden. Their rights were deemed expendable when balanced against the greater good. Indeed, with their foreign "ideas and sentiments," the Germans were the main targets of English-only legislation. An attorney for the state of Nebraska, sounding a lot like today's advocates for Official English, argued before the U.S. Supreme Court: "Nebraska cannot be divided and made part English and part German. It is the ambition of the state to have its entire population 100 percent American."

This was a worthy objective, agreed Justice McReynolds, writing for the court. "The desire of the Legislature to foster a homogeneous people with American ideals prepared readily to understand current discussions of civic matters is easy to appreciate." But Anglo-conformity could not be imposed by state fiat:

> The protection of the Constitution extends to all, to those who speak other languages as well as to those born with English on the tongue. Perhaps it would be highly advantageous if all had ready understanding of our ordinary speech, but this cannot be coerced with methods which conflict with the Constitution—a desirable end cannot be promoted by prohibited means.[4]

Federal courts had previously invoked the Fourteenth Amendment to shield corporations from state regulation. But up to now, as far as individual liberties were concerned, they had been extremely literal in their reading of the Constitution. Freedom of speech, assembly, press, religion—these were clear enough. But freedom to teach a foreign language? *Meyer v. Nebraska* blazed a new trail of judicial analysis, relying on the Due Process Clause. "The liberty thus guaranteed," the court said, "denotes not merely freedom from bodily restraint but also the right of the individual to contract, to engage in any of the common occupations of life, to acquire useful knowledge, to marry, establish a home and bring up children, to worship God according to the dictates of his own conscience, and generally to enjoy those privileges long recognized at common law as essential to the orderly pursuit of happiness by free men." In other words, due process was not just a question of procedure; it also encompassed *substantive* rights, values, and traditions. Simply put, there were certain liberties the state could not restrict without very good reason. Among these Justice McReynolds counted Meyer's right to pursue his calling as a modern-language teacher and German parents' right to engage him to instruct their children.

Later courts have relied on "substantive due process" to establish a general right of privacy, for example, in reproductive choice cases such as *Griswold v. Connecticut* and *Roe v. Wade.* Yet the doctrine remains controversial. Majoritarians like Robert Bork have attacked it as an "unprincipled" way for judges to substitute their own "value preferences" for those of elected legislatures. It all began with *Meyer v. Nebraska,* Bork says, a case he believes was "wrongly decided."[5]

Meyer also helped to lay the foundation for a more generous interpretation of the Equal Protection Clause. Traditionally courts have held that the Fourteenth Amendment allows government to treat certain groups differently from others, provided that it is acting reasonably to further legitimate goals. To take an extreme example, a state might declare itself to be officially right-handed, outlaw the teaching of left-handed penmanship in all schools, and ban expenditures to accommodate left-handers who fail to conform—as long as Official Rightness bore some rational relationship to achieving a worthwhile civic purpose (promoting a sense of national unity, controlling sinister thought patterns, bringing Lefties into the mainstream). If so, left-handers would have no recourse under the Fourteenth Amendment.

Since the rational-basis test is relatively easy to pass, minority groups have often found themselves unprotected. States long found it easy to justify "separate but equal" and other discriminatory laws as "reasonable," until the Supreme Court began to expand its view of equal protection. For the first time in 1938, it noted that "prejudices against discrete and insular minorities"—such as those based on race, national origin, or religion—may "curtail the operation of those political processes ordinarily to be relied upon" to safeguard fundamental rights. When states treated such groups differently, their actions warranted "more exacting judicial scrutiny." Thus began a legal revolution against majoritarian excesses.

A 1954 decision, *Hernández v. Texas,* illustrates the principles at work. A Mexican American defendant was convicted of murder in Jackson County, Texas, by an all-Anglo jury. Even though Mexican Americans made up 14 percent of the local population, not one had served as a juror in the past twenty-five years; citizens with Hispanic surnames were systematically excluded, a practice common in Texas at the time. The Supreme Court found such methods of jury selection to be unconstitutional, ruling that Mexican Americans were a "distinct class" for equal protection purposes—a group that his-

torically had been singled out for adverse treatment and deprived
of political power. While "color" was one obvious marker, the court
said, "Spanish names" were another. State actions that use these
categories to discriminate are automatically "suspect" and cry out
for strict scrutiny. The court left the door open to define further
suspect classes (for example, minority language speakers), noting
that "community prejudices are not static, and from time to time
other differences from the community norm may define other groups
which need the same protection."

Discrimination is rarely so blatant today. More often, a minority
feels a disproportionate impact under a law or policy that appears
neutral "on its face." English Only legislation treats all groups
"equally," even though it affects some differently from others. But
a discriminatory *result* does not necessarily denote a violation of
the Equal Protection Clause, which requires proof of discriminatory
intent: that the state acted "at least in part 'because of,' not merely
'in spite of,' its adverse effects upon an identifiable group." Moreover, there is a difference between state interference with protected
rights, as in *Meyer,* and failure to provide special help—for example, to overcome language barriers. In 1983, a federal appeals
court found nothing unconstitutional about the Social Security Administration's practice of limiting most forms and proceedings to
English because there was no evidence it had singled out linguistic
minorities (in this case, Spanish speakers) for adverse treatment. In
other words, the Fourteenth Amendment grants no blanket right to
public services in languages other than English, and government
agencies do not necessarily violate equal protection by failing to
offer them. A blanket termination of bilingual programs, however,
or a law ruling out new ones, might be another matter.[6]

Here is where strict scrutiny comes in. When suspect classes are
involved, state actions must be "precisely tailored to serve a compelling government interest." They may not abridge minority rights
in pursuit of some trivial objective or employ measures that are
more drastic than necessary.

In connection with Official English, one might ask whether there
is any "compelling" need for all Americans to speak the same language, considering the nation's ability to cope with diversity in the
past. Even more dubious: Is a mandate that government operate
only in English the means best "tailored" to promote a common

tongue? Would it not be more efficient (not to mention more humane) to expand opportunities to learn English? If bilingual assistance is eliminated, wouldn't that harm those who are struggling to learn English just as much as those who resist doing so? In sum, is there any overarching reason to deny the existence of minority language rights? If Official English fervor continues to spread, these questions are likely to come before the Supreme Court some day. But an important hurdle remains—the question of defining linguistic minorities as a "suspect class."

No federal court has yet gone that far. In most cases there has been no need to consider language as a characteristic apart from national origin. For example, in 1991 the Supreme Court stopped short of defining language as a criterion for equal protection analysis in another decision involving jury selection. Dionisio Hernández was charged with attempted murder following a shootout in a Latino neighborhood in Brooklyn, New York. Several witnesses were scheduled to testify in Spanish through an interpreter, and the prosecutor expressed concern that jurors who understood Spanish might heed the direct testimony rather than the English translation that forms the official court record. (The two are not always consistent and controversies sometimes arise.[7]) So he used peremptory challenges to disqualify prospective jurors who were bilingual.[8] The trial judge accepted this procedure, over defense objections, and Hernández was later convicted by the all-Anglo jury. On appeal, the Puerto Rican Legal Defense and Education Fund argued that because a high percentage of New York's Latinos speak both Spanish and English, barring bilingual jurors amounted to discrimination on the basis of race and ethnicity. Less drastic solutions were available, such as allowing jurors to raise questions if they disputed the official translation. Certainly, the net effect was to deny Hernández a jury of his peers.

On a six-to-three vote, the Supreme Court accepted the prosecutor's "race-neutral" explanation. It found no proof of intentional discrimination; therefore, no violation of the Equal Protection Clause. But Justice Kennedy, writing for the court's conservative majority, added a caveat: "Our decision today does not imply that exclusion of bilinguals from jury service is wise, or even that it is constitutional in all cases. It is a harsh paradox that one may become proficient enough in English to participate in trial [a requirement for federal jurors], only to encounter disqualification because he knows a second language as well." As for the suspect class issue, Kennedy summarized the court's thinking since *Meyer v. Nebraska:*

> Language elicits a response from others, ranging from admiration and respect, to distance and alienation, to ridicule and scorn. Reactions of the latter type all too often result from or initiate racial hostility. . . . It may well be, for certain ethnic groups and in some communities, that proficiency in a particular language, like skin color, should be treated as a surrogate for race under an equal protection analysis. And, as we make clear, a policy of striking down all who speak a given language, without regard to the particular circumstances of the trial or the individual responses of the jurors, may be found by the trial judge to be a pretext for racial discrimination. But that case is not before us.

Under this standard, state or local English Only measures would be unconstitutional to the extent they are motivated by animus toward specific groups, such as Latinos or Southeast Asians. Or, by extending the legal reasoning, courts could apply equal protection to linguistic minorities directly and overrule initiatives like Proposition 106 to the extent they discriminate *on the basis of language*. Although the latter approach is foreign to American traditions, it is well established in international law, for example, in the United Nations Charter and the Universal Declaration of Human Rights. Such treaties, once ratified by the Senate, become part of U.S. law.

Several legal scholars have argued that non-English speakers should be regarded as a suspect or "quasi-suspect" class.[9] Antonio Califa of the American Civil Liberties Union reasons that "the English Only movement is fueled by cultural insecurity and prejudice against Hispanics" and other linguistic minorities. Official English legislation abridges "important rights such as education and nondiscriminatory work environments, as well as the right to vote, which the [Supreme] Court recognizes as fundamental." Moreover, non-English speakers have historically been singled out for unequal treatment. "The strict scrutiny test would be appropriately applied . . . because the class deprived of rights is *defined by language*—a proxy for national origin." Finally, "language discrimination is an area where the majoritarian political process may not adequately reflect or protect concerns of the minority. Prejudice disguised as national unity wins popular support. If the proposal is enacted, the Constitution will be the only refuge for America's linguistic minorities."

Should Official English ever become a part of the U.S. Constitution, all bets are off. It is possible that such a measure would forever exclude non-English speakers from the protections of the Fourteenth Amendment and add a footnote, in effect, to the First Amendment guarantee of free speech: *except in languages other than English*. As numerous analysts have concluded, however, the precise impact is impossible to predict. A simple declaration—"The English language shall be the official language of the United States"—might have no legal effect whatsoever unless Congress chose to enforce it. (So far, this has been the fate of Official English in states where it has passed.) But other versions of the amendment, such as those sponsored by Senator Hayakawa and Representative Norman Shumway, incorporate the restrictive features of Proposition 106. With a few exceptions, they would appear to ban any use of other languages by federal, state, or local governments.[10] And this time linguistic minorities could count on no constitutional safety net. An English Language Amendment would override statutes and case law at all levels. Where conflicts arose with the First, Fifth, Sixth, Fourteenth, or Fifteenth amendments, the more recent and more explicit English Only mandate would likely take precedence.

In its most proscriptive form, Official English would settle the issue of minority language rights in the United States—there would be none left to debate. Even now their status is uncertain. For the most part, state and federal governments are just beginning to address language barriers in such fields as civil liberties, social services, and business regulation.

One exception is California, where the Dymally-Alatorre Act of 1973 requires state agencies that deal directly with the public to accommodate non-English speakers, where the need is sufficient, by hiring bilingual employees. The demand for assistance is greatest in Spanish, Cantonese, Vietnamese, Tagalog, Korean, and American Sign Language, with nearly one million such "contacts" recorded annually. Under other California laws, government must print minority-language pamphlets on subjects including food stamps,

Medi-Cal insurance, workers' compensation, labor and fair employment laws, the rights of the disabled, motor vehicle regulations, and consumer protection, to name a few. State-funded programs in job training, special education, low-income housing, energy conservation, waste recycling, pesticide spraying, and disaster relief must offer translation services. Property tax forms, various legal notices, and information in state courts must be provided in Spanish as well as English.

On the other hand, states like Ohio, Pennsylvania, Louisiana, and Colorado have repealed virtually all of their nineteenth-century statutes authorizing official uses of minority languages. Even New Mexico, whose 1912 constitution provided for the publication of state laws in Spanish, discontinued the practice in 1949. In addressing today's diversity, few legislatures have followed California's lead in requiring bilingual services. For its part, the U.S. Code includes only a handful of such statutes, generally enacted in response to judicial precedents.

Minority language rights—to the extent they exist in this country—are found largely in federal court decisions that ban invidious discrimination, ensure rights otherwise guaranteed, or provide access to certain government functions. The last category is quite small. The most significant of these "access rights" is the Supreme Court's 1974 ruling in *Lau v. Nichols* that public schools must take "affirmative steps" to compensate for a child's lack of English skills:

> There is no equality of treatment merely by providing students with the same facilities, textbooks, teachers, and curriculum; for students who do not understand English are effectively foreclosed from any meaningful education. Basic English skills are at the very core of what these public schools teach. Imposition of a requirement that, before a child can effectively participate in the educational program, he must already have acquired those basic skills is to make a mockery of public education.

Nevertheless, the court created no federal entitlement to bilingual education.[11] A handful of states like Illinois, Massachusetts, Texas, and, until recently, California have mandated bilingual classrooms where schools have a critical mass of limited English speakers from the same language group. Still, a large percentage of such students receive nothing more than remedial English instruction, the minimum standard under *Lau*.

Because language rights have been manufactured piecemeal by judges, they are inconsistent and contradictory. Only in recent years have linguistic minorities been guaranteed liberties that other Americans consider their birthright. Until 1970, a non-English-speaking defendant in a criminal trial had no assurance that an interpreter would be available to translate the proceedings. The case that established this right involved Rogelio Negrón, a Puerto Rican farm laborer who had killed a fellow worker during a drunken brawl. At his trial there was an interpreter hired by the prosecutor to translate Spanish testimony into English, but no one bothered to translate for Negrón, a monolingual Spanish speaker, who had little idea of what was happening during the four-day proceeding. (His court-appointed attorney, unable to speak Spanish, could offer no help.) On two occasions during breaks, the court interpreter briefed Negrón informally on what had transpired. But generally, he was unable to comprehend damaging testimony against him or to confer with his lawyer about how to cross-examine witnesses. Convicted of second-degree murder, he was sentenced to prison for twenty years to life.

Although Negrón was indigent and uneducated, acting as his own lawyer he persisted in filing habeas corpus petitions. Finally, after three years he won a new trial. A federal appeals court ruled that the defendant had been denied his Sixth Amendment right to confront his accusers. "Not only for the sake of effective cross-examination," wrote Judge Irving Kaufman,

> but as a matter of simple humaneness, Negrón deserved more than to sit in total incomprehension as the trial proceeded. Particularly inappropriate in this nation where many languages are spoken is a callousness to the crippling language handicap of a newcomer to its shores, whose life and freedom the state by its criminal processes chooses to put in jeopardy. . . . The least we can require is that a court, put on notice of a defendant's severe language difficulty, make unmistakably clear to him that he has a right to a competent translator to assist him, at state expense if need be, throughout his trial.

Congress has since adopted this principle for federal criminal and immigration proceedings. State courts generally observe it as well. But no comparable rule has been defined in civil or administrative cases, such as welfare and child custody actions, in which non-English-speaking parties may have higher personal stakes than in criminal matters.

On one thing Official English advocates and opponents are agreed. A constitutional English Language Amendment would outlaw bilingual ballots, currently required by the 1975 amendments to the Voting Rights Act. In its earliest campaigns in California, U.S. English tapped resentments about this intrusion of bilingualism into a primal rite of citizenship. For many Anglo-Americans, the new law epitomized the lengths to which government would go in appeasing militant minorities. Voting in foreign languages—was nothing sacred? When the San Diego registrar wrote to half a million county residents to see if they would need Spanish-language ballots, thousands of prepaid postcards came back with angry comments: "I'm sick of this damn pampering of Mexicans"; "Speak English in America or get out"; "Stop wasting our taxes on Chicanos and aliens"; "Send mine in Italian and my husband's in Polish, and you may as well put us on welfare, too, and we can live it up."

There were also less bigoted objections. Considering that candidates for U.S. citizenship had to pass an English literacy test, wasn't it contradictory to allow them to vote in other tongues? Wouldn't it cost enormous sums to accommodate all immigrants in this way? Then, too, there were the standard Anglo anxieties: could bilingual ballots create a disincentive to learning English, divide Americans along language lines, erode the nation's social glue, et cetera? When put to a popular vote, these arguments prevailed, first in San Francisco, where Proposition O passed easily in 1983, and the following year statewide, as 71 percent of Californians approved Proposition 38, "Voting Materials in English Only." Both measures were advisory, simply calling for repeal of the bilingual provisions of the Voting Rights Act. So far, that has not occurred, but most of these requirements will expire in 1992 unless Congress votes to renew them.

Bilingual ballots have never enjoyed much public support because the public has never known much about their origin and rationale. For instance, it is often assumed that any non-English speaker is entitled to vote in his or her native tongue. The reality is that this right applies only to linguistic minorities who have historically faced discrimination at the polls—Hispanics, Asians, and Native Americans—and only in areas where they meet strict requirements. A language group must represent more than 5 percent of the local population and have below-average rates of voter turnout and English literacy. Moreover, the cost of assisting non-English-speaking voters is quite modest. San Francisco officials have estimated that the annual expense of trilingual English-Spanish-Chinese ballots comes to less than three cents per household. In 1984, a federal survey of eighty-three "covered" jurisdictions found that it cost them a grand total of $388,000, or 7.6 percent of election expenses, to provide bilingual ballots. Hardly an exorbitant price to safeguard what the Supreme Court has called a "fundamental right because it is preservative of all rights."

The trend toward bilingual ballots originated in the Voting Rights Act of 1965. This law suspended literacy requirements for voting in southern states where they had been systematically used to disfranchise African-Americans. A related provision, sponsored by Senator Robert F. Kennedy, prohibited such tests elsewhere for voters who had completed the sixth grade on U.S. soil in a school whose "predominant classroom language was other than English." In other words, native-born U.S. citizens could no longer be prevented from voting simply because they had grown up in a non-English-speaking environment. Puerto Ricans were the main beneficiaries of this section, particularly in New York, where a 1921 amendment to the state constitution (aimed principally at Yiddish-speaking Jews) had denied the franchise to anyone unable to read English.

Federal courts soon went further. Banning English literacy tests was a hollow gesture, they reasoned, if formerly excluded voters still faced a language barrier at the polls. Accordingly, they mandated bilingual election materials for Puerto Rican voters in Philadelphia, Chicago, and New York. "It is simply fundamental," wrote one judge, "that voting instructions and ballots, in addition to any other material which forms part of the official communication to registered voters prior to an election, must be in Spanish as well as in English, if the vote of Spanish-speaking citizens is not to be seriously impaired."

Mexican Americans faced more complex barriers to empowerment in the Southwest. If awards were given for obstructing the right to vote, the state of Texas would undoubtedly win in the creative subterfuge category. Until it was overruled on equal protection grounds in 1970, the Texas election code prohibited poll workers from assisting voters who were illiterate in English (while encouraging them to assist the physically handicapped). The poll tax, another restraint on Hispanic voting—or, more accurately, on Hispanic voting independent of political machines[12]—survived in Texas until 1966. After it was struck down, the legislature devised an inconvenient system requiring voters to reregister each year. When that, too, was ruled unconstitutional, a new law dropped voters from the rolls if they missed an election and failed to return a registration form in English. Smaller discriminations were perpetrated as well: locating polling places on the Anglo side of town, using police to intimidating effect on election day, and violating the secrecy of the ballot.

Throughout the Southwest the English-only nature of the system was the most pervasive, if not always the most severe, obstacle. As a federal judge observed in 1972, "This cultural and language impediment, conjoined with the poll tax and the most restrictive voter registration procedures in the nation, [has] operated to effectively deny Mexican Americans access to the political processes in Texas even longer than the blacks were formally denied access by the white primary." Yet Congress, preoccupied with barriers against African-American voters in the Deep South, had virtually ignored the plight of Mexican Americans. Under the original Voting Rights Act, jurisdictions that had used literacy tests to discriminate now came under close supervision; they had to clear any proposed changes in voting districts or election procedures with the U.S. Department of Justice. But Texas, despite its broad array of tactics for disfranchising Chicanos (as well as blacks), had not relied on the literacy test. So the state escaped "preclearance" coverage under the act.

The 1975 amendments were intended to correct such oversights. First, federal supervision was extended to districts where the English-only ballot had limited the participation of linguistic minority voters. That took care of Texas, Alaska, and parts of Arizona, California, New York, Florida, and a few scattered counties elsewhere. Second, bilingual ballots were required in these and other districts where at least 5 percent of the population belonged to a single minority language group.[13]

Here was a meat-ax, as opposed to a surgical approach, to remove a complex cancer. The symptoms of discrimination were far more obvious than the cure. Spanish speakers accounted for 16.4

percent of Texas residents, but only 2.5 percent of elected officials; in New York they represented 7.4 percent of the population but held less than 0.1 percent of elected positions. Yet language was neither the only, nor the worst barrier to voting by these groups, as hearings on the legislation made clear. This has led critics like Abigail Thernstrom to charge that "ethnic activists" and their allies in Congress "speciously equated an English-only ballot with a fraudulent literacy test" to prove intentional discrimination where none existed. As compared with the black experience, there was "little evidence of basic disfranchisement" for Hispanics, she insists. "The electoral ineffectiveness of Mexican Americans" was due at least in part "to internal disunity and a culture of political passivity."

Once again Thernstrom is not averse to rewriting the public record, which supports none of the trickery she alleges. Representative Barbara Jordan of Texas, chief sponsor of the 1975 amendments, acknowledged at the outset of the hearings:

> The *purpose* of providing English-only elections where significant numbers of Mexican Americans reside may not be discriminatory, but the *effect* is discriminatory, especially when combined with the low educational attainment of the population. . . . Just as Congress seized upon literacy tests as *characteristic* of the voting problems facing blacks in the South, so too are English-only ballots among a substantial Spanish-speaking population. . . . I have incorporated the use of an English-only ballot as a "test or device" because it is a readily identifiable, objective criterion [that] the Justice Department can easily apply nationally. [Her emphasis.]

Bilingual voting, like bilingual education, was designed to compensate for decades of inequality,[14] a goal that could not be achieved through strictly "equal" treatment. Simply prohibiting the English literacy test, or ending the segregation of Mexican and Chinese American students, was insufficient to restore rights that linguistic minorities had lost through no fault of their own. For such groups, affirmative measures were needed to guarantee equal opportunity. Clearly, this approach can lead to anomalies, as when naturalized citizens of "Spanish origin" are entitled to bilingual ballots but their Portuguese- or French-speaking neighbors are not. Congressional critics of the expanded Voting Rights Act have argued that its effect is "to mandate an 'unequal protection of the laws,'" privileging some minority voters over others from non-English-speaking backgrounds—namely, that it favors nonwhite immigrants and indigenous minorities over white Euro-ethnics.

Under current law an individual's need for a bilingual ballot does not enter into the equation. Perhaps it should. Why encourage immigrants to become U.S. citizens and then limit their ability to participate in our political system? Why not make every effort to eliminate language barriers to voting? It is true that most applicants for naturalization must pass an English literacy test (except for those aged fifty or older who have been legal U.S. residents for at least twenty years). But the level of proficiency required is quite low. In 1982, an average year, the Immigration and Naturalization Service turned down only twenty-nine out of 201,507 petitions for citizenship because of inability to speak, read, or write the English language. The literacy skills required to decipher voter registration notices or complex ballot propositions are normally the last to be acquired in a second language.

Official English advocates have also attacked bilingual ballots as an invitation to ethnic bossism. In 1984, sponsors made the following argument for California's Proposition 38: "Citizens who have limited or no knowledge of English do not have access to essential information for independent decision-making. They are easily led into block [sic] voting by opportunistic political leaders." This is precisely the type of problem that bilingual ballots were designed to solve. Increasing voters' ability to make informed choices increases their independence from ward bosses, ethnic or otherwise. On the other hand, there is nothing un-American about bloc voting, a tactic that every immigrant group—except for those denied the franchise—has used to secure its rights. One gets the impression that what English Only advocates dread most is not uninformed voting, but minority empowerment.

Since the 1975 amendments became law, few statistics have been gathered on the relationship between bilingual ballots and voter turnout. In one survey by Robert Brischetto of the Southwest Voter Research Institute, 72 percent of monolingual Spanish speakers in Texas and California said they would be less likely to vote without them. Yet a majority of Hispanics live in areas outside the coverage of the Voting Rights Act, which applies the same 5 percent standard to every jurisdiction regardless of size. In sparsely populated Texas counties, a few Mexican American families are sufficient to trigger coverage; in cities like Chicago, huge barrios are insufficient to do so. The effect has been to limit the availability of bilingual ballots in urban areas, except where they are ordered by courts or provided voluntarily. Under a more equitable formula, any voting district with, say, ten thousand members of a single linguistic minority might be required to offer assistance. But proposals to expand coverage, and perhaps even to continue coverage, are expected to face strong resistance in Congress.

Official English advocates have often disavowed any interest in restricting private speech. In 1988, John Tanton asserted that "no one, no one at all, wants to prohibit or outlaw the use of any language in America. No one wants to regulate the languages used in homes, businesses, or churches, or to prevent newspapers or books from being published in any language." In the post-Tanton era, U.S. English still defines its goal as designating "one language for use in official public business," nothing more. Yet even if its sponsors' motives were so pure—they are not—the plain wording of the English Language Amendment threatens the right to speak other tongues in private contexts. In particular, it would overrule fair employment and contracting laws to the extent they "require . . . the use in the United States of languages other than English." Such a constitutional provision might restrain courts from treating language discrimination as a proxy for national-origin discrimination, jeopardizing numerous precedents on free speech, both large and small.

Take the case of the English-only barroom. This lawsuit concerned, in the words of the trial judge, "nothing more—nor less—lofty than the right of some American citizens to enjoy a bottle of beer at . . . a nondescript little tavern . . . and to speak in Spanish while doing so." On August 23, 1972, Gilberto Hernández and two Chicano friends were drinking beer and speaking their native tongue at the Taffrail Tavern in Forest Grove, Oregon, when some Anglo customers became agitated. What if the Spanish speakers were talking about them? They complained to the bartender, who then invoked a house rule:

Do not allow a foreign language to be used at the bar, if it interferes with the regular trade. If there should be a chance of a problem, ask the "Problem" people to move to a table and turn the juke box up.

When the Spanish-speaking drinkers protested the order to move, the bartender poured out their beers and refused to refund their money. Police were called and the Chicanos left peaceably. A similar scenario was replayed two days later, except that three Anglo regulars followed the "problem" customers outside and assaulted them with a fire extinguisher. Both groups of Hispanics filed suit against the tavern, charging that the English-only rule violated Reconstruction-era civil rights laws that guarantee racial equality in private contracts and purchases.

In their defense the bar owners explained that the language policy was designed solely to keep the peace. About one-quarter of their customers were Mexican Americans, recent arrivals in the community, and some locals resented the presence of these "foreigners," the defendants testified. So they required bar customers to speak English as a way to reduce friction and mistrust. But the federal court found this to be a "lame justification" indeed:

> Just as the Constitution forbids banishing blacks to the back of the bus so as not to arouse the racial animosity of the preferred white passengers, it also forbids ordering Spanish-speaking patrons to the "back booth or out" to avoid antagonizing English-speaking beer-drinkers. . . . Catering to prejudice out of fear of provoking greater prejudice only perpetuates racism. Courts faithful to the Fourteenth Amendment will not permit, either by camouflage or cavalier treatment, equal protection to be so profaned.

Whether the bar owners intended to discriminate against Chicanos was "irrelevant," the court added. "The rule's results are what count." It cited a recent Supreme Court precedent in *Griggs v. Duke Power,* a job discrimination case, which held that only a well-established "business necessity" can justify employer actions that have a disparate impact on racial or ethnic minorities. This has become a key tenet in adjudicating English-only restrictions on private speech, though an increasingly embattled one.

Thus far, the only court test of Proposition 63, California's Official English amendment, has come in such a case. In 1984, three municipal court judges in Huntington Park, a predominantly Latino suburb of Los Angeles, adopted a policy forbidding court employees to speak languages other than English during working hours, except when necessary to communicate with non-English-speaking members of the public. (The ban was later amended to exempt breaktime conversations.) The employees most directly affected were Spanish-speaking court clerks who, ironically, had been hired for their bilingual skills so that they could translate for Latinos from the community. As usual the English-only rule was rationalized as a way to promote ethnic harmony in the workplace—Anglo employees had feared they were the butt of jokes in Spanish—and to keep the municipal court from becoming a "Tower of Babel" unable to function for lack of a common language. After the state's Official English amendment passed in November 1986, it too was cited as a justification, since the court is a public-sector employer.

Alva Gutiérrez, a bilingual clerk, sued to overturn the policy as a form of national-origin discrimination. In response the Huntington Park judges denied any such intent. They argued that because the plaintiff was fluent in English and had no trouble complying with the rule, there was no disparate impact. Lawyers for Gutiérrez countered that preventing employees from speaking their native tongue had a discriminatory effect, whether monolingual Anglos appreciated it or not. Besides creating a burden in expressing certain thoughts and emotions, an English-only rule made "Hispanics feel belittled" and not unreasonably so, since English speakers had voiced ethnic slurs against them. On the other hand, there was no evidence that Spanish had ever been used to express animosity toward Anglos—only that it made them feel threatened.[15]

The U.S. Equal Employment Opportunity Commission had recently issued a set of guidelines for such situations. While not formally binding, the policy put employers on notice that any speak-English-only rule would have to meet stringent standards or face an E.E.O.C. lawsuit. A language restriction had to be "necessary to safe and efficient job performance." It might be justified when workers were performing dangerous or difficult tasks and close coordination was essential, but not when they were doing routine chores or taking coffee breaks. Moreover, an English-only policy had to be communicated and applied uniformly; it could not be used to harass or isolate certain groups of employees. Appeasing anti-Hispanic prejudices would not qualify as a bona fide business necessity.

Applying the E.E.O.C. guidelines to the Huntington Park case, the Ninth U.S. Circuit Court of Appeals could find no grounds to sustain the English-only restriction. The argument that requiring employees to speak a common language would minimize disruptions sounded reasonable in the abstract. But Spanish was a fact of life in Huntington Park; hence the need to hire bilingual clerks like Alva Gutiérrez. "Babel" already seemed to be "part of the normal press of court business," the appellate panel observed. "[Thus] its elimination in the area of intra-employee communication cannot be termed essential to . . . efficient operation[s]." Nor was there any evidence that the English-only rule had improved relations among employees; to the contrary, it seemed to be fostering racial tension. Responding to a claim that the use of Spanish undercut supervisors' authority, the court suggested that the municipal judges might consider hiring a few supervisors who spoke Spanish.

Finally, the Ninth Circuit rejected the argument, advanced by the defendants and by U.S. English, that Proposition 63 required an English-only policy for public employees. The amendment said no such thing, the court ruled. It was "primarily a symbolic statement concerning the importance of preserving, protecting, and strengthening the English language." Furthermore, what was at issue in this case was "private speech in Spanish during on-duty periods." That the employer happened to be the County of Los Angeles was incidental to the decision, which struck down a prevalent type of English-only rule in both private and public workplaces.

Yet the precedent in *Gutiérrez v. Municipal Court* survived only briefly. Issued in early 1988, it was dismissed a year later by the Supreme Court—not on its merits, but because the lawsuit was judged to be moot (the plaintiff had quit her job and accepted a cash settlement).[16] This has thrown the issue up for grabs, owing to a 1980 decision in the Fifth Circuit that held precisely the opposite—it was permissible to fire a bilingual hardware clerk for making a casual remark in Spanish—although that case, *García v. Gloor,* predated the E.E.O.C. guidelines. Further muddying a murky pond, the Supreme Court has abandoned the *Griggs* standard, making it tougher to prove a civil rights violation when "innocent" employment practices have a disparate impact on minorities. This move, in turn, has stirred a political conflict over "racial quotas" and equal opportunity that seems likely to persist through the 1990s.[17]

Amid the legal uncertainty, English-only rules seem to be spreading. They have already appeared in "hospitals, universities, the U.S.

Postal Service, hotels, electronics manufacturing firms, insurance companies, banks, and even nonprofit charitable organizations," according to Edward Chen, an A.C.L.U. litigator in California. He credits Proposition 63 for this trend. Various linguistic minorities have been affected, but for reasons as yet unexplained, Filipinos seem to be disproportionately targeted. Perhaps it is because many of them hold entry- and mid-level jobs in health care, a field where English-only policies are popular with employers.

Hospital employees at the University of California at San Francisco complained to the E.E.O.C. in 1988 after they were disciplined for speaking Tagalog or Spanish on the job, either among themselves or with patients. Yolanda Cortez, a shop steward for the American Federation of State, County, and Municipal Employees, says management would sometimes call upon bilingual workers to serve as translators (with no added compensation) but otherwise banned speech in their native tongues. The policy was apparently inspired by a "customer relations" concern: fear of alienating upscale Anglo patients. "It got to be pretty ridiculous," Cortez recalls. "You'd have cook-helpers chopping beets all day—everybody on that shift may have been Filipino—and they're all Tagalog speakers. But it was necessary that they 'communicate in a common language,' English." Or secretaries would be reprimanded for speaking Spanish on the telephone because any English speaker within earshot "had to understand what you said at all times." Supervisors often used the rule to harass or humiliate active union members, she charges. Intentional or not, the effect was to widen ethnic divisions among employees and produce a tense work environment. Following months of unfavorable publicity, the hospital agreed to rescind its policy.

As the Proposition 63 experience demonstrates, Official English inevitably encroaches on the terrain of private speech. This is not a case of good intentions gone awry. U.S. English abandoned its attacks on Spanish advertising only after they raised First Amendment concerns, and it has continued to work through regulatory agencies to obstruct business operations in minority languages. In 1986, the group protested to the California Public Utilities Commission when Pacific Bell introduced a system that gave Spanish- and Chinese-speaking customers direct access to telephone operators in their native tongue. Meanwhile it petitioned the Federal Communications Commission to limit broadcasting in languages other than English, claiming that English stations were being "crowded off the dial" in certain areas. Neither of these campaigns was successful.

Several California communities have taken Proposition 63 as a green light to regulate non-English business signs. Usually the targets have been Chinese, Korean, and other Asian establishments, whose "foreign" appearance offends some natives' sensibilities. In 1988, the Pomona City Council passed an ordinance requiring that signs displaying "foreign alphabetical characters" devote at least half their space to "English alphabetical characters." Officials claimed the law was necessary to help identify buildings in case of fire or other emergencies. Yet there was no comparable requirement that a business advertising only in English display its name or even a street number. The law's sponsor, Councilman Clay Bryant, shed further light on his intentions by observing that "a proliferation of signs and advertising [in] oriental characters" had "caused dissent and strife" in nearby communities. "I think it's totally out of hand over there in Monterey Park," he added. "I fought in two wars to keep this country the way it is, and I'll be damned if I'm going to let any part of America be turned into Little Saigon or whatever."

A federal court agreed with Asian business owners who challenged Pomona's ordinance: they were being singled out for harassment. The safety argument was a mere pretext for restricting First Amendment rights. As the plaintiffs' attorney, Elizabeth Brancart, noted, the city had not only abridged free speech; it had "compelled speech" by requiring English advertising. The judge also ruled the measure unconstitutional on equal protection grounds. Nevertheless, city councils in nearby Arcadia, San Gabriel, and San Marino subsequently refused to repeal similar ordinances.

These officials are not alone in their intransigence. In California, Official English seems to encourage a conviction that rights to use other languages in any context have been limited. While no court has yet endorsed this view—nor is one likely to do so—elected leaders are less immune to such influences. So the major impact of Proposition 63 has been indirect, political rather than legal. Instead of directly terminating services for linguistic minorities, it has weakened support for such programs in the legislature. Bilingual education has been the most notable casualty.

Eight

Problem or Resource?

An eye-catching full-page advertisement appeared in the *New York Times* for July 25, 1989. "IF SOME N.Y. EDUCATORS GET THEIR WAY," warned the 96-point headline, "THIS IS THE KIND OF FUTURE MANY OF OUR CHILDREN WILL FACE." Underneath was the picture of a stereotypical low-status worker: a dishwasher.

U.S. English thereby launched a furious lobbying campaign against bilingual education in New York State. Its target was the Board of Regents, the overseer of public schools and universities, then considering a proposal to keep limited-English-proficient (LEP) children a little longer in bilingual classrooms. Previously students had been reassigned as soon as they achieved minimal competence in English. But there were growing indications that this practice could be harmful. Students often lacked the language skills to keep up in all-English classrooms and many were falling behind, never to catch up. So the state Division of Bilingual Education recommended a more gradual transition to English.[1] It noted that "the child's first language should be regarded as an important cultural asset as well as a useful tool in learning English and school subjects. Research over the past two decades . . . lends strong support for developing students' native language and literacy skills while they learn English." Among other things, it asked the Regents to adopt a policy "that all students in New York State become proficient in English, and to the extent possible, in another language."

For readers of the *Times,* U.S. English painted a different picture:

Under this plan, children will be forced to study all subjects in their native languages, with very limited instruction in English.

The result—hundreds of thousands of children will be denied the opportunity to participate fully in the American dream.

Don't be fooled. This plan will handicap, not help, children with a limited knowledge of English.

We at U.S. ENGLISH believe that all children should be guaranteed the right to learn English.

You can help. But time is running out. Call the Regents' office, (518) 474-5889. Insist that they stop this from going forward. Do it now. We cannot afford to be silent.

Over the next few days, the Board of Regents received thousands of calls from members of the public who were understandably concerned. In response it scheduled a series of hearings thoughout the state to clarify and discuss the proposed changes. U.S. English spent at least $72,000 to fly in critics of bilingual education, place newspaper ads, and otherwise attempt to influence the Regents' decision. It accused the Division of Bilingual Education of promoting the "ideological goal of a multilingual America." It staged a nationwide petition drive, calling on U.S. Secretary of Education Lauro Cavazos to withhold federal funds from New York programs that "hinder non-English speakers from learning English." And its P.R. apparatus churned out position papers and news advisories featuring additional erroneous claims: for example, that the plan would lead to the hiring of non-English-speaking teachers and allow students to graduate from high school without speaking English.[2] In the end, the lobbying blitz failed to convince the Regents—they adopted the new regulations intact—but U.S. English did succeed in rallying public hostility against bilingual instruction.

This was not the first time the group had sought to shape education policy. Three years earlier it had timed Proposition 63 to coincide with the expiration of California's bilingual education law. Governor George Deukmejian, sensing the populist fervor behind the English Only amendment, vetoed two attempts to extend the bilingual mandate—in effect, removing all strings on state subsidies for the education of LEP students. Districts that had previously resisted the mandate were emboldened in their preference for "alternative" (read: English-only) programs. One result was a lawsuit against the Berkeley school system, which a parents' group charged with failing to hire qualified teachers in either bilingual education or English as a second language and relying largely on uncertified tutors and aides to instruct LEP children. U.S. English came to the aid of the school district, issuing press advisories and amicus briefs praising Berkeley's "innovative English-based instruction." Meanwhile it financed groups of disgruntled teachers in organizing against bilingual programs elsewhere in California and began to finance research by academic enthusiasts of alternative methodologies.

Attacks on bilingual education have always served a propaganda function for Official English proponents. Increasingly, however, the schools themselves are becoming the focus of English Only campaigns, in which simplistic charges and media hype are impeding efforts to determine what is best for children.

Monolinguals have enough trouble as it is with the concept of learning in two languages. Set aside the ethnic politics, the melting-pot mythology, the nativist impulses, and bilingual education still offends the conventional wisdom. Opinion polls are consistent. While few Americans object to short-term help in the vernacular for children who come to school without English—that seems only humane—most fail to see why students should continue to receive such instruction for two, three, or more years. The idea is jarring to pragmatist habits of mind. Isn't English the newcomer's ticket to success in this country? Outside of a few places like Miami, foreign languages seem about as useful in the U.S. job market as foreign currency. Can it benefit linguistic minorities to isolate them in separate classrooms and prolong their reliance on Spanish or Chinese? In the past immigrant children appeared to pick up English right away. But nowadays most live in ethnic enclaves, often poor and crime-ridden, where everyone seems to speak their native tongue. The odds are already against these kids. If the schools won't teach them English, who will?

This is the altruistic voice of American pragmatism. Then there's the self-interested voice, which asks: Is it wise to encourage language diversity, considering the societal costs? Isn't bilingualism wasteful, impractical, and divisive? In the United States we have the good fortune to speak one dominant language, which is fast becoming a universal language as well. Rather than squander this advantage, why not engage in a benevolent form of linguistic imperialism? Helping others to acquire English would appear to profit everyone, not least of all ourselves.

George Bush espoused this latter view when he dispatched the Peace Corps into post-Communist Poland and Hungary. As much as dollars, the President suggested, the fledgling capitalists needed a world-class medium of communication. He told the departing volunteers:

> The key you carry with you will be the English language . . . the language of commerce and understanding. And just as national literacy has long been the key to power, so today English literacy has become the key to progress. Like your liberty, your language came to you as a birthright and a credit to the dreams and sacrifices of those who came before. . . . Your investment is America's investment in the consolidation of democracy and independence in central and eastern Europe.

A birthright, indeed. It seemed fitting that the greatest nation would possess the greatest language: carrier of high-minded ideals, unchallenged medium of diplomacy, not to mention a handy business tool. Bush's sales force could be proud of its product. English had come to represent affluence, potency, dynamism—everything that others envied about this country. An inspiring legacy, which we could now afford to share with less fortunate peoples.

No doubt the Poles and Hungarians welcomed the President's noblesse oblige, if not the sentiments behind it. English is truly a valuable commodity. More impressive than the world total of English speakers—estimates range from 700 million to one billion—is the fact that a sizable percentage, perhaps a majority, learned English as a second language. It has become the lingua franca of international trade, politics, and popular culture. John Adams would be gratified at the advance of Anglo-American prestige and influence, achieved without benefit of an official language academy.

At the same time, he would be displeased to see the effect on American attitudes. Empire has bred complacency. Why learn other languages when the world is learning ours? Monolingualism has become an ideal, an emblem of national strength, whereas bilingualism is seen as a curse, an oddity, a mark of low social status, or an expectation for foreign visitors to our shores.[3] Few Anglo-Americans ever attempt to learn a second language, much less succeed, leaving the United States an underdeveloped country when it comes to linguistic resources. During the 1980s a trend toward stiffer requirements has yielded a substantial increase in foreign language study. Still, in 1990 fewer than two in five U.S. high school students were enrolled in a foreign language course. Normally this involved one or two years of Spanish, French, or sometimes German, but rarely Russian, Chinese, or Arabic.[4]

Unlike educated Europeans, Asians, Africans, and Latin Americans, U.S. college graduates are seldom expected to speak any tongue but their own. The State Department has long since dropped its second-language requirement for Foreign Service recruits because too many promising applicants were thus disqualified. It even has trouble finding competent translators, a failing manifested by President Jimmy Carter when he visited Poland and tried to express, in his hosts' language, an interest in better relations. "I desire the Poles carnally" is how Carter's words came out. A decade later, when George Bush sent in the English teachers, European entrepreneurs were already negotiating deals in Polish, German, and French. As English penetrates the former Soviet bloc, it will facilitate trade and investment not only by Americans and British, but also by Japanese, Taiwanese, Koreans, and other competitors. The world's willingness to learn our language is no longer an unmixed blessing.

What accounts for Americans' obstinate monolingualism? Some argue that geographical isolation limits our opportunities to use other tongues. Foreign language skills learned in school almost always go to waste unless the student has a chance to live abroad. But if location is determinant, why are the Japanese and Australians so far ahead of us in language abilities? Why are tens of millions of Chinese studying English, while only a few thousand Americans are studying Mandarin? Another popular excuse is that U.S. residents have limited economic incentives to become bilingual. Few of our jobs require proficiency in languages other than English, and those that do (teaching, translating) pay modest salaries. On the other hand, the need for bilingual skills is growing with changing demography. Public employees, especially in law enforcement and social services, are now called upon to use Spanish, Vietnamese, or Creole—though generally without extra compensation.

While to some extent a matter of practicality, American monolingualism is principally a matter of values. It is supported by attitudes that emphasize the negative aspects of linguistic diversity and ignore the potential benefits. "Language-as-problem" is our dominant orientation, argues Richard Ruíz of the University of Arizona, as opposed to "language-as-resource." Hence the treatment of bilingual education as a compensatory program for disadvantaged children. The prevailing *transitional* emphasis focuses on overcoming a disability—students' lack of English—rather than on cultivating abilities that could be useful to this society.

Take the example of Korean, a language of growing commercial importance that is relatively difficult for English speakers to acquire. The Defense Language Institute in Monterey, California, offers an intensive forty-seven-week course for military personnel, providing some 1,400 hours of instruction at a cost of $12,000 per student (in addition to salaries and benefits). While the D.L.I. is reputed to be among the most successful language schools anywhere, its graduates achieve lower levels of oral proficiency in Korean than a five-year-old native speaker brings to school. Nevertheless, Korean children are rarely encouraged to maintain or develop these skills. While they may be enrolled in a so-called bilingual program, the instructional goal is not bilingualism, but an expeditious transition to English. In U.S. public schools there are virtually no *developmental* bilingual programs in Korean (or in most other languages; there are a handful in Spanish). As the problem of English acquisition is solved, a valuable resource is squandered.

Monolinguals naturally cherish a number of myths about how a second language is acquired. On the one hand, the task seems terribly onerous. Americans who struggled to learn a foreign language in school recall the drudgery of memorizing vocabulary and grammar, not to mention the embarrassment of attempting actual communication. (Woe unto those who tried to use their high school French in Quebec!) As adults with little to show for the experience, they tend to despair of the whole idea of language learning. On the other hand, children make it look so effortless. They seem to "pick up" a strange tongue within a few weeks, chattering away with new playmates before their parents can utter a respectable sentence.

Although these perceptions reflect real phenomena, they are distorted by social prejudices. Many Americans conclude, for example, that the most effective way to learn a second language is to be "totally immersed" in it. Necessity seems the best motivator. Conversely, the option of relying on one's mother tongue appears to weaken the incentive to learn another. This *immersion fetish*—the idea that maximum exposure and maximum will are what count in language acquisition—inspires much of the skepticism surrounding bilingual education. According to this reasoning, if children are allowed to keep their life-preservers, they will never swim unassisted.

"I got the total immersion method," claims Mark LaPorta, chairman of the Florida English Campaign. A second-generation American, he grew up speaking English, although "a big chunk of my people spoke Italian as the primary language. My father would rather have a conversation in Italian than in English." To uphold the tradition LaPorta was sent to learn Italian from relatives in the old country. "My father put me on an airplane for southern Italy when I was five and my brother was four, kissed us on the forehead, and said, 'Speak or don't eat.' For thirty to forty days, there was no English, and we ate fine. My family on that side were all schoolteachers. We didn't have to sit down for an hour and make a class out of it. But I was dumped in and I learned good Italian." LaPorta is fortunate for the experience. Today, in contrast to most Euroethnics, he can communicate freely with his elders in their favored language. What child would not benefit from a similar opportunity? Yet he is mistaken to generalize lessons for non-English-speaking children in American schools. Too often, their experience is to be "dumped" into a strange environment, without relatives who can help them, and expected to use a poorly grasped language in learning to read and other challenging pursuits. Intimidation and confusion are hardly ideal conditions for acquiring English. Furthermore, the stakes are considerably higher. For minority students, falling behind means being labeled a slow learner (perhaps even "learning disabled"[5]), and greatly increases their likelihood of dropping out. Life chances can hinge on school performance at an early age.

Over the past generation, research has cast increasing doubt on the immersion fetish. Psycholinguistics—the study of language development and its role in cognitive growth—has strengthened the rationale for bilingual schooling. Yet science has been slow to penetrate the thicket of opinionated discourse about language. One reason is that the study of bilingualism is an evolving discipline whose findings are sometimes tentative. For example, researchers have discredited the notion that learning in two languages will confuse a child's mind but have yet to establish what many suspect: that "balanced" bilingualism can be an intellectual advantage. Kenji Hakuta, a Stanford University psychologist, traces the history of this puzzle in his highly readable *Mirror of Language: The Debate on Bilingualism.*

Generally speaking, however, the results of such research have been poorly communicated to the public. As yet, we have no Carl Sagan of linguistics ("Billions and billions of sentences . . ."). Many otherwise informed Americans seem oblivious to the field's existence. Journalists, frequently unable to determine who the experts are, tend to spread more confusion than enlightenment. Because bilingual education is controversial, it is reported less as a pedagogical field than a political issue, with opposing "sides" given equal time. The result has been to lend credibility to critics whose expertise approximates that of the Flat Earth Society. "We think that native-language instruction holds kids back," says Kathryn Bricker of U.S. English, and her words are broadcast to the millions via network television. Yet Bricker has no training or experience in the subject; her career has consisted of advocacy for English Only and immigration restrictions. By contrast, bona fide experts in second-language acquisition tend to have little patience with these simplistic debates or their media impresarios, and thus avoid them. This is unfortunate.

If science is often counterintuitive, psycholinguistics is especially so. Recent findings about bilingualism contradict many of our perceptions drawn from immediate experience. To wit: the detour of native-language instruction is often the best route to English acquisition. Accepting this kind of go-west-to-get-east idea means abandoning one worldview and embracing another.

Largely unbeknownst to the American public, a conceptual revolution has taken place in this field since passage of the 1968 Bilingual Education Act. Two of its leaders are Stephen Krashen, of the University of Southern California, and Jim Cummins, of the Ontario Institute for Studies in Education. Neither researcher began with any "ideological" agenda favoring multilingualism. Krashen was seeking more effective ways to teach English as a second language, while Cummins was unconvinced by the traditional rationale for native-language instruction. Initially bilingual education was conceived as a temporary measure to cope with a "language mismatch" between home and school—a way to keep minority students from falling behind in other subjects while they learned English. But the researchers discovered a more significant benefit: a firm command of the first tongue facilitates the acquisition of a second.

While that may sound paradoxical, it makes good sense when the underlying principles are revealed. Krashen explains that "humans acquire language in only one way—by understanding messages, or by receiving *comprehensible input.*" That is, the more exposure to intelligible messages in a second language, the more second language will be acquired.[6] Without quality input, however, quantity is meaningless. Students learn very little English in a sink-or-swim classroom, where the teacher's words sound like undifferentiated noise. The brain does not process what it cannot understand; hence any benefit of second-language exposure is lost.

Here is the first way in which bilingual education can promote English acquisition. It provides *context* that makes English more comprehensible. Krashen illustrates this principle with what he calls the "Paris argument":

> Pretend that you have just received, and accepted, an attractive job offer in Paris. Your French, however, is limited. (You had two years of French in high school and one semester in college, and it was quite a while ago.) Before your departure, the company that is hiring you will send you the following information, in English: What to do when you arrive in Paris, how to get to your hotel, where and how to find a place to live, where to shop, what kinds of schools are available for your children, how French companies function (how people dress in the office, what time work starts and ends, etc.), and specific information about the functioning of the company and your responsibilities.
>
> It would be very useful to get this information right away in English, rather than getting it gradually as you acquire French. If you get it right away, the world around you will be much more comprehensible, and you will thus acquire French more quickly. Anyone who agrees with this, in my opinion, agrees with the philosophy underlying bilingual education.

It is important to bear in mind, however, that children starting school differ from adults in their mastery of language. They have not finished acquiring the basic skills, literacy in particular, on which future academic achievement will depend. Here is the second way in which bilingual education can help. Instead of discarding children's foundation in their native tongue and starting over from scratch, it facilitates a "transfer" of these proficiencies to English.

Two reading experts, Frank Smith and Kenneth Goodman, have postulated that acquiring literacy is analogous to acquiring language: "We learn to read by reading," by making sense of print. Extending this logic, Krashen reasons that "it will be much easier to learn to read in a language one already knows, since written material in that language will be more comprehensible." If anything defies common sense, it is teaching children to read in English before they have acquired English, needlessly complicating the task. Better to build on their strengths rather than their weaknesses. Literacy, mastered in the first tongue, never needs to be relearned in a second. "Once you can read, you can read. This ability transfers to other languages that may be acquired," Krashen explains.[7] "Reading is the major source of our competence in vocabulary, spelling, writing style, and grammar." Print also expands the child's background knowledge and exposure to understandable messages, compounding the benefit.

Besides comprehensible input there is another variable that affects the brain's response to second-language stimuli. Krashen calls it the *affective filter,* a term for all the subjective barriers—high anxiety in a new environment, low motivation to learn the language, fear of sounding foolish—that can keep comprehensible input from reaching our "language acquisition device." Simply put, the right attitude is essential. Smith suggests that it involves two things: an expectation of success and a desire to join "the club" of those who speak that language. Defeatism almost ensures that one will fail, and so do feelings of estrangement (whether condescension or inferiority) toward speakers of the second tongue. Among adults these are common obstacles. Here is where young children sometimes have an advantage, with their prepubescent lack of self-consciousness and their eagerness to make new friends. More open and motivated than their elders, they tend to pick up simple conversational skills more easily.

Yet this is not always the case. A positive attitude can be destroyed by insensitive educators. To devalue a minority child's language is to devalue the child—at least, that's how it feels on the receiving end. The longtime policy of punishing Chicano students for speaking Spanish is an obvious example. While such practices are now frowned upon, more subtle stigmas remain. Children are quick to read the messages in adult behavior, such as a preference for English on ceremonial occasions or a failure to stock the school library with books in Chinese. The "early-exit" approach to bilingual education, with its haste to push children into all-English tracks, may have a similar effect. Whatever the cause, minority students frequently exhibit an alienation from both worlds. Jim Cummins calls it *bicultural ambivalence:* hostility toward the dominant culture and shame toward one's own. Though the idea of enhancing students' self-esteem has been much ridiculed of late, it is especially germane to the problem of English acquisition. If Cummins and Krashen are correct, a negative sense of self can be a formidable obstacle to language learning.

Richard Rodríguez stands out as an interesting exception. In his autobiography, *Hunger of Memory,* he describes a personal odyssey from "socially disadvantaged child" to Milton scholar to apostate Chicano with a disdain for bilingual education. Prolonging children's reliance on their native language is a trap, Rodríguez believes, because Hispanics cannot have it both ways—they must choose between treasuring a Spanish identity and advancing in Anglo society. "Bilingual enthusiasts bespeak an easier world. They seek a linguistic solution to a social dilemma. They seem to want to believe that there is an easy way for the child to balance private and public." For Rodríguez, there is no avoiding the psychological turmoil and sense of loss: "I was that child! I faced the stranger's English with pain and guilt and fear. Baptized to English in school, at first I felt myself drowning—the ugly sounds forced down my throat—until slowly, slowly (held in the tender grip of my teachers), suddenly the conviction took: English was my language to use."

This is the Americanization myth internalized, the same either/or mentality that induced many European immigrants to prevent their children from becoming bilingual in the pathetic hope of improving their English. But Rodríguez is a compelling writer when he recalls sitting mute and helpless in the classroom, as strange words buzzed around his head. It is hard to fault his parents for instituting, on the advice of concerned teachers, an English-only policy in the home, even though their own proficiency was limited:

At first, it seemed a kind of game. After dinner each night, the family gathered to practice "our" English. . . . Laughing, we would try to define words we could not pronounce. We played with strange English sounds, often overanglicizing our pronunciations. And we filled the smiling gaps of our sentences with familiar Spanish sounds. . . .

Again and again in the days following, increasingly angry, I was obliged to hear my mother and father: "Speak to us *en inglés.*" *(Speak.)* Only then did I determine to learn classroom English. Weeks after, it happened. . . . I spoke out in a loud voice. And I did not think it remarkable that the entire class understood. That day, I moved very far from the disadvantaged child I had been days earlier. The belief, the calming assurance that I belonged in public, had at last taken hold. . . .

But the special feeling of closeness at home was diminished by then. . . . The family's quiet was partly due to the fact that, as we children learned more and more English, we shared fewer and fewer words with our parents. Sentences needed to be spoken slowly when a child addressed his mother or father. (Often the parent wouldn't understand.) The child would need to repeat himself. (Still the parent misunderstood.) The young voice, frustrated, would end up saying, "Never mind"—the subject was closed. Dinners would be noisy with the clinking of knives and forks against dishes. My mother would smile softly between her remarks; my father at the other end of the table would chew and chew at his food, while he stared over the heads of his children.

Published to literary acclaim in 1982, *Hunger of Memory* also produced political excitement. Here was a paean to assimilation, notwithstanding its dilemmas; the ordeal of cultural adjustment made it seem all the more heroic. Here was testimony—Hispanic testimony, no less—that children can learn English without bilingual education and grow up to become best-selling writers. (Rodríguez explains that he dropped out of academic life rather than be perceived as a beneficiary of affirmative action.) No doubt some LEP children do succeed without special help, but how representative are their stories? " 'Selection bias' is a problem," observes Stephen Krashen. "We hear from those who've made it. We haven't heard from those who didn't. They don't write letters to the editor and they don't write books, because they can't."

Yet, in another way, the experience of Richard Rodríguez is instructive. What so alarmed his teachers was "a typical *silent period*," Krashen says. It is "not pathological, but normal" for a non-English-speaking child to go for as long as six months without "producing" speech in the second language. As long as there is comprehensible input in English, English acquisition is taking place. Then one day the child suddenly starts showing off his or her new knowledge. This, rather than any coerced "determination to learn classroom English," probably accounts for the breakthrough that Rodríguez describes. In the meantime it is unlikely that he received much useful second-language exposure at home because his parents' English was quite poor. Nor is it clear that he got much in class. He probably benefited most from two other sources of English mentioned in *Hunger of Memory:* after-school tutoring by a kindly teacher and interaction with children in his predominantly Anglo neighborhood. Krashen suspects that "Rodríguez would have succeeded quite well without giving up Spanish at home, [a decision that] resulted only in estrangement from his family and did not contribute to his English-language acquisition."

For worried parents and teachers, recent research on bilingualism provides some welcome news. "A sense of urgency in introducing English to non-English-speaking children and concern about postponing children's exit from bilingual programs" are unfounded, according to Kenji Hakuta and Catherine Snow, a professor at the Harvard Graduate School of Education. Despite appearances, it turns out that adults and adolescents acquire languages more efficiently than children. Canadian studies have shown that one year of second-language study in the seventh grade is worth three years of study beginning in the first grade. The researchers add that "starting to speak English even as late as high school is no barrier to learning to speak it very well." These findings confirm Krashen's "input hypothesis." Older learners receive more comprehensible input because they understand more of what they hear and read, drawing on their greater knowledge and intellectual attainment. On the other hand, it makes sense to begin English instruction early for the simple reason that learning a second language takes time—indeed, a good deal more time than is commonly realized.

Conversely, there is no evidence that "native-language instruction holds kids back," as U.S. English claims. Quite the reverse. A premature transition to all-English classrooms seems to retard academic achievement. This is true not only for the sociocultural reasons noted above, but also for linguistic reasons. "Language is not a unitary skill, but a complex configuration of abilities," write Hakuta and Snow. "Language used for conversational purposes is quite different from language used for school learning." In other words, there are *two types of proficiency*. One is exemplified by the speech children use on the playground, interpersonal communication that is high in context and low in cognitive demands. The other is more complex, involving the ability to manipulate verbal symbols without the aid of physical gestures or oral feedback, the kind of language needed for abstract reasoning. Jim Cummins, who first elaborated and tested this distinction, concludes that children need much less time to develop conversational proficiency in a second language (one to two years) than academic proficiency (five to seven years).

This creates a quandary for the schools. After a relatively brief exposure to English, many students sound fluent enough to make it in an all-English classroom. So there is often pressure to "mainstream" them at that point, although few have acquired the kind of English they need to keep up in class. Until the age of ten or eleven, *all* children are continuing to acquire complex grammatical structures in their first language, along with vocabulary, literacy, semantics, and a repertoire of linguistic styles appropriate for various occasions. Moreover, they are using these tools to cover academic terrain of increasing difficulty. As Cummins observes, English-speaking students "do not stand still waiting for the minority student[s] to catch up." So when the latter are placed in a regular classroom without fully developed English skills, they inevitably fall behind. This is the problem that the New York Regents were seeking to address. Raising the standard for English proficiency, the point at which bilingual students are reassigned to regular classrooms, was designed to avoid a premature transition.

Far more than academic speculation, the theories of Cummins and Krashen have shaped a number of innovative bilingual programs. One example is known as the Eastman model, after a school in East Los Angeles, in which instruction shifts gradually from Spanish to English, but students continue to develop skills in their native tongue through the sixth grade. Barrio children who once scored far below citywide norms now surpass them in language, reading, and mathematics. The curriculum has been so successful that in 1988 the L.A. school board approved a $20 million plan to replicate it throughout the district. Similar developmental approaches have also yielded remarkable gains.

All that said, it would be misleading to claim that recent advances in understanding bilingualism have been "proven" beyond all doubt. Research continues and so does debate. Such is the case with all science. Hypotheses are tested, discarded, refined, and retested on the basis of empirical data. Knowledge gradually accumulates until one day the reigning theory is overthrown. Given the intuitive prejudices about language and the novelty of psycholinguistics (not to mention the hold of Americanization ideology), the continuing skirmishes over bilingual education are unsurprising. What is disconcerting, however, is the fixation of policymakers on a single, narrow issue: does bilingual education "work"? For the vast majority of researchers and practitioners in second-language acquisition, this is no longer a serious question. For the critics, it remains the only question.

After a decade of sniping, in 1985 came the frontal assault. Secretary of Education William Bennett denounced the Bilingual Education Act as "a failed path," "a bankrupt course," and a scandalous waste of the taxpayers' money: "After seventeen years of federal involvement, and after $1.7 billion of federal funding, we have no evidence that the children whom we sought to help—that the children who deserve our help—have benefited." According to Bennett's diagnosis, the program "had lost sight of the goal of [teaching] English" in favor of "enhancing students' knowledge of their native language and culture." Meanwhile there were "alternative methods of special instruction using English," such as so-called "structured immersion" programs, that looked promising. Yet these nonbilingual approaches were denied federal funding under the Bilingual Education Act. The law should be changed, he argued, to give school districts "local flexibility" to choose instruction tailored to their students' needs.

With its stress on anti–Big Government themes, Bennett's attack was transparently political. The fact that there was no federal "mandate" for bilingual education got lost in the demagoguery. Competition for grants had always been stiff because, in a normal year, funding was available to serve only 5 to 10 percent of the nation's eligible students. But methodological requirements were minimal; schools merely had to make *some* use of the students' native language to qualify for grants under the Bilingual Education Act. If districts wanted subsidies for all-English approaches, they could apply under other federal programs (Chapter 1, emergency immigrant assistance, or migrant education, to name a few).

Nevertheless, the Secretary's call for "flexibility" sounded reasonable when combined with his argument that research on the effectiveness of bilingual instruction remained inconclusive. In some studies, he asserted, "the mandated method . . . seemed to be no better than [a regular classroom] without *any* special help." He charged that "too many children have failed to become fluent in English," while the Hispanic dropout rate remained "tragically as high now as it was twenty years ago." As long as no one knew what worked, Bennett reasoned, schools should be encouraged to experiment with alternative, English-only programs.[8]

How can this reading of the research be reconciled with the diametrically opposite findings of Cummins, Krashen, Hakuta, Snow et al.? Is someone hallucinating here? fabricating evidence? Or are the two sides talking about different studies? In fact, there are two types of research at issue: *basic research* on the cognitive process of second-language acquisition and *evaluation research* of actual programs in actual schools. There is no question that the former has provided stronger support for bilingual education than the latter. The clarity and consistency achieved in small, controlled experiments has yet to be matched in large-scale comparisons of student progress.

Clearly, it is unfair to judge an approach where it is poorly executed, suffers from a shortage of qualified teachers, or faces conditions—crime, drugs, poverty, homelessness—that make any kind of learning a challenge. Proof of universal effectiveness, with every child in every school, is a standard that no other pedagogy is expected to meet. On the other hand, it is undeniable that students in many bilingual programs are still scoring below national norms, and this could mean there is something wrong with the concept. Perhaps the success stories are aberrations, a tribute to dedicated teachers and involved parents rather than to the value of native-language instruction. Hakuta and Snow put the question this way: either bilingual education is no better than English-only approaches or "the evaluation studies are doing a poor job of measuring" its superiority. The researchers make a convincing case for the latter hypothesis.

Everyone complains about the poor quality of evaluation research. One perennial problem has been limited support from the federal government. In the first decade federal expenditures under the Bilingual Education Act totaled approximately $500 million, but of this amount less than one-half of one percent went for research. To make matters worse, early standards were slipshod. Evaluators often lacked expertise in linguistics or language education, and political pressures sometimes came into play, both for and against bilingual instruction.

Furthermore, there are inherent difficulties in designing studies of bilingual programs. Educational evaluations will almost invariably show that children have learned *something* between fall and spring, but they might well have learned more (or less) in a different program. So an independent basis for comparison is essential. While it is possible to chart student progress against normal curves, which predict "average" rates of achievement, it is hard to generalize from such findings because there are many variables that can distort the outcome (an exceptionally bright group of children, the presence of books in their homes, a school principal's incompetence, drug shootouts in the neighborhood). The optimum approach is to study a comparable group of children—in socioeconomic status, language background, achievement level, and other traits—who are receiving an alternative treatment from teachers of equivalent abilities, ideally in the same school, over a period long enough to gauge program effects. Needless to say, a perfect match is rarely found. While there are statistical techniques to adjust for preexisting differences between groups, these are imperfect, especially as variables multiply.

Some of the methodological pitfalls are obvious in the first large-scale evaluation of bilingual programs, conducted in 1975–76 by the American Institutes for Research. After reviewing the progress of 7,000 students in Spanish-English classrooms in 150 schools, then averaging the results, the study found no "consistent significant impact" for bilingual instruction. Hence Secretary Bennett's claim that it "seemed no better" than sink-or-swim. But one reason may have been a built-in bias that favored the comparison group. At least two-thirds of students in all-English classrooms had previously been enrolled in bilingual classrooms—apparently, many had "graduated" after having been deemed fluent in English—and they naturally tended to outperform LEP students who had yet to be mainstreamed. But the researchers made no attempt to compensate for this anomaly. In effect, the successes of bilingual education were held up as evidence of its failure.

A 1981 "review of the literature" by the U.S. Department of Education was even cruder in its approach. The researchers, Keith Baker and Adriana de Kanter, sorted through more than three hundred evaluation studies and threw out all but twenty-eight as methodologically flawed. Reaching into this grab bag of educational treatments, they added up the verdicts on bilingual education, pro and con, then took an average. Not surprisingly, their conclusions were a wash. Results from poorly designed programs canceled the results from well-designed programs. And because pedagogies varied widely, it was never clear what was being compared.

For the critics of bilingual education, however, this remains the preferred type of research. Like Secretary Bennett, they assume that language of instruction, ipso facto, defines an educational "method." Programs that use two languages are lumped together as *transitional bilingual education,* while English-only programs are labeled *immersion* (if geared to students' level of proficiency) or *submersion* (if not). Other features of program design and execution—how languages are integrated in the curriculum, how children are assessed and reassigned, how teachers approach E.S.L. instruction—fade into insignificance. With the pedagogical details out of the way, quantitative analysis is then performed on a selected group of program evaluations. In head-to-head competition between bilingual education and its alternatives, the outcome is usually "no difference."[9]

A leading practitioner of this type of research, Christine Rossell, of Boston University, sounds quite authoritative when she concludes: "In second language learning 29 percent of the studies show transitional bilingual education to be superior, 21 percent show it to be inferior, and 50 percent show it to be no different from submersion—doing nothing. Altogether, 71 percent show T.B.E. to be no different or worse than the supposedly discredited submersion technique."[10] There is only one problem with Rossell's procedure. Computer programmers call it *gigo,* or "garbage in, garbage out."

Research that relies on simplistic program labels is worse than useless: it offers no guidance to educators, while sowing confusion among policymakers. As we shall see, it also conspires in politicizing the debate, by encouraging participants to choose sides "for" or "against" bilingual education, immersion, and E.S.L. The pedagogical reality is that there are various ways to teach children in their native language, some better than others, and there is considerable overlap among bilingual, immersion, and E.S.L. methodologies. Some of the most successful approaches, such as the Eastman model, use all three. Some of the least successful are bilingual in name only.[11] As in the case of Berkeley, children get mostly E.S.L., with sporadic tutoring from bilingual teacher aides. A 1985 survey in California determined that students' first language was being used, on average, only 8 percent of the time in so-called "bilingual" classrooms; sometimes it was never used. On the other hand, some programs labeled "immersion" feature substantial amounts of native-language instruction.

Further confusing the issue is the analogy often drawn with *total immersion* in Canada, a remarkably successful approach in teaching French to middle-class, anglophone children. Students start school entirely in the second language, with English introduced gradually. By the end of elementary school, most reach fluent (if not quite nativelike) levels of French—at no cost to academic achievement or competence in English. From modest beginnings in an English-speaking suburb of Montreal, French immersion has spread throughout Canada in the past twenty years. By 1988, 224,000 students were enrolled, or about 5 percent of the elementary and secondary school population. Such programs dispel any doubts about whether it is possible for children to learn in a second language, provided that instruction is made comprehensible.

The question is whether an all-English immersion approach is advisable for linguistic minority children in the United States. Absolutely not, according to the researcher who pioneered Canadian immersion programs. Wallace Lambert, of McGill University, explains that because English is a high-status language in Canada, French immersion poses no threat to students' native-language development. Even in Quebec, anglophone children have strong social and economic incentives to become proficient in English (not to mention help from well-educated parents). But minority children in the United States, who are more likely to live in poverty and to feel the stigma attached to their culture, have limited opportunity or motivation to develop their native-language skills outside of school. For these students, Lambert warns, English-only immersion tends to displace "the critical linguistic system associated with the development of basic concepts from infancy on." He calls this *subtractive bilingualism,* an approach that can leave children "in a psycholinguistic limbo where neither the home language nor English is useful as a tool of thought and expression." By contrast, the Canadian children are the beneficiaries of *additive bilingualism;* they learn French without giving up English and without falling behind academically.

Lambert and his colleague Richard Tucker have formulated a simple guideline for teaching children in a bilingual environment: "Priority in early years of schooling should be given to the language . . . least likely to be developed otherwise—in other words, the language most likely to be neglected." In this way students can emerge proficient in both tongues, and their achievement in other subjects will not suffer; it may even be enhanced.

By a happy accident, the Canadian immersion model can be adapted to the United States in a way that benefits both majority-language and minority-language students. *Two-way bilingual education* offers total immersion for English speakers learning Spanish, say, and developmental bilingual education for Spanish speakers learning English. The main difference is that children learn from each other, as well as from the teacher. Only a few such programs exist,[12] but they show promise in turning out fluent bilinguals who also do well in other subjects. And there is an added dividend for minority students. Instead of being treated as deprived children in need of remedial education, they enjoy the status of "peer tutors," encouraged to share valuable skills with English-speaking classmates. This can make an enormous difference in their attitudes toward school and toward themselves.

In sum, bilingual educators are no longer groping in the dark. There are some remarkable approaches that are "working" just fine. What's more, an evolving theory of second-language acquisition has illuminated *why* these models are effective, an essential step in replicating them elsewhere. Stephen Krashen and Douglas Biber have compiled a volume entitled *On Course,* describing seven bilingual programs in California and analyzing their successes. While there are significant variations among these and other exemplary approaches—supporting the idea that no one method works best—all seem to share an important emphasis: they seek to cultivate, not replace, children's native-language abilities.

Two things are striking about the academic opponents of bilingual education. First is their refusal to engage the pedagogical theory underlying bilingual instruction, other than to claim that it remains "unproven." Keith Baker spent a career, first at the Department of Education and later as a consultant for U.S. English, poring over evaluations of program effectiveness. At one point he claimed to have reviewed more than four thousand studies and concluded that "not one credible bilingual education program has ever been implemented in spite of all the time, money, and effort given over to it." Yet Baker never delved into the reasons why. It was only "common sense," he argued, "that English is learned by exposure to English, not by exposure to another language." This was all the theory he needed.[13]

Christine Rossell, while employing a similar modus operandi, at least elaborates a hypothesis to explain her view that bilingual education is inferior to all-English approaches. "Time on task—the amount of time spent learning a subject—is . . . a good predictor of achievement" generally she reasons. Immersion provides larger quantities of English exposure; therefore, it must be a superior way to teach English. Yet she ignores the competing hypothesis: that language acquisition is a special case of learning, which depends on quality, *comprehensible* exposure, and that cognitive growth depends on native-language skills. Herbert J. Walberg, another proponent of time-on-task, was once asked to respond to the linguistic arguments for bilingual instruction. "I don't see where linguistics has much to do with learning theory," Walberg replied. He dismissed the work of Cummins and Krashen as lacking "empirical support."

Time-on-task, however, remains no more than a debatable explanation of the evidence. Numerous researchers dispute its reliance on Canadian immersion, which is bilingual in both methods and goals, to claim the superiority of English-only approaches. What scientists normally do in this situation is to *test* their hypothesis. Rather than merely gathering data to support their own interpretation, they design and carry out experiments in which it could be disproven. Yet neither Rossell, Walberg, nor anyone else has subjected time-on-task to rigorous scrutiny as a theory of second-language acquisition. Despite their contemptuous statements about existing research ("wretchedly planned and executed," says Walberg), they seem disinclined to lead by example.

This is the second striking thing about the critics. With few exceptions, they come from outside the fields of applied linguistics, language education, E.S.L., and bilingual education. Baker is a sociologist by training; Rossell a political scientist. Walberg, though an educational psychologist, shows little acquaintance with the literature on bilingualism. None of them can claim any practical expertise in the programs they are judging.

Challenged on this point when appearing as an "expert witness" in the Berkeley bilingual education case, Rossell advanced the novel argument that her lack of background was a virtue. "Applied linguistics is a field of fads," she testified. "Linguists tend to be ardent supporters of language-maintenance programs because they themselves love languages and, as a result, frequently succumb to wishful thinking. . . . They think that everyone can be bilingual." Rossell went on to describe her own evaluation of Berkeley's programs for LEP children, which gave the district a clean bill of health. She found that students who received bilingual instruction in Berkeley did no better than those who received E.S.L. and individual tutoring; so she saw no need to expand bilingual programs. Under cross-examination, however, Rossell admitted that her conclusions were based on (1) three minutes of classroom observation, (2) brief conversations with teachers, and (3) a partial comparison of test results for about 20 percent of the district's LEP students. She had little idea of what methodologies were used in either program. As usual Rossell merely compared programs *labeled* bilingual or E.S.L. This is not how educational experts conduct evaluations.

Baker has distanced himself even further from researchers and practitioners in second-language acquisition, whom he describes as "a vested interest group." In 1989 testimony before the New York Regents, he mocked the views of professional organizations like the New York State Association for Bilingual Education. "They are *for* bilingual education because bilingual education lines their pockets with state money," he charged. Walberg has also rejected "the opinions of teachers and others" employed in the field as "suspect because their jobs depend on such programs. Getting information from such sources is like asking your barber if you need a haircut." Asked why a researcher like Stephen Krashen, who long specialized in E.S.L., would have a vested interest in bilingual education, Walberg responded with a sly smile: "Consulting fees."

As it happens, the critics have been less than reticent about seizing such opportunities for themselves. Christine Rossell has turned her court testimony into something of a cottage industry, appearing in numerous cases on behalf of school districts being sued by minority parents. In *Teresa P. v. Berkeley* alone, she collected $129,049 in fees and expenses. Paid at the same rate—$125 an hour—Keith Baker allowed his pockets to be lined with $40,950, while Rosalie Porter, another detractor of the "bilingual bureaucracy," took home $12,937. Not bad for part-time consulting work (all three had other jobs at the time).[14] This sort of gravy train is unheard of among advocates for bilingual education. In the Berkeley case the plaintiffs' expert witnesses—including Krashen, Hakuta, James Alatis of Georgetown University, and Courtney Cazden of Harvard—were reimbursed for travel expenses but were paid nothing for their time. Researchers who evaluate bilingual programs or conduct teacher-training workshops do not get rich, either.

No one has suggested that the academic critics of bilingual education are in it solely for the money. Why do they hurl this ad hominem charge at their opponents? Why condemn an entire profession as biased by a desire to secure funding and perpetuate a bureaucracy? One seldom if ever hears such complaints about math teachers, science teachers, or foreign language teachers, not to mention the researchers who evaluate them. (Nor are questions raised about whether these pedagogies "work," despite perennial concerns about U.S. student performance.) Either bilingual educators are uniquely venal, willing to sell out the interests of children to protect their own, or there is a double standard at work. Why is this field being singled out? Does it have anything to do with a belief that bilingual education is little more than a Hispanic "jobs program," in which professional opinion is contaminated by ethnic politics?

That is the implication of Rosalie Porter in her 1990 book, *Forked Tongue: The Politics of Bilingual Education.* Formerly director of bilingual and E.S.L. programs in Newton, Massachusetts, Porter is one of the few critics who have spent more than three minutes in a bilingual classroom. Having started school as a monolingual Italian speaker, she can claim personal acquaintance with the sink-or-swim method. Unlike Richard Rodríguez, she does not recommend this treatment for LEP students today. But based on her experience as a bilingual teacher, Porter believes that special help should consist largely of English instruction. In her book she recalls the frustration of having to teach children in Spanish when they were beginning to speak English: "I doubted that [there was a] magic transfer of reading skills from Spanish to English. . . . I decided, quite on my own, and based on this firsthand experience, to devote most of the teaching time to intensive work on English-language skills." Porter's thinking developed further along these lines as an administrator. By the early 1980s she began to promote what she called "a flexible approach to the education of limited-English children"— English-only alternatives to bilingual education—first in Newton and later in lobbying the Massachusetts legislature.

Porter's rebellion against her school's instructional policy is hardly unique. Teachers often feel they know better—sometimes they do— and many follow their own instincts in the classroom (to the despair of researchers seeking program consistency). Bilingual educators are not immune to social pressures favoring a rapid transition to English. Some start out impatient to get native-language instruction "over with," then change their minds after learning more about second-language acquisition or after witnessing a successful bilingual approach. On the other hand, where children are making little progress, teachers have reason to be concerned. Something must be wrong with the program, and every effort should be made to diagnose and correct it. This necessitates a vigorous and uninhibited exchange of ideas, as Porter correctly points out. Yet that cause is hardly advanced by her own tactics.

Forked Tongue devotes an entire chapter to detailing "corrupt, discriminatory practices" by "the bilingual establishment in Massachusetts." Several tales involve Porter's own alleged victimization by militant Hispanics.[15] (Obviously, one of her objectives is to settle scores with numerous enemies she has made during her career.) She makes repeated reference to a "political ideology" of bilingual educators that warps their pedagogical judgment. When her opponents are not "misdefining students' needs" or using "unfounded conclusions as a basis for decisions," their "entrenched biases" are limiting parental choices, "suppressing" reports on English-only alternatives, and "squelching legislative change." At the end of her diatribe, Porter still wonders at the "siege mentality" of bilingual educators and "the atmosphere of distrust" toward well-meaning liberals like herself.

There is no doubt that polarization has distorted the pedagogical debate. Under fire from English Only zealots, researchers and practitioners are increasingly cautious about discussing the shortcomings of bilingual programs, because their comments are easily twisted. To take one recurrent example, Kenji Hakuta, in *Mirror of Language,* makes a forthright comment about the state of evaluation research: "An awkward tension blankets the lack of empirical demonstration of the success of bilingual education programs. Someone promised bacon, but it's not there." Hakuta is nevertheless an articulate advocate for nurturing native-language skills, and he makes a convincing case that the evaluation research is misleading. His opinions are based not on "political ideology," but on psycholinguistic research—his own and that of others. Hakuta is not uncritical of transitional bilingual education. (Nor should he be: researcher-cheerleaders provide little guidance for classroom teachers.) Yet he has come to regret his choice of words. The quotation has been cited repeatedly by Porter, Rossell, Baker, and assorted spokesmen for U.S. English to argue that bilingual education supporters have no proof for their claims. In the Berkeley case it was used to undercut Hakuta's own testimony for the plaintiffs; in New York State, to oppose the Regents' plan; and on Capitol Hill, to advocate cuts in bilingual education spending.

In this adversarial climate, professionals in bilingual education feel the pressure to act like politicians—to mince their words or risk harming the field. Debates over the benefits of transitional versus developmental approaches, which were quite lively in the 1970s, have died down now that all forms of native-language instruction are under attack. The slightest criticism of pedagogical practice can be used to indict the theory of bilingual instruction by enemies seeking to abolish it. A researcher's candor can have unforeseen effects in the policymaking process. Polemics like *Forked Tongue* serve as a kind of Miranda warning: anything you say can and will be used against you in a partisan struggle. The effect is to discourage free discussion about how to improve the schools.

Yet what is most disingenuous about Porter's complaints of political bias is her own intimate association with U.S. English. While posturing as a "moderate," unaligned with either of "the extremist camps—the doctrinaire official-English supporters and the strident proponents of full bilingualism," she does not hesitate to accept financial support from English Only advocates. In 1991, Porter took over the Institute for Research in English Acquisition and Development (READ), founded by Keith Baker with a $62,000 grant from U.S. English. READ's board chairman is Robert Rossier, a longtime activist for U.S. English, who has called bilingual education "the new Latin hustle." The operation continues to receive major support from the Laurel Foundation, the benefactor behind John Tanton's numerous projects; English Language Advocates, a California group that campaigned for Proposition 63; and U.S. English itself.

"We are unaffiliated and entirely independent," Porter insists. "These grants are without strings. We are free to research and publish what we deem to be reliable work done by respected people." Porter declines to divulge the organization's budget but says that "less than half" of its funding comes from U.S. English. She maintains that READ has endorsed no political agenda. "We have no relationship with U.S. English and no obligation except to put the money they give us to good use and to report back on how we spend it." Nevertheless, one academic adviser to READ resigned after learning of the U.S. English connection. Guadalupe Hamersma, a Chicago elementary school principal, has her own reservations about bilingual education but believes that READ's funding sources have compromised its pretense of objectivity.[16]

If only some wise and disinterested researcher would perform the study-to-end-all-studies, supply indisputable data to prove or disprove the rationale for bilingual education, and bring this unproductive debate to a close. Congress could finally settle the question "Does it work?" with an up-or-down vote. Educators could focus on educating and politicos could move on to other campaigns. Applied linguists could concentrate on improving instruction rather than fending off ideologues. Children could get on with learning. Unfortunately, such a study is unlikely to appear anytime soon. But there is some important new evidence to consider.

A long-awaited report on bilingual and alternative programs, by Aguirre International under contract with the U.S. Department of Education, was released in February 1991. The study's design, which overcame many limitations of earlier evaluation research, has drawn

praise from partisans on both sides. Its principal investigator was
David Ramírez, a researcher associated with neither camp, and during data-gathering (1984–1988) the contract's federal overseer was
none other than Keith Baker. Commissioned in 1983 at a cost of
$4.1 million, the study involved more than two thousand LEP stu-
dents, all Spanish speakers, enrolled in nine school districts in California, Florida, New Jersey, New York, and Texas. Its objective
was to compare the relative merits of three instructional models:
structured immersion in English, "early-exit" (transitional) bilingual
education, and "late-exit" (developmental) bilingual education. Ramírez paid close attention to program detail, so that each label meant
something consistent. He also took pains to achieve comparability
among students, teachers, and classrooms, and to compensate for
disparities in parents' income and education, students' years in the
United States, teachers' experience and training, and so on. Rather
than take a brief snapshot of student achievement, Ramírez followed its ups and downs over four years. Finally, he sought out the
best examples of each approach, so as to minimize the problem of
poor execution.

On release, however, the Ramírez study brought less clarity than
many had hoped. The Department of Education muddied the findings by declaring "the three most common bilingual education
methods" (sic) to be "effective." Therefore, "school administrators
can choose the method best suited to their students, confident that,
if well implemented, it will reap positive results." Not much help
for the perplexed.

What the study actually found was more illuminating. First, there
were few significant differences in achievement between immersion
and early-exit programs, that is, between children taught almost exclusively in English and those taught mostly in English.[17] Second,
children in late-exit programs, taught primarily in Spanish, had the
most sustained growth in achievement. Third, students in all three
groups took five or more years to acquire academic proficiency in
English. The second and third findings—and, arguably, the first—
are consistent with the hypotheses of Cummins (linguistic interde-
pendence) and Krashen (comprehensible input).

The Ramírez study's impact was weakened by a decision not to
include late-exit programs in the direct comparisons of student
progress.[18] Nevertheless, its vote of confidence for additive bilingualism was quite strong. In the two subtractive approaches, early-

exit and immersion, children made reasonable gains in English language, reading, and math. But their growth slowed down by the third grade, leveling off parallel to (but well below) the "normal curves" of English-proficient children. By contrast, in the late-exit programs, academic growth accelerated over time. By the sixth grade, these students had yet to reach national norms but showed promise of doing so. For Ramírez, the implications are clear:

> If your instructional objective is to help kids stay where they are—around the 25th percentile—then give them immersion or early exit and they'll keep their place in society. If your concern is to help kids catch up to the norming population, use more primary language. In the late-exit programs, they're growing faster in content areas and in English, too. It's really clear that you will not slow down a child's acquisition of English by providing large amounts of native-language instruction.

These findings were further confirmed by patterns of achievement among the late-exit programs: a direct and consistent correlation between Spanish-language development and student gains. In one district that lapsed into an early-exit model during the study, scores fell off dramatically. In another, where the native language was used most extensively, progress was most dramatic.

This last program, the highest performing in the study, is located in one of the poorest sections of Brooklyn, New York. Enrollment is 99 percent black and Latino. Known as School District 19, by all external criteria it is the proverbial dead end for minority children. "A bombed-out area," in the words of David Ramírez. Muggers and drug dealers control the streets. The district's headquarters, which also houses an elementary school, resembles a fortress with its chains and grates, metal shields over the doors, and guards to frisk each visitor for weapons. "Teachers are really remarkable to work under these conditions," the researcher adds. "I've never seen a district that faced as many challenges." Yet its bilingual program has distinguished itself as among the best in the United States. Ramírez credits Frank Arricale, the former superintendent, for resisting pressures to mainstream children quickly and building "one of the rare late-exit models."

Carmen Dinos, a Brooklyn College professor who helped to coordinate the study in District 19, cites several reasons for the program's success. Foremost, she believes, is its "supportive atmosphere. Children have to be given an opportunity to grow at their own pace, instead of being cut off at grade 3," as early-exit programs do. Where learning in Spanish is encouraged, "they don't feel like outsiders." She also cites Arricale's success in assembling a well-trained staff, with sufficient numbers of fluent bilingual teachers. Then there is the transfer of Spanish proficiency itself. "Allowing children to continue in the bilingual strategy doesn't hurt their ability to learn English; it enhances it." A final factor, found in all the late-exit programs, is that Latino parents are more likely to help children with schoolwork in a language they understand.

As for structured immersion, Ramírez offers very qualified support. *If* teachers are proficient in their students' native tongue, *if* they have been specially trained in oral language development, *if* they have mastered "sheltered English" techniques, immersion may be appropriate for some LEP children in the United States. "Quality immersion programs are better than doing nothing," he says. "But the danger is in lifting the cap [on funding for English-only alternatives to bilingual instruction] without any clear specifications. When most districts talk about immersion, they mean taking regular teachers and placing them in a bilingual classroom, looking for a way to exit kids as quickly as possible." In such treatments students receive little more than sink-or-swim, with some E.S.L. on the side. "We know that doesn't work," Ramírez emphasizes. In a few situations—for example, where bilingual teachers are unavailable or where students speak numerous languages—an immersion approach "may be all we can do," he concedes. "But is it really what we want? It doesn't cost you any more to provide a late-exit program than an immersion program. It's just a philosophical or political question."

If research on bilingualism has demonstrated anything over the past twenty years, it is that there are no shortcuts to English proficiency. Subtractive approaches, whether immersion or short-term bilingual, cannot speed up the process. Even under the best of circumstances, the average LEP child needs five years or more to complete the transition. A fixation on teaching English as quickly as possible fails to prepare students to compete on equal terms. As a group they remain "at risk," disadvantaged, stigmatized. On the other hand, additive approaches promise to break the cycle of underachievement. When their first language is cultivated along with

English, students are equipped to develop normally. They enter the mainstream later, but with improved chances of success and with the added dividend of fluency in two languages.

Pedagogically this should not be a complicated choice. As Ramírez notes, however, there are political questions. English Only advocates insist that "prolonged bilingual education" is unacceptable, irrespective of its pedagogical virtues, because it "threaten[s] to divide us along language lines." This fear outweighs any solicitude about students' life chances. English must always come first: "If the standard of success in educating immigrant children is going to be 'no dropouts, no academic failures,' " says U.S. English, "then frankly we can't afford immigration." In other words, subtractive bilingualism may have its costs, but consider who is paying them. Besides, if minority students excel in school, who will be left to wash the dishes?

Nine

Babel in Reverse

When bilingualism is mentioned, thoughts turn to Quebec, home to the most celebrated language conflict in North America. It is a place where opening one's mouth becomes a declaration of allegiances. No message, however mundane, seems without political symbolism. A shopkeeper can run afoul of the provincial language police (a.k.a. the *Commission de protection de la langue française*) by posting a sign that reads Merry Christmas rather than Joyeux Noël. Virtually all employers, private as well as public, are required to operate in French. Children are forbidden to attend English-language schools unless at least one of their parents did so, in Quebec. These are among the mandates of Bill 101, a 1977 law that defines "fundamental language rights" in every phase of life—but only for francophones. It appears that every effort is being made to inconvenience the anglophone minority, about 13 percent of the population, until it either surrenders to "francization" or moves elsewhere. Meanwhile an English Only movement is spreading in Ontario and western Canada, to the distress of francophone minorities there. The 1969 Official Languages Act, among whose goals was to transform an English-speaking civil service into a bilingual one, continues to meet with anglophone resistance. In 1990, the refusal of other provinces to recognize Quebec as a "distinct society" derailed the Meech Lake Accord, on which hopes for a new constitution had been riding. Canada's future as a federation has never looked so doubtful.

This is the surface that American visitors see. Most come away shaking their heads at the pettiness, incivility, alienation—apparent byproducts of bilingualism. The lesson they take home can be summed up "One language unites, two languages divide." That slogan has been popularized by the Alliance for the Preservation of English in Canada, a militant anglophone group subsidized by U.S. English. It has also been an effective sales pitch for Hayakawa's "insurance policy." If French speakers are disrupting Canada's social order, according to this logic, think what Spanish speakers might do in the United States. Ronald Saunders, executive director of U.S. English, appealed to such fears in a 1991 fundraising letter:

> Bilingualism was instituted in Canada during the 1970s to ap-
> pease the French-speaking separatists. By making the country
> officially bilingual, the government hoped to create a sense of
> fairness and equality among all Canadians.
>   But instead they created a monster.
>   During the 1960s and 1970s, terror bombs, murders, and
> kidnapping wracked the nation. Today, billions of dollars are
> spent on translation services by both government and industry.
> The national anthem has two distinctly different sets of lyrics,
> and even cereal boxes have to be printed in both lan-
> guages! . . .
>   As I write this letter to you, experts now believe we face a
> real possibility of seeing three Canadas: An East Canada and a
> West Canada, separated by the sovereign nation of Quebec! It's
> a frightful mess. But it can never happen here, right? WRONG!
> It not only can happen here, it is happening here.

In other words, Canadians are fighting over language, so language must be responsible. To avoid a similar plight, Americans must give English "legal protection." This is about as insightful as blaming religion for the troubles in Northern Ireland and calling for a crackdown on Catholicism in the United States. If, as John Tanton likes to say, "language and religion are the ultimate dividers of Mankind," why not establish a single state church along with a single official tongue to guard against future strife? Of course, history has taught us the consequences, not just for minorities but for the larger society, of government attempts to dictate belief. It has yet to teach us the comparable lesson about linguistic intolerance: that choice of language, like choice of religion, is a matter of *self-definition*. To abridge either freedom is to invite conflict.

Grappling with our own questions of diversity, but lacking much tradition of language politics, Americans are prone to draw superficial parallels with Canada's. When Walter Cronkite quit the U.S.

English advisory board, he felt compelled to note, "I remain firmly opposed to bi-lingualism in the Canadian pattern." As if American policy options were somehow analogous. Alistair Cooke, who remains a U.S. English loyalist, has described bilingual voting rights as "the opening Quebec gambit" by ethnic separatists in this country. Spanish ballots today, Aztlán tomorrow. Jacques Barzun has also endorsed Hayakawa's amendment, hoping "it will prevent . . . the kind of split we see in Belgium or in Canada, where the existence of two official languages has increased hostilities." Barzun does not explain how declaring a single official language would overcome divisions. Through compulsory anglicization, perhaps? Or does he expect minority tongues to wither and die without state support? All three commentators seem to conflate the reality of bilingualism with governmental attempts to accommodate it. Canada has given equal status to English and French; anglophones and francophones are divided; ergo, official bilingualism spells trouble. This is a bit like attributing American race conflicts to civil rights laws. Cause and effect are confounded.

Official bilingualism was not "instituted to appease the French-speaking separatists" but to end two centuries of second-class status for francophone Canadians. Despite constitutional guarantees of linguistic equality,[1] in practice francophones outside of Quebec had little access to government unless they spoke English. Within Quebec their career prospects were limited by anglophone dominance of business and the professions. A federal commission in the mid-1960s reported that one-third of French Canadians were bilingual, as compared with only 5 percent of English Canadians. Yet, by every measure of social status—education, income, occupation—francophones lagged behind anglophones and even recently arrived immigrants.[2] Meanwhile falling birthrates in Quebec enhanced fears that French was endangered. These factors underlay the *opposition* to official bilingualism by Québécois militants, who passed Bill 101 to shore up the status of their language. Since 1977, English-speaking Quebeckers have felt the tyranny of the majority to which French speakers were long subjected, and to similar effect: ethnic polarization. Canada's experience is certainly no advertisement for English Only policies in the United States.

Quebec nevertheless remains a cautionary example for anxious Americans. One need not be a cultural chauvinist to appreciate the advantages of a common language or to dread the fate of linguistic balkanization. There is no question that language differences can exacerbate ethnic tensions. Yet anxiety offers a shaky foundation for public policy. Our own response to bilingualism must be grounded in American realities, not in alarmist visions of what *could* happen, should U.S. Hispanics start acting like Québécois. It is true that Mexican Americans, long victimized by discrimination, have struggled to maintain their cultural heritage. But it is also true that, compared with French speakers in Quebec, native-born Spanish speakers in the Southwest are thirty times more likely to adopt English as their dominant language.[3] Calvin Veltman projects that, were it not for immigration from Latin America, Spanish would disappear within a generation or two, except in remote rural and border areas. Other than the short-lived La Raza Unida of the early 1970s, there have been no Chicano political parties; even in its heyday Aztlán was more a state of mind than a separatist program. Certainly, the United States has nothing to compare with the Parti Québécois, which held power in the province of Quebec from 1976 until 1985 and actively sought political autonomy. Nor is there a single Hispanic organization that advocates official bilingualism, much less Spanish Only laws, in this country.

At the same time, Spanish is clearly on the march, and not just in the Southwest, creating for some Anglo-Americans the impression that English is losing ground. While this may seem contradictory, the statistical reality is not hard to grasp. The *rate* of anglicization is increasing in the United States, but so is the *number* of minority language speakers. Hispanics are switching to English faster than ever before, but not as fast as new Spanish speakers are arriving. Similar patterns hold for other linguistic minorities. Pockets of Amharic, Farsi, Gujarati, and Hmong are appearing in unlikely places. Yet there is no indication that language shift is slowing in the United States, a process of such brutal efficiency that the linguist Einar Haugen has termed it "Babel in reverse." Minority tongues are simply more noticeable today. After a fifty-year hiatus in immigration, an explosion of diversity is posing formidable problems in education, law, and community relations, while contributing valuable, though unexploited, assets.

Under the circumstances our tradition of ad hoc responses is outmoded. The lack of a clear, coordinated, national policy means that whenever a language issue arises—whether it be an English Only sign ordinance or a demand for bilingual health care—an unproductive debate is likely to ensue, pitting a knee-jerk Anglo-conformity against assertions of ethnic militancy. Without a set of standards to settle such disputes, antagonism is inevitable. A philosophical approach is needed to guide decisionmaking, one that would consider the benefits as well as the costs of diversity, minority rights as well as majority prerogatives, democratic principles as well as pragmatic self-interest, language-as-resource as well as language-as-problem. Provided that we avoid simplistic parallels, there is much to learn from the experience of other countries.

In 1986, U.S. English published a survey of 161 constitutions from around the world, reporting that sixty-four—nearly 40 percent—designate an official language. The point being that an English Language Amendment is not such a crazy idea. If other countries can have an official tongue, why not the United States? U.S. English has organized a membership drive around the shocking disclosure that "14 Nations Call English Their National Language. We're Not One of Them." Its full-page newspaper spread, featuring the flags of Gambia, Sierra Leone, Vanuatu, Western Samoa, and the Seychelles, among others, suggests that these countries understand something the U.S. Congress has failed to grasp: "Democracy, more than any other system of government, requires that the people and their elected representatives communicate with each other. A common language is essential." More skillful than the text is the image conveyed: *one flag, one language.*

U.S. English commissioned the survey, by Professor Albert Blaustein of Rutgers University Law School, to provide a basis for such claims. But it demonstrates instead how problematic international analogies can be. After a bit of digging through the text, one discovers that, of the sixty-four constitutions that explicitly declare an official language, all but seventeen protect the rights of linguistic minorities, either by naming more than one official (or "national") language or by incorporating various antidiscrimination guarantees. In addition, twenty-eight countries provide such safeguards without designating any official tongue.

How these provisions translate into policy is another matter. Just as language situations and political structures vary, so do the meanings of constitutional clauses. While Austria's official language has a largely symbolic significance, Turkey's signals a determination to repress public expression and instruction in ethnic languages. India is officially bilingual in Hindi and English, although most Indians speak neither; state governments rely on fifteen regional tongues, each with several million speakers. Official multilingualism, a force for stability in Switzerland, is a focus of contention in Belgium, despite a comparable system of territorial language rights. Irish is designated the national language of Ireland, although it is rarely used by citizens. In contrast, the national language of Haiti (Creole) is spoken widely, while the official language (French) is monopolized by elites. In France, where cultural paranoia runs so high that advertisers can be fined for importing foreign words and phrases, there is no constitutional provision of any kind regarding language. Finally, for what it's worth, not a single country has named English its *sole* official tongue. About the only pattern one can discern in this patchwork is that "one flag, one language" is the world exception rather than the rule.

The ideal of the unilingual nation-state is precisely that: a myth that may serve to inspire patriotism or to justify ethnic chauvinism but that accurately describes only a few small countries. One can list Iceland, Portugal, Liechtenstein . . . before the mind starts to go blank. Not a single major power lacks for minority tongues. Multilingualism is the norm, not the exception, for the simple reason that languages greatly outnumber human societies. In a world with approximately 160 national flags and some 3,000 languages,[4] the odds weigh heavily against unilingualism.

While languages of state have existed since ancient times, until the modern era there was limited success in imposing them on people. Latin survived as an official language in medieval Europe long after it had died out as a vernacular. Gradually rulers began to employ their own dialects for administrative convenience as well as political symbolism. To help consolidate their newly won hegemony, Ferdinand and Isabella designated Castilian as Spain's official language and promoted it as a literary medium. In 1492, Antonio de Nebrija presented the Queen with his *Gramática sobre la lengua castellana*, the first grammar of a modern European tongue. When Isabella asked, "What is it for?" the Bishop of Avila answered on Nebrija's behalf: "Your Majesty, language is the perfect instrument of empire."

Taking this advice to heart, over the next three centuries Spanish monarchs issued periodic edicts on the imperative of Castilianizing the New World.[5] Yet these instructions lacked any relationship to reality, either demographic or political. Priests found it easier to save souls in Indian vernaculars, while civil authorities preferred to rule through translators. Enslaved masses had little motivation to learn Castilian and were slow to do so. (In Latin America to this day, there remain sizable indigenous groups whose Spanish is limited.) Conversely, linguistic unity with the mother country did nothing to inoculate Spanish Creoles against the revolutionary ideas of Bolívar and San Martín, just as it made no difference in our own war of independence.

As a coherent ideology and a mass phenomenon, linguistic nationalism first emerged in Europe. Its intellectual midwife, Johann Gottfried Herder, conceived language as a people's "collective treasure," a repository of "the history, the poetry, and songs about the great deeds of its forefathers." It embodied a *Volksgeist,* or national spirit, that not only symbolized group experience but shaped a thought process and "inner being" distinct from all others. In short, each language defined a natural political unit.

Though Herder's philosophy was influential, providing an impetus for German unification, it remained a historical fantasy. Before the advent of mass literacy, European languages were too fragmented into regional dialects to unify anyone (except gentry and literati) on a broad scale. For the unschooled peasant, whose patois might be incomprehensible in a village twenty miles away, the language of king and court was a matter of indifference. By the same token, elites were rarely concerned with the speech choices of the powerless, so long as taxes were efficiently collected. In 1789, fully half the French population knew no French at all, a mere 12 to 13 percent spoke the Parisian dialect, and fewer still commanded the elegant variety favored by the *Académie française.* Only with the rise of modern states came the means and motivation to popularize a standard tongue. Languages do not mold nations, but vice versa.

Still, the myth of linguistic solidarity can be a powerful unifier— or not, depending on the circumstances. As we have seen, English has played at best a walk-on role in the pageant of American nationalism. Our early leaders conceived language as a lever of national strength, but hardly its essence. Their approach to linguistic diversity was equally pragmatic. During a 1795 debate on whether to print federal laws in German, a Pennsylvania congressman noted that "many honest men, in the late disturbances [the Whiskey Rebellion], were led away by misrepresentation; ignorance of the laws laid them open to deception, when some counties . . . were in a state of insurrection." Government would be well advised to communicate "in the language understood" by a sizable group of citizens. The proposal for German translations was narrowly defeated, apparently because of another utilitarian concern: cost.

Around the same time, a different approach was emerging in revolutionary France. A decree of January 14, 1790, ordered official documents translated into provincial languages and dialects so as to extend the reach of republican ideas. But by 1793, the Jacobins were suppressing these same tongues in the name of *liberté, égalité, fraternité,* while exalting French as "the most reliable agent" of the Revolution. To keep the masses powerless and divided, "the monarchy had reason to emulate the Tower of Babel," declared Bertrand Barère, a member of the Committee for Public Safety. But "the language of a free people ought to be one and the same for all. . . . We have revolutionized the government, the habits, the customs, commerce, and thought; let us also revolutionize the language which is their daily instrument. . . . It is treason to *la Patrie* to leave the citizens in ignorance of the national language." Accordingly, the National Convention mandated French schooling and banned official uses of other languages in provinces like Alsace.

How to explain the contradiction—two national-democratic revolutions, one virtually oblivious to linguistic unity, the other obsessed with it? Simply stated, the answer lies in a clash of political traditions. The essence of nation-building is drawing boundaries; to unite a people, one must differentiate it from others. Native languages were salient identifiers in Europe, where they defined competitive markets and political domains. In France the francophones had rivals who spoke Basque, Breton, Provençal, Flemish, Italian, or German; hence their stake in language loyalty. Moreover, a linguistic standard was essential in rationalizing the state to serve the needs of a rising bourgeoisie. As "the instrument of public thought" throughout the country, French was hailed as the key to defeating reactionary ideas and consolidating the Revolution. In reality, francization was the key to centralizing government under the hegemony of a new national elite headquartered in Paris. Partial interest cloaked itself in egalitarian rhetoric.

By contrast, our own Founders did not perceive Germans and other immigrant groups as serious economic or political competitors. Even if they had, the language of King George III would have been a poor choice as patriotic icon. Rather than crushing minorities, Americans cultivated their allegiance to the commonweal by promising (if not always delivering) safeguards against "interested combinations of the majority." Hence our tradition of linguistic libertarianism—with notable exceptions in the case of conquered peoples and, to a lesser extent, immigrants. Until recently, language has seldom been regarded as a proper subject for federal legislation. The American "policy not to have a policy," as Shirley Brice Heath describes it, has tended to neutralize language, both as a source of conflict and as a unifying symbol.

While one may quarrel with the wisdom of either tradition, Jacobin unilingualism or Madisonian pluralism, one must acknowledge both for what they are: political responses to political conditions. There is no organic relationship between a common language and national unity—neither ensures the other. Nor is there any all-purpose policy wisdom for coping with diversity. Context is crucial. To declare the dominant language official would mean one thing in Iceland, where bilingual services are not at issue, and another in the United States, where there is a growing animus toward immigrants. And it means something else again when a "commonwealth," long denied political or cultural self-determination, moves to assert its linguistic independence.

Puerto Rico took this extraordinary step on April 5, 1991, restoring Spanish as its sole official language. Bilingualism had been official since 1902, not by popular choice, but for the convenience of the colonizers. Virtually no residents of Puerto Rico spoke English when the law was passed—even today, fewer than 20 percent are fully fluent—but North American administrators could not be bothered to learn Spanish. Although the two languages were declared coequal, it was the English version of the laws that governed. The island's legislature operated in Spanish, while the U.S.-appointed governor and executive council (who exercised a veto power over elected officials) functioned in English. This brand of official bilingualism, with the rulers speaking one language and the people another, came to symbolize the denial of self-government.[6] On that basis alone it would have remained unpopular among Puerto Ricans. More than an expression of colonial arrogance, however, the law was part of a systematic attempt to replace Spanish with English, beginning with the language of public instruction.

Students struck, parents protested, teachers rebelled, and still the Americanization policy persisted. José Padín, Puerto Rico's commissioner of education in the 1930s, recognized its disastrous consequences for children. Why not "give pupils such a working knowledge of English as may be justified by their social and vocational needs," he asked, while allowing them to get an education in their native language? Hardly a radical, Padín saw Spanish as a pedagogical, not a political, imperative. In the same spirit, he criticized the slavish elevation of English as "a sort of sacred symbol embodying our loyalty to the United States" and resolved "to adjust its place and function in the curriculum, in the same manner as any other educational subject." The commissioner was asking for trouble.

Padín was fired in 1937, on the advice of Secretary of the Interior Harold Ickes. In appointing a replacement, President Franklin Roosevelt took the opportunity to express his "regret" that Puerto Ricans were resisting English:

> The American citizens of Puerto Rico should profit from their unique geographical situation and the unique historical circumstance which has brought to them the blessings of American citizenship by becoming bi-lingual. But bi-lingualism will be achieved by the forthcoming generations of Puerto Ricans only if the teaching of English throughout the insular educational system is entered into at once with vigor, purposefulness and devotion, and with the understanding that English is the official language [sic] of our country.

The new commissioner, José Gallardo, reimposed English as the language of instruction but had no more success than his predecessors in anglicizing the island.

Under Luis Muñoz Marín, the first Puerto Rican to serve as governor of Puerto Rico, vernacular instruction was finally restored.[7] As founder of the Popular Democratic Party (Populares), Muñoz Marín had initially been an independence advocate. But in 1952, he settled for half a loaf—a commonwealth, or "free associated state"— which expanded cultural autonomy while withholding political freedom. As if to justify the deal, Muñoz Marín put an increasing stress on linguistic nationalism. In a famous speech he criticized Agapito's Bar, a Puerto Rican establishment that chose to identify itself in English: "Why did you do this, Agapito? Not even once in a year will you see on your street of this small town a single customer whose vernacular is the English. Is it that you feel better expressing it in a language that is not yours? And if you despise your own language, are you not despising yourself?"

Under the new commonwealth status, official bilingualism remained in place even though island residents remained largely monolingual in Spanish. The main beneficiaries were U.S. corporations, whose dealings with the insular government could be conducted entirely in English. Not until 1965 was Spanish established as the official language of Puerto Rican courts. (The U.S. District Court in San Juan still operates solely in English.) Nilita Vientos Gastón, a former attorney general of Puerto Rico, has observed: "Only in a nation without sovereignty does the right to place its own language above any other come up for discussion."

Against this background the declaration of Official Spanish becomes easier to appreciate. By 1991, Congress and the Bush administration were moving to authorize a binding plebiscite on the options of statehood, independence, or "enhanced" commonwealth. It appeared that Puerto Ricans might get a chance to choose their own government for the first time since Columbus claimed the island for Spain in 1493.[8] But as always, the question of political status was overshadowed by the question of language—this time the threat of English Only legislation.

Senator Hayakawa once said his constitutional amendment was intended to "keep [Puerto Rico] a territory indefinitely, unless English became the pervading language of the government." But how would Official English affect a State of Puerto Rico if ratified after the fact? Would Spanish have to be abandoned or subordinated? No one could say with certainty. Senator J. Bennett Johnston of Louisiana, chief sponsor of the plebiscite bill, had previously supported the English Language Amendment. But now, hoping to avoid a divisive floor debate over bilingualism, he ruled out provisions that would either mandate English or protect Spanish on the island. Statehood proponents went along with this strategy, while assuring their constituents that "Spanish is not negotiable." But the pro-commonwealth *Populares*, joined by *Independentistas* in Puerto Rico's legislature, insisted on their own insurance policy: Spanish must be *el idioma oficial*. If Puerto Ricans did vote to become the fifty-first state, there would be no ambiguity about their intent to retain a Hispanic heritage.

Known as Bill 417, the Official Spanish measure was not without controversy. Opponents characterized it as "Spanish Only," equating it with the hated English Only movement. Mainland *políticos* asked, "How can we attack language restrictions here while supporting them on the island?" There was special concern for return migrants, Puerto Ricans raised in New York or Bridgeport or Camden, whose Spanish is often limited and whose children encounter difficulties in Puerto Rican schools.

But supporters of Bill 417 stressed its nonrestrictionist character. All branches of government could still use English when "convenient, necessary, or indispensable"—a rather large loophole—and public schools were expressly encouraged to teach English as a subject. Awilda Palau, a political sociologist and leader in the campaign for Bill 417, explains that the objective was not to make life difficult for anyone, but to guard against a specific threat to Spanish. "It is an issue of what we are," she says. "We are not attacking English. We just want to be ourselves. Spanish is our most important single characteristic that differentiates us from the United States. If instead we were a colony of Venezuela, Spanish would not be such an important issue. But as part of a nation with a different culture, a different way of thinking and expressing itself . . . the people of Puerto Rico have been fighting to maintain their identity since 1898. They need to reassert themselves by speaking Spanish."

Sponsors of Bill 417 knew that ethnocentrists in Congress would never accept these terms. Senator Kent Conrad of North Dakota was typical. "If we bring Puerto Rico in as a state," he warned, "I fear that we may create a Quebec." One might ask why Puerto Ricans would join the Union in order to hatch separatist plots. Or how granting equal representation to a cultural minority a thousand miles offshore could threaten the unity of a great power. Or by what right the United States had forced its language on Puerto Rico in the first place. Yet such questions were overlooked by the World's Greatest Deliberative Body. The plebiscite bill died in Johnston's committee, as the *Populares* had hoped. While statehood supporters were properly incensed, they had offered no tangible safeguards for Spanish; moreover, their charges of *Español Solamente* were misplaced. That some sponsors of Bill 417 had ulterior motives does not invalidate the legislation. The confluence of political events brought to the surface a deeply felt issue for Puerto Ricans: who would control their linguistic destiny? Official Spanish was a reassertion of popular preferences—not against internal minorities but against external overlords.

Linguistic self-determination is also a matter of growing concern to American Indians. While an estimated 206 indigenous languages still survive in the United States, a majority of these are in extremely poor health, spoken by dwindling groups of elders. Many lack writing systems and will leave no trace when their remaining speakers die. (This was the fate of several hundred New World languages that have become extinct since white settlers arrived.) Already the cultures these tongues once sustained are disappearing. Storytelling, the traditional pastime on remote reservations, is giving way to V.C.R.'s and cable television. Nowadays it hardly matters that Bureau of Indian Affairs schools have stopped suppressing Indian vernaculars, because students often prefer the language of the Teenage Mutant Ninja Turtles to that of their ancestors.

In 1970, it was hard to find a member of the Navajo Nation unable to speak Navajo; twenty years later it is not unusual for children to grow up speaking only English, even in isolated communities. Until now the tribe's success in preserving its language, unsurpassed by other Native Americans, has been a source of great pride. As U.S. Marines during World War II, Navajo "code-talkers" played a vital role at Guadalcanal and Iwo Jima; the Japanese were never able to decipher signals encoded in their language. Previously, few Navajos had ventured far from the reservation—indeed, it was literally to defend this sacred land that most volunteered—and speaking English had rarely been essential. That situation has changed dramatically, with an influx of whites to exploit uranium, coal, and other Indian resources and with an exodus of tribal members to find jobs elsewhere. The Navajos' isolated way of life is passing and, with it, the security of their tongue. The oral tradition remains strong, preserved through tribal politics, radio stations, and religious ceremonies. But as young Indians encounter a world in which languages of power are *written down,* Navajo literacy is a marginal force.

This poses a painful dilemma, and not just for Navajos. While English provides access to the dominant society, it also weakens the hold of the minority tongue.

Attempting to halt linguistic erosion, a number of tribes—including the Navajo, Red Lake Band of Chippewa, Northern Ute, Arapahoe, Pasqua Yaqui, and Tohono O'odham (Papago)—adopted official language policies during the 1980s. While particulars vary, all share an insistence on teaching their languages in the schools. On other reservations bilingual education programs have supported the cause of language revival, for example, financing the first dictionary in Crow and computer programs in Hualapai. Academic experts have assisted in these projects, along with a number of Indian linguists, and have lobbied successfully for federal help. One result was the Native American Language Act of 1990, a broad policy statement endorsing the preservation of indigenous tongues and requiring government agencies, in particular the Interior and Education departments, to review their activities to make sure they advance this objective. The law commits no additional resources, however, leaving language education to compete with other priorities for scarce tribal dollars.

All these efforts were responses (direct or otherwise) to the English Only movement. Ironically, in its anti-Hispanic zeal, U.S. English has paid little attention to Native Americans, preferring to couch bilingualism as a purely immigrant issue. Yet Native Americans are no less vulnerable to its restrictionist agenda; Arizona's Proposition 106 jeopardized numerous state services on which they rely. And for Indians, unlike immigrants, cultural genocide is forever. "English Only has hit very hard in Indian country," says Ofelia Zepeda, a Papago linguist at the University of Arizona. "There was a sudden fear that an outside entity could come in and cut off your language—like cutting off your hand."

So far, however, language codes have been enacted on only a handful of reservations, and even there obstacles remain. While formal instruction in ancestral tongues is far more available today than in the past, tribal sovereignty over education is fragmented. Public and parochial schools are under no obligation to honor Indian wishes and frequently they do not. Moreover, B.I.A. and tribally controlled schools are subject to a variety of political pressures and Anglo-conformist influences. Bilingual education is often blocked or sabotaged. On the other hand, traditional elders—not to be confused with tribal council members—have resisted policies formulated by outside consultants. Some Utes, for example, have opposed writing the tribe's language, feeling this would open its last cultural bastion to whites. Elsewhere factionalism has undercut good intentions; the Navajo language policy looks ambitious on paper but was largely shelved in 1986 when the tribal chairman, Peterson Zah, lost a close election to Peter MacDonald.

Perhaps some controversy is inevitable wherever language is concerned. Being regular users, we all feel like experts entitled to assert our preferences. Albert Alvarez, who helped to develop an orthography of his native Papago in the late 1960s, was surprised by the opposition he encountered from fellow members of the Tohono O'odham tribe.[9] Still, having worked earlier with Bible translators who had their own ideas about the language, Alvarez could appreciate the resistance to decisions imposed from without. After studying linguistics with Kenneth Hale at the Massachusetts Institute of Technology, he went to every O'odham village to explain the new writing system "until everyone was satisfied." Since the 24,000 tribal members are spread over four reservations in southern Arizona, a land area totaling 2.8 million acres, this was an enormous task. But it paid off in terms of acceptance; the tribe formally adopted the Alvarez-Hale orthography in 1974.

Similarly, the Tohono O'odham language policy has been successful because it reflects a broad consensus, says Ofelia Zepeda, who helped draft the document. "We had six or seven months of public hearings, going to village meetings and asking for opinions and endorsements. We went to wedding dances and made announcements during breaks. When we explained the possible impact, people got very excited." As adopted in 1986, the policy's overriding objective is the maintenance of the tribal *Himdag,* or cultural heritage. Toward that end, elders are enlisted to help train teachers, so that education remains truly bicultural as well as bilingual. The language is taught in all twelve grades in reservation schools and is used officially in tribal proceedings. Classes are also available for adults who wish to become literate in Papago; Alvarez himself has taught many teachers to read the language.

About three-quarters of the O'odham remain orally fluent in their native tongue—a high proportion, compared to most other tribes, no doubt reflecting the isolation of Sonoran Desert life. But there has been a noticeable decline in recent years. In Sells, the seat of tribal government, it is now common to find young Papagos unable or un-willing to speak the language, and that worries Albert Alvarez. "My desire," he says, "was to teach others [to read and write], so they could teach the kids, because I felt that was the most important thing we have, the language. As long as it's alive, it's a part of us, it's our life. [It expresses] that respect when we see mountains, when we see trees, when we see anything that grows—we don't just go and start chopping it down for our own satisfaction. When we lose that, we're just walking in the dark, trying to search our way around. We may be fluent, as far as English is concerned, but it's just on the surface."

This is a very Indian view of language—not as a neutral instru-ment, but as a conveyor of values. The O'odham regard their tongue as "a gift from our Creator," part of the *Himdag* that defines the tribe and its reverence for the earth. Preserving it is no less a duty than preserving the unique features of the natural world. Dick Lit-tlebear, a Northern Cheyenne educator, feels much the same: "We need our land and we need our language. The two are inseparable. . . . There are references to the land that can be articulated only in the Cheyenne language. I believe that once those sacred references can no longer be expressed, the Northern Cheyennes will start view-ing the land much as the dominant culture views it. These vital links will no longer exist in the tribal consciousness."

Littlebear estimates that seven in ten members of his Montana tribe have largely lost the Cheyenne language, often at great cost to their self-image. Coercive anglicization has taken more from Native Americans than a set of linguistic skills. It has isolated them from cultural resources they need to define themselves, leaving many un-prepared to enter a wider society, still far from color-blind, that is likely to reject them regardless of their English-speaking ability. Alienated from both cultures, Indian youths may be attracted to substance abuse, violence, and other self-destructive behavior. It is significant that alcoholism is associated not with those who observe traditional ways, but with those who renounce them and find no place in the white world.

What is sad about all this is that there is no reason, other than social prejudice, to give up one language while learning another. Subtractive bilingualism is entirely unnecessary. Furthermore, it is a waste of human capital.

Not all nations regard language diversity as an unmitigated curse. In casting about for international analogies, Americans might consider Australia, a country whose linguistic heritage and makeup are quite similar to our own, but whose policy responses provide an instructive contrast. English is indisputably dominant, the de facto (but unofficial) national language, spoken as a native tongue by 83 percent of Australians, who, like Americans, are notorious for their monolingualism. But numerous Asian and European languages are also represented, thanks to levels of immigration considerably higher than our own. Melbourne is now the third largest Greek-speaking city in the world. There are also sizable pockets of Italian, Serbo-Croatian, German, Dutch, Chinese, Polish, Maltese, Spanish, French, and Vietnamese. Meanwhile about 150 indigenous tongues are still spoken, although many are threatened; about fifty remain viable among Aborigines. As in the United States, language barriers create practical headaches for schools, courts, and social service agencies; illiteracy is a particular problem. Traditionally, speaking a language other than English has been viewed as a handicap rather than a skill to be valued. Opportunities for maintaining minority cultures have been limited until recently, and language loss is common among immigrant as well as indigenous minorities.

The major difference is that Australia has no second language as pervasive as Spanish in the United States.[10] This may help to explain the striking difference in attitudes toward bilingualism. Rather than organizing English Only campaigns, Anglo-Australians tend to support, or at least accept, the idea of minority language maintenance. So government has been free to take a dispassionate, no-nonsense approach to language planning. It has funded developmental bilingual education, for example, without provoking conflicts over melting pots and salad bowls. A state-run television network has been set aside for multilingual programming, along with public radio stations that broadcast in more than fifty languages. Most significant, in 1987 Australia adopted a comprehensive National Policy on Languages, a model of linguistic pluralism that the United States would do well to study.

Briefly stated, the policy's principal aim is "to ensure that Australia derives maximum benefit from its rich linguistic resources." The idea is not only to cope with diversity, but to exploit it on behalf of national objectives in external relations and trade, political communication, and cultural expression. The policy incorporates four "guiding principles":

- competence in *English for all* Australians;
- *a language other than English for all,* either through the maintenance of existing skills or opportunities for Anglo-Australians to learn a second language;
- *conservation of languages* spoken by Aborigines and Torres Strait Islanders; and
- equitable and widespread *services in languages other than English,* including intrepreters, libraries, and media.

So far the major impact has been to increase support for language education of all kinds. New programs have been created, or existing ones expanded, in adult literacy, English as a second language, Asian studies, bilingual and multicultural schooling for immigrants, Aboriginal language revival, and foreign language instruction. In elementary and secondary programs, special emphasis has been given to nine "languages of wider learning"—Arabic, Chinese (Mandarin), French, German, Greek, Indonesian/Malay, Italian, Japanese, and Spanish—deemed vital to "Australia's domestic and external needs."

Without introducing any new requirements for Australian students—indeed, there are no mandatory features of any kind—the policy promotes *individual bilingualism* as a national asset. It argues that depending on English alone is shortsighted in a competitive world. With its Pacific Rim location, Australia enjoys advantages in attracting Asian business and tourism, but only if it can overcome cultural barriers. Moreover, Australia needs diplomats trained in "languages of world significance." One obvious solution to both problems is to tap the resources of immigrant communities. Besides the cultural and intellectual opportunities afforded by proficiency in more than one language, the policy emphasizes the goals of "social justice and overcoming disadvantages." Immigrant and Aboriginal children experience acute educational problems—not unlike those of their U.S. counterparts—because of limited English proficiency and the erosion of native-language skills. Australia is responding with *additive* bilingual education, designed to provide access to the English mainstream while conserving and developing other tongues. For Aborigines in particular, the policy recognizes that social equality cannot be achieved through cultural genocide, that indigenous languages deserve protection because they are "central to individual and group identity."

Clearly, decades of neglecting minority tongues will not be remedied overnight. Despite notable achievements since 1987—in language-learning opportunities, expanded enrollments, professional training and research, and Aboriginal programs—the practical effects of the new policy are only beginning to be felt. Many Australians remain unaware of its existence. Thus far, as might be expected, efforts have largely involved language educators, ethnic advocates, and government bureaucrats. Yet the policy represents an important intervention by government: a comprehensive approach that balances majority and minority interests, while relying on consensus rather than coercion to influence behavior.

For Americans worried about the impact of bilingualism, Australia's experience demonstrates that language contradictions need not be antagonistic but can instead provide opportunities for enrichment. This, in essence, is the English Plus philosophy. Rather than language-as-problem, it stresses language-as-resource. A coalition of education and civil rights groups—including the National Education Association, the Teachers of English to Speakers of Other Languages, the National Association for Bilingual Education, the American Jewish Committee, the American Civil Liberties Union, and the Mexican American Legal Defense and Educational Fund— has united behind English Plus as a policy alternative to English Only. In the late 1980s the idea won the support of state legislatures in New Mexico, Oregon, and Washington State, city councils from Cleveland to Tucson, numerous newspaper editors, civic leaders, and even the odd chamber of commerce.

English Plus recognizes that "English is and will remain the primary language of the United States" and that good English skills are required for full participation in American life. For the significant portion of U.S. residents with other native tongues, it supports expanded public funding for adult E.S.L. instruction. At the same time, it emphasizes that while people are learning English, they need bilingual assistance to guarantee access "to the electoral process, education, the legal system, social services, and health care." But there is no reason for government to stop there. As a nation we have a growing need for "multiple language skills . . . to promote our position in the world marketplace and to strengthen the conduct of foreign relations." Instead of focusing solely on immigrants' *dis*abilities in English, why not nurture their abilities in other tongues? They could even be enlisted to help Anglo-Americans overcome their monolingualism. English Only intolerance not only harms linguistic minorities; it defies national self-interest.

The case for English Plus boils down to a simple question: Why throw away valuable knowledge? If there is any pedagogical reason to do so, it has yet to be discovered. Psycholinguists have long since debunked the myth that bilingualism confuses the brain; more likely, it enhances cognitive flexibility. No one can deny that individuals benefit in numerous ways—occupational, cultural, psychological—by maintaining their native tongues as they learn English. For the country as a whole, the benefits may be less obvious, but they are no less substantial. Language conservation offers a more realistic hope of increasing our pool of linguistic talent than the current reliance on foreign language instruction. Native speakers not only enjoy a head start but usually have strong incentives to cultivate their skills. What they need are opportunities to do so, such as developmental bilingual education and, for older students, academic courses taught in the mother tongue. While Anglo-Americans may be enticed to study a second language, they seldom acquire fluency without compelling personal or professional motivations, as well as occasions to speak it regularly. Yet these could be expanded, again by drawing on minority resources. For English-speaking children, two-way bilingual programs are among the most effective ways to acquire a second language, because they combine immersion techniques and close contact with native speakers.

To be sure, English Plus will not come free. It will mean, for example, expenditures to train instructors in numerous languages. In California, where one out of five schoolchildren is limited in English, public schools faced a shortage of eleven thousand bilingual teachers in 1990, and that number is expected to rise through the decade. The state's late bilingual education law tried (with little success) to address this problem on the cheap, requiring mid-career teachers to become bilingual on their own time—as if a few months of classes in Khmer or Portuguese could qualify anyone to teach in those languages. (Needless to say, the requirement did little to endear English-speaking teachers to the concept of bilingual education.) It is now clear that any solution must involve financial incentives to attract linguistic minorities to the profession. Such spending will no doubt be unpopular in fiscally troubled times.

Yet, as Catherine Snow and Kenji Hakuta observe, "subtractive bilingualism" also has its costs, and these are rarely factored into the policy equation. This society must spend considerable sums to teach English speakers the same skills that linguistic minorities are encouraged to forget. In 1991, the Senate Intelligence Committee was so dubious about the recruiting pool for American spies that it established a $150 million National Security Education Fund to improve college programs in foreign languages and international studies. But why insist on manufacturing linguistic and cultural expertise from scratch while ignoring "immigrant gifts" that could be adapted or developed? English Plus would seem a more rational and cost-effective approach.

Indeed, all of this makes such good educational sense that it is hard to see how anyone could object, much less the U.S. Department of Education. But federal programs for limited-English-proficient students remain, in Snow and Hakuta's words, "efficient revolving doors between home-language monolingualism and English monolingualism." Although funding for developmental bilingual education was restored in 1984 after a six-year ban, the Reagan and Bush administrations have generally refused to spend the modest subsidies allowed by Congress. In 1989, Secretary of Education Lauro Cavazos justified this policy as a way to "maximize instructional resources" for teaching English "as quickly as possible." Reserving grants for transitional bilingual and English-only immersion programs did not, in his carefully worded opinion, imply an "objective of encouraging children to abandon their native language." (Presumably, they would continue to study in their free time.) Cavazos hastened to make respectful noises about "the ability to use two languages . . . a highly desirable goal . . . a skill critical to the Nation's future economic competitiveness. However, other Departmental programs . . . are designed to foster second language acquisition."[11]

In short, schizophrenia continues to guide federal policy. "Foreign language" proficiency, a worthy objective, is promoted for English speakers; "bilingualism," an unfortunate social problem, is addressed with remedial education.

English Plus would seem, at first glance, an effective counterpoint to English Only. Judged by their results, bilingual programs are a superior method of teaching English and they could be a great deal more. A national policy of encouraging *individual* bilingualism—English, plus another language for all Americans—would go a long way toward mitigating the complications of *societal* bilingualism. Moreover, a language-as-resource philosophy would finally begin to attack the problem, widely bemoaned but seldom addressed, of being a "tongue-tied" nation. As trade barriers fall and the world economy becomes more integrated, our disability becomes increasingly apparent. If there was ever an occasion for pragmatism, this is it. Rather than worry about immigrants getting the "wrong message" when government provides bilingual services, we should consider the message an Official English amendment would send American youth about the value of learning other tongues. English Only is a Know-Nothing movement in the fullest sense of the phrase.

Yet, however sensible on the high plane of public policy, English Plus has been a weak political strategy. At its core today's language debate is not about human resources—or about language, for that matter. It is about rights, status, and belonging. Should all Americans be guaranteed equality under the law regardless of their English skills, or should they remain less than full citizens until they have learned the common tongue? Should our sense of national identity be expansive, a cornucopia of languages and cultures, or should the title *American* be reserved for those who speak good English?

Despite its appeals to pluralism, English Plus has largely sidestepped these questions and the strong feelings they arouse. It may win elite endorsements, but if electoral experience is any guide, it inspires little popular enthusiasm. Anglo-Americans are apt to ask, "English Plus *what?*"—suspecting a sly attempt to impose Spanish. Whereas Hispanics, facing an attack from bigots, often find the slogan apologetic: "*Con permiso,* we're learning English; just let us keep our language." By not directly addressing majority fears or minority aspirations, English Plus can lapse into a bland multiculturalism that satisfies no one. An analogous approach to school desegregation would be to focus on the waste of intellectual skills when children are denied a quality education. Entirely true, yet beside the point.

Conclusion

Democracy and Language

As a political issue, bilingualism has two dimensions in the
United States, one that can be addressed within our constitutional traditions and another that poses conceptual challenges. First, it is a question of *individual rights*. How far should
we extend freedom of expression and equality of opportunity for
linguistic minorities? One answer is Official English, a policy of limiting such liberties in the name of national unity—to what extent
remains in dispute, but there is no doubt about its English Only
thrust. An alternative response, advanced by language rights advocates, would expand current laws against discrimination and rationalize the hit-or-miss approach to bilingual services. Though not necessarily easy to resolve, these are familiar issues of free speech, due
process, and equal protection.

Language choice is secondly a question of *self-determination,* of
ethnic democracy. Here we enter the less explored realm of "group
rights," of extraordinary laws like the Voting Rights Act designed
to overthrow tyrannies of the majority—not case by case, but by
more expeditious means. Should certain minorities, because of their
history and current circumstances, be entitled to state assistance in
preserving their native languages and cultures? Or should laissez-
faire, a principled nonintervention by government, continue to guide
our approach to cultural pluralism? These are among the questions
a comprehensive U.S. language policy would have to decide. Before
proceeding to consider them, however, it is important to determine
what is *not* at issue.

U.S. English has always had trouble providing a plausible answer
to the question: Why does the United States need an English Language Amendment? Clarifying "the primacy of English" would seem

superfluous in a country where it is spoken as a native tongue by seven residents out of eight and where immigrants adopt it rapidly as their usual language. Reaffirming our "common bond" as Americans makes little sense, either, considering that English has rarely played that symbolic role in the past, except as a surrogate for racism or xenophobia. Finally, the idea of taking out an "insurance policy" against language strife seems like a neurotic exercise, a kind of Strategic Defense Initiative against "foreign" cultures. These lame rationales for Official English led many to suspect a hidden agenda even before the Tanton scandal broke. In its aftermath U.S. English has been desperately seeking to articulate a clear and present danger, something that would justify "the legal protection of English" without resorting to rude phrases like "the Latin onslaught." Hence its 1991 advertising campaign, run in newspapers throughout the country. A knife slashes through a map of the United States, its handle bearing the sinister legend: *Official Bilingualism.*

But who are the leaders and organizations promoting official bilingualism or linguistic separatism in the United States today? When pressed during an interview, U.S. English director Ronald Saunders declined to name names. He would only hint that one must speak Spanish to ferret out the conspirators—ethnic politicians who would like to keep their constituents ignorant of English. As evidence of "calls for official bilingualism," a U.S. English publication cites: (1) statements by educators about the virtues of multiple language skills, (2) an English Plus resolution passed by the Oregon legislature, (3) a civil rights attorney's criticism of coercive assimilation in the Southwest, and (4) an offhand comment by former mayor Maurice Ferré about the dominance of Spanish in Miami. If there is a movement to declare Spanish a coequal language in the United States, a reasonable person might ask, why isn't a single prominent Hispanic willing to endorse it?

"I have not heard of anyone promoting such an agenda," says Antonia Hernández, president of the Mexican American Legal Defense and Educational Fund. "It's definitely not a part of MALDEF's agenda. There are so many more pressing, urgent problems that need to be addressed. It would be foolish to spend our time on that." The relevant demand is not equal status for Spanish, she says, but equal access for Spanish speakers who have yet to acquire English. Bilingual education offers limited-English-proficient children a means to become productive members of society, while bilingual ballots enable LEP adults to participate in the democratic process. As for the importance of English, "who's denying that?" Hernández asks. "Who's saying, 'Don't let the kids learn English'? English is the language you need to make it here." On the other hand, why shouldn't Americans "speak more than one language, whatever it is?" Believing that bilingual skills should be valued, MALDEF has filed lawsuits seeking extra compensation for employees whose jobs require them to use Spanish or other minority tongues. It has challenged English-only rules in the workplace, prodded school districts to improve instruction for LEP students, and led efforts to extend bilingual voting rights. Finally, MALDEF has joined with other Hispanic organizations, such as the National Council of La Raza, in lobbying to increase federal subsidies for adult English instruction. For these ethnic advocates, the common threads are civil rights and educational advancement, not official bilingualism.

If U.S. English were seriously interested in speeding English acquisition among immigrants, it would work closely with Hispanic and Asian leaders, who are virtually unanimous in supporting this goal. Instead, it raises the specter of linguistic separatism, relying not on the statements or actions of real opponents, but on racial fears and stereotypes. One can only conclude that the Official English campaign has less to do with shaping language policy than with exploiting the politics of resentment.

What is at issue for policymakers is how to address the practical reality of bilingualism within a framework of democratic principles. While this is partly a matter of managing resources— balancing costs and benefits—it is primarily one of defining rights. By nature the process will be political; that is, it will involve conflicting interests and symbols. Yet, to be productive, it must dispense with global analogies and focus on tangible problems.

For individuals there are two kinds of rights that must be clarified: freedom from discrimination on the basis of language and affirmative steps to overcome language barriers. The first category would seem rather straightforward and noncontroversial. As we have seen, the Supreme Court has increasingly treated language discrimination as a surrogate for national-origin discrimination, which is prohibited both by statute and by the U.S. Constitution. It should be a simple matter to codify these precedents in federal law so that they are widely understood. Who would oppose this basic principle of fairness? Senator Richard Shelby, for one. At the behest of U.S. English, the Alabama Democrat has proposed legislation that would, among other things, amend the Civil Rights Act of 1964 to include an explicit ban on language-based discrimination, *but for English speakers only*. How courts would interpret this implied departure from equal protection is uncertain. Some might now question the E.E.O.C.'s fair-practice guidelines for linguistic minorities; even the *Lau v. Nichols* precedent on special help for LEP students could be subject to challenge. Private-sector employers could be vulnerable to lawsuits if they hired or promoted workers for their bilingual skills. Shelby's so-called Language of Government Act would also prohibit any "official act"[1] by federal agencies or employees "that requires the use of a language other than English"—in effect, requiring the government itself to discriminate. At minimum, Americans should reject such mean-spirited restrictions.

A more difficult, though no less urgent, task is to formulate an affirmative policy for bilingual public services that is both equitable and realistic. There is no question of accommodating 160 languages at once, as some obstructionists have suggested, or of creating an entitlement to language assistance for any non-English speaker at any time. A sound policy must reflect both numbers and need. Naturally these will vary, depending on the languages spoken in a given community and the government services at issue. Take a hypothetical American city, recently transformed by newcomers whose English is limited, and assume that 20 percent of local residents are native speakers of Spanish, 5 percent speak Vietnamese, and another 5 percent speak either Cantonese, Tagalog, Gujarati, Armenian, or Polish. Should the city ensure that court interpreters and 911 operators are available in all these languages? Definitely. In which tongues besides English should it provide brochures on low-income energy assistance? Probably in Spanish and Vietnamese and in the others if practical, since non-English speakers are among those likely to need help. Should it translate property tax bills into every language? Probably not, considering the expense and the alternatives for providing assistance, although printing them in Spanish might prove cost-effective.

It would be best to leave such decisions to local or state governments, which are already responding to these needs (if somewhat haphazardly). No doubt many jurisdictions would welcome guidance on what kinds of accommodations are reasonable. Yet in areas where minorities remain powerless to secure help through normal political channels, federal mandates may be necessary, especially where due process or public safety is involved. Neither cost nor administrative convenience can excuse policies that result in the denial of fundamental rights or essential services. Less vital needs may be balanced against practical exigencies. Demographic formulas could be devised, as under the Voting Rights Act, to trigger a jurisdiction's obligation to provide certain kinds of help, say, bilingual drivers' tests, and special oversight could be authorized in localities with a documented history of discrimination. The operative principle, which should be applied wherever possible, is one of simple equality under the law. Rights that individuals would otherwise enjoy, including free access to government, must not be limited on account of language ability.

More complex questions of democracy arise regarding minorities whose native tongues have been excluded or repressed or both, yet survive as valued means of self-expression. Does justice demand that such communities be granted extraordinary rights—beyond equality as individuals and freedom of communication in private contexts? Should they be offered, in effect, an exemption from "the primacy of English," with guarantees of native-language services and assistance in undoing the damage wrought by forced "Americanization"? On the other hand, can we extend these special rights without fostering resentment and divisiveness, not only between Anglos and non-Anglos, but among linguistic minorities who are treated differently? Can we create legal privileges on the basis of ethnicity without encouraging tribalism?

In jurisdictions where a single minority language has been historically dominant and continues to be so, these questions are easily settled. Residents of Puerto Rico—whether they choose statehood or not—should have every right to preserve their Spanish heritage and to resist further attempts to anglicize the island. Or they should be able to move toward bilingualism, appeasing a growing stratum of Puerto Ricans that favors greater use of English. But whatever the outcome, it should be a decision by Puerto Ricans, not by outsiders.

This same principle should apply on the Navajo, Tohono O'odham, and other reservations where Indian tongues remain viable. In addition, as past targets of cultural genocide, indigenous Americans should have a special claim on subsidies to maintain or revive their languages and teach them to their young. The Hawaiian language, reduced to fewer than two thousand native speakers, is now beginning to make a comeback, thanks to private efforts like the Pûnana Leo ("Language Nest") immersion program for preschoolers. But preventing the extinction of indigenous tongues must be understood as preserving cultural treasures that belong, in a sense, to all Americans—a public responsibility. Besides expanding educational assistance, the federal government should finance tribally controlled projects in language revival.

The question of linguistic self-determination is a much closer one for Spanish speakers in the Southwest, now reduced to minority status in all but a few locales. A substantial percentage of these Hispanics are recent immigrants, and in any case, they are rapidly becoming anglicized. Nevertheless, Spanish remains a significant, if not a dominant, tongue in many parts of the region, where it antedates English by nearly three centuries. Surveys have repeatedly shown that Mexican Americans (like most other linguistic minorities) want their children to learn English, but not to lose their native tongue in the process. For this sizable group of U.S. citizens, it would seem hard to justify a restriction of language choice—to insist that maintaining Spanish should be a private matter, not a public right—purely on the basis of "majority rule" by relative newcomers to their homeland. To do so would be equivalent to justifying an Official Spanish policy for Dade County, or an Official Chinese policy for Monterey Park, should local voters decide to enact them.

Such acts of retribution against English speakers seem unlikely. Yet tomorrow's balkanization thrives on today's denial of minority rights. This remains the essential folly of English Only, whether it affects immigrants or indigenous Americans, groups or individuals, people with historic claims or newcomers seeking a modicum of fairness. Tyrannies of the majority are ultimately self-defeating. At a juncture in our national experience when ideals of community seem elusive and fellow countrymen seem fractioned into selfish clans, it is worth remembering, to paraphrase the Supreme Court in *Meyer v. Nebraska*, that—however advantageous the goal may appear—national unity cannot be coerced. "American" identity cannot be propagated, nor ethnic harmony assured, by means that contradict our founding principles.

Notes

Chapter 1

1. Whether any cut was actually made remains in dispute. A group known as Friends of the Monterey Park Library contends that, following Hatch's comments, the foreign materials budget was reduced from $11,000 to $3,000. Librarian Elizabeth D. Minter has strongly denied this, adding: "If the council had adopted a policy restricting the library to purchasing only English-language books and subscriptions, my professional ethics would have required that I work to get the policy rescinded immediately or resign my position in protest"; see "Monterey Park Library Caught in Political Crossfire," *Library Journal,* Dec. 1988, p. 20.

2. In the 1950s the top five countries of origin were Germany, Canada, Mexico, the United Kingdom, and Italy; in the 1980s they were Mexico, the Philippines, Vietnam, Korea, and China (including Taiwan). Asian immigration increased from 6 percent of the total in the 1950s to 43 percent in 1986.

3. Incredible as this may seem, Dr. Robert Melby, chairman of the Florida English campaign, called for the abolition of bilingual 911 assistance during a public debate in Miami, as reported by United Press International (*Diario Las Américas,* March 22, 1985). A year later he reiterated the same argument during an interview: "Everybody calling the emergency line should have to learn enough English so they can say 'fire' or 'emergency' and give the address. I would [learn that much Spanish] if I was living in Mexico." Asked whether his proposal might not lead to needless tragedies, the Tampa optometrist responded that "loss of life" had already occurred in cases where bilingual operators were unavailable. It was "an unrealistic dream," Melby added, for non-English speakers to expect emergency services in numerous languages; see James Crawford, "Conservative Groups Take Aim at Bilingual-Education Programs," *Education Week,* March 19, 1986, pp. 1, 14.

4. The signatures were never verified, however, because the ballot issue was later disqualified.

5. Although the council had tentatively decided to submit CHaMP's counter-proposal to the voters, it, too, was dropped after the Official English petitions were rejected.

6. Beginning in 1981, bilingual instruction was mandated in elementary schools with at least ten LEP students from the same minority-language background at the same grade level. To avoid segregation by language and to provide role models for LEP children, at least one-third of students assigned to a bilingual classroom had to be fluent in English. The law expired in 1987 after Governor George Deukmejian vetoed a bill to extend it.

7. The Mexican national holiday commemorates an 1862 victory against a French expeditionary force that slowed Maximilian's invasion.

8. Nebraska and Illinois passed such measures in 1920 and 1969, respectively. Hawaii, sometimes counted in the Official English column, declared itself bilingual in 1978 with a constitutional amendment recognizing Native Hawaiian as a second official tongue.

9. This dialect is spoken by ethnic Chinese from Vietnam.

10. Yet this can be said of a dwindling number of Monterey Park voters. Tired of polarization, in 1990 they elected three new council members dedicated to restoring harmony. Barry Hatch received the fewest votes in a field of six candidates; the other remaining English Only proponent, Pat Reichenberger, came in fifth.

Chapter 2

1. One persistent legend, popularized after the Civil War and revived by the German-American Bund in the 1930s, is that German failed by a single vote to become the official language of the United States. Apparently the tale draws on two unrelated events involving Frederick A. C. Muhlenberg, a Pennsylvania German who served as the first Speaker of the U.S. House of Representatives. One involved a petition by Virginia Germans seeking the publication of important federal laws in their language. In 1795, the House defeated this proposal on a 42–41 vote, in which Muhlenberg may have stepped down from the Speaker's chair to break a tie. Existing records, however, make it impossible to ascertain what role, if any, the Speaker played. It is known that he was never fluent in German and was widely suspected of Anglophilia. In a second, well-documented episode, Muhlenberg broke a tie vote in favor of executing the Jay Treaty, which authorized payment of a ransom for American sailors held by the British. This act brought the Speaker both political and personal grief. Pennsylvania voters, who regarded the treaty as a humiliating sellout, defeated Muhlenberg in the 1796 election; whereupon his own outraged brother-in-law attacked him with a knife. A combination of poor record keeping, Muhlenberg's reputation as an ethnic Judas, and German cultural pride breathed life into this captivating but absurd story. English has never had to weather a challenge, serious or otherwise, in the U.S. Congress. See Feer, "Official Use of the German Language," pp. 394–401.

2. A pidgin is a simplified (though hardly simpleminded) language that eliminates irregular features to make it broadly accessible. A Creole is a pidgin that has acquired native speakers. Black English is an example of "decreolization," or encroachment by the higher status language. Gombo, a French Creole, became well established among Louisiana slaves before English speakers arrived, and in rural enclaves it remains a viable tongue today.

3. This work, *Observations Concerning the Increase of Mankind*, would later influence Malthus himself. It analyzed the economic conditions, notably the demand for labor on the frontier, that favored rapid population growth in the New World. What worried Franklin, however, was not the *quantity*, but the *quality* of humankind: "The number of purely white people in the world is proportionably very small. . . . I could wish their numbers were increased." And his conception of preferred breeding stock was Anglocentric, to say the least. "In Europe, the Spaniards, Italians, French, Russians, and Swedes, are generally of what we call a swarthy Complexion; as are the Germans also, the Saxons only excepted, who with the English, make up the principal Body of White People on the Face of the

Earth." For immigration policy, the implication was clear: "Why increase the sons of Africa by planting them in America, where we have so fair an opportunity, by excluding all blacks and tawnys, of increasing the lovely red and white?" Regretting his intemperate remarks, Franklin excised this passage from later editions of his writings.

4. According to the census of 1806, 52,998 persons lived in what would become the state of Louisiana, including 23,574 slaves, 3,355 free people of color, and 26,069 whites. Of this last group, 13,500 were natives of Louisiana, 3,500 were natives of the United States, and the rest were of European birth: French, Spaniards, English, Germans, and Irish.

5. Because the Republican party had pledged to admit New Mexico, Beveridge had to go to great lengths to prevent it, even hiding out for ten days to avoid a Senate floor vote (which protocol prevented in a committee chairman's absence). Later he suggested joint statehood with Arizona, an alternative that would leave "the Mexican population in the middle, masses of Americans to the east of them, masses of Americans to the west of them—a situation ideal for Americanizing within a few brief years every drop of the blood of Spain"; Senate floor speech, Feb. 5, 1905. Congress backed this proposal in 1906, subject to separate approval by both territories. While New Mexico voters were agreeable, Arizonans showed no interest in the missionary role that Beveridge had assigned them. Fearful of being overwhelmed by Spanish speakers, they defeated the referendum by a vote of nearly eight to one.

6. In 1910, 40 percent of New Mexicans had been born in other states of the Union, as opposed to only 21 percent in 1900. Combined with the Anglo-Americans already there, the total of English speakers slightly surpassed that of Spanish speakers. See Kloss, *American Bilingual Tradition*, p. 128.

7. Such legislation passed Congress four times beginning in 1897 but consistently met with presidential vetoes. Finally, in 1917, restrictionists mustered a two-thirds majority to enact the literacy requirement over Woodrow Wilson's opposition, but by that time its effectiveness as a barrier had declined.

8. Originally the naturalization bill required new citizens to be able to read both English and their native tongue, but this provision was dropped after it was pointed out that 80 percent of Americans, including Representative Bonynge, could not meet the standard of literacy in two languages. The current requirement—ability to read and write English as well as speak it—dates from the McCarran-Walter Act of 1952.

9. This restriction, imposed in October 1917, proved so burdensome that its effect was to bar most foreign-language publications from the U.S. mail unless they could qualify for an exemption. Naturally, those willing to serve as cheerleaders for government policy were favored; almost no socialist periodicals received a permit to use the mails without submitting translations. While some German newspapers began to publish in English, many others went out of business. See Wittke, *German-Americans and the World War*, pp. 173–77, and Park, *Immigrant Press and Its Control*, pp. 439–42.

10. According to the *Dakota Freie Presse*, a German-language newspaper in New Ulm, Minnesota, of 17,908 charges by January 1, 1921, 5,720 had led to convictions, 2,924 had been dismissed for lack of evidence, and 9,259 had yet to be tried; cited in Rippley, *The German-Americans*, p. 126.

Chapter 3

1. Explaining his change of heart, Van de Kamp cited a single source, a previous attorney general's opinion that found no conflict between the Treaty of Guadalupe Hidalgo and California's English-literacy requirement for voting, later ruled unconstitutional in *Castro v. State of California* (1970). According to this narrow reading, the treaty guaranteed no rights for anyone other than "Mexican nationals residing in the ceded territories" in 1848. In other words, their descendants got nothing; Attorney General Stanley Mosk to Assemblyman James B. Mills, Aug. 23, 1961.

2. Mexican nationals living on the ceded lands had three options: (1) moving to Mexican territory, as about two thousand chose to do; (2) remaining on U.S. soil and becoming citizens of the United States automatically after one year; or (3) staying put and declaring themselves Mexican citizens. Before ratification, the U.S. Senate deleted Article X, which concerned the validity of Mexican land titles, although such claims were generally upheld (in principle, if not in practice) under other provisions of the treaty. The Senate also revised Article IX, which had initially contained a more detailed statement regarding the status of Mexican Americans: "With respect to political rights, their condition shall be on an equality with that of the inhabitants of the other territories of the United States; and at least equally good as that of the inhabitants of Louisiana and the Floridas, when these provinces, by transfer from the French Republic and the Crown of Spain, became territories of the United States." To assuage Mexican concerns about the removal of this guarantee, a protocol was signed on May 26, 1848, stating that the Senate's changes were technical in nature and would result in no loss of rights. See *Treaties and Other International Acts*, V: 217–19, 241–43, 254–56, 380–81.

3. In 1849, native *Californios* accounted for 13,000 out of an estimated 100,000 white residents of California. New immigrants included about 8,000 Mexicans and 5,000 Chileans and Peruvians, while Indians numbered approximately 72,000; Bancroft, *History of California*, V: 643; Pitt, *Decline of the Californios*, p. 43.

4. Rather than any challenge to bilingual state operations, the cases brought under this provision generally involved creative attempts to invalidate laws or criminal charges in which foreign words appeared. Only a few of these were successful. The California Supreme Court dismissed one indictment because it included an untranslated exhibit in Chinese; *People v. Ah Sum* (1892). On another occasion it invalidated an oral sodomy law because fastidious legislators had listed the prohibited sex act in Latin, without further explanation in English; *In re Lockett* (1919). But judges otherwise upheld the use of foreign terms in statutes (e.g., *prima facie, cannabis sativa*), as long as translations were provided or were easily accessible. Ironically, the mandate for English-language proceedings had the effect of *expanding* minority language rights in the courtroom by necessitating the use of interpreters for non-English-speaking witnesses; *People v. Pechar* (1955).

5. It should be noted that not all Mexican American leaders were so eager for assimilation, or so sanguine about racial progress. Those with continuing ties to Mexico and its revolutionary traditions put a strong emphasis on maintaining their native tongue. El Congreso Nacional del Pueblo de Habla Hispana, representing more than a million members, actively campaigned for bilingual instruction in the late 1930s. La Fraternal Asociación por el México Americano, with chapters

throughout the Southwest, sponsored Spanish-language summer schools as a way to preserve and strengthen children's cultural identity.

6. Out of 144 witnesses in the House and Senate hearings combined, 70 had Hispanic surnames. The occupational breakdown is as follows:

	House	Senate	Total
Independent experts (educators, academics, government staff)	13	61	74
Lobbyists (representing advocacy or community groups)	3	23	26
Elected officials (federal, state, local)	7	18	25
Miscellaneous (private sector, social welfare, unidentified)	0	19	19
Total	23	121	144

Numerous other individuals and organizations submitted written materials for the record.

7. In distributing federal funds, Title VII gave priority to school districts with concentrations of families living below the poverty line, then $3,000 a year. Since more than a third of Mexican Americans and Puerto Ricans met this criterion (dropped in 1974), it served Yarborough's purpose of channeling most available resources to Spanish speakers. No separate vote was taken on the bill, which passed overwhelmingly in an "omnibus" package of education measures. Only Lyndon Johnson, Yarborough's ancient adversary, raised any serious opposition. As a young man, Johnson had taught at a "Mexican" school in Cotulla, a town not far from Crystal City, where he ruthlessly enforced an English-only policy. But the President's qualms about the Bilingual Education Act were financial, not ideological. He favored funding bilingual programs through existing mechanisms rather than creating a new drain on the federal treasury. Hispanics lobbied against this approach, however, fearing it would put them in competition with blacks for compensatory education dollars. Finding no support for his position on Capitol Hill, Johnson relented, and on January 2, 1968, he signed the Bilingual Education Act into law.

Chapter 4

1. On civil rights grounds, the U.S. Department of Transportation ordered the county's transit system to end its English Only policy in 1985.

2. Jeffrey Browne, the organization's political consultant, says he sometimes "felt more in common" with opponents like Mark LaPorta than with his own Cuban allies. By the end of the campaign, Jon Weber and LaPorta had become friends. It was Unidos, the unofficial executive committee of Miami's Cuban elite, that had recruited Weber to head English Plus, Inc., the initial campaign organization. Conscious of their strong accents, Unidos members felt it would be advantageous to

have a dynamic young Anglo as public spokesman. Still, they had no intention of abdicating control. Frustrated with this arrangement, after two months Weber and Browne left to set up SUN for Florida. The lack of involvement by influential Cubans posed a major problem for fundraising. Little Havana was accustomed to shelling out generously for political causes (the more Castrophobic, the better), but this time the requisite blessings were not forthcoming. Many leaders felt that, with no hope of winning, an aggressive campaign might compound the defeat by stirring up added animosity. "The heavy hitters said 'this is a non-issue,' " Weber complains. "It's very difficult to get Cubans to identify themselves as victims of discrimination. They just don't think of themselves as a minority: 'We're white. How could we be discriminated against?' "

3. According to reports filed with the Federal Election Commission, ELPAC spent $97,188 in "independent expenditures" to oppose Ros-Lehtinen, along with a $5,000 contribution to Richman, the maximum allowed by law. Its total investment equaled nearly 20 percent of what Richman spent in a costly general election.

4. The final vote was 53–47 percent. Though slightly outnumbered in registration, Hispanic voters more than compensated with a 58 percent turnout, as compared with 42 percent for Anglos. According to various exit polls, 94 percent of Hispanics and more than two-thirds of Hispanic Democrats supported Ros-Lehtinen. Richman carried 88 percent of Anglos, 55 percent of Anglo Republicans, and 96 percent of blacks.

Chapter 5

1. Some restrictionists have claimed that immigration is now at its highest level in U.S. history. This is untrue in both absolute and relative terms. About 8 million immigrants arrived during the 1980s, including 2 million undocumented, according to Census Bureau estimates. This compares with 8.8 million between 1901 and 1910, a period when the U.S. population was little more than a third of today's size. An estimated 7 percent of U.S. residents were foreign-born in 1989, versus 14.6 percent in 1910; Woodrow, "Undocumented Immigrants Living in the United States."

2. The 1990 Census figure of 11 percent is an egregious undercount, according to city officials and community organizations.

3. Although a lack of baseline data for earlier immigrants makes direct comparisons impossible, Veltman calculates the rising rates of English dominance by comparing language use among age groups in the 1976 sample; *Future of the Spanish Language*, pp. 3, 46, 49.

4. Veltman computes these values for immigrants aged fourteen and above by using a weighted sample to reflect arrivals between 1960 and 1970. Similar rates prevailed among immigrants arriving before 1960 and in the period between 1970 and 1976; *Language Shift*, pp. 48–58.

5. In analyzing results from the 1980 High School and Beyond study, Veltman found almost no measurable effect of native-language instruction in delaying the movement of Spanish-speaking children toward dominance in English "Each additional year of bilingual education is associated with . . . a net decline of 0.5 percent in [the anglicization rate] of the children of Spanish mother tongue"; *Language Shift*, p. 204. That is, the students lost their Spanish rapidly, regardless of the language used in school. Yet becoming anglicized does not necessarily mean

becoming *fluent* in English. In the 1978 Children's English and Services Study, more than half of linguistic minority students reported to be dominant in English were also judged to be limited-English-proficient; Dorothy Waggoner, *NABE Journal* 13, no. 3 (Spring 1989): 253–61.

6. "Illiterate minors" had to present cards signed by their English teacher as a condition of employment. By some accounts, Lowell mill owners were unusually cooperative. But at a time when child labor was common in the textile industry, state officials were less than zealous in enforcing such laws.

7. A small Puerto Rican community formed in Lowell in the late 1950s; more recent Hispanic arrivals include Dominicans, Mexicans, Nicaraguans, and Ecuadorans.

Chapter 6

1. In 1988, there was a nasty exchange of letters in the *Washington Post* when a Georgetown University professor, Charles Keely, pointed out the associations between U.S. English, FAIR, and the Center for Immigration Studies, a FAIR spin-off. Writing to correct Keely's "serious errors," C.I.S. director David E. Simcox insisted that his group had "no connection with U.S. English." In fact, Tanton's U.S. Inc., the umbrella under which U.S. English then operated, had funneled more than $100,000 to FAIR and C.I.S. over the past three years. A few months previously, when U.S. English filed for independent corporate status, Simcox himself had signed on as one of its "incorporators."

2. This figure is derived from I.R.S. Forms 990 or 990-PF for the Federation for American Immigration Reform, U.S. Inc., U.S. English Foundation, the Environmental Fund (now Population-Environment Balance), and the Laurel Foundation for tax years 1983 through 1989. No doubt the total is incomplete, because it does not reflect filings by Cordelia Scaife May's own charitable trust, which—unlike those of tax-exempt organizations—are not in the public domain.

3. The second largest, after May, has been Sidney Swensrud, a retired chairman of Gulf Oil and a longtime associate of the Mellon family.

4. Laughlin worked closely with John B. Trevor, the New York lawyer who devised the national-origins quota system enacted in 1924 and became a prominent Nazi sympathizer in the 1930s. His son, John B. Trevor, Jr., continues to serve as treasurer of the Pioneer Fund. In 1965, on behalf of the far-right American Coalition of Patriotic Societies, the younger Trevor testified against eliminating racial criteria in U.S. immigration law. To do so, he warned, would foster "biologic fusion . . . a conglomeration of racial and ethnic elements [that] renders a serious culture decline inevitable." This was a polite way of restating Laughlin's argument that uncontrolled immigration would pollute the American gene pool.

5. A year later Tanton came to the defense of another Pioneer Fund grantee, Linda Gottfredson of the University of Delaware. One of Gottfredson's colleagues, William Frawley, had protested a $174,000 Pioneer grant to support her research on educational "ability differences" among racial and ethnic groups. Frawley asked, "Does the University of Delaware wish to lend its name—wittingly or unwittingly—to an organization that unabashedly promotes intolerance?" In a letter supporting Gottfredson, Tanton responded: "If the new standard being promulgated is that funds can be received only from sources that pass some social litmus test, then this is a stringent requirement indeed. No organization could receive

funds from the Ford Foundation unless it approved of Henry Ford's anti-Semitism, or of Ford's use of Harry Bennett and his goons to break union heads at the Battle of the Overpass, [or of] Mr. Ford's continuing to run his factories in Nazi Germany up until the time that the U.S. declared war on the country." Unconvinced, University of Delaware president E. A. Trabant decided to accept no additional grants from the Pioneer Fund as long as it "remains committed to . . . a pattern of activities incompatible with the university's mission."

6. Gregory Curtis, who runs the foundation for Cordelia Scaife May, had a good answer: "The Raspail novel makes the point in a hard-hitting way that Tanton has been trying to make. It is the worst case scenario: How does an ethical man living in an affluent country respond to the demands of an overwhelming number of poor people? It raises issues pertaining to American immigration policy"; quoted in Eleanor Bergholz, "Bad Language over Official U.S. Tongue," *Pittsburgh Post-Gazette,* Nov. 5, 1988, p. 5.

7. Tanton has not gone uncompensated for his civic activism. In 1986, for example, he received a salary of $46,803 from U.S. Inc., for his part-time work.

8. Chávez believes her involvement with U.S. English was an important (if not the only) factor in her failure to receive a high-level job offer from the Bush administration. Since leaving the organization in 1988, she has worked out of her home in suburban Maryland, writing a syndicated column. In 1991, with support from the neoconservative Manhattan Institute, she published a book, *Out of the Barrio: Toward a New Politics of Hispanic Assimilation.*

9. For 25 percent this was a "major reason," for 17 percent a "minor reason," for 53 percent "not a reason," and 5 percent had no opinion. No inquiry was made about attitudes toward Asians or other linguistic minorities. The telephone survey, conducted by the Gary C. Lawrence Co. of Santa Ana, Calif., was based on a random sample of 400 U.S. English members conducted in April 1988, with a margin of error of plus or minus 5 percent.

10. It could hardly be called a mass organization. Anyone who had given at least $10 in the past two years was considered a member, according to the group's government relations director, Steve Workings. In April 1988, U.S. English spent more than $100,000 to convene a two-day "national membership meeting" in Los Angeles. But according to an internal report, only 79 actual members showed up, not counting staff, board members, and guests.

11. None have done so, although in 1986 Saul Bellow said through his literary agent that he had never agreed to serve. U.S. English continues to use his name in fundraising, along with an alleged quotation from his endorsement letter: "Melting Pot, yes. Tower of Babel, no!" Bellow has declined to comment further.

12. This idea seems to have captured John Tanton's imagination as well. One of the numerous projects he has launched through U.S. Inc., is Pro-Wild, an experiment in "game ranching."

13. Despite its limited staff, English First sent out millions of pieces of direct mail in its first year and claimed to have recruited 250,000 members. By 1991, it had raised and spent $7.1 million, according to lobbying reports filed with the U.S. Senate. Something of an entrepreneur in conservative causes, Pratt runs several operations that compete with more established lobbies: Gun Owners of America, a National Rifle Association look-alike; U.S. Border Control, a counterpart of FAIR; and the Committee to Protect the Family, which resembles a number of New Right groups active on social issues. Naturally, Pratt's activities are resented by those

who feel he is exploiting their successes and making away with loot that is rightfully theirs. In a 1989 letter Kathryn Bricker accused Pratt of "consistently [taking] credit for activities that have been spearheaded, primarily funded, and followed through by U.S. English." She challenged him to provide "documentation" of anything English First had contributed to the cause. Pratt wrote back to say that John Tanton's indiscretions had been "quite a blow" to the Official English movement. Under the circumstances it was "outrageous" of U.S. English to demand "that we explain English First programs and policies." At this point Tanton himself intervened, advising Bricker that it was best not to "air our dirty linen in public." More important, "it's useful . . . to have another organization to the right of us. It opens up the center for more maneuvering and grants us the centrist position."

14. This was not Mrs. Bush's first impression. In a September 1986 speech at the National Press Club and in a subsequent interview, she said she had been "appalled" to learn that English was not the official language of the United States. "Foreign languages are very important, but English First!" Endorsing the English Language Amendment, she cited the problem of linguistic diversity in the schools: "Wouldn't it be terrible if you had to teach them in all those languages? How can each child have [that] privilege?" Barbara Bush reversed this position in a written statement during the 1988 presidential campaign.

15. From 1984 through 1989, the U.S. English Legislative Task Force reported spending $1,149,767. Over the same period its income from the "charitable" U.S. Inc., and U.S. English Foundation totaled $1,150,208. The National Unity Fund, a similar organization, also received substantial funding from the 501(c)(3) side of U.S. English. Mauro Mujica, a U.S. English board member, said in 1992 that such pass-throughs were no longer used to fund lobbying.

16. Zall identifies himself as "designated assistant treasurer"; his wife, Jan C. Zall, is titular head of ELPAC as well as ImmPAC, the Immigration Political Action Committee. Another familiar name turns up in both PACs' reports to the Federal Election Commission—Cordelia Scaife May—who has donated the legal maximum of $5,000 in nearly every election since the PACs were created. Among its activities, ELPAC sent out a letter attacking the Democratic standard-bearer in 1988: "I'm furious and I'm scared," wrote Barnaby Zall. "I'm furious that the presidential nominee of a major American political party delivered a large portion of his acceptance speech in a foreign language. . . . Dukakis crossed a line that has never been crossed before. He signaled to all Americans that, in his search for Hispanic votes, he is willing to embrace a new way of life for us all—official bilingualism"; Daniels, *Not Only English*, pp. 4–5.

17. Such expressions of new allegiances, however, proved insufficient to guarantee his job security. Diamond fired Saunders as executive director in February 1992, a few weeks before he himself was forced to resign as chairman. Amid the scandal over U.S. English political expenditures, former Representative Norman Shumway took the helm, pledging to restore the organization's reputation and "fiscal health."

Chapter 7

1. On the other hand, an outraged Navajo Nation threatened to exercise its tribal sovereignty and restore the original names of reservation tourist spots like *Tsébii'nidzisgai* (Monument Valley) and *Tségháhoodzáni* (Window Rock).

2. The judge noted that in specifying exceptions to its coverage, Proposition 106 defined "acting in English" to include mundane pursuits like foreign-language teaching. Therefore, Corbin had no basis to claim that it applied only to "sovereign acts."

3. By contrast, Canada is officially bilingual. Its 1982 constitution proclaims: "English and French are the official languages of Canada and have equality of status and equal rights and privileges as to their use in all institutions of the Parliament and government of Canada." In effect, francophones are granted an absolute right to preserve their minority culture—as Canada's Commissioner of Official Languages once put it, "the right *not* to assimilate, the right to maintain a certain difference"; Yalden, "The Bilingual Experience in Canada," p. 79.

4. The court invalidated the Nebraska law on a seven-to-two vote, along with similar statutes in Iowa and Ohio. The decision remained ambiguous, however, on the right to bilingual instruction: "The power of the state to compel attendance at some school and to make reasonable regulations for all schools, including a requirement that they shall give instructions in English, is not questioned. Nor has challenge been made of the state's power to prescribe a curriculum for institutions which it supports. Those matters are not within the present controversy. Our concern is with the prohibition [on foreign language teaching]."

5. Bork's candor in this area clearly damaged his chances for confirmation to the Supreme Court. In a report to the Senate Judiciary Committee, the American Civil Liberties Union summed up a widespread complaint: "Judge Bork's view of the Constitution is that it creates a governmental structure designed, with few exceptions, to promote the majority will at the expense of individual rights." Of the latter, he believed that only specified guarantees should be honored. In *Meyer*, Bork argued, the court could have reached the same result on religious-freedom grounds. During his confirmation hearing he acknowledged that substantive due process had been applied earlier to protect property rights (e.g., to strike down worker-protection laws). But characteristically, Bork was more upset about "judicial activism" on behalf of individual liberties.

6. The Supreme Court has taken a dim view of majority attempts to "place special burdens on racial minorities within the governmental process." For example, it struck down a 1964 ballot initiative in California that prohibited the legislature from enacting fair housing laws—not unlike Proposition 63's attempt to limit bilingual accommodations; *Reitman v. Mulkey* (1967).

7. In a California case, for example, the following exchange occurred over translated testimony:

> *Dorothy Kim (Juror No. 8)*: Your Honor, is it proper to ask the interpreter a question? I'm uncertain about the word La Vado [sic]. You say that is a bar.
>
> *The Court*: The Court cannot permit jurors to ask questions directly. If you want to phrase your question to me—
>
> *Dorothy Kim*: I understood it to be a restroom. I could better believe they would meet in a restroom rather than a public bar if he is undercover.
>
> *The Court*: These are matters for you to consider. If you have any misunderstanding of what the witness testified to, tell the Court now what you didn't understand and we'll place the—

Dorothy Kim: I understand the word La Vado [sic]—I thought it meant restroom. She translates it as bar.

Ms. Ianziti: In the first place, the jurors are not to listen to the Spanish but to the English. I am a certified court interpreter.

Dorothy Kim: You're an idiot.

After further questioning, the witness clarified that none of the conversations occurred in a restroom, and Dorothy Kim explained that she had said, "It's an idiom," rather than "You're an idiot." Nevertheless, she was dismissed from the jury; *U.S. v. Pérez*, 658 F.2d 662–63.

8. Because the challenges were peremptory, the prosecutor had no duty to disclose his reasons for excluding the jurors. But when the defense alleged discrimination against Latinos (in violation of a 1986 Supreme Court decision in *Batson v. Kentucky*), he volunteered that the bilinguals were excluded because they had expressed uncertainty about being able to ignore Spanish-language testimony.

9. Thus far, strict scrutiny has been reserved for government acts that discriminate on the basis of race, national origin, or alien status or that abridge a "fundamental right," such as freedom of interstate travel. But this is not the only level of "heightened" judicial review. As a commentary in the *Harvard Law Review* explains: "The Supreme Court has found other legislative classifications, such as those based on gender and illegitimacy, to be 'quasi-suspect,' for they sometimes are a valid basis for different treatment, but more often are employed for improper purposes and violate contemporary notions of equality. For these classifications a court will apply 'intermediate' scrutiny, inquiring into whether the state action is *substantially* related to legitimate or even *important* governmental objectives. A strong argument can be made for treating language minorities as a quasi-suspect class"; " 'Official English,' " p. 1353.

10. Representative William Dickinson of Alabama reintroduced Shumway's proposal in 1991. Designated as H.J. Res. 81, it reads as follows:

Section 1. The English language shall be the official language of the United States.

Section 2. Neither the United States nor any State shall require, by law, ordinance, regulation, order, decree, program, or policy, the use in the United States of any language other than English.

Section 3. This article shall not prohibit any law, ordinance, regulation, order, decree, program, or policy

(1) to provide educational instruction in a language other than English for the purpose of making students who use a language other than English proficient in English,

(2) to teach a foreign language to students who are already proficient in English,

(3) to protect public health and safety, or

(4) to allow translators for litigants, defendants, or witnesses in court cases.

Section 4. The Congress and the States may enforce this article by appropriate legislation.

11. What Justice Douglas said was: "Teaching English to the students of Chinese ancestry who do not speak the language is one choice. Giving instructions to this group in Chinese is another. There may be others. Petitioners ask only that the Board of Education be directed to apply its expertise to the problem and rectify the situation." As a practical matter, the San Francisco Unified School District, the defendant in the case, agreed to establish bilingual programs in Cantonese, Spanish, and Tagalog. Some opponents of bilingual education have interpreted the court's words as an endorsement of instructional "flexibility"—i.e., carte blanche to pursue English-only alternatives. In fact, the court did not mandate a pedagogical approach because it was not asked to do so. Similarly, it did not reach the constitutional issues of equal protection but relied on the Civil Rights Act of 1964, as elaborated in regulations by the Department of Health, Education, and Welfare.

12. Anglo *patrones* often paid the poll tax when they wanted to "vote their Mexicans." South Texas machines delivered an estimated 35,000 such votes for "Landslide" Lyndon Johnson in his 1948 Senate race, which he won by a final margin of 87 votes statewide; Caro, *Means of Ascent*, pp. 182–83, 310–11.

13. In 1982, under the so-called Nickles amendment, the criterion was narrowed to 5 percent of potential voters who "do not speak or understand English adequately enough to participate in the electoral process." As a result, the number of jurisdictions required to provide bilingual materials was cut from 369 to 160. Los Angeles, for example, with its huge population of Spanish monolinguals, no longer meets the criteria for coverage, although it has continued to provide bilingual ballots on a voluntary basis, prompting threats of litigation by U.S. English.

14. In its rationale for bilingual ballots, Congress cited three related factors: a history of discrimination, high rates of illiteracy, and low rates of political participation. It noted that, among Latino citizens over the age of twenty-five in 1970, 18.9 percent had not completed the fifth grade, as compared with 5.5 percent of the population as a whole (for Mexican Americans in Texas, the rate was 33 percent). The House Judiciary Committee reported that "these high illiteracy rates are not the result of choice or happenstance. They are the product of the failure of state and local officials to afford equal educational opportunities to members of language minority groups." Besides Spanish speakers, the victims included Chinese Americans, who had been legally segregated in California public schools until 1947, and Native Americans, whose unequal schooling had been well documented in recent court decisions. The committee also found "overwhelming evidence of voting discrimination against language minorities" that limited their impact at the polls. For example, 46 percent of Mexican Americans were registered in 1972, as compared with 73.4 percent of white Anglos (and only 37.5 percent actually voted, as compared with 64.5 percent). This pattern did not prevail for European immigrant groups, mostly anglicized by now, whose rates of registration and voting were generally above average. In the 1972 presidential election, these rates for Germans were 79 percent and 70.8 percent, respectively; for Italians, 77.5 percent and 71.5 percent; for Poles, 79.8 percent and 72 percent; for Russians, 85.7 percent and 80.5 percent. Thus Congress saw no reason to require special assistance for these groups.

15. Even where speaking Spanish is associated with hostile acts, according to the U.S. Equal Employment Opportunity Commission, the employer should correct the offending behavior or otherwise attempt to mediate ethnic conflicts, rather

than impose an English Only rule that penalizes all Spanish-speaking employees; E.E.O.C. Compliance Manual, §623.6(d)(3).

16. What message the high court intended to send remains unclear. Obviously, it could have withheld judgment and left the Ninth Circuit precedent intact by simply refusing to hear the case; vacating the decision implied disapproval. U.S. English claimed a "great victory for Proposition 63." But Professor Bill Piatt of Texas Tech University argues that *Gutiérrez* "is still persuasive for other language rights cases which will undoubtedly follow"; ¿*Only English?*, pp. 71–72. Indeed, its logic has since been cited to void restrictions on foreign-language business signs.

17. In 1991, after much political posturing, Congress and the Bush administration agreed on a partial restoration of the *Griggs* standard. At this writing, the new law awaits judicial interpretation.

Chapter 8

1. Specifically, the plan was to raise the "exit criterion" for bilingual programs from the 23rd percentile in English proficiency to the 40th percentile.

2. Under existing regulations, LEP students arriving in New York after the eighth grade had the option of taking the required Regents' Competency Tests in their native tongue. To graduate, however, they still had to pass a test in English as a second language.

3. The commentator John McLaughlin once complained that Mexican presidents Miguel de la Madrid and Carlos Salinas had spoken through interpreters when interviewed on his TV show. "When are they going to get into the twentieth century down there?" McLaughlin raged. "Somebody should tell the President of Mexico that when he appears on American television, he should speak English"; quoted in Eric Alterman, "Pundit Power," *Washington Post Magazine,* March 18, 1990, p. 33.

4. In 1990, a survey by the American Council on the Teaching of Foreign Languages reported the following public-school enrollments in grades 9–12: Spanish, 2,611,367; French, 1,089,355; German, 295,398; Latin, 163,923; Italian, 40,402; Japanese, 25,123; and Russian, 16,491. (In grades 7–12, there were a total of 6,738 enrolled in Mandarin and 478 in Arabic.) Assuming no overlap in these figures, ACTFL concludes that 38.4 percent of U.S. high school students were studying a foreign language that year, up sharply from 22.6 percent in 1982; Draper, "Foreign Language Enrollments." Yet only about 3 percent of secondary students "achieve meaningful proficiency in a second language—and many of these students come from bilingual homes"; ACTFL *Public Awareness Network Newsletter* 6, no. 3 (May 1987).

5. It is still commonplace to find LEP children classified as retarded on the basis of English-language I.Q. tests. A 1980 study in Texas found that Hispanic children were overrepresented in the learning-disabled category by 315 percent; Alba A. Ortiz and James R. Yates, "Incidence of Exceptionality among Hispanics: Implications for Manpower Training," *NABE Journal* 7, no. 3 (Spring 1983): 41–53.

6. The terms *acquisition* and *learning* are used interchangeably here. Krashen draws a distinction to denote "two independent ways of developing ability in second languages. 'Acquisition' is a subconscious process identical in all important ways to the process children utilize in acquiring their first language, while 'learn-

ing' is a conscious process that results in 'knowing about' language." He hypothesizes that while learned knowledge—e.g., memorized grammatical rules—can serve a "monitor," or editing function, naturally acquired language is essential to a full range of communicative competencies; *Input Hypothesis,* p. 1.

7. The "transfer" effect varies depending on "surface" differences between languages. According to Cummins, researchers "have reported highly significant correlations for written grammatical, discourse, and sociolinguistic skills in Portuguese and English" and slightly lower, yet still meaningful correlations between Japanese and English. Similar results have been documented for Spanish and English, Hebrew and English, Finnish and Swedish, and Turkish and German; Cummins, *Empowering Minority Students,* pp. 46–48.

8. In 1988, Congress acceded in part to Bennett's wishes, diverting up to 25 percent of bilingual education funding to nonbilingual programs.

9. One significant exception is a "meta-analysis" by Ann Willig, of the University of Texas at Austin, covering the same studies reviewed in the Baker–de Kanter report. When Willig adjusted statistically for differences in program, student, and teacher characteristics, as well as research methods—183 variables in all—the end results were moderately favorable to bilingual education. More important, she determined that the better the study, the better the measured outcome of bilingual education: "In every instance where there did not appear to be crucial inequalities between experimental and comparison groups, children in the bilingual programs averaged higher than the comparison children" on achievement tests.

10. Another way to look at this is that 79 percent show bilingual approaches to be as good or better than English-only approaches. This conclusion is more telling, Krashen argues, "since it means that the children have acquired just as much English with significantly less exposure to English. This confirms the underlying theory of bilingual education"; Krashen, "The Case against Bilingual Education," paper presented to the National Association for Bilingual Education, Tucson, Ariz., April 22, 1990.

11. Or when the native language is used, it is used poorly. In an early method known as *concurrent translation,* teachers would simply repeat each idea in two languages. With everything translated on the spot, students had no incentive to pay attention during the English parts of the lesson and simply tuned out. Conversely, teachers had no reason to tailor the second language to their students' level. The end result was little comprehensible input in English. Thanks to advances in basic research, concurrent translation has been widely discredited. Theoretically grounded techniques are taking its place, in which subjects are taught alternately in the native tongue and in "sheltered English," but not in both at once.

12. A nationwide search in 1987 by U.C.L.A.'s Center for Language Education and Research turned up only thirty-two bilingual programs that could be described as fully "two-way." All were Spanish-English, with the exception of one Greek-English and one Arabic-English. Despite prodding from members of Congress, the Reagan and Bush administrations have shown little interest in funding this approach. Bilingual and foreign language programs are administered by entirely separate offices at the U.S. Department of Education.

13. In an August 1991 interview, Keith Baker did an about-face, contradicting his statements of the past decade. His latest conclusion: "Bilingual education works, but not the way Cummins says it does. It works in the first three years, but after that point it flips—children do better in all-English programs." Ever the empiricist,

Baker attributed his conversion to new patterns he had discerned in students' test scores. Though he had yet to work out any theoretical explanation, he said the phenomena could be due to "mental fatigue" among LEP children in English-only classrooms.

14. Although the Berkeley school district faced a major fiscal crisis in 1988, it dipped into an emergency reserve fund for approximately $1.5 million to defend the lawsuit. By comparison, the district spent $480,000 each year to educate its 571 LEP students; all but $35,000–$40,000 of this amount came from the state of California. In the end Judge D. Lowell Jensen ruled for the school district. He cited testimony by Berkeley's consultants that "a good teacher is a good teacher," whether bilingual or not. This decision reversed a string of victories for the plaintiffs' public-interest law firm, Multicultural Training, Education, and Advocacy (META). Still, it was hardly the "landmark decision" that U.S. English has hailed. In declining to mandate bilingual education, Judge Jensen accepted META's legal reasoning but disagreed that the facts of the case justified such an order.

15. As a "gringo" attending the University of Massachusetts at Amherst, she describes being brushed aside in favor of "unqualified latino students" (who allegedly received preferential treatment in grades and fellowships). As the director of an alternative program in Newton, she claims to have been the target of "unrelenting attack" by an evil state bureaucracy (which terminated financial aid after finding the district out of compliance with state law). As a bilingual education adviser to Secretary Bennett, she describes a political smear by Hispanic critics (who called her a Reagan appointee, of all things). Only Porter's side is presented; where the truth lies in these incidents is anybody's guess.

16. READ's other board members are Abigail Thernstrom, of Boston University, and Esther Eisenhower, former director of E.S.L. programs for Fairfax County, Va. Its "academic advisory panel" includes Christine Rossell, Herbert Walberg, Charles Glenn, of the Massachusetts Department of Education, and Richard Estrada, a syndicated columnist and former research director of the Federation for American Immigration Reform. Keith Baker was forced out as director of READ in January 1991; he and Porter both say they cannot comment on the reasons for his departure. Baker adds, however, that given Porter's "bias against bilingual education, I would look closely at any research she comes out with. She's just trying to prove that bilingual education doesn't work." After another internal dispute at READ, Porter resigned as director in October 1991.

17. Children's achievement was compared on basis of English-language tests in reading, language, and mathematics. Immersion programs were taught in English 94 to 98 percent of the time, with Spanish used only for clarification. Early-exit programs featured English instruction two-thirds of the time in kindergarten, three-fourths of the time in second grade, and almost exclusively by fourth grade. The one statistically significant difference came in kindergarten and first grade, when the early-exit bilingual students outperformed the immersion students in English reading, despite their lesser "time on task" in English.

18. Late-exit programs used English less than 10 percent of the time in kindergarten, with the proportion rising to 33 percent in second grade and 60 percent in grades 4–6. Ramírez explains that because of the controversial nature of the study, he decided on a conservative statistical approach. The school districts offering late-exit programs had no early-exit or immersion programs that met the study's criteria. So he ruled out direct comparisons across districts, although indirect com-

parisons were possible by plotting academic growth rates in all three programs against national norms.

Chapter 9

1. The Royal Proclamation of 1763 and the Constitutional Act of 1791 granted French coequal status with English as a language of government. Canada's first constitution, the British North America Act of 1867, recognized "both English and French as legislative and judicial languages in federal and Quebec constitutions; the right to denominational schooling (which was closely associated with the French-English distinction); and the official character of both languages in the various Canadian territories"; Yalden, "The Bilingual Experience in Canada," p. 73.

2. In 1961, yearly incomes in Quebec averaged $5,502 for monolingual anglophones, $4,772 for bilinguals (mainly of French origin), and $3,099 for monolingual francophones; Schmid, "Quebec in the 1970s–1980s," p. 274.

3. Veltman has calculated an anglicization rate of 1.5 percent for francophones in Quebec; for Spanish speakers, the comparable figures are 34.6 percent in Texas, 41.8 percent in New Mexico, 51.4 percent in Arizona, 69.2 percent in California, and 74.0 percent in Colorado. These data reflect the 1976 Survey of Income and Education and the 1971 Canadian census.

4. The total obviously depends on how one differentiates languages from dialects. Using rather conservative criteria, the *Académie française* has calculated 2,796 known languages worldwide.

5. The Archbishop of Mexico, Antonio Lorenzana y Buitrón, explained the policy in 1769: "Tumults, insurrections, civil seditions grow much larger when they are hatched among subject people speaking a foreign language. Indeed, this very difference in customs itself inflames them with a recollection of their former lords and with that mischievous notion to which human nature is prone, that their own languages, dress, liberties, heathenism, and other vices are superior to others'. A nation's speaking a single language, that of its sovereign and only monarch, engenders true love and good will among individuals, an ease of intercourse not found among those who do not understand each other, and a fellowship, brotherhood, civility, and politeness that is very favorable to spiritual government, domestic dealings, commerce, and politics. Moreover, it is very conducive to a conquered people's gradually forgetting their enmities, their divisions, their partialities, and their aversion to those who rule"; "Pastoral V: In Order that the Indians Learn Castilian," reprinted in Heath, *Telling Tongues,* p. 209.

6. In a series of decisions known as the Insular Cases, the U.S. Supreme Court gave its approval to the new colonialism. After some tortuous reasoning, the justices concluded that the Constitution and Bill of Rights did not necessarily follow the flag. It was the sole prerogative of Congress to determine the rights and status of "dependencies" acquired in the Spanish-American War. For example, in *Balzac v. Porto Rico,* Chief Justice William Howard Taft found no constitutional right to a jury trial on the island. He explained there were special standards for "distant ocean communities *of a different origin and language* from those of our continental people"; 258 U.S. 311 (emphasis added). Earlier, in *Downes v. Bidwell,* the court responded to those who worried about the abuse of American power: "There are

certain principles of natural justice inherent in the Anglo-Saxon character which need no expression in constitutions or statutes to give them effect"; 182 U.S. 280.

7. This followed a drawn-out legal battle that began when the House of Delegates enacted the change in 1946 over the veto of an appointed governor. President Truman then vetoed the measure, but after the statutory deadline had passed. The matter wound up in a federal appeals court, which found technical grounds to rule against the legislature. Puerto Ricans still had no right to designate the medium of their children's instruction. In 1949, a commissioner of education appointed by Muñoz Marín reinstated Spanish instruction through administrative regulations, while promising that "English [would] be taught at all levels of our school system."

8. A nonbinding plebiscite was held in 1967. The commonwealth option was endorsed by 60 percent of Puerto Rican voters, while statehood won 39 percent. Independence advocates boycotted the election, denouncing it as a sham designed to legitimize colonialism.

9. Tohono O'odham, "People of the Desert," is the tribe's preference. Papago was a name bestowed by Spaniards and is translated loosely as "Bean Eater."

10. Italian speakers, the largest linguistic minority, represented 3.9 percent of the population in 1983, about half the percentage of Spanish speakers in the United States.

11. In 1990, the administration finally agreed to spend $2.8 million on developmental bilingual education out of a $116 million program budget. By law, it could have spent up to $29 million.

Conclusion

1. As in Arizona's Proposition 106, much unclarity surrounds this term. Shelby's bill, S. 434, and a similar measure sponsored by Representative Bill Emerson, H. R. 123, include the following definition:

> (2) The term 'official' means governmental actions, documents, or policies that are enforceable with the full weight and authority of the Government, but does not include—
>
> (A) actions, documents, or policies that are purely informational or educational;
>
> (B) actions, documents, or policies that are not enforceable in the United States;
>
> (C) actions that protect the public health or safety;
>
> (D) actions that protect the rights of victims of crimes or criminal defendants; and
>
> (E) documents that utilize terms of art or phrases from languages other than English.

This wording raises more questions than it answers. As "enforceable actions" would federal civil and administrative proceedings—e.g., immigration hearings—be included in the ban? As "informational documents," would bilingual voter aids be exempted? What about contracts, treaties, and trade negotiations with foreign governments—would the U.S. government have to act in English only? Once again the philosophy seems to be: let the courts sort it out.

Sources

Interviews

Albert Alvarez, Papago linguist, Sells, Ariz.
Frank Arcuri, English Only activist, Monterey Park, Calif.
Susan Armsby, People for the American Way, Washington, D.C.
Keith Baker, former researcher, U.S. Department of Education; director, Research on English Acquisition and Development, Silver Spring, Md.
Joe Bernal, former Texas state senator; school administrator, San Antonio
Gerda Bikales, executive director, U.S. English
Elizabeth Brancart, attorney for Asian American Business Group, Pomona, Calif.
Javier Bray, founder, Spanish-American League Against Discrimination, Miami
Robert Brischetto, director, Southwest Voter Research Institute, San Antonio
Barbara Bush
José Calderón, University of California at Los Angeles; community activist, Monterey Park, Calif.
Robert Canino, South Florida director, League of United Latin American Citizens
José Cárdenas, director, Intercultural Development Resource Association, San Antonio
Juan Cartagena, legal director, Department of Puerto Rican Community Affairs in the United States
Max Castro, executive director, Greater Miami United
Linda Chávez, president, U.S. English
Edward Chen, staff counsel, American Civil Liberties Union of Northern California
Judy Chu, mayor and city council member, Monterey Park, Calif.
Yolanda Cortez, shop steward, American Federation of State, County, and Municipal Employees, Council 10, San Francisco
Fernando de la Peña, president, Cambria English Institute, Los Angeles
Stanley Diamond, chairman, U.S. English and California English Campaign
Carmen Dinos, Brooklyn College (retired)
Mark Gallegos, attorney and spokesman for Unidos, Miami
Charles Gargiulo, cochair, Coalition for a Better Acre, Lowell, Mass.
Ghislain Gouraige, assistant vice-president, Citicorp, Miami
Kenji Hakuta, Stanford University
Guadalupe Hamersma, principal, Plamondon School, Chicago
Barry Hatch, mayor and city council member, Monterey Park, Calif.
S. I. Hayakawa, U.S. senator from California (1977–1983); cofounder and honorary chairman, U.S. English

Antonia Hernández, president, Mexican American Legal Defense and Educational Fund
Katherine Holmes, former director of research, U.S. English
John Horton, University of California at Los Angeles
Richard Howe, mayor, Lowell, Mass.
Alex Huertas, Lowell chapter president, Parents United for the Education and Development of Others
Kathryn Imahara, director, language rights project, Asian Pacific American Legal Center of Southern California
Anton Jungherr, associate superintendent for business, Berkeley (Calif.) Unified School District
Charles Keely, Georgetown University
George Kouloheras, member, Lowell School Committee
Stephen Krashen, University of Southern California
Daniel Lam, director, Massachusetts Office of Refugees and Immigrants
Mark LaPorta, chairman, Florida English Campaign
Dick Littlebear, Northern Cheyenne educator, Busby, Mont.
Raúl Martínez, executive director, Aspira of Florida
Robert Melby, chairman, Florida English Campaign
Ernest Morales, former mayor and city council member, Fillmore, Calif.
Mauro Mujica, board member, U.S. English
Tom Olson, former director of public relations, U.S. English
Awilda Palau, University of Puerto Rico (retired)
Albar Peña, former director, U.S. Office of Bilingual Education
Camilo Pérez-Bustillo, Multicultural Education, Training, and Advocacy, Inc.
Carmen Pérez Hogan, director, New York State Education Department, Division of Bilingual Education
Rosalie Porter, executive director, Institute for Research in English Acquisition and Development, Washington, D.C.
Larry Pratt, president, English First, Springfield, Va.
J. David Ramírez, Aguirre International, San Mateo, Calif.
Terry Robbins, U.S. English activist and founder, Dade Americans United To Protect the English Language, Miami
Joe Rubin, chairman, Residents' Association of Monterey Park
Fabiola Santiago, managing editor, *El Nuevo Herald,* Miami
Ronald Saunders, executive director, U.S. English
Enos Schera, vice-president, Citizens of Dade United, Miami
Leo Sorensen, former board member, U.S. English
Osvaldo Soto, attorney and former president, Spanish-American League Against Discrimination, Miami
Ross Steele, member, Australian Advisory Council on Languages and Multicultural Education
John Tanton, cofounder and chairman, U.S. English
Elma Vaidya, Cambodian Mutual Assistance Association, Lowell, Mass.
Calvin Veltman, Université du Québec à Montréal
Herbert J. Walberg, University of Illinois at Chicago
Ruth Willner, cochair, Coalition for Harmony in Monterey Park; member, Friends of the Monterey Park Library
Steve Workings, director of government relations, U.S. English

Ravuth Yin, Cambodian Mutual Assistance Association, Lowell, Mass.
Martin Yoffe, coordinator of cable television services, Dade County Public Schools
Lou Zaeske, president, American Ethnic Coalition, Bryan, Tex.
Ofelia Zepeda, University of Arizona

Books and Pamphlets

Acuña, Rodolfo. *Occupied America: The Chicano's Struggle for Liberation.* San Francisco: Canfield Press, 1972.

Adams, Karen L., and Daniel T. Brink, eds. *Perspectives on Official English: The Campaign for English as the Official Language of the USA.* Berlin: Mouton de Gruyter, 1990.

Anderson, Benedict R. O'G. *Imagined Communities: Reflections on the Origin and Spread of Nationalism.* London: Verso, 1983.

Baker, Keith A., and Adriana A. de Kanter, eds. *Bilingual Education: A Reappraisal of Federal Policy.* Lexington, Mass.: Lexington Books, 1983.

Balibar, Renée, and Dominque Laporte. *Le Français national: Politique et pratique de la langue nationale sous la Révolution.* Paris: Hachette Littérature, 1974.

Bancroft, Hubert Howe. *History of California.* San Francisco: History Co., 1886.

Baron, Dennis E. *The English-Only Question: An Official Language for Americans?* New Haven: Yale University Press, 1990.

———. *Grammar and Good Taste: Reforming the American Language.* New Haven: Yale University Press, 1982.

Beer, William, and James E. Jacob, eds. *Language Policy and National Unity.* Totowa, N.J.: Rowman & Allanheld, 1985.

Bellant, Russ. *Old Nazis, the New Right, and the Reagan Administration: The Role of Domestic Fascist Networks in the Republican Party and Their Effect on U.S. Cold War Politics.* 2d ed. Cambridge, Mass.: Political Research Associates, 1989.

Bikales, Gerda, and Gary Imhoff. *A Kind of Discordant Harmony: Issues in Assimilation.* U.S. English Discussion Series, no. 2. Washington, D.C.: U.S. English, 1985.

Blaustein, Albert P., and Dana Blaustein Epstein. *Resolving Language Conflicts: A Study of the World's Constitutions.* Washington, D.C.: U.S. English, 1986.

Boorstin, Daniel J. *Hidden History: Exploring Our Secret Past.* New York: Vintage Books, 1989.

Boswell, Thomas D., and James R. Curtis. *The Cuban-American Experience: Culture, Images, and Perspectives.* Totowa, N.J.: Rowman & Allanheld, 1983.

Bowers, Claude G. *Beveridge and the Progressive Era.* Boston: Houghton Mifflin, 1932.

Brown, Everett S. *The Constitutional History of the Louisiana Purchase.* Berkeley: University of California Press, 1920.

Busey, Samuel C. *Immigration: Its Evils and Consequences.* New York: DeWitt & Davenport, 1856.

Butler, R. E. "Rusty." *On Creating a Hispanic America: A National Within a Nation?* Washington, D.C.: Council for Inter-American Security, 1985.

California State Department of Education, Office of Bilingual Bicultural Education. *Schooling and Language Minority Students: A Theoretical Framework.* Los Angeles: California State University, 1981.

————. *Studies on Immersion Education: A Collection for United States Educators*. Sacramento: California State Department of Education, 1984.

Campbell, Russell N., and Kathryn J. Lindholm. *Conservation of Language Resources*. Educational Report Series, no. 6. Los Angeles: University of California, Center for Language Education and Research, 1987.

Caro, Robert A. *The Years of Lyndon Johnson*. Vol. 1, *The Path to Power*. Vol. 2, *Means of Ascent*. New York: Alfred A. Knopf, 1982, 1990.

Claiborne, W. C. C. *Official Letter Books, 1801–1816*, ed. Dunbar Rowland. Jackson, Miss.: State Department of Archives and History, 1917.

Conklin, Nancy Faires, and Margaret A. Lourie. *A Host of Tongues: Language Communities in the United States*. New York: Free Press, 1983.

Connor, Walker, ed. *Mexcian-Americans in Comparative Perspective*. Washington, D.C.: Urban Institute Press, 1985.

Crawford, James, ed. *Language Loyalties: A Source Book on the Official English Controversy*. Chicago: University of Chicago Press, 1992.

Cummins, Jim. *Empowering Minority Students*. Sacramento: California Association for Bilingual Education, 1989.

Daniels, Harvey A., ed. *Not only English: Affirming America's Multilingual Heritage*. Urban, Ill.: National Council of Teachers of English, 1990.

Daniels, Roger. *Asian America: Chinese and Japanese Immigrants in the United States since 1950*. Seattle: University of Washington Press, 1988.

Dargo, George. *Jefferson's Louisiana: Politics and the Clash of Legal Traditions*. Cambridge, Mass.: Harvard University Press, 1975.

Dillard, J. L. *Black English: Its History and Usage in the United States*. New York: Random House, 1972.

Edwards, John. *Language, Society, and Identity*. Oxford: Basil Blackwell, 1985.

Edwards, John Carver. *Patriots in Pinstripe: Men of the National Security League*. Washington, D.C.: University Press of America, 1982.

Eno, Arthur L., Jr., ed. *Cotton Was King: A History of Lowell, Massachusetts*. [Somersworth, N.H.]: New Hampshire Publishing Co., 1976.

Epstein, Erwin H., ed. *Politics and Education in Puerto Rico: A Documentary Survey of the Language Issue*. Metuchen, N.J.: Scarecrow Press, 1970.

Epstein, Noel. *Language, Ethnicity, and the Schools: Policy Alternatives for Bilingual-Bicultural Education*. Washington, D.C.: Institute for Educational Leadership, 1977.

Fairchild, Henry Pratt. *Greek Immigration to the United States*. New Haven: Yale University Press, 1911.

The Federalist Papers. New York: New American Library, 1961.

Feldstein, Stanley, and Lawrence Costello. *The Ordeal of Assimilation: A Documentary History of the White Working Class, 1830s to the 1970s*. Garden City, N.Y.: Anchor Books, 1974.

Ferguson, Charles A., and Shirley Brice Heath, eds. *Language in the U.S.A.* Cambridge: Cambridge University Press, 1981.

Fishman, Joshua A., et al. *Language Loyalty in the United States: The Maintenance and Perpetuation of Non-English Mother Tongues by American Ethnic and Religious Groups*. The Hague: Mouton Publishers, 1966.

Franklin, Benjamin. *Observations Concerning the Increase of Mankind, Peopling of Countries, &c*. In *Papers*, vol. 4, ed. Leonard W. Labaree. New Haven: Yale University Press, 1961.

García, Mario T. *Mexican Americans: Leadership, Ideology, and Identity, 1930–1960.* New Haven: Yale University Press, 1989.

Gayarré, Charles. *History of Louisiana.* Vol. 4, *The American Domination.* 5th ed. Gretna, La.: Pelican Publishing Co., 1974.

Glazer, Nathan. *Affirmative Discrimination: Ethnic Inequality and Public Policy.* New York: Basic Books, 1975.

Gordon, Milton M. *Assimilation in American Life: The Role of Race, Religion, and National Origins.* New York: Oxford University Press, 1964.

Gould, Stephen Jay. *The Mismeasure of Man.* New York: W. W. Norton, 1981.

Graeff, Arthur D. *The Relations Between the Pennsylvania Germans and the British Authorities.* Norristown: Pennsylvania German Society, 1939.

Graham, Hugh Davis. *American Liberalism and Language Policy: Should Liberals Support Official English?* Washington, D.C.: U.S. English, 1990.

Graham, Otis, Jr. *Illegal Immigration and the New Reform Movement.* Washington, D.C.: Federation for American Immigration Reform, 1980.

Grant, Lindsey, and John H. Tanton. *Immigration and the American Conscience.* Washington, D.C.: The Environmental Fund, 1982.

Grosjean, François. *Life With Two Languages: An Introduction to Bilingualism.* Cambridge, Mass.: Harvard University Press, 1982.

Hakuta, Kenji. *Mirror of Language: The Debate on Bilingualism.* New York: Basic Books, 1986.

Handlin, Oscar. *Race and Nationality in American Life.* Garden City, N.Y.: Anchor Books, 1957.

———. *This Was America: As Recorded by European Travelers in the Eighteenth, Nineteenth, and Twentieth Centuries.* New York: Harper Torchbooks, 1964.

Hansen, Marcus Lee. *The Atlantic Migration, 1607–1860: A History of the Continuing Settlement of the United States.* New York: Harper Torchbooks, 1961.

Hardin, Garrett. *An Ecolate View of the Human Predicament.* Washington, D.C.: The Environmental Fund, 1984.

Hartmann, Edward George. *The Movement to Americanize the Immigrant.* New York: Columbia University Press, 1948.

Haugen, Einar. *The Ecology of Language: Essays by Einar Haugen,* ed. Anwar S. Dil. Stanford, Calif.: Stanford University Press, 1972.

———. *The Norwegian Language in America: A Study in Bilingual Behavior.* Bloomington: University of Indiana Press, 1969.

Hawgood, John A. *The Tragedy of German-America.* New York: Putnam, 1940.

Hayakawa, S. I. *One Nation . . . Indivisible? The English Language Amendment.* Washington, D.C.: Washington Institute for Values in Public Policy, 1985.

Heath, Shirley Brice. *Telling Tongues: Language Policy in Mexico, Colony to Nation.* New York: Teachers College Press, 1972.

Heizer, Robert T., and Alan F. Almquist. *The Other Californians: Prejudice and Discrimination under Spain, Mexico, and the United States to 1920.* Berkeley: University of California Press, 1971.

Hersh, Burton. *The Mellon Family: A Fortune in History.* New York: William Morrow, 1978.

Higham, John. *Send These to Me: Jews and Other Immigrants in Urban America.* New York: Atheneum, 1975.

———. *Strangers in the Land: Patterns of American Nativism, 1860–1925.* 2d ed. New Brunswick, N.J.: Rutgers University Press, 1988.

Hitchens, Christopher. *Blood, Class, and Nostalgia: Anglo-American Ironies.* New York: Farrar, Straus & Giroux, 1990.

Hobsbawm, E. J. *Nations and Nationalism Since 1780: Programme, Myth, Reality.* Cambridge: Cambridge University Press, 1990.

Isaacs, Harold R. *Idols of the Tribe: Group Identity and Political Change.* New York: Harper & Row, 1975.

Jefferson, Thomas. *Notes on the State of Virginia* (1785). In *Works,* vol. 2, ed. Albert Ellery Bergh. Washington, D.C.: Thomas Jefferson Memorial Association, 1903.

Jones, Maldwyn Allen. *American Immigration.* Chicago: University of Chicago Press, 1960.

Karas, Nicholas V. *Greek Immigrants At Work: A Lowell Odyssey.* Lowell, Mass.: Meteora Press, 1986.

————. *The Greek Triangle of the Acre, Then and Now.* Lowell, Mass.: Meteora Press, 1984.

Kenngott, George F. *The Record of a City: A Social Survey of Lowell, Massachusetts.* New York: Macmillan Co., 1912.

Kevles, Daniel J. *In the Name of Eugenics: Genetics and the Uses of Human Heredity.* New York: Alfred A. Knopf, 1985.

Kloss, Heinz. *The American Bilingual Tradition.* Rowley, Mass.: Newbury House, 1977.

Krashen, Stephen D. *Bilingual Education: A Focus on Current Research.* Occasional Papers in Bilingual Education, no. 3. Washington, D.C.: National Clearinghouse for Bilingual Education, 1991.

————. *The Input Hypothesis: Issues and Implications.* London: Longman, 1985.

Krashen, Stephen D., and Douglas Biber. *On Course: Bilingual Education's Success in California.* Sacramento: California Association for Bilingual Education, 1988.

Kucera, Daniel W. *Church-State Relationships in Education in Illinois.* Washington, D.C.: Catholic University of America Press, 1955.

Lambert, Wallace E., and G. Richard Tucker. *Bilingual Education of Children: The St. Lambert Experiment.* Rowley, Mass.: Newbury House, 1972.

Larson, Robert W. *New Mexico's Quest for Statehood, 1846–1912.* Albuquerque: University of New Mexico Press, 1968.

Laughlin, Harry H. *Conquest by Immigration: A Report of the Special Committee on Immigration and Naturalization.* New York: Chamber of Commerce of the State of New York, 1939.

Leibowitz, Arnold H. *The Bilingual Education Act: A Legislative Analysis.* Arlington, Va.: National Clearinghouse for Bilingual Education, [1980].

Lewis, Gordon K. *Puerto Rico: Freedom and Power in the Caribbean.* New York: M.R. Press, 1963.

Lindholm, Kathryn J. *Directory of Bilingual Immersion Programs: Two-Way Bilingual Education for Language Minority and Majority Students.* Educational Report Series, no. 8. Los Angeles: University of California, Center for Language Education and Research, 1987.

LoBianco, Joseph. *National Policy on Languages.* Canberra: Australian Government Publishing Service, 1987.

McCarthy, Kevin F., and R. Burciaga Valdez. *Current and Future Effects of Mexican Immigration in California.* Santa Monica, Calif.: Rand Corporation, 1986.

McKay, Sandra Lee, and Sau-ling Cynthia Wong, eds. *Language Diversity: Problem or Resource?* Cambridge, Mass.: Newbury House, 1989.

Mackey, William Francis, and Von Nieda Beebe. *Bilingual Schools for a Bicultural Community: Miami's Adaptation to the Cuban Refugees.* Rowley, Mass.: Newbury House Publishers, 1977.

McWilliams, Carey. *North From Mexico: The Spanish-Speaking People of the United States.* Philadelphia: J. P. Lippincott, 1949.

Maldonado-Denis, Manuel. *Puerto Rico: A Socio-Historic Interpretation.* New York: Vintage Books, 1972.

Mann, Arthur. *The One and the Many: Reflections on the American Identity.* Chicago: University of Chicago Press, 1979.

Mencken, H. L. *The American Language,* ed. Raven I. McDavid, Jr. New York: Alfred A. Knopf, 1985.

Milroy, James, and Lesley Milroy. *Authority in Language: Investigating Language Prescription and Standardisation.* London: Routledge and Kegan Paul, 1985.

Montejano, David. *Anglos and Mexicans in the Making of Texas, 1836–1986.* Austin: University of Texas Press, 1987.

Moquin, Wayne, ed. *A Documentary History of the Mexican Americans.* New York: Bantam Books, 1972.

Morris, Richard B. *The Forging of the Union, 1781–1789.* New York: Harper & Row, 1987.

———. *Witnesses at the Creation: Hamilton, Madison, Jay, and the Constitution.* New York: Holt, Rinehart and Winston, 1985.

National Center for Education Statistics. *The Retention of Minority Languages in the United States: A Seminar on the Analytic Work of Calvin J. Veltman.* Washington, D.C.: U.S. Government Printing Office, 1980.

National Education Association. *The Invisible Minority: Report of the NEA–Tucson Survey.* Washington, D.C.: National Education Association, 1966.

Negrón de Montilla, Aída. *Americanization in Puerto Rico and the Public-School System, 1900–1930.* Río Piedras, P.R.: Editorial Edil, 1971.

Newton, Lewis William. *The Americanization of French Louisiana: A Study of the Process of Adjustment Between the French and the Anglo-American Populations of Louisiana, 1803–1860.* New York: Arno Press, 1980.

Osuna, Juan José. *A History of Education in Puerto Rico.* Río Piedras: Editorial de la Universidad de Puerto Rico, 1949.

Park, Robert E. *The Immigrant Press and Its Control.* New York: Harper, 1922.

Pitt, Leonard. *The Decline of the Californios: A Social History of the Spanish-Speaking Californians, 1846–1890.* Berkeley: University of California Press, 1966.

Piatt, Bill. *¿Only English? Law and Language Policy in the United States.* Albuquerque: University of New Mexico Press, 1990.

Porter, Bruce, and Marvin Dunn. *The Miami Riot of 1980: Crossing the Bounds.* Lexington, Mass.: Lexington Books, 1984.

Porter, Rosalie Pedalino. *Forked Tongue: The Politics of Bilingual Education.* New York: Basic Books, 1990.

Portes, Alejandro, and Rubén G. Rumbaut. *Immigrant America: A Portrait.* Berkeley: University of California Press, 1990.

Powell, Philip Wayne. *Tree of Hate: Propaganda and Prejudices Affecting United States Relations with the Hispanic World.* New York: Basic Books, 1971.

Prucha, Francis Paul. *American Indian Policy in Crisis: Christian Reformers and the Indian, 1865–1900.* Norman: University of Oklahoma Press, 1976.

Ramírez, J. David, Sandra D. Yuen, and Dena R. Ramey. *Final Report: Longitudinal Study of Structured Immersion Strategy, Early-Exit, and Late-Exit Transitional Bililngual Education Programs for Language-Minority Children.* San Mateo, Calif.: Aguirre International, 1991.

Raspail, Jean. *The Camp of the Saints.* New York: Charles Scribner's Sons, 1975.

Ravitch, Diane. *The Schools We Deserve: Reflections on the Educational Crises of Our Time.* New York: Basic Books, 1985.

Renshaw, Patrick. *The Wobblies: The Story of Syndicalism in the United States.* Garden City, N.Y.: Doubleday, 1967.

Ridge, Martin, ed. *The New Bilingualism: An American Dilemma.* New Brunswick, N.J.: Transaction Books, 1981.

Rieff, David. *Going to Miami: Exiles, Tourists, and Refugees in the New America.* Boston: Little, Brown, 1987.

Rippley, La Vern J. *The German-Americans.* Boston: Twayne Publishers, 1976.

Rivera, Feliciano. *A Mexican American Source Book.* Menlo Park, Calif.: Educational Consulting Associates, 1970.

Rodríguez, Richard. *Hunger of Memory: The Education of Richard Rodríguez.* Boston: David R. Godine, 1982.

Saloutos, Theodore. *The Greeks in the United States.* Cambridge, Mass.: Harvard University Press, 1964.

Sandmeyer, Elmer Charles. *The Anti-Chinese Movement in California.* Urbana: University of Illinois Press, 1939.

San Miguel, Guadalupe, Jr. *"Let All of Them Take Heed": Mexican Americans and the Campaign for Educational Equality in Texas, 1910–1981.* Austin: University of Texas Press, 1987.

Shockley, John Staples. *Chicano Revolt in a Texas Town.* Notre Dame, Ind.: University of Notre Dame Press, 1974.

Simcox, David E., ed. *U.S. Immigration in the 1980s: Reappraisal and Reform.* Boulder, Colo., and Washington, D.C.: Westview Press and Center for Immigration Studies, 1988.

Simon, Paul. *The Tongue-Tied American: Confronting the Foreign Language Crisis.* New York: Continuum, 1980.

Strategy Research Corporation. *U.S. Hispanic Market Study, 1989.* Miami: S.R.C., 1989.

Tanton, John H. *Rethinking Immigration Policy.* Washington, D.C.: Federation for American Immigration Reform, 1979.

Taylor, Paul S. *An American-Mexican Frontier: Nueces County, Texas.* Chapel Hill: University of North Carolina Press, 1934.

Thernstrom, Abigail M. *Whose Votes Count? Affirmative Action and Minority Voting Rights.* Cambridge, Mass.: Harvard University Press, 1987.

Thernstrom, Stephan, ed. *Harvard Encyclopedia of American Ethnic Groups.* Cambridge, Mass.: Harvard University Press, 1980.

Turner, Lorenzo D. *Africanisms in the Gullah Dialect.* Chicago: University of Chicago Press, 1949.

Veltman, Calvin. *The Future of the Spanish Language in the United States.* Washington, D.C.: Hispanic Policy Development Project, 1988.

————. *Language Shift in the United States.* Berlin: Mouton Publishers, 1983.

Villeré, Sidney Louis, *Jacques Philippe Villeré: First Native-Born Governor of Louisiana, 1816–1820.* New Orleans: Historic New Orleans Collection, 1981.

Warner, W. Lloyd, and Leo Srole. *The Social Systems of American Ethnic Groups.* New Haven: Yale University Press, 1945.

Walsh, Catherine E. *Pedagogy and the Struggle for Voice: Issues of Language, Power, and Schooling for Puerto Ricans.* South Hadley, Mass.: Bergin and Garvey Publishers, 1991.

Weber, David J., ed. *Foreigners in their Native Land: Historical Roots of the Mexican Americans.* Albuquerque: University of New Mexico Press, 1973.

Webster, Noah. *Dissertations on the English Language: With Notes, Historical and Critical.* Boston: Isaiah Thomas & Co., 1789. Rpt. Meniston, England: Scolar Press, 1967.

Weinstein, Brian. *The Civic Tongue: Political Consequences of Language Choices.* New York: Longman, 1983.

Winslow, Ola Elizabeth. *John Eliot: "Apostle to the Indians."* Boston: Houghton Mifflin, 1968.

Wittke, Carl. *German-Americans and the World War: With Special Emphasis on Ohio's German-Language Press.* Columbus: Ohio State Archaeological and Historical Society, 1936.

————. *The German-Language Press in America.* Lexington: University of Kentucky Press, 1957.

Wood, Ralph, ed. *The Pennsylvania Germans.* Princeton, N.J.: Princeton University Press, 1942.

Wright, Louis B. *The Cultural Life of the American Colonies, 1607–1763.* New York: Harper & Row, 1957.

Zepeda, Ofelia. *A Papago Grammar.* Tucson: University of Arizona Press, 1983.

Articles

Adams, John. "Letter to the President of Congress," Sept. 5, 1780. In *Works,* ed. Charles Francis Adams (Boston: Little, Brown, 1852), VII: 249–50.

American Civil Liberties Union of Northern California. "Bilingual Public Services in California." In Crawford, *Language Loyalties,* pp. 303–11.

"American Council of Learned Societies Report of the Committee on Linguistic and National Stocks in the Population of the United States." In *Annual Report of the American Historical Association for the Year 1931* (Washington, D.C.: A.H.A., 1932), pp. 103–441.

Bell, Whitfield J., Jr. "Benjamin Franklin and the Pennsylvania Germans." *Proceedings of the American Philosophical Society* 99, no. 6 (Dec. 1955): 381–87.

Benally, AnCita, and T. L. McCarty. "The Navajo Language Today." In Adams and Brink, *Perspectives on Official English,* pp. 237–45.

Bikales, Gerda. "Maximum Feasible Misunderstanding: Bilingual Education in Our Schools." *Imprimis* 15 (Oct. 1989): 1–5.

————. "We Must Make English Our Official Language." *Washington Jewish Week,* March 19, 1987, p. 25.

Blewett, Peter F. "The New People: An Introduction to the Ethnic History of Lowell." In Eno, *Cotton Was King,* pp. 190–217.

Bush, George. "Remarks at a White House Ceremony Marking the Entry of the Peace Corps into Central Europe." *Weekly Compilation of Presidential Documents,* June 15, 1990.

Califa, Antonio J. "Declaring English the Official Language: Prejudice Spoken Here." *Harvard Civil Rights–Civil Liberties Law Review* 24, no. 2 (Spring 1989): 293–348.

Chávez, Linda. "The World View of a Radical Racist." *New America,* (Dec. 1975): p. 10.

Chen, Edward M. "Language Rights in the Private Sector." In Crawford, *Language Loyalties,* pp. 269–77.

Combs, Mary Carol, and John Trasviña. "Legal Implications of the English Language Amendment." In *The 'English Plus' Project* (Washington, D.C.: League of United Latin American Citizens, [1986]), pp. 24–31.

Conzen, Kathleen Neils. "Germans." In Thernstrom, *Harvard Encyclopedia of American Ethnic Groups,* pp. 405–25.

Crystal, David. "How Many Millions: The Statistics of English Today." *English Today* 1 (Jan. 1985): 7–9.

Cummins, Jim. "The Role of Primary Language Development in Promoting Educational Success for Language Minority Students." In California State Department of Education, *Schooling and Language Minority Students,* pp. 3–49.

Dale, Charles V. "Legal Analysis of H.J. Res. 169 Proposing an Amendment to the U.S. Constitution to Make English the Official Language of the Untied States," June 27, 1983. Rpt. in U.S. Senate, *English Language Amendment,* pp. 89–95.

———. "Legal Analysis of S.J. Res. 167 Proposing an Amendment to the U.S. Constitution to Make English the Official Language of the United States," June 13, 1984. Rpt. in U.S. Senate, *English Language Amendment,* pp. 32–35.

Diamond, Stanley. "New York's Blueprint for Disaster." *U.S. English Update* 7, no. 2 (March–April 1989): 4.

Dorpalen, Andreas. "The Political Influence of the German Element in Colonial America." *Pennsylvania History* 6 (1939): 147–58, 224–39.

Esman, Milton J. "The Politics of Official Bilingualism in Canada." In Beer and Jacob, *Language Policy and National Unity,* pp. 45–66.

Fedynskyj, Jurij. "State Session Laws in Non-English Languages: A Chapter of American Legal History." *Indiana Law Journal* 46, no. 4 (Summer 1971): 464–78.

Feer, Robert A. "Official Use of the German Language in Pennsylvania." *Pennsylvania Magazine of History and Biography* 76 (1952): 394–405.

Fishman, Joshua A. " 'English Only': Its Ghosts, Myths, and Dangers." *International Journal of the Sociology of Language* 74 (1988): 125–40.

———. "Language Maintenance." In Thernstrom, *Harvard Encyclopedia of American Ethnic Groups,* pp. 629–38.

Forbes, Susan S., and Peter Lemos. "History of American Language Policy." In Select Commission on Immigrant and Refugee Policy, *U.S. Immigration and the National Interest,* Staff Report, April 30, 1981, Appendix A.

Franklin, Benjamin. Letter to Peter Collinson, May 9, 1753. In *Papers,* IV: 483–85.

Fuchs, Lawrence H. "Cultural Pluralism and the Future of American Unity: The Impact of Illegal Aliens." *International Migration Review* 18, no. 3 (Fall 1984): 800–13.

Glazer, Nathan. "The Process and Problems of Language-Maintenance: An Integrative Review." In Fishman, *Language Loyalty in the United States,* pp. 358–68.

Guerra, Sandra. "Voting Rights and the Constitution: The Disenfranchisement of Non-English Speaking Citizens." *Yale Law Journal* 97 (1988): 1419–37.

Gutiérrez, José Angel. "Mexicanos Need To Control Their Own Destinies." In *La Causa Política: A Chicano Politics Reader,* ed. F. Chris García (Notre Dame, Ind.: University of Notre Dame Press, 1974), pp. 226–33.

Guy, Gregory. "International Perspectives on Linguistic Diversity and Language Rights." *Language Problems and Language Planning* 13, no. 1 (1989): 45–53.

Hafford, William E. "The Navajo Code Talkers." *Arizona Highways* 65 (Feb. 1989): 36–45.

Hakuta, Kenji, and Catherine Snow. "The Role of Research in Policy Decisions about Bilingual Education." *NABE News* 9, no. 3 (Spring 1986): 1, 18–21.

Hardin, Garrett. "Population and Immigration: Compassion or Responsibility?" *The Ecologist* 7 (Aug.–Sept. 1977); 268–72.

———. Address to the World Wilderness Congress. Excerpted in *Balance Report,* no. 57 (Nov.–Dec. 1987), pp. 4–5.

Hayakawa, S. I., J. William Orozco, and Stanley Diamond. "Argument in Favor of Proposition 38." In California voter information packet, "Voting Materials in English Only; Initiative Statute," 1984.

———. "Argument in Favor of Proposition 63." In California voter information packet, "Official State Language; Initiative Constitutional Amendment," 1986.

Hayes, Harold. "A Conversation with Garrett Hardin." *Atlantic* 247 (May 1981): 60–70.

Heath, Shirley Brice. "A National Language Academy? Debate in the New Nation." *International Journal of the Sociology of Language* 11 (1976): 9–43.

Hill, Howard C. "The Americanization Movement." *American Journal of Sociology* 24 (May 1919): 609–42.

Huddy, Leonie, and David O. Sears. "Qualified Public Support for Bilingual Education: Some Policy Implications." *Annals of the American Academy of Political and Social Science* 508 (March 1990): 119–34.

Imhoff, Gary. "The Position of U.S. English on Bilingual Education." *Annals of the American Academy of Social and Political Science* 508 (March 1990): 48–61.

Jefferson, Thomas. Letter to John Dickinson, Jan. 13, 1807. In *Works,* XI: 136–37.

Kellogg, Louise Phelps. "The Bennett Law in Wisconsin." *Wisconsin Magazine of History* 2 (1918): 3–25.

Kimura, Larry Lindsey. "The Hawaiian Language and Its Revitalization." In Freda Ahenakew and Shirley Fredeen, eds., *Our Languages: Our Survival,* Proceedings of the 7th Annual Native American Languages Issues Institute (Saskatoon: Saskatchewan Indian Languages Institute, 1987), pp. 117–23.

Kjolseth, Rolf. "Cultural Politics of Bilingualism." *Society* (May–June 1983): 40–48.

Kloss, Heinz. "German-American Language Maintenance Efforts." In Fishman, *Language Loyalty in the United States,* pp. 206–52.

Lambert, Wallace E. "An Overview of Issues in Immersion Education." In California State Department of Education, *Studies on Immersion Education,* pp. 8–30.

Language Policy Task Force. "Language Policy and the Puerto Rican Community." *Bilingual Review/La Revista Bilingüe* 5, nos. 1–2 (1978): 1–39.

Leibowicz, Joseph. "The Proposed English Language Amendment: Sword or Shield?" *Yale Law & Policy Review* 3, no. 2 (Spring 1985): 519–50.

Leibowitz, Arnold H. "English Literacy: Legal Sanction for Discrimination." *Notre Dame Lawyer* 45, no. 7 (1969): 7–67.

———. "The Imposition of English as the Language of Instruction in American Schools." *Revista del Derecho Puertorriqueño*, no. 38 (1970): 175–244.

Lemann, Nicholas. "Growing Pains." *Atlantic* 261 (Jan. 1988): 57–62.

Lexion, Valerie A. "Language Minority Voting Rights and the English Language Amendment." *Hastings Constitutional Law Quarterly* 14 (1987): 657–81.

Loo, Chalsa M. "The 'Biliterate' Ballot Controversy: Language Acquisition and Cultural Shift among Immigrants." *International Migration Review* 19, no. 3 (Fall 1985): 493–515.

Loret de Molac, Alex. "Hispanic Hollywood." *New Miami* 2 (Oct. 1989): 40–43.

Macías, Reynaldo F. "Language Choice and Human Rights in the United States." In *Language in Public Life,* ed. James E. Alatis (Washington, D.C.: Georgetown University Press, 1979), pp. 86–101.

Marshall, David F., ed. "The Question of an Official Language: Language Rights and the English Language Amendment." *International Journal of the Sociology of Language* 60 (1986).

Matsui, Robert, Estéban Torres, and Don Edwards. "Argument Against Proposition 38." In California voter information packet, "Voting Materials in English Only; Initiative Statute," 1984.

Mealey, Linda M. "English-Only Rules and 'Innocent' Employers: Clarifying National Origin Discrimination and Disparate Impact Theory Under Title VII." *Minnesota Law Review* 74 (1989): 387–436.

Medicine, Bea. " 'Speaking Indian': Parameters of Language Use among American Indians." *Focus* [National Clearinghouse for Bilingual Education], March 1981, pp. 1–8.

Morgan, Thomas B. "The Latinization of America," *Esquire* 99 (May 1983): 47–56.

Nunberg, Geoffrey. "The Official English Movement: Reimagining America." In Crawford, *Language Loyalties,* pp. 479–94.

" 'Official English': Federal Limits on Efforts to Curtail Bilingual Services in the States." *Harvard Law Review* 100, no. 6 (April 1987): 1345–62.

Ortiz Toro, Arturo. "Language and Statehood." In Epstein, *Politics and Education in Puerto Rico,* pp. 31–44.

Pedraza-Bailey, Silvia. "Cubans and Mexicans in the United States: The Functions of Political and Economic Migration." *Cuban Studies/Estudios Cubanos* 11–12 (July 1981–Jan. 1982): 79–97.

Pérez-Bustillo, Camilo. "The Return of the Nativists: Law, Language, and Liberation." *Justicia y Derecho* [Arizona State University Law School] 1 (in press).

Portes, Alejandro, Juan M. Clark, and Manuel M. López. "Six Years Later, the Process of Incorporation of Cuban Exiles in the United States: 1973–1979." *Cuban Studies/Estudios Cubanos* 11–12 (July 1981–Jan. 1982): 1–24.

Pratt, Larry. "English Should Be Official Tongue." *Winter Haven News Chief,* Oct. 29, 1988.

"¡Qué Lástima!" In Texas Association for Bilingual Education, *Ever Vigil por Nuestros Niños,* vol. 2 (Dallas: TABE, 1988), pp. 34–35.

Ramírez, David. "Study Finds Native Language Instruction Is a Plus." *NABE News* 14, no. 5 (March 15, 1991): 1, 20–22.

Read, Allen Walker. "American Projects for an Academy to Regulate Speech." *Publications of the Modern Language Association* 51 (Dec. 1936): 1141–79.

———. "Bilingualism in the Middle Colonies, 1725–1775." *American Speech* 12 (1937): 93–99.

Rodríguez, Richard. "Bilingualism, Con: Outdated and Unrealistic." *New York Times,* Nov. 10, 1985, sec. 12, p. 83.

Roosevelt, Franklin. Letter to José M. Gallardo, April 17, 1937. In *The Public Papers and Addresses of Franklin D. Roosevelt, 1937* (New York: Macmillan, 1941), pp. 160–61.

Roosevelt, Theodore. Speech to Knights of Columbus, Oct. 12, 1915; message to American Defense Society, Jan. 3, 1919. In *Works,* Memorial Edition (New York: Charles Scribner's Sons, 1923–1926), XX: 456; XXIV: 554.

Rossell, Christine H., and J. Michael Ross. "The Social Science Evidence on Bilingual Education." *Journal of Law and Education* 15 (Fall 1986): 385–419.

Ruíz, Richard. "Orientations in Language Planning." In McKay and Wong, *Language Diversity: Problem or Resource?,* pp. 3–25.

Rush, Benjamin. "To the Citizens of Pennsylvania of German Birth and Extraction: Proposal of a German College," Aug. 31, 1785. In *Letters,* ed. L. H. Butterfield (Princeton, N.J.: Princeton University Press, 1951), I: 364–68.

Sagarin, Edward, and Robert J. Kelly. "Polylingualism in the United States of America: A Multitude of Tongues Amid a Monolingual Majority." In Beer and Jacob, *Language Policy and National Unity,* pp. 20–43.

Sánchez, George I. "History, Culture, and Education." In *La Raza: Forgotten Americans,* ed. Julian Samora (Notre Dame, Ind.: University of Notre Dame Press, 1966).

Schmid, Carol L. "Quebec in the 1970s–1980s: Submerged Nation or Canadian Fringe?" *Research in Political Sociology* 2 (1986): 269–91.

Snow, Catherine E., and Kenji Hakuta. "The Costs of Monolingualism" In Crawford, *Language Loyalties,* pp. 384–94.

Stolz, James. "The Dangerous Chemistry of Dade County." *Geo* 3 (Aug. 1981): 99–104.

Tanton, John. "U.S. English—It's Being Victimized by the 'Big Lie.'" *Houston Chronicle,* Oct. 30, 1988.

Thernstrom, Abigail. "E Pluribus Plura—Congress and Bilingual Education." *Public Interest* 60 (Summer 1980): 3–22.

Troike, Rudolph C. "Improving Conditions for Success in Bilingual Education." In U.S. House, *Compendium of Papers on the Topic of Bilingual Education,* pp. 1–15.

Urquides, María. "Tucson's Tale of Two Cultures." *N.E.A. Journal,* Feb. 1967, pp. 62, 88–89.

Van de Kamp, John, Willie L. Brown, Jr., and Daryl F. Gates. "Argument against Proposition 63." In California voter information packet, "Official State Language; Initiative Constitutional Amendment," 1986.

Vientos Gastón, Nilita. "The Supreme Court of Puerto Rico and the Language

Problem." *National Lawyers Guild Practitioner* 46, no. 4 (Fall 1989): 104–13.

Walsh, Michael. "Language Policy—Australia." *Annual Review of Applied Linguistics*, 1981, pp. 21–32.

Weaver, Glenn. "Benjamin Franklin and the Pennsylvania Germans." In Leonard Dinnerstein and Frederick Jaher, eds., *The Aliens: A History of Ethnic Minorities in America* (New York: Appleton-Century-Crofts, 1970), pp. 47–64.

Weinstein, Brian. "Francophonie: Purism at the International Level." In *The Politics of Language Purism*, ed. Björn H. Jernudd and Michael J. Shapiro (Berlin: Mouton de Gruyter, 1989), pp. 53–79.

Whyte, William F. "The Bennett Law Campaign in Wisconsin." *Wisconsin Magazine of History* 10 (1927): 363–90.

Willig, Ann C. "A Meta-Analysis of Selected Studies on the Effectiveness of Bilingual Education." *Review of Educational Research* 55, no. 3 (Fall 1985): 269–317.

Yalden, Maxwell F. "The Bilingual Experience in Canada." In Ridge, *The New Bilingualism*, pp. 71–87.

Zall, Barnaby. "The U.S. Refugee Industry: Doing Well by Doing Good." In Simcox, *U.S. Immigration in the 1980s*, pp. 258–68.

Zentella, Ana Celia. "Language Politics in the U.S.A.: The English-Only Movement." In Betty Jean Craige, ed., *Literature, Language, and Politics* (Athens: University of Georgia Press, 1988), pp. 39–53.

Zepeda, Ofelia. "American Indian Language Policy." In Adams and Brink, *Perspectives on Official English*, pp. 247–56.

Government Documents

American State Papers, 1789–1809. Vol. 1, *Miscellaneous.*

Arizona Attorney General. Opinion no. I89–009, Jan. 24, 1989.

Australia, Department of Employment, Education, and Training. *Australia's Policy on Languages.* Canberra: Australian Government Publishing Service, [1988].

Australia, Senate Standing Committee on Education and the Arts. *Report on a National Language Policy.* Canberra: Australian Government Publishing Service, 1984.

Australian Advisory Council on Languages and Multicultural Education. *The National Policy on Languages, December 1987–March 1990: Report to the Minister for Employment, Education, and Training.* Canberra: AACLAME Secretariat, 1990.

Dade County (Fla.) Attorney. Opinion nos. 81–29 (July 2, 1981); 82–21 (Sept. 10, 1982); 80–37 (Dec. 18, 1980); 81–28 (July 2, 1981); 82–26 (Nov. 18, 1982); 85–15 (Aug. 9, 1985).

Debates and Proceedings of the Constitutional Convention of the State of California, 1878–1879. Sacramento: 1880–1881.

Indian Peace Commission. *Report to the President,* House Exec. Doc. no. 97, 40th Cong., 2d sess. (1868).

Lowell (Mass.) School Committee. Annual report, 1903–1904.

Massachusetts Commission on Immigration. *The Problem of Immigration in Massachusetts,* March 1914.

Massachusetts Department of Education. *State Conference on Immigrant Education in Massachusetts Industries,* Plymouth, Sept. 17–18, 1920.

Monterey Park (Calif.) City Council. Selected minutes, 1985–1988.

New York State Education Department. *Regents Policy Paper and Proposed Action Plan for Bilingual Education,* Sept. 20, 1989.

Official Report of Debates in the Convention of Louisiana, 1844–45.

President's Commission on Foreign Languages and International Studies. *Strength Through Wisdom: A Critique of U.S. Capability.* Washington, D.C.: U.S. Government Printing Office, 1979.

Report of the Commissioner of Indian Affairs, 1887. House Exec. Doc. no. 1, pt. 5, 50th Cong., 1st sess., serial 2542.

Territorial Papers of the United States. Vol. 9, *Orleans Territory.*

Texas Superintendent of Education. *A Hand Book of Information as to Education in Texas, 1918–1922.* Austin: Texas Department of Education, 1923.

Tohono O'odham Education Standards, October 1987. Sells, Ariz.: Tohono O'odham Education Department, 1987.

Treaties and Other International Acts of the United States of America. Washington, D.C.: U.S. Government Printing Office, 1937.

U.S. Commission on Civil Rights. *The Excluded Student: Educational Practices Affecting Mexican Americans in the Southwest.* Mexican American Education Study, Report III. Washington, D.C.: U.S. Government Printing Office, 1972.

U.S. Congress, Joint Economic Committee. *Economic and Demographic Consequences of Immigration,* 99th Cong., 2d sess. (1986).

U.S. Department of Education. *The Condition of Bilingual Education in the Nation: A Report to Congress and the President,* June 30, 1991.

U.S. Department of the Interior. *Americanization as a War Measure: Report of a Conference Called by the Secretary of the Interior and Held in Washington, April 3, 1918.* Bulletin of the Bureau of Education, no. 18 (1918).

U.S. Equal Employment Opportunity Commission. *Compliance Manual,* §623, "Speak-English-Only Rules and Other Language Policies."

U.S. General Accounting Office. *Bilingual Education: A New Look at the Research Evidence.* GAO/PEMD-87-12BR (1987).

———. *Bilingual Voting Assistance: Costs of and Use During the November 1984 General Election.* GAO/GGD-86-134BR (1986).

U.S. House, Committee on Education and Labor. *Compendium of Papers on the Topic of Bilingual Education.* Serial No. 99-R, 99th Cong., 2d sess. (1986).

———, General Subcommittee on Education. *Hearings on Bilingual Education,* 90th Cong., 1st sess. (1967).

———, Subcommittee on Elementary, Secondary, and Vocational Education. *Hearings on H.R. 15.* Pt. 3, *Bilingual Education,* 95th Cong., 1st sess. (1977).

U.S. House, Committee on the Judiciary. *Voting Rights Act Extension.* House Rpt. no. 94–196 (1975).

———, Subcommittee on Civil and Constitutional Rights. *Hearings on Extension of the Voting Rights Act,* 94th Cong., 1st sess. (1975).

U.S. Immigration Commission. *Reports of the Immigration Commission.* 42 vols. Washington, D.C.: Government Printing Office, 1911.

U.S. Immigration and Naturalization Service. *Statistical Yearbook,* 1982, 1986.

U.S. Senate, Committee on the Judiciary. *Hearings on the Nomination of Robert*

Bork to be Associate Justice of the Supreme Court of the United States, 100th Cong., 1st sess. (1987).

————, Subcommittee on the Constitution. *The English Language Amendment: Hearing on S.J. Res. 167,* 98th Cong., 2d sess. (1984).

U.S. Senate, Committee on Labor and Public Welfare, Special Subcommittee on Bilingual Education. *Hearings on Bilingual Education,* 90th Cong., 1st sess. (1967).

————, Subcommittee on Indian Education. *Indian Education: A National Tragedy, A National Challenge,* 91st Cong., 1st sess. (1969).

U.S. Senate, Committee on Territories. *New Mexico Statehood Bill,* 57th Cong., 2d sess., Senate Rpt. no. 2206 (1902), serial 4410.

U.S. Senate, Select Committee on Equal Educational Opportunity. *Hearing on Mexican American Education,* 91st Cong., 2d sess. (1970).

Court Cases

Asian American Business Group v. City of Pomona, 716 F.Supp. 1328 (C.D.Cal. 1989)

Batson v. Kentucky, 476 U.S. 79 (1986)

Balzac v. Porto Rico, 258 U.S. 298 (1922)

Castro v. State of California, 2 C.3d 223; 85 Cal.Rptr. 20, 466 P.2d 244 (1970)

Cruz v. Domínguez, 8 P.R.R. 551 (1905)

Downes v. Bidwell, 182 U.S. 244 (1901)

García v. Gloor, 618 F.2d 264 (5th Cir. 1980), *cert. denied,* 449 U.S. 1113 (1981)

Garza v. Smith, 320 F.Supp. 131 (W.D.Tex. 1970)

Graves v. Barnes, 343 F.Supp. 704 (W.D.Tex. 1972)

Griggs v. Duke Power Co., 401 U.S. 424 (1971)

Gutiérrez v. Municipal Court, 838 F.2d 1031 (9th Cir. 1988), *en banc rehearing denied,* 861 F.2d 1187 (9th Cir. 1988), *vacated as moot,* 109 S.Ct. 1736 (1989)

Hernández v. Erlenbusch, 368 F.Supp. 752 (D.Ore. 1973)

Hernández v. New York, 111 S.Ct. 1859 (1991)

Hernández v. Texas, 347 U.S. 475 (1954)

Katzenbach v. Morgan, 384 U.S. 641 (1966)

Lau v. Nichols, 414 U.S. 563 (1974)

In re Lockett, 179 Cal. 581 (1919)

Meyer v. Nebraska, 107 Neb. 657, 187 N.W. 100 (1922), *rev'd,* 262 U.S. 390 (1923)

People v. Ah Sum, 92 Cal. 648 (1892)

People v. Pechar, 130 Cal. App.2d 616 (1955)

Puerto Rican Organization for Political Action (PROPA) v. Kusper, 490 F.2d 575 (7th Cir. 1973)

Reitman v. Mulkey, 387 U.S. 369 (1967)

Soberal-Pérez v. Heckler, 549 F.Supp. 1164 (E.D.N.Y. 1982), *aff'd,* 717 F.2d 36 (2d Cir. 1983), *cert. denied,* 466 U.S. 929 (1984)

Torres v. Sachs, 381 F.Supp. 309 (S.D.N.Y. 1974)

U.S. ex rel. Negrón v. New York, 434 F.2d 386 (2d Cir. 1970)

U.S. v. Pérez, 658 F.2d 654 (9th Cir. 1981)

Yñiguez v. Mofford, 730 F.Supp. 309 (D.Ariz. 1990)

Unpublished Materials

Baker, Keith A. Testimony before the New York State Board of Regents, Schenectady, Oct. 17, 1989; Buffalo, Nov. 9, 1989.

Bennett, William J. Speech to the Association for a Better New York, Sept. 26, 1985.

Bikales, Gerda. Presentation to Georgetown University Round Table on Languages and Linguistics, March 12, 1987.

Bricker, Kathryn. "Tanton Defense," Oct. 25, 1988.

Calderón, José, and John Horton. "The English Only Movement: Sources of Support and Opposition." Paper presented to the American Sociological Association, Atlanta, Aug. 1988.

Cárdenas, Blandina. "Defining Equal Access to Educational Opportunity for Mexican-American Children: A Study of Three Civil Rights Actions Affecting Mexican-American Students and the Development of a Conceptual Framework for Effecting Institutional Responsiveness to the Educational Needs of Mexican-American Children." Ed.D. diss., University of Massachusetts, 1974.

Chávez, Linda. "English: Our Common Bond." Speech to the Los Angeles World Affairs Council, Dec. 4, 1987.

Clyne, Michael. "The Uniqueness of the Language Situation in Australia: Its Policy and Research Implications," Aug. 18, 1987.

Cohen, Linda M. "New Mexico: The Thorn or the Rose?" National Clearinghouse for Bilingual Education, Jan. 9, 1984.

Diamond, Stanley. "What's Happened to Proposition 63, the English Language Amendment" [Spring 1987].

Draper, Jamie B. "Foreign Language Enrollments in Public Secondary Schools, Fall 1989 and Fall 1990." American Council on the Teaching of Foreign Languages, Oct. 1991.

Florida English Campaign. "The Florida English Language Amendment Initiative Drive: Some Questions and Answers" [1985].

Frawley, William. Memorandum to E. A. Trabant, president, University of Delaware, Oct. 31, 1989.

Gary C. Lawrence Co. "National Telephone Membership Study for U.S. English." Santa Ana, Calif., April 1988.

González, Martín. "Language and Conflict in California: The Case of Fillmore, 1984–1986." University of California, Santa Barbara, Nov. 28, 1988.

Gray, Tracy C., and M. Beatriz Arias. "Challenge to the AIR Report." Press statement, Center for Applied Linguistics, 1978.

Hardin, Garrett. "A Foundation for Immigration Policy." Memorandum for WITAN VI, Cambridge, Mass., Oct. 23, 1987.

Hayakawa, S. I. "Questions Often Asked about State Campaigns to Make English Their Official Language," May 1987.

Horton, John. "Ethnicity and the Politics of Growth." Paper presented at the Conference on Comparative Ethnicity, Los Angeles, June 1988.

Judd, Elliot L. "Factors Affecting the Passage of the Bilingual Education Act of 1967." Ph.D. diss., New York University, 1977.

Kiang, Peter Nien-chu. "Southeast Asian Parent Empowerment in Lowell, Massachusetts." Paper delivered to the Sixth National Conference of the Association for Asian American Studies, New York, June 1–3, 1989.

Lam, Daniel. Testimony at a forum on Official English, Middlesex Community College, Lowell, Mass., Nov. 1, 1989.

Littlebear, Dick. "*Natsèhesenèstsestòtse:* Cheyenne, My Native Language" [1989].

Locke, Pat. "Indian Language Codes." Presentation at the Native American Language Issues Institute, Billings, Mont., June 10, 1989.

Macías, Reynaldo F. "Cauldron, Boil and Bubble: United States Language Policy towards Indigenous Language Groups during the Ninteenth Century." University of Southern California, Sept. 1984.

Perlmann, Joel. "Bilingualism and Ethnicity in American Schooling before 1960: An Historical Perspective." Paper presented at the Institute on Bilingual Education, Harvard Graduate School of Education, Dec. 11, 1987.

Pioneer Fund. "Outline Proposed for First Year's Work of the Foundation" [1937].

———. Memoranda in response to William Frawley, University of Delaware, Nov. 1, 15, 1989.

Robbins, Terry. "An Open Letter to All the Governors in the United States," March 30, 1985.

———. Speech at Florida International University, Oct. 8, 1987.

Robinson, Genevieve. "The Acropolis of Hellenism in America: First Generation Greeks in Lowell, Massachusetts, 1895–1922." Ph.D. diss., Boston College, 1986.

Sgouros, Adam Demetrios. "The Greek-American Community of Lowell, Massachusetts, and Its Educational Institutions." Ph.D. diss., Florida State University, 1979.

Shimomura, Floyd D. [Deputy Attorney General, State of California.] "English as 'Official Language'—Effect on S.F.'s Trilingual Ballots," April 9, 1987.

Simmons, Thomas E. "The Citizen Factories: The Americanization of Mexican Students in Texas Public Schools, 1920–1945." Ph.D. diss., Texas A&M University, 1976.

Spanish-American League Against Discrimination, "Not English Only, English *Plus!*: Bilingual Education Issue Analysis," Miami, Oct. 15, 1985.

John Tanton. "Answering the Charge of Racism." Memo to Kirby Seminar Attendees, Feb. 19, 1985.

———. "Commentary on the Frawley Letter," Nov. 15, 1989.

———. "FAIR: Quo Vadis" [1986].

———. "Fundamentals," Jan. 13, 1989.

———. "Memorandum to WITAN IV Attendees," Oct. 10, 1986.

———. "The Mis- and Mal-interpreted Tanton Memo: A Note on Its Purpose and the Circumstances under Which It Was Written," Dec. 27, 1988.

Tatalovich, Raymond. "English Language Statutes in Six Midwestern States: A Comparative Analysis." Paper presented at the Western Political Science Association meeting, Newport Beach, Calif., March 22–24, 1990.

U.S. English. "Frequently Used Arguments against the Legal Protection of English" [1987].

———. "U.S. English Policy Position: Native American Languages," March 27, 1984.

Weber, Jon, and Jeffrey Browne. Presentation to English Plus Information Clearinghouse (EPIC), Washington, D.C., Dec. 2, 1988.

Woodrow, Karen. [U.S. Census Bureau.] "Undocumented Immigrants Living in the United States." Paper presented to the American Statistical Association, Anaheim, Calif., Aug. 1990.

References

Preface

One million Yiddish speakers: Leibowitz, "English Literacy," pp. 34–35. "Mindless drift": Bikales, presentation to Georgetown University Round Table. 41 percent: Current Population Survey, Nov. 1989, cited in *Numbers and Needs* 2, no. 1 (1992): 2–4. "Greater reproductive powers": Tanton, "Memorandum to WITAN IV."

1. Guardians of English

Pressed to limit expenditures: Monterey Park City Council budget hearing, July 23, 1988; Willner interview. "Encroach on space": Richard Springer, "New Monterey Park Mayor Battles with Councilmember Judy Chu," *East West News*, Sept. 29, 1988, p. 8. "This little library": Hatch interview.

"English is under attack": U.S. English brochure, "In Defense of Our Common Language." $28 million: U.S. English annual reports, internal memoranda, and tax returns, 1983–1990. Elizabeth, N.J.: Mayor Thomas G. Dunn, memo of June 16, 1983. San Diego grand jury: 1984 report quoted in Butler, *On Creating a Hispanic America*, p. 9. Koreans in Philadelphia: Vince Kasper, "Korean Signs in Olney Spark Harsh Language," *Philadelphia Daily News*, July 24, 1986. Broward County: "English-Only Condominium Angers Hispanics in South Florida," *Tampa Tribune*, March 4, 1988, p. 11-B. Concert near Boston: "Boston's English-only Audience," *Phoenix Gazette*, Aug. 19, 1988. Alderman in Chicago: "Ald. Henry to Grocers: Speak My Language," *Chicago Sun-Times*, Dec. 6, 1989.

51 percent: 1986 test census, analyzed in Calderón and Horton, "The English Only Movement," p. 13. $5 a square foot: Mark Arax, "Asian Influx Alters Life in Suburbia," *Los Angeles Times*, April 5, 1987, p. 30. "Acceptance of ethnic diversity": Kathy Seligman, "Monterey Park, Calif.: Ethnic Mix a Success," *USA Today*, March 27, 1985, p. 7A. "Discriminating against Americans": Arcuri interview. "English as a foreign language": Monterey Park city council minutes, Nov. 12, 1985, 33-346–48. "If we want a civil war": ibid., 33-330–35. "Has anybody here read the Constitution?": Arcuri interview. "Where am I?": Hayakawa statement read by Stanley Diamond, city council minutes, 33-348–49.

Charging students: Dave Brackney, "School Board Cancels Transit Fees," *Fillmore Herald*, May 2, 1985, p. 1. Mayor Hub Cloyd: statement reprinted in *Ventura County Star-Free Press*, May 14, 1985, p. A-10. Three hundred demonstrators: González, "Language and Conflict in California," p. 17. "Good Hispanic": Morales interview. "Linguistic scholar": Kathleen Bohland, "Hispanics Vent Anger," *Ventura County Star-Free Press*, May 15, 1985, pp. A1–2. Tried to get Ernest Morales fired: Stanley Diamond to Commanding Officer, Pt. Mugu, June 29, 1985; Captain J. M. Hickerson, Commander, Pacific Missile Test Center, to Diamond, July 10, 1985.

Twenty-eight percent settled there: U.S. Immigration and Naturalization Service, *Statistical Yearbook*, 1986, pp. 32–35. Thirty-seven state houses: survey by *Education Week*, June 17, 1986. 64 percent of Americans: Hearst Corp. survey on the Constitution reported in "Survey: Most Think English Is Official U.S. Language," Associated Press, February 14, 1987. "Advertising in English only": Felix Gutiérrez, "U.S. English Members Targeting Companies Advertising in Spanish," Associated Press, Dec. 25, 1985. Proposition 63 might outlaw: Van de Kamp et al., "Argument against Proposition 63." "Recognizes in law": Hayakawa et al., "Argument in Favor of Proposition 63." The day after: William Trombley, "Assemblyman Vows to Carry to Ball for English-Only Action," *Los Angeles Times*, Nov. 6, 1986, Pt. I, pp. 3, 31. Survey commissioned by U.S. English: Hamilton, Frederick & Schneiders, "Summary of Poll Results, Floridians' Opinions on English as official Language," May 7, 1987. "THE PEOPLE": Diamond, "What's Happened to Proposition 63." "Trouble on your hands": Hayakawa interview.

75 percent of Hispanic immigrants: Veltman, *Future of the Spanish Language*, pp. iii–iv. Status or solidarity: Milroy and Milroy, *Authority in Language*, pp. 55–59. "Necessary evil": Haugen, *Norwegian Language in America*, p. 2. "Social mobility": Fishman, "Language Maintenance," p. 630. "What then is the American?": quoted in Gordon, *Assimilation in American Life*, p. 116.

2. Polyglot Boarding-House

"Band of national union": Webster, *Dissertations on the English Language*, p. 397. Apocryphal accounts; "Make the English speak Greek": Baron, *Grammar and Good Taste*, pp. 11–13. "Buckskin, moccasins": *Nation* 116 (1923): 408. Chicago Irish: Mencken, *American Language*, pp. 92–93. "American Academy": Adams, "Letter to the President of Congress," Sept. 5, 1780. "Hardly any thing": Sen. Samuel Latham Mitchill to Noah Webster, Jan. 7, 1807, quoted in Read, "American Projects," pp. 1149–50. Courted rebellion: Baron, *Grammar and Good Taste*, p. 95. "To padlock the language": Rep. David A. DeArmond, quoted in Read, "American Projects," p. 1171. 8.7 percent: 1790 Census figures analyzed in "American Council of Learned Societies." "Perfect and complete": Boorstin, *Hidden History*, pp. 76–93. "Sunny side": Higham, *Strangers in the Land*, p. 337.

Jay's rationale: *Federalist Papers*, p. 38. "All civilized societies": Madison comments at Federal Convention, quoted in Morris, *Witnesses at the Creation*, p. 121. "Interested combinations": *Federalist Papers*, p. 324. "Those who own the country": Abram Elting Bennett, *Huguenots Migration: Descendants' Contributions to America* (Washington, D.C.: National Huguenot Society, 1984), p. 57.

60 percent of the white population: Morris, *Forging of the Union*, p. 16. "Whole counties": Handlin, *This Was America*, p. 45. Eighteen different languages: Hansen, *Atlantic Migration*, pp. 38–39. Indigenous tongues: Sagarin and Kelly, "Polylingualism in the United States," p. 22. "Praying towns": Winslow, *John Eliot*, pp. 88–91, 137–47. Slave ship's captain: William Smith, *A New Voyage to Guinea* (1744), quoted in Dillard, *Black English*, pp. 73–74. Thirty-eight German-language newspapers: Conzen, "Germans," p. 409. Private schools in Philadelphia: Wright, *Cultural Life of the American Colonies*, p. 109. "Run away . . . ": cited

in Read, "Bilingualism in the Middle Colonies," 93–99. **Distinctions other than ethnicity:** Jones, *American Immigration*, pp. 53–63. **"Swedish language is doomed":** Wright, *Cultural Life of the American Colonies*, p. 51.

"They begin of late": Franklin to Peter Collinson, May 9, 1753. **First German-language newspaper:** Wittke, *German-Language Press*, pp. 13–14. **"Dutch under-live":** Graeff, *Relations Between the Pennsylvania Germans and the British Authorities*, p. 31. **Hailing from Württemburg:** Dorpalen, "The Political Influence of the German Element," p. 234–35. **En masse:** Weaver, "Benjamin Franklin and the Pennsylvania Germans," p. 57. **"Only possible means":** Rush, "To the Citizens," p. 366.

"They will bring": Jefferson, *Notes on Virginia* (1785), p. 120. **"Incapable of self-government":** Jefferson to DeWitt Clinton, Dec. 2, 1803, quoted in Newton, *Americanization of French Louisiana*, p. 41. **"Not one in fifty":** *Official Letter Books*, I: 328, 330. **"No two parishes":** Rep. Joseph Nicholson, *Annals of Congress*, 8th Cong., 1st Sess. (1803–1804), p. 1229. **Creoles had been intrigued:** Dargo, *Jefferson's Louisiana*, pp. 10–11. **"Are truths, then":** "Remonstrance of the People of Louisiana Against the Political System Adopted by Congress for Them," Dec. 31, 1804, *American State Papers*, I: 397, 399. **Jefferson instructed:** Jefferson to Claiborne, Dec. 2, 1804; Claiborne to Jefferson, Jan. 10, 1805; in *Territorial Papers*, IX: 343, 366–67. **Thirty thousand English speakers:** Jefferson to John Dickinson, Jan. 13, 1807. **Second governor:** Villeré, *Jacques Philippe Villeré*, pp. 70–72. **Half of Louisiana's white population:** Newton, *Americanization of French Louisiana*, p. 193. **"That population":** *Official Report of Debates*, p. 839. **When Democrats returned:** Kloss, *American Bilingual Tradition*, pp. 112–22, 158.

"Not as Indians": Thomas Jefferson Morgan, address to the Lake Mohonk Conference of Friends of the Indian, 1889, quoted in Prucha, *American Indian Policy*, p. 299. **Literacy rate:** U.S. Senate, *Indian Education*, p. 19. **"Immersing the Indians":** 1883 address to World Convention of Baptists, quoted in Prucha, *American Indian Policy*, p. 275. **"Utterly subversive":** *Congressional Globe*, vol. 40, pt. 2, pp. 1821, 1842. **600,000 elementary-school children:** Kloss, *American Bilingual Tradition*, p. 76.

Chinese immigrants: Sandmeyer, *Anti-Chinese Movement in California*, pp. 71–72; Heizer and Almquist, *The Other Californians*, pp. 46–48. **"Bigoted ultramontane sectaries":** Kucera, *Church-State Relationships*, pp. 114–15. **"Let us never forget":** Kellogg, "Bennett Law in Wisconsin," pp. 24–25. **"Iron rule":** Kloss, "German-American Language Maintenance," p. 230. **"Indeed means war":** "Col. Krez on the Bennett Law," *Milwaukee Sentinel*, Jan. 1, 1890, p. 4. **"No more a foreign language":** Christian Koerner, cited in Kellogg, "Bennett Law in Wisconsin," p. 12. **"Menace":** Whyte, "Bennett Law Campaign," p. 389.

"System where chaos reigns": Bowers, *Beveridge and the Progressive Era*, pp. 74–76, 121. **"Extension of ordered liberty":** Lewis, *Puerto Rico*, p. 100. **"Passive and plastic":** Negrón de Montilla, *Americanization in Puerto Rico*, p. 13; Osuna, *History of Education in Puerto Rico*, p. 342. **"Colonization carried forward":** Negrón de Montilla, *Americanization in Puerto Rico*, p. 62; Osuna, *History of Education in Puerto Rico*, p. 344. **3.6 percent of Puerto Ricans:** survey of island residents over the age of ten, cited in Language Policy Task Force, "Language Policy and the Puerto Rican Community," pp. 8–9. **"Inalienable right":** Negrón de Montilla, *Americanization in Puerto Rico*, p. 160.

Later translated: Leibowitz, "Imposition of English," p. 202. **Two of fourteen**

counties: Larson, *New Mexico's Quest for Statehood*, p. 124. **5 percent:** 1874 territorial report cited in Kloss, *American Bilingual Tradition*, p. 130. **33 percent could read:** Cohen, "New Mexico," pp. 18–19. **"Identical in language":** U.S. Senate, *New Mexico Statehood Bill*, p. 9. **"Curious continuance":** *Congressional Record*, 61st Cong., 2d sess. (1910), p. 8225. **Enabling legislation:** U.S. Commission on Civil Rights, *Excluded Student*, pp. 78, 80.

"Wide open": Boorstin, *Hidden History*, p. 213. **"Race suicide":** Higham, *Strangers in the Land*, pp. 143, 147. **"So deficient":** House Rpt. no. 1789, 59th Cong., 1st sess. (1906). **"Safeguarding and elevating":** *Congressional Record*, 59th Cong., 1st sess., 7775–76, 7782 (June 2, 1906).

"Strikes and plots": "Americanization by Industry," *Immigrants in America Review* 2, no. 1 (1916): 24. **"English First":** Hartmann, *Movement to Americanize the Immigrant*, pp. 128–31. **"Induced to give up":** Rea and Ford quoted in Hill, "Americanization Movement," pp. 630–31, 638. **550 publications:** Conzen, "Germans," p. 420. **"Forced uniformity":** Goebel, *Kampf um deutsche Kultur in Amerika*, quoted in Park, *Immigrant Press and Its Control*, p. 62. **"Pan-German" plot:** Hawgood, *Tragedy of German-America*, pp. 292–95. **"Hyphenated American":** Roosevelt, speech to Knights of Columbus, Oct. 12, 1915. **Sweeping restrictions:** Wittke, *German-Americans and the World War*, pp. 184–87. **"Westerners Do Things":** *New York Times*, June 1, 1918, p. 10. **Fifteen states:** Hartmann, *Movement to Americanize the Immigrant*, pp. 253–54. **Unprecedented expansion:** Baron, *English Only Question*, pp. 141–42. **Shocking confirmation:** Gould, *Mismeasure of Man*, pp. 165–66, 195–200, 227–28. **"Inborn socially inadequate qualities":** Handlin, *Race and Nationality in American Life*, p. 105.

3. Strangers in Their Own Land

Spanish language rights: Associated Press, "Van de Kamp Says 'Official English' Efforts Ignore 1849 [sic] Pact Asserting Status of Spanish," *Los Angeles Daily Journal*, Oct. 10, 1986, p. 2. **"California's oneness":** Hayakawa et al., "Argument in Favor of Proposition 63." **"Governed by the same principles":** "U.S. English Policy Position: Native American Languages," March 27, 1984. **"Stole it fair and square":** quoted in Alan Ehrenhalt, *Politics in America: Members of Congress in Washington and at Home* (Washington, D.C.: Congressional Quarterly Press, 1982), p. 86.

"Extranjeros": U.S. Senate Exec. Doc. no. 52, 30th Cong., 1st sess., serial 509, pp. 291–92, 342–43, 374. **Some recognition:** Acuña, *Occupied America*, pp. 27–30; Rivera, *Mexican American Source Book*, pp. 184–86. **"Lamentable exception":** Powell, *Tree of Hate*, p. 11. **"Cruel streak":** *Texas Rangers*, excerpted in Weber, *Foreigners in Their Native Land*, p. 77. **California's native population:** Heizer and Almquist, *The Other Californians*, p. 59. **"Greatest misfortunes"**; **"Castilian race":** Weber, *Foreigners in Their Native Land*, pp. 135, 145. **14 million acres:** Pitt, *Decline of the Californios*, pp. 86, 91–94; McWilliams, *North From Mexico*, p. 91. **"Kanaka":** *El Clamor Público*, March 7, 1857, quoted in Weber, *Foreigners in Their Native Land*, p. 152. **"All laws of the State":** *Debates and Proceedings*, II: 801-2. **Official state translator:** William Trombley, "Prop. 63—A New Battle in Historical War of Words," *Los Angeles Times*, Oct. 21, 1986, pp. 3, 26.

"Why not Mexicans?": Pitt, *Decline of the Californios*, pp. 187–88. **"Means or**

facilities": Weber, *Foreigners in Their Native Land,* pp. 254–55. **Coercive anglicization:** Texas Superintendent of Education, *Hand Book,* p. 23. **Fewer than one in twenty:** 1928 study by Hershel Manuel, cited in Simmons, "Citizen Factories," p. 116. **"If the Mexicans get educated":** Taylor, *American-Mexican Frontier,* pp. 195–96, 217. **Civil rights movement:** San Miguel, *"Let All of Them Take Heed,"* p. 67, 78–80, 123–26; Cárdenas, "Defining Equal Access," p. 80. **"Acquisition of the English language":** LULAC Constitution, Art. II, §4 (May 1929), in Moquin, *Documentary History of the Mexican Americans,* p. 365. **"Learn to handle with purity":** García, *Mexican Americans,* pp. 30, 44. **"If they can't talk English":** Simmons, "Citizen Factories," p. 172. **"The time has come":** San Miguel, *"Let All of Them Take Heed,"* p. 107. **"Child's introduction":** García, *Mexican Americans,* p. 261.

"Our culture superimposed upon them": U.S. Senate, *Bilingual Education,* p. 37. **"Window-dressing":** Thernstrom, "E Pluribus Plura," pp. 6–8. **"Regardless of its educational effectiveness":** Ravitch, *Schools We Deserve,* pp. 272–73. **"Part of a political movement":** Diamond, "New York's Blueprint," p. 4. **"Submersing" students:** Sánchez, "History, Culture, and Education," pp. 10–13. **"Confusion, failure, and frustration":** Urquides, "Tucson's Tale of Two Cultures," p. 62. **Only 5 percent:** U.S. Commission on Civil Rights, *Excluded Student,* p. 26. **"Just about anything":** Cárdenas interview. **"Rejection of one":** Bernal interview. **"I come from a small town":** "¡Qué Lástima!" pp. 34–35. **New wave of school boycotts:** U.S. Senate, *Mexican American Education,* pp. 2463–2516; Cárdenas interview. **"Handful of gringos":** Gutiérrez, "Mexicanos Need To Control Their Own Destinies," pp. 227, 229. **3.1 years:** 1970 Census. **Pedagogically grounded:** Shockley, *Chicano Revolt,* pp. 117, 245–50.

"Best of both worlds": *Congressional Record,* 90th Cong., 1st sess. (Dec. 1, 1967), pp. 34702, 34703, 35053. **Thirty-six bilingual education bills:** Judd, "Factors Affecting," pp. 121, 172, 177–80. **"Ultimate goal":** Epstein, *Language, Ethnicity, and the Schools,* p. 20. **"An obsession":** Peña interview. **50 percent lacked:** Gray and Arias, "Challenge to the AIR Report." **"Affirmative ethnicity":** Epstein, *Language, Ethnicity, and the Schools,* passim. **"Like Canada":** U.S. House, *H.R. 15,* p. 83. **"Curse for a nation":** Bikales, presentation to Georgetown University Round Table.

4. Tribal Politics

"Capital of the Spanish language": Soto interview. **"You can be born here":** Morgan, "Latinization of America," p. 55. **Forbidden by law:** Dade County Attorney, Opinion no. 80–37 (Dec. 18, 1980). **Spanish-language programming:** Yoffe interview.

"Less attractive place": Fredric Tasker, "Anti-Bilingualism Measure Approved in Dade County," *Miami Herald,* Nov. 5, 1980, p. 11A. **Cuban Refugee Program:** Pedraza-Bailey, "Cubans and Mexicans in the United States," p. 88. **Language census; 8,500 businesses:** Mackey and Beebe, *Bilingual Schools,* pp. 30, 41. **Spanish speakers outnumbered:** Boswell and Curtis, *Cuban-American Experience,* p. 79. **Cuban American elite:** Liz Balmaseda, "Tossing Power With Pride," *Miami Herald,* Jan. 31, 1981, p. 1C. **"Appealing way":** Bray interview. **Full 45 percent:** Portes et al., "Six Years Later," pp. 6–10. **"In gestation":** Castro interview.

98 percent of Hispanic parents: Strategy Research Corporation study, cited in

Combs and Trasviña, "Legal Implications of the English Language Amendment," p. 30.

"Overuse of Spanish": Schera interview. "Not a mongrel nation": Robbins, speech at Florida International University. "Will not be tolerated": Jay Ducassi, "Burger King to Workers: 'Hold the Spanish,' " *Miami Herald*, Oct. 26, 1983, p. 1B. "Hotel managers": T. Willard Fair, "Blacks Must Help Themselves," *Miami Herald*, Feb. 14, 1982, p. E1. $7.86 to Hispanics: Porter and Dunn, *Miami Riot*, pp. 196–97. "Everything is done in Spanish": Gouraige interview. Eighteen lives: Stolz, "Dangerous Chemistry of Dade County," p. 101. "I don't see why": Celia W. Dugger, "2 Don't Know Spanish, Denied Jobs," *Miami Herald*, Oct. 25, 1984, pp. 1B, 3B.

Non-English-speaking muggers: Boswell and Curtis, *Cuban-American Experience*, pp. 54–55. Move elsewhere: Tasker, "Anti-Bilingualism Measure," p. A11. "I don't feel like I'm in America": Sara Rimer, "How Anti-Bilingual Crusade Began," *Miami Herald*, Oct. 26, 1980, pp. 1A, 14A. Budget for bilingual services: Dade County Division of Latin Affairs, fact sheet on the Antibilingual Ordinance [1980]. "Cuban-pandering": Emmy Shafer, "On Anti-Bilingual Ordinance," *Miami Herald*, Oct. 10, 1987, p. 23A. Spent $50,000: Michael Browning, "Anti-Bilingual Backers Celebrate Early," *Miami Herald*, Nov. 5, 1980, p. A11.

"Unity from diversity": Florida English Campaign, "Florida English Language Amendment Initiative," p. 1. "No longer a bond": testimony by Gerda Bikales, U.S. Senate, *English Language Amendment*, p. 6. "Rednecks": LaPorta interview. "Extremely tough race": Howard M. Burkholz to Jeff Browne et al., Aug. 7, 1988. "Feel comfortable": SUN for Florida, "Vote No Language Enforcement," Aug. 6, 1988. "Over my dead body": Schera interview. "Bunch of neanderthals": Weber, presentation to EPIC.

"Main effect": Castro interview. "¿Dónde está Jorge?": Luciano García, "Publix Disciplines Worker for Speaking Spanish on Job," *Miami Herald*, Nov. 12, 1988, pp. 1D, 2D. High-school administrator: Ronnie Ramos, "Official English Raises Bias Fears," *Miami Herald*, Nov. 15, 1988, pp. 1D, 3D. Telephone orders: Marshall Ingwerson, "English-Only Laws: How Broad?" *Christian Science Monitor*, Nov. 29, 1988, p. 3. Not a single complaint: Canino interview. "Smoldering coal": Gallegos interview.

"American seat": Luis Feldstein Soto, "Richman Trounces Kennedy," *Miami Herald*, Aug. 16, 1989, p. 22A. "Richman's racist view": Ileana Ros-Lehtinen, " 'Bigotry' Is Not Debatable," *Miami Herald*, Aug. 23, 1989, p. 17A. "Malicious state senator": Tom Fiedler, "A Warning, in English Only," *Miami Herald*, Aug. 9, 1989, p. 2B. Preelection polling: Tom Fiedler, "Poll: Ethnic Groups' Turnout Is Key to Tight House Race," *Miami Herald*, Aug. 23, 1989, pp. 1A, 13A. Puerto Rican community: Martínez interview.

"First-class citizens": Loret de Molac, "Hispanic Hollywood," p. 43. 84 percent: Luisa Yañez, "Young Cuban-Americans Speaking Less Spanish, M-DCC Professor Warns," *Miami News*, Feb. 24, 1986, p. 5A. Third of Hispanics: Strategy Research Corporation, *U.S. Hispanic Market Study, 1989*, pp. 89, 134. "Front doors": *Miami News*, Feb. 16, 1985, p. 14A. "Rooms with Views:" Tom Fiedler, "Memo to Candidates," *Miami Herald*, Aug. 27, 1989, p. 3C.

5. Old Ethnics and New

"Don't come here": Kouloheras interview.
"Assimilation has been slow": U.S. Immigration Commission, *Reports,* I: 14, 42. "Yiddish world": Henry James, *The American Scene* (New York: Harper & Bros., 1907), pp. 86, 138. "Poor questions": Veltman, *Future of the Spanish Language,* pp. 16–20. Verdict: Grosjean, *Life with Two Languages,* pp. 54–57. "World doesn't change": Veltman interview. "Two-generation model": Veltman, *Language Shift,* pp. 58–62. The younger an immigrant: Veltman, *Future of the Spanish Language,* pp. 38–45. Speak English with their children: Veltman, *Language Shift,* p. 214.
13 percent: Perlmann, "Bilingualism and Ethnicity in American Schooling."
Twenty thousand Greeks: Robinson, "Acropolis of Hellenism," p. 3. "Killing bequest": Blewett, "New People," p. 208. $3 to $4 a week: Kenngott, *Record of a City,* pp. 55, 124. "When I stepped into the Appleton": Karas, *Greek Immigrants at Work,* p. 11. "Gave light to the world": Saloutos, *Greeks in the United States,* p. 71. Ottoman rule: Sgouros, "Greek-American Community of Lowell," pp. 83–85, 115. Bilingual classes for adults: Lowell School Committee, Annual Report, 1903–1904, p. 15. Nine hundred Greek students: Fairchild, *Greek Immigration,* p. 145. "Padrone System": U.S. Immigration Commission, *Reports,* II: 401. "70,000 to 100,000": Massachusetts Commission on Immigration, *Problem of Immigration,* p. 114. "Un-American tendencies": John J. Mahoney, Massachusetts Supervisor of Americanization, "Principles and Procedures Suggested to the Industrial Group," in *State Conference on Immigrant Education,* p. 62. "BECOME AN AMERICAN": Robinson, "Acropolis of Hellenism," p. 378. Old World politics: Sgouros, "Greek-American Community of Lowell," pp. 63–69. "Greeks must recognize": Saloutos, *Greeks in the United States,* p. 235. Begining to hold functions in English: Warner and Srole, *Social Systems of American Ethnic Groups,* pp. 222–28. Crime, vandalism: Karas, *Greek Triangle of the Acre,* p. 48. "Survivors": Karas, *Greek Immigrants at Work,* p. 88.
"I missed my own food": Yin interview. "We hide our faces": Sommanee Bounphasaysonh, Laotian Association of Greater Lowell, quoted in Kiang, "Southeast Asian Parent Empowerment," p. 8. "Anybody who was school-age": Vaidya interview. 40 percent and growing: Kiang, p. 4. 2,000 of 12,650 children: Nancy Costello, "Lowell Schools in Space Crisis," *Lowell Sun,* May 26, 1987, p. 15. Nearly 70 percent: M. E. Malone, "In Many Classrooms, Needs Are Going Unmet," *Boston Globe,* Jan. 23, 1989, p. 8. "Civil liberties of the majority": Sharon Britton, "School Committee Turns Down 'Pairing' Desegregation Plan," *Lowell Sun,* March 27, 1987. "Hispanics are the worst": Nancy Costello, "Kouloheras Sparks Racial Clash at Meeting," *Lowell Sun,* May 7, 1987; Pérez-Bustillo interview. "True immigrants": Kouloheras interview. "Everybody who comes here": Huertas interview. "No true desegregation": Multicultural Education, Training, and Advocacy, Inc., press statement, June 27, 1987; Pérez-Bustillo, letter to Lowell School Committee, May 21, 1987.
One day in mid-September: Doris Sue Wong, "Day of Fishing Ends in Violent Death for Lowell Boy," *Boston Globe,* Sept. 23, 1987, pp. 25, 28. Rebuke: *Lowell Sun,* Nov. 6, 1989, p. 12. "Ethnic landscape": Gargiulo interview. Diversion: Howe interview. "Don't want you here": Lam, testimony at a forum on Official English. "Eliminate our mother tongue": Yin interview.

6. Hispanophobia

"U.S. English is to Hispanics": Imhoff, "Position of U.S. English on Bilingual Education," p. 49. "My people": *U.S. English Update,* Jan.–Feb. 1988, p. 1. 73 percent: Chávez, presentation at Harvard Graduate School of Education, Dec. 11, 1987. "Professional Hispanics": Tanton memo, Feb. 19, 1985. "Naturalized immigrants": Hayakawa interview. Hayakawa's political career: Charles Claffey, "Say it Again, Sam," *Boston Globe,* March 18, 1988, pp. 33–34.

"Gobernar es poblar": Tanton, "Memorandum to WITAN IV." "Congenital conservationist": Tanton interview. "Their 'huddled massess' ": Tanton, *Rethinking Immigration Policy,* p. 8. "Go home and take a shower": William Trombley, "Prop. 63 Roots Traced to Small Michigan City," *Los Angeles Times,* Oct. 20, 1986, Pt. I, p. 3. "The taboo": Tanton, "FAIR: Quo Vadis." "Certain intellectuals": Graham, *Illegal Immigration and the New Reform Movement,* pp. 7–8. Shying away: Roger Conner, executive director of FAIR, memo of July 11, 1986. "Inextricably intertwined": Tanton, "Fundamentals," p. 2. "Whimsical name": Tanton interview. "White man in Druid": LaPorta interview. Political involvement in Latin America: George E. Delury, ed., *World Encyclopedia of Political Systems and Parties* (New York: Facts on File, 1987).

"Never, ever": Elizabeth Llorente, "Linda Chávez: Thriving on Controversy," *Vista,* Nov. 8, 1987. "The libertarian in me": Chávez interview. $500 million: "The Forbes Four Hundred," *Forbes,* Oct. 23, 1989, p. 223. $650,000: I.R.S. Form 1023 filed by U.S. English Foundation, Inc., July 22, 1987. Entirely from "membership": Bikales interview. "Stop the Stork": Hersh, *Mellon Family,* p. 538. "Only nine hundred million": Raspail, *Camp of the Saints,* preface. "Genocide as well": Chávez, "World View of a Radical Racist," p. 10. "Prophetic work": Zall, "The U.S. Refugee Industry," p. 258. "America, like invaded France": Hardin, *An Ecolate View,* [n.p.].

"Germ plasm": Kevles, *In the Name of Eugenics,* p. 103. "Practical population control": Laughlin to Wickliffe P. Draper, Dec. 23, 1936. "Applied Genetics": Pioneer Fund, "Outline Proposed for First Year's Work." Lebensborn: Kevles, *In the Name of Eugenics,* p. 117. "Mainstream of U.S. thought": Pioneer Fund, unsigned memo in response to Frawley, Nov. 15, 1989. Other intimates; Arthur Jensen and William Shockley: Grace Lichtenstein, "Fund Backs Controversial Study of 'Racial Betterment,' " *New York Times,* Dec. 11, 1977, p. 76. "Study of human variation": Harry F. Weyher, president, Pioneer Fund, memo in response to Frawley, Nov. 1, 1989. Antibusing seminars: Dick Kaukas, "Fund Aids Race Intelligence Studies, Busing Foes," *Louisville Courier-Journal,* Oct. 16, 1977. Modern Ku Klux Klan: *Southern Horizons: The Autobiography of Thomas Dixon* (Alexandria, Va.: I.W.V. Publishers, 1984). Professed to know nothing: Tanton interview. A bit of persuading: Olson interview; Holmes interview. "Character assassination": Tanton, "U.S. English: It's Being Victimized." Forty-two ethnic organizations: U.S. English, "Partial List of Ethnic Organizations Supporting the Proposed English Language Amendment," April 19, 1985. Republican Heritage Groups: Bellant, *Old Nazis, the New Right,* pp. 23, 43, 59, 61. Significant cause: Bikales, "We Must Make English Our Official Language," p. 25. "Nothing, says Plato": Tanton quoting *The Spectator,* no. 557, "Comment on the Frawley Letter," Nov. 15, 1989. "Early diagnosis": Tanton, "Fundamentals," p. 3. "Mc-

Carthyite tactics": Tanton resignation statement, Oct. 17, 1988. "Nearly fatal": Tanton, "U.S. English: It's Being Victimized."
"So foreign": Chávez interview. "The guy is a racist": Holmes interview. "White political caucus": Tanton to Leon F. Bouvier, May 2, 1988. "Redneck factor": Gary C. Lawrence Co., "National Telephone Membership Study," April 1988. "I do not believe": Bikales interview. "Ugly core": People for the American Way, press release, Oct. 19, 1988. Liberals like you: Armsby interview; Olson interview. "Blighting and withering": Busey, *Immigration*, p. 9.
WITAN's 1989 roster: Tanton memo on WITAN IX, March 9, 1989. " 'Sanctity of life' ": Hardin, *An Ecolate View;* see also Hardin, "Foundation for Immigration Policy." Two-thousand-mile electronic fence: Hardin, "Population and Immigration," p. 270. "Repugnant": Keely interview. "Obscene": Hayes, "A Conversation with Garrett Hardin," p. 63. "Cultural carrying capacity": Hardin, Address to the World Wilderness Congress. "Caught in a vise": Bikales, "Maximum Feasible Misunderstanding," p. 6. "Patterns of success": Lamm comments on WAMU-FM, Washington, D.C., Nov. 26, 1990. "Demography is destiny": U.S. Congress, *Economic and Demographic Consequences of Immigration*, pp. 361, 364. "Political patrones: Zaeske interview. "New generation": Pratt interview. "Spanish-only requirement": Pratt, "English Should Be Official Tongue."
Formerly gung-ho: Olson interview. "Racial slur": Barbara Bush remarks on *Good Morning America,* quoted in *U.S. English Update* 8, no. 2 (March–April 1990): 1. $135-an-hour: Bricker, memo on "Tanton defense," Oct. 25, 1988. WITAN meeting: Holmes interview. 99.2 percent: Arizonans for Official English, campaign disclosure form, March 24, 1989. Two inquiries: Zall to Alva E. Smith, Federal Election Commission, March 16, 1988; Zall to Reports Analysis Division, Nov. 13, 1989. "Illegal activites of U.S. English": Diamond, draft letter to Non-Profit Section, Internal Revenue Service, Nov. 8, 1990. Blackmail: Sorensen interview. "Reflection of some inner problems": Sheila Kaplan, "Hasta la Vista, U.S. English?" *Legal Times*, Mar. 9, 1992, p. 18.
"Revolving loan program": de la Peña interview. "Moral obligation": Bikales interview. Project Golden Door: *U.S. English Update* 5, no. 4 (July–Aug. 1987): 1. From $700,000: Sophia Nieves, "U.S. English Leader Says State Initiatives Will Continue," *Hispanic Link Weekly Report,* Nov. 21, 1988. "To change the perception": Saunders interview. Tanton is no longer connected: Saunders to Henry Lesnick, Teachers of English to Speakers of Other Languages, May 7, 1991.

7. Language Rights and Wrongs

"Will not make": James F. Henderson, memo to Arizona attorney general, Jan. 13, 1989. "Administration of justice": Andy Hall, "English Measure Disturbs Judges," p. A12. "New constitutional 'right' ": *Arizona Update Supplement*, no. 1 [June 1988], p. 1. "Proposition 106 requires": Arizona Attorney General, Opinion no. I89–009, Jan. 24, 1989, p. 12. "One fell swoop": Bricker, interviewed on KABC-AM, Los Angeles, Feb. 1990.
"The law affects few": *Meyer v. Nebraska,* 187 N.W. 102. "Nebraska cannot be divided": "Hold Nebraska Law Is Curb on Religion," *New York Times,* Feb. 24, 1923, p. 5. "A homogeneous people": 262 U.S. 401–2.
"Discrete and insular minorities": *U.S. v. Carolene Products Co.,* 304 U.S. 153

n. 4 (*dictum*). "**Community prejudices**": *Hernández v. Texas,* 347 U.S. 478. "**At least in part 'because of'**": *Personnel Admin. v. Feeney,* 442 U.S. 256. **Nothing unconstitutional:** *Soberal-Pérez v. Heckler,* 717 F.2d 41. "**Precisely tailored**": *Plyler v. Doe,* 457 U.S. 217. "**Harsh paradox**": *Hernández v. New York,* 111 S.Ct. 1872–73. **International law:** Macías, "Language Choice," pp. 87–90. "**Cultural insecurity**": Califa, "Declaring English the Official Language," pp. 347–48.

Precise impact: see, e.g., Dale, "Legal Analysis of H.J. Res. 169"; "Legal Analysis of S.J. Res. 167." **Under other California laws:** A.C.L.U. of Northern California, "Bilingual Public Services in California." **Repealed virtually all:** Fedynskyj, "State Session Laws in Non-English Languages," pp. 464–78. "**No equality of treatment**": *Lau v. Nichols,* 414 U.S. 566. "**Simple humaneness**": *U.S. ex rel. Negrón v. New York,* 434 F.2d 390–91.

"**Pampering of Mexicans**": Nancy Skelton, "Spanish Forms Prompt Anger," *Los Angeles Times,* Oct. 19, 1978, p. 3. **San Francisco officials:** Matsui et al., "Argument Against Proposition 38." **7.6 percent:** U.S. General Accounting Office, *Bilingual Voting Assistance,* p. 16. "**Simply fundamental**": *Torres v. Sachs,* 381 F.Supp. 312. **Overruled on equal protection:** *Garza v. Smith,* 320 F.Supp. 131. **New Texas law:** testimony of Leonel Castillo, U.S. House Judiciary Committee, *Extension of the Voting Rights Act,* pp. 823–24. "**Language impediment**": *Graves v. Barnes,* 343 F.Supp. 731. **16.4 percent of Texas:** U.S. House, *Voting Rights,* p. 18. "**Ethnic activists**": Thernstrom, *Whose Votes Count?* pp. 54–55, 57, 61–62. "**Unequal protection**": dissenting views of Rep. Robert McClory and seven other Republicans, U.S. House, *Voting Rights,* p. 88. **Twenty-nine out of 201,507:** U.S. Immigration and Naturalization Service, *Statistical Yearbook,* 1982, pp. 108, 162. "**No knowledge**": Hayakawa et al., "Argument in Favor of Proposition 38."

"**No one, no one at all**": Tanton, "U.S. English: It's Being Victimized." "**Nothing more—nor less**": *Hernández v. Erlenbusch,* 368 F. Supp. 752. **Reconstruction-era:** Piatt, *¿Only English?,* pp. 130–31. "**Hispanics feel belittled**": *Gutiérrez v. Municipal Court,* 838 F.2d 1051. **Bilingual hardware clerk:** *García v. Gloor,* 618 F.2d 264. "**Hospitals, universities**": Chen, "Language Rights," p. 269. "**Pretty ridiculous**": Cortez interview.

Public Utilities Commission: *U.S. English Update* 4, no. 6 (Nov.–Dec. 1986): 6. "**Crowded off**": *U.S. English Update* 4, no. 1 (Jan.–Feb. 1986): 2. "**Proliferation**": Councilmember Clay Bryant, memo to Pomona City Council, Oct. 18, 1988. "**Out of hand**": Jeffrey Miller, "Lawsuit Filed over Pomona Sign Law," *Los Angeles Times,* San Gabriel Valley ed., Feb. 16, 1989, Pt. IX, pp. 1, 4. "**Compelled speech**": Brancart interview. **Equal protection:** *Asian American Business Group v. City of Pomona,* 716 F.Supp. 1328. **Nearby towns:** Imahara interview.

8. Problem or Resource?

"**Child's first language**": New York State Education Department, *Regents Policy Paper,* pp. A-11–12, A-15. **At least $72,000:** U.S. English, New York State lobbying report for 1989, filed Feb. 23, 1990. "**Ideological goal**": Diamond, "New York's Blueprint," p. 4. **Timed Proposition 63:** Bikales interview. "**Innovative**": "Berkeley Decision May Alter Nation's Approach to Bilingual Education," *U.S. English Update* 7, no. 2 (March–April 1989), p. 1.

Opinion polls: see, e.g., Huddy and Sears, "Qualified Public Support for Bilingual Education." **"Key you carry":** Bush, "Remarks at a White House Ceremony." **700 million:** Crystal, 'How Many Millions," pp. 7–9. **Foreign Service recruits:** Simon, *Tongue-Tied American*, pp. 4, 9. **"Language-as-problem":** Ruíz, "Orientations in Language Planning," pp. 3–25. **Oral proficiency in Korean:** Campbell and Lindholm, *Conservation of Language Resources*, pp. 3–6.

"**Total immersion**": LaPorta interview. "**Holds kids back**": *ABC World News Tonight*, July 4, 1989.

"**One way**": Krashen, *Input Hypothesis*, p. 2. "**Paris argument**": Krashen, *Bilingual Education*, pp. 2–3. "**We learn to read**": ibid., p. 2, citing Frank Smith, *Understanding Reading* (Hillsdale, N.J.: Erlbaum, 1988) and Kenneth Goodman, *Selected Writings* (London: Routledge and Kegan Paul, 1982). **Bicultural ambivalence:** Cummins, "Role of Primary Language Development," pp. 34–37.

"**Bilingual enthusiasts**": Rodríguez, "Bilingualism, Con," p. 83. "**En inglés**": Rodríguez, *Hunger of Memory*, pp. 21–23. "**Selection bias**": Krashen interview. "**Typical silent period**": Krashen, *Input Hypothesis*, pp. 9–11.

"**Sense of urgency**": Hakuta and Snow, "Role of Research," p. 19. **First elaborated:** Cummins, "Role of Primary Language Development," pp. 7–17.

"**Failed path**": Bennett, speech to the Association for a Better New York. **At least two-thirds:** Willig, "A Meta-Analysis," p. 305. "**Review of the literature**": Baker and de Kanter, "Federal Policy and the Effectiveness of Bilingual Education." "**29 percent of the studies**": Rossell and Ross, "Social Science Evidence," p. 399. **1985 survey in California:** Troike, "Improving Conditions," p. 3. **Immersion tends to displace:** Lambert, "An Overview of Issues in Immersion Education," p. 20. "**Priority in early years**": Lambert and Tucker, *Bilingual Education of Children*, p. 216.

"**Common sense**"; "**not one credible**": Baker, New York Regents testimony, Oct. 17 and Nov. 9, 1989. "**Time on task**": Rossell and Ross, "Social Science Evidence," p. 407. "**Learning theory**": Walberg interview. "**Field of fads**": Rossell, oral testimony in *Teresa P. v. Berkeley Unified School District*, trial transcript, pp. 12-2074, 2075 (Sept. 1988). "**Like asking your barber**": Walberg, letter to Frederick Mulhauser, Sept. 22, 1986, in U.S. G.A.O., *Bilingual Education*, p. 71. **$129,049:** Jungherr interview.

"**Magic transfer**": Porter, *Forked Tongue*, p. 23. "**Awkward tension**": Hakuta, *Mirror of Language*, p. 219. **$62,000 grant:** U.S. English, I.R.S. Form 990 for 1989. "**Unaffiliated**": Porter, memo of June 18, 1991. "**Less than half**" Porter interview. **Academic adviser:** Hamersma interview.

Long-awaited report: Ramírez et al., *Final Report: Longitudinal Study*. "**Instructional objective**": Ramírez interview. "**Supportive atmosphere**": Dinos interview. "**Standard of success**": U.S. English, "Frequently Used Arguments."

9. Babel in Reverse

"**Ultimate dividers**": Tanton, letter to supporters, Dec. 7, 1988. "**Opening Quebec gambit**": Dick Kirschten, "Defending the Primacy of the English Language," *National Journal*, April 29, 1989, p. 1064. "**In Belgium**": William Trombley, "Norman Cousins Drops His Support of Prop. 63," *Los Angeles Times*, Oct. 16, 1986, Pt. I, p. 3. **Francophones lagged:** Esman, "The Politics of Official Bilingualism in

Canada," p. 46. **Thirty times more likely:** National Center for Education Statistics, *Retention of Minority Languages,* p. 9. **"Babel in reverse":** Haugen, *Ecology of Language,* p. 1.

Survey of 161 constitutions: Blaustein and Epstein, *Resolving Language Conflicts,* p. 3. **Advertisers can be fined:** Weinstein, "Francophonie," pp. 62–65, 69. **"Perfect instrument of empire":** Heath, *Telling Tongues,* p. 6. **"Collective treasure":** Edwards, *Language, Society, and Identity,* pp. 23–26. **Half the French population:** Hobsbawm, *Nations and Nationalism,* pp. 60–61. **"Many honest men":** Rep. Thomas Hartley, *Annals of Congress,* 3rd Cong., 2nd sess. (Feb. 16, 1795), pp. 1228–29. **"Language of a free people":** Balibar and Laporte, *Le Français national,* p. 94. **"Not to have a policy":** Heath, "A National Language Academy?" p. 10.

Fewer than 20 percent: Palau interview; 1980 Census. **English version:** *Cruz v. Domínguez.* 8 P.R.R. 551. **"Sacred symbol":** Osuna, *History of Education in Puerto Rico,* pp. 370–71. **"American citizens of Puerto Rico":** Roosevelt to Gallardo, April 17, 1937. **Agapito's Bar:** Ortiz Toro, "Language and Statehood," p. 35. **"Nation without sovereignty":** Vientos Gastón, "Supreme Court of Puerto Rico," p. 105. **"A territory indefinitely":** Hayakawa interview. **"What we are":** Palau interview. **"Create a Quebec":** Bill McAllister, "Puerto Rico Referendum Killed," *Washington Post,* Feb. 28, 1991, p. A6.

206 indigenous languages: Medicine, "Speaking Indian," p. 4. **Grow up speaking:** Benally and McCarty, "Navajo Language Today," p. 239. **Japanese intelligence:** Hafford, "Navajo Code Talkers," p. 45. **Official language policies:** Locke, "Indian Language Codes." **"Hit very hard":** Zepeda interview. **To every O'odham village:** Alvarez interview. **24,000 tribal members:** Zepeda, "American Indian Language Policy," p. 255. **Three-quarters:** Zepeda, *Papago Grammar,* p. xiv. **"Gift from our Creator":** *Tohono O'odham Education Standards,* p. 6. **"We need our land":** Littlebear, "*Natsêhesenestsêstôtse,*" pp. 16–17. **Seven in ten:** Littlebear interview.

83 percent: Parliament of Australia, *Report on a National Language Policy,* p. 9. **Greek-speaking city:** Walsh, "Language Policy—Australia," p. 21. **State-run television:** Clyne, "Uniqueness of the Language Situation in Australia." **"Guiding principles":** LoBianco, *National Policy on Languages,* p. 4; AACLAME, *Report to the Minister,* pp. 6–10. **"Languages of wider learning":** Australia, Department of Employment, Education, and Training, *Australia's Policy on Languages,* p. 7.

"English is and will remain": English Plus Information Clearinghouse, "Statement of Purpose," Oct. 1987. **One out of five:** California State Department of Education, "Language Census Report for California Public Schools, 1991," p. 13. **"Efficient revolving doors":** Snow and Hakuta, "Costs of Monolingualism," p. 390. **"Maximize instructional resources":** Cavazos to Augustus F. Hawkins, House Education and Labor Committee, Jan. 30, 1989.

Conclusion

One must speak Spanish: Saunders interview. **"Calls for official bilingualism":** *U.S. English,* vol. 1, no. 1 [1991]. **"I have not heard":** Hernández interview. **Fewer than two thousand:** Kimura, "The Hawaiian Language and Its Revitalization," pp. 117–23.

Acknowledgments

This is a story to which I came as a journalist, an outsider. It could not have been told without the help of numerous insiders—in particular, bilingual educators and civil rights advocates. Besides those who gave me formal interviews, scores of people have contributed insights, opened doors, set up interviews, sent clippings, loaned books, offered hospitality, and provided encouragement over the past six years. I am especially grateful to:

Ron Wolk, my former editor at *Education Week,* who assigned me to cover bilingual education, a fascinating and largely unexplored beat, and supported my efforts;

professionals who introduced me to language pedagogy and politics: Ellen Riojas Clark, of the University of Texas, San Antonio; Virginia Collier, of George Mason University; Kenji Hakuta, of Stanford University; Sandra Johnson, consultant on Indian education; Stephen Krashen, of the University of Southern California; Dick Littlebear, of the Alaska Multifunctional Resource Center; James J. Lyons, of the National Association for Bilingual Education; Ricardo Martínez, former staff member of the U.S. House Education and Labor Committee; Norm Gold, of the California State Department of Education; Carlos Ovando, of Indiana University; Shelly Spiegel-Coleman, of the Los Angeles County Department of Education; and Concepción Valadez, of the University of California at Los Angeles;

activists who kept me informed through the English Plus Information Clearinghouse: Susan Armsby, Gloria Barajas, Maurice Belanger, Marilyn Braveman, Antonio Califa, Steve Carbo, Donna Christian, Mary Carol Combs, Denise De La Rosa, Jamie Draper, Martha Jiménez, Suzanne Ramos, Richard Tucker, and Arturo Vargas;

in Arizona: Perry Baker, Connie Bertoldo, Armando Ruíz, and Richard Ruíz;

in California: Ed Chen, Sally Chou, Chuck Cota, Lily Wong Fillmore, J Craig Fong, Michael Genzuk, Helen George, Shirley Brice Heath, John Horton, Kathy Imahara, Reynaldo Macías, Natalia Martínez, Ernest Morales, Geoffrey Nunberg, Roger Olsen, Amado Padilla, David Ramírez, Ruth Willner, and Linda Wong;

in Florida: Ellis Berger, Joanne Bretzer, Max Castro, Rosa Castro Feinberg, and Mark Gallegos;

in Massachusetts: Deborah Gaines, Joan Gendron, Alex Huertas, Camilo Pérez-Bustillo, Mac Pritchard, and Catherine Walsh;

in New York: Peter Byron, Diana Caballero, Juan Cartagena, Carmen Pérez Hogan, Henry Lesnick, Luis Reyes, Elaine Ruíz, María Torres-Guzmán, and Ana Celia Zentella;

in Texas: Joe Bernal, José Cárdenas, Josie Garza, Angel Noë González, Antonio González, Celso Guzmán, Charles Kilpatrick, and Gloria Zamora;

in Washington, D.C.: Charlie Ericksen, Jonathan Lemco, Wes McCune, Sara Meléndez, Bill Montague, Félix Pérez, Keith Sinzinger, John Trasviña, and Dorothy Waggoner;

elsewhere: Russ Bellant, Richard Castro, Jim Cummins, José Delgado, Ricardo Fernández, William Frawley, Diamond Navarro, Steve Orlov, Jon Reyhner, Carol Schmid, and Raymond Tatalovich.

I also want to acknowledge the assistance of Linda Chávez and Mark LaPorta, who, despite our principled differences, were more than cooperative in providing an inside view of U.S. English.

During my research, I benefited from frequent discussions with Geoffrey Nunberg, who was generous in sharing his provocative ideas. María Torres-Guzmán taught me to appreciate biculturalism, and much more. Joanne Bretzer, Ed Chen, Mary Carol Combs, Stephen Krashen, and Camilo Pérez-Bustillo no doubt spared me numerous embarrassments by carefully reading and critiquing portions of the manuscript.

My literary agent, Lisa DiMona, not only got my foot in the door but supplied expert guidance throughout the publishing process. My editor at Addison-Wesley, Amy Gash, and her predecessor, Jane Isay, approached my work with a welcome balance of enthusiasm, firmness, and sensitivity.

Finally, I want to add a special thanks to Mary Carol Combs, who first drew my attention to the English Only phenomenon and became an encyclopedic source, constructive critic, and valued friend.

—James Crawford

Index